THE ARAB BUREAU

ALSO BY EAMONN GEARON

The Sahara: A Cultural History
(Signal, 2011)

Turning Points in Middle Eastern History
(The Great Courses series, 2016)

The History and Achievements of the Islamic Golden Age
(The Great Courses series, 2017)

The Middle East in the Twentieth Century
(The Great Courses series, 2021)

Winnie-the-Pooh at 100
(Audible series, 2026)

The Silk Roads
(The Great Courses Series, 2026)

The Arab Revolt: The Lost Chronicle from Lawrence of Arabia's Intelligence War
(Hurst Publishers, forthcoming)

EAMONN GEARON

The Arab Bureau

The Story of Britain's Most Ingenious Intelligence Unit

HURST & COMPANY, LONDON

First published in the United Kingdom in 2026 by
C. Hurst & Co. (Publishers) Ltd.,
New Wing, Somerset House, Strand, London, WC2R 1LA
© Eamonn Gearon, 2026
All rights reserved.

The right of Eamonn Gearon to be identified as the author of this publication is asserted by him in accordance with the Copyright, Designs and Patents Act, 1988.

A Cataloguing-in-Publication data record for this book is available from the British Library.

ISBN: 9781805264255

EU GPSR Authorised Representative
Easy Access System Europe Oü, 16879218
Address: Mustamäe tee 50, 10621, Tallinn, Estonia
Contact Details: gpsr.requests@easproject.com, +358 40 500 3575

Cover image courtesy of James A. Cannavino Library, Archives & Special Collections, Marist College, USA.

Cover image, taken in Aqaba, clockwise from standing figure on left: Sub-Lieutenant Langbeim, Royal Naval Reserve (in khaki service tunic); Captain H.C. Hornby, Royal Engineers (in drab service tunic with Military Cross ribbon); Major W.E. Marshall, Royal Army Medical Corps (tropical service tunic); Captain Raymond Goslett, Royal Army Service Corps (on Lawrence's camel saddle, petting a saluki called Shorter); Major Scott of the Royal Inniskilling Fusiliers (Aqaba base commander, wearing a cuff rank drab tunic and holding a terrier named Robert); T.E. Lawrence; and Major P.G.W. Maynard, Royal Irish Rifles.

This book is printed using paper from registered sustainable and managed sources.

www.hurstpublishers.com

Printed and bound in Great Britain by Bell and Bain Ltd, Glasgow

CONTENTS

Acknowledgements   ix
Foreword by Rob Johnson   xiii
Preface   xvii

Introduction   1

PART I
CRISIS

1. The Gallows at Dawn: Damascus and Beirut   13
2. Unprepared for War: Black Sea, Constantinople, Egypt, India   35

PART II
RESPONSE

3. "British Desiderata in Turkey and Asia": Foreign Office, Whitehall, London   61
4. The Scholar Spies: Oxford   81
5. Rooms at the Savoy: Cairo   97

PART III
INTELLIGENCE AND INNOVATION

6. Networks of Knowledge: Middle East, North Africa, India   113
7. "Reading the Enemy's Mail": Intelligence Breakthroughs: Hijaz   129
8. The *Arab Bulletin* as Intelligence Innovation: Cairo   149

PART IV
PROPAGANDA AND ARAB ALLIES

9. *Thawrat al-Arab*: Creating an Arabic-Language Propaganda Masterpiece: Cairo   179
10. The Paper War: London–Cairo–Mecca   205

PART V
IMPACT AND LEGACY

11. Post-War Postmortem: Modern Middle East   229
12. Seven Pillars of Intelligence Wisdom: Lessons from the Arab Bureau   247

Notes   269
Bibliographic Essay   303
Index   309

To my wife, for her boundless love, constancy, and support, and my son, for his endless curiosity and for helping me see the world anew. Thanks for joining me on this literary adventure.

Also in loving memory of Roger Owen (1935–2018), my dear friend and mentor. He inspired this scholastic quest, and I like to think he would have enjoyed the result.

ACKNOWLEDGEMENTS

Although my DPhil was written by me alone, the myth of such an undertaking being an entirely solitary pursuit is belied by the following list of people from whom I received invaluable guidance, encouragement, insights, and corrections, and who all have my heartfelt thanks.

It is perhaps customary to acknowledge and give thanks first to the living, not the dead, but I wish to record my deepest thanks to the late Professor Roger Owen, former Director of the St Antony's College Middle East Centre at the University Oxford, as well as A.J. Meyer Professor of Middle East History at Harvard University. Roger was the first person with whom I discussed my ideas for this research, and he offered support and stimulating suggestions from the start. More important than all his professional achievements, Roger was my friend, whose company and counsel I continue to miss.

The staff of both academic and public libraries perform remarkable feats on a daily basis, and they do so with apparent ease, grace, patience, and good manners. They and the institutions in which they work are priceless; they are a treasure worth guarding, the heart of learning, and the measure of a healthy community. Thank you to the staff of the Howe and Etna Libraries, Hanover, New Hampshire; the Baker-Berry Library, Sherman Art Library, and Jones Media Centre of Dartmouth College; the many libraries and archives at the University of Oxford, not least the Middle East Centre Library at St Antony's; the British Library, London; and the staff and collections of the National Archives at Kew, London.

Without the guidance of a supervisor, it is unlikely that any research degree would ever reach a successful conclusion. I was most fortunate in having the ear and intellect of more than one counsellor. Informally—which is to say on a friendly and unstintingly generous footing—Christopher Andrew, Corpus Christi College, Cambridge, provided

ACKNOWLEDGEMENTS

essential guidance in the field of Intelligence Studies. Formally, Eugene Rogan, Director of the University of Oxford's Middle East Centre, St Antony's College, was my first supervisor. Eugene's friendship and candour allowed me to keep moving forward, as we explored and eliminated numerous possible paths for my research.

> "Two roads diverged in a wood, and I –
> I took the one less traveled by,
> And that has made all the difference."

Having at last found that less-travelled road, bridging Middle East Studies and Intelligence Studies, I was only able to navigate it thanks to Rob Johnson, Pembroke College, Oxford. "Supervisor" is altogether too passive a word for the man who served as my guide, navigator, and bastion of support.

Sincere thanks also to: Roderick Bailey, Wellcome Unit for the History of Medicine, Oxford; Jamie Belich, Baliol, Oxford; Maya Blackwell, Faculty of History, Oxford; Debbie Challis, Petrie Museum, University College London (UCL); Erica Charters, Wolfson, Oxford; Rory Cormac, University of Nottingham; John Darwin, Nuffield, Oxford; Richard Davenport-Hines, Quondam Fellow of All Souls, Oxford; Juliette Desplat, National Archives, Kew; Neil Faulkner, University of Bristol, Great Arab Revolt Project (deceased); Avalon Floyd, Faculty of History, Oxford; Adrian Gregory, Pembroke, Oxford; Miles Larmer, St Antony's, Oxford; Dan Larsen, University of Glasgow; Katherine Lebow, Christ Church, Oxford; Margaret MacMillan, St Antony's, Oxford; James McDougall, Trinity, Oxford; Erin O'Halloran; Hussein Omar, Pembroke, Oxford; Roger Owen, Harvard (deceased); Tim Paris, independent scholar and author; Thomas Powers, independent scholar and author, South Royalton, Vermont; Nick Saunders, UCL, Great Arab Revolt Project; my dearest friend, William Sheward, University of Winchester; Avi Shlaim, St Antony's, Oxford; Hew Strachan, Oxford and St Andrews; Nick Stargardt, Magdalen, Oxford; Debbie Usher, archivist in the Middle East Centre at St Antony's, Oxford; Philip Walker, independent scholar (deceased); and Rupert Allason, the author better known as Nigel West.

"So the last shall be first, and the first last." It is also entirely apt and appropriate to thank one's family above all others. My wife and our son

ACKNOWLEDGEMENTS

have been patient and considerate throughout the process of researching and writing this DPhil. My name is on the cover, but any laurels awarded must be shared equally with them.

FOREWORD

Dr Rob Johnson

In the October 1920 issue of *The Army Quarterly and Defence Journal*, T.E. Lawrence 'of Arabia' wrote: "The printing press is the greatest weapon in the armoury of the modern commander". He understood, as a member of the Arab Bureau, that intelligence *and* propaganda were vital in war. Eamonn Gearon's research, which unearths a previously hidden dimension of the First World War in the Middle East, shows that this statement was put into practice with some effect.

In the information age, there has been a tendency to assume that only with the latest technologies can an accurate assessment of an adversary's intentions and sentiments be made, and ideas injected into their consciousness. Lawrence's reference to the printing press tells us that this 'presentism' is misplaced. The problem is that we tend to forget that information has long been an enabling and sometimes decisive element of warfare. Around 468 BCE King Archidamus of Sparta wanted to assess the strength of the Athenians. It is said he used merchants to make enquiries about the military capabilities and the 'will to fight' of his chief rivals, and used opportunities to demoralise his enemies by spreading stories of the prowess of the Spartan warriors. Too often, successes like these have been overlooked. This is especially true of Britain's Arab Bureau, whose innovations during the First World War have been curiously neglected by both intelligence practitioners and historians alike.

This oversight is particularly striking given the Arab Bureau's brief but transformative existence from 1916 to 1920. Operating out of the

FOREWORD

Savoy Hotel, Cairo, this small unit fundamentally reimagined how intelligence services could operate in culturally complex environments. Yet despite its remarkable achievements and even more colourful staff, the Arab Bureau has, like many other aspects of the Great War in the Middle East, been overshadowed by the story of T.E. Lawrence's exploits. It deserves more attention as an intelligence innovation on a par with 'Station X' of the Second World War. Gearon's book moves us beyond the familiar Lawrence-centric narrative to reveal the Arab Bureau as a sophisticated institution whose significance extends far beyond any single personality.

This meticulously researched study remedies our historical amnesia with an engaging verve. Drawing upon previously unexplored Arabic sources, most notably the complete text of *Thawrat al-Arab* (*The Arab Revolt*), Gearon transforms our understanding of what was arguably Britain's most ingenious intelligence unit. That this substantial piece of wartime propaganda has escaped scholarly attention until now highlights the linguistic and archival barriers that have long impeded serious intelligence historiography. The oversight is all the more remarkable given that *Thawrat al-Arab* represents one of the longest sustained pieces of British propaganda from the entire war, and predates the better-known Ministry of Information which emerged later in the war.

The Arab Bureau grew out of the catastrophic intelligence failures at Gallipoli and Kut al-Amara as a radical experiment in cultural intelligence. Freed from the institutional constraints that typically stifle innovation within established intelligence services, it created what Gearon aptly terms a self-conscious "imperial epistemic community"—a knowledge production system that transformed academic expertise into operational capability. This was intelligence work of an entirely different order from the conventional military intelligence of the period. Nor was it limited to the secret espionage that focusses on individual leaders. The Arab Bureau's approach represented a fundamental shift from seeing intelligence as mere information gathering to understanding it as a sophisticated analytical discipline requiring deep cultural knowledge and from which tangible effects could be produced.

Central to the Arab Bureau's success was the *Arab Bulletin*, which Professor Christopher Andrew of Cambridge University described as containing the best-written intelligence reports in British history. Gearon's analysis reveals how this remarkable publication evolved over its

FOREWORD

114 issues from simple military reporting into a detailed regional analysis that foregrounded modern intelligence methods. The Arab Bureau's unique composition of scholars, linguists, and regional specialists enabled a multidisciplinary approach to intelligence that remains exemplary. What emerges from Gearon's careful study is a picture of intelligence officers who were as comfortable discussing Islamic jurisprudence as they were analysing Ottoman military dispositions, a breadth of expertise that modern intelligence services sometimes struggle to replicate.

The personnel themselves were extraordinary: alongside Lawrence, the Arab Bureau included figures such as Gertrude Bell, David Hogarth, Ronald Storrs, and Kinahan Cornwallis. Yet as Gearon demonstrates, their effectiveness lay not in individual brilliance but in their collective function as an epistemic community that created new frameworks for understanding complex regional dynamics.

Equally impressive was the Arab Bureau's approach to what we would now call information operations, not conceived as a separate branch, but as an intrinsic element of creating strategic effects. Their propaganda efforts went far beyond slogans, narratives, or messaging and created complex and interdependent information ecosystems working through authentic Arab voices. From carefully targeted Arabic newspapers with different registers for different audiences to postage stamps incorporating genuine Islamic artistic elements, they understood that effective influence required cultural authenticity, a lesson repeatedly forgotten in subsequent conflicts. This sophisticated approach to information warfare anticipated modern methods by decades.

Lawrence's complementary autobiographical book *Seven Pillars of Intelligence Wisdom*, distilled from the Arab Bureau's experience, offers a practical framework for understanding how all this worked in practice and has enduring relevance. The first principles of the Bureau's work, from cultural understanding as operational capability to the cultivation of continuous institutional learning, speak directly to challenges facing intelligence services today. The tragic irony is that many of these lessons have been relearned at considerable cost in Iraq, Afghanistan, and elsewhere, rather than drawn from this rich historical precedent.

The author does not romanticise his subject. He carefully acknowledges the fundamental contradictions within the Arab Bureau's position. Its cultural sophistication ultimately served imperial objectives that constrained the very Arab aspirations it claimed to understand. This was,

FOREWORD

after all, an institution that served the exercise of power during an existential war. Yet within these limitations, the Bureau's approach to intelligence gathering, analysis, and dissemination was revolutionary for its time and remains remarkably relevant today.

This book makes an essential contribution to intelligence history by recovering forgotten innovations and demonstrating their contemporary relevance. It serves as a salutary reminder that effective intelligence work requires not merely technical competence but cultural fluency, a lesson that resonates powerfully in our current era of global interconnectedness. The Arab Bureau succeeded because it recognised that understanding people and their motivations was as crucial as intercepting their communications, correlating armed forces, or mapping their positions. The work also illuminates broader questions about the relationship between knowledge and power in intelligence operations. The Arab Bureau's scholars were not mere academic advisors but operational actors whose intellectual frameworks directly shaped policy outcomes. This integration of scholarship and statecraft offers important lessons for contemporary intelligence communities grappling with complex global challenges that demand both analytical rigour and cultural sensitivity. The Arab Bureau's brief but brilliant existence offers a masterclass in adaptive intelligence that deserves far wider recognition.

At a time when cultural intelligence remains as crucial as ever to international security, Gearon's study provides both historical insight and practical wisdom. It is a work that should be read not only by historians but by anyone seeking to understand how intelligence can succeed in complex cultural environments—and why best practice, and success, are so often forgotten.

Dr Rob Johnson, Director of the Changing Character of War Centre,
Pembroke College, University of Oxford

PREFACE

Academic monographs are often seen as boring—as is the word 'monograph'—mainly because many of them are. This book started life as a 100,000-word DPhil. The point of a DPhil (that is, a PhD from the University of Oxford), is for the researcher to find a gap—'lacuna' is the beloved term—in the existing scholarship, and in filling it make an 'original contribution to the field'. This thesis is read by one's supervisor, who offers advice and suggestions along the way. For the last two years of this process, my supervisor was the brilliant Dr Rob Johnson, Pembroke College.[1] Of course, should I fail my oral defence, or *viva voce*—Latin (what else?) for "with the living voice"—he should obviously be considered a fool who deserves to be fired.[2]

Upon completion and submission, the thesis is read by two examiners: one from the candidate's own university and one from another. These are the only three people who have to read the manuscript. Not long ago, there was an expectation that an academic publisher would publish such a manuscript, often without significant changes. The manuscript would then go on to gather dust in a few hundred university libraries, and academia would be richer for having it.

Things have changed in recent years. Now, dear reader, you can read the fruits of a researcher's labour, but typically only after they've made some effort to make the text faintly interesting. Ursula K. Le Guin, the great author of speculative fiction, when interviewed in *Vogue* spoke about revising her book on writing fiction, *Steering the Craft*,[3] nearly 20 years after it was first published. She said, "It's substantially the same book, but almost every sentence is rewritten."[4]

The Arab Bureau: The Story of Britain's Most Ingenious Intelligence Unit is substantially the same text as my DPhil[5] but entirely recrafted in the hope of producing a book that would appeal to more than three readers. In doing so, I have tried to follow Elmore Leonard's dictum on writing: "Try to leave out the parts that people skip."[6] If I have fallen short in

PREFACE

this aspiration, I'm sure I will hear all about it, but thank you either way for buying this book.

Beyond T.E. Lawrence: A Personal Reflection

Like many, I first encountered the Arab Bureau indirectly, through the sweeping desert panoramas and enigmatic gaze of Peter O'Toole in David Lean's *Lawrence of Arabia*.[7] Many years later, just weeks after 9/11, I found myself teaching that very film to Egyptian students attending the American University in Cairo as part of a course I was teaching on Orientalism. It led to a series of fascinating discussions as my students grappled with this Western portrayal of their region's history and geography: scenes in the film depicting the Arab Bureau headquarters and other scenes set in Cairo (as well as Jerusalem and Damascus) were shot in Seville, Spain. The undergraduates' responses ranged from fascination to indignation, but more than anything revealed the enduring power of imperial narratives and the complex legacy of British involvement in the Arab world.

The film's singular focus on Lawrence was an entirely understandable oversimplification on Lean's part. He was making the film he wanted to make, despite the fact that in his autobiographical book *Seven Pillars of Wisdom* Lawrence listed nearly forty colleagues—members of the Arab Bureau and others who, as Lawrence wrote, "also did their best"—whose collective efforts naturally outweighed his individual, not to say singular, contribution. But none of those have the fame, or notoriety, that is attached to Lawrence's name, and they have faded from popular memory.

As for historical accuracy, as Lawrence blandly says in the introduction, "In these pages the history is not of the Arab movement, but of me in it."[8] This tension between the romantic myth of the lone hero and the reality of the collaborative intelligence effort was one catalyst for my exploration of the Arab Bureau's complex legacy.

From Historical Study to Contemporary Relevance

Over the years, my pursuit of the story of the Arab Bureau has taken me from Cairo to the Hejaz, and many wind-swept Arabian desert locations; to Aqaba, Wadi Rum, and other sites in Jordan; on to Jerusalem,

PREFACE

and Damascus; to the Foreign Office in London; the National Archives at Kew; and libraries and archives in Oxford, Cambridge, and many places besides.

The journey has been filled with unexpected personal connections, from doing my DPhil at the University of Oxford—where the History Faculty's offices are housed in the former Oxford High School for Boys, which Lawrence and his brothers attended—to conducting research at the Middle East Centre Library and Archive in St Antony's College, not two minutes from Lawrence's family home, 2 Polstead Road. Walking the same streets, studying in the same buildings, as he once had, I often felt the strange resonance between past and present that makes history come alive, and had to remind myself to return my focus to the Arab Bureau as a whole.

Along the way I was also working with the US Department of State and Britain's Foreign and Commonwealth Office, now the Foreign, Commonwealth and Development Office, training British and American diplomats and others about the Middle East and North Africa (MENA) region, passing on—among other things—lessons in cultural engagement picked up in the field, so to speak. Here, I saw firsthand the shadows of the century-old intelligence approaches of the Arab Bureau still informing Western interactions with the region.

What began as a matter of personal historical curiosity became increasingly relevant to my work. In creating MENA area studies training for diplomats, it is impossible not to hear echoes of Arab Bureau approaches in contemporary frameworks, sometimes knowingly adopted, often unconsciously repeated: a lesson learned here and a point noted there, but for now best set aside.

Imperial Contradictions and Ethical Complexities

Having lived across the region—from the bustle of Cairo to Riyadh's quieter compounds, from Kabul to Casablanca—I've confronted the lasting consequences of the imperial contradictions embodied by the Arab Bureau. Teaching Middle Eastern history to Western audiences, I've witnessed how difficult it is for many to reconcile the Arab Bureau's cultural sophistication with its imperial function. My Arab students and colleagues have often pressed me on this point, challenging any narrative that celebrates these intelligence innovations without acknowledging their ultimate purpose.

PREFACE

Over time, I've observed how contemporary officials unconsciously reproduce this contradiction, developing sophisticated cultural understanding while in some cases advancing policies that lack a proper understanding of local aspirations or needs. Across the region and in London and Washington, DC, in discussions with diplomats, soldiers, journalists, and academics—a professional cross-section mirroring the Arab Bureau's own roll call—I've often seen how, and also understood why, institutional imperatives may override the insights provided by cultural specialists, in much the same way they did a century ago.

The Arab Bureau's Unexpected Afterlives

As we've already seen, the Arab Bureau may have been shuttered in 1920, but its influence extended far beyond its brief institutional existence. Its methodological innovations resurfaced repeatedly across the twentieth century, often without explicit acknowledgement of their origins.

By 1942, as Allied forces prepared for North African operations, the Political Warfare Executive (PWE) had established reading rooms in Cairo and distributed carefully crafted materials through seemingly independent Arab cultural channels—a direct echo of the Arab Bureau's newspaper strategy—while America's Office of Strategic Services was also on the scene. The noted British-Italian explorer and travel writer Freya Stark (1893–1993), who worked for Britain's Ministry of Information during the Second World War, and played an important part in numerous propaganda efforts, was both aware and admiring of the work done by the Arab Bureau.

During the Cold War, Central Intelligence Agency (CIA) activities in the Middle East similarly reflected Arab Bureau methodologies. The American University of Beirut became a hub for regional intelligence in ways that mirrored the Arab Bureau's academic networks, while Radio Free Europe's approach to cultural programming drew directly from the Arab Bureau's strategies.

Most striking is how the Arab Bureau's approach resurfaced during recent conflicts in Iraq and Afghanistan. The US Army's Human Terrain System, despite its troubled implementation, conceptually echoed the Arab Bureau's integration of academic expertise with military operations. Indeed, General David Petraeus's counterinsurgency doctrine, published in 2008, explicitly acknowledged Lawrence's influence, and Provincial

PREFACE

Reconstruction Teams attempted to recreate the Arab Bureau's flexible organisational structure.

Beyond Intelligence, Education

My work as an educator has also revealed how the Arab Bureau's approach continues to influence contemporary understanding of the Middle East. Speaking with audiences across the region and around the world, I've observed how academic programmes still struggle with certain of the same methodological questions that confronted the Arab Bureau: How do we integrate different disciplinary approaches? How do we balance academic rigour with practical application? How do we ensure that Western theoretical frameworks don't overshadow local perspectives?

During my time at the University of London's School of Oriental and African Studies, and when conducting research at the Middle East Centre, Oxford, and at Kew, I traced methodological connections between the Arab Bureau's approach and later institutions. The creation of the Middle East Centre for Arab Studies (MECAS) in Lebanon after the Second World War represented an institutional attempt to recapture what the Arab Bureau had achieved, combining linguistic immersion with cultural and political understanding. Though rarely acknowledging its wartime predecessor directly, MECAS adopted strikingly similar approaches to language training and cultural immersion, preparing officials for regional service through methods that echoed the Arab Bureau's interdisciplinary collaboration.

I've witnessed similar continuities in cultural diplomacy, and discussions with British Council officials have revealed approaches to cultural engagement that parallel methods pioneered by the Arab Bureau, including working through local networks, adapting messaging to cultural contexts, and emphasising authentic partnerships. These continuing echoes of Arab Bureau approaches, often unrecognised by practitioners themselves, reveal how deeply certain methodological innovations have been institutionalised in British engagement with the region.

Reader, an Invitation

Last year, I was in Cairo once again, walking the streets where the Savoy Hotel had once stood, and which address, perhaps predictably, has no historical marker to indicate the site's significance to British intelligence activities in the First World War. Sheltering in the shadows of modern concrete and glass buildings, where the Arab Bureau once discussed tribal alliances and crafted propaganda, I watched locals walk past, either engrossed in their smartphones or navigating the traffic—several doing both at the same time—entirely unaware of how decisions made in that space had helped shape the borders and geopolitical structures in the place they and others across the MENA region now inhabit.

After three decades living and working across the Middle East and North Africa, I've increasingly come to see the Arab Bureau's legacy as profoundly human. During countless discussions with innumerable Arabs and others—of all faiths and of none—I have seen first-hand how the consequences of imperial machinations remain alive in contemporary consciousness not as distant history, but as living context for present struggles.

My years training Western diplomats have shown me both the promise and peril of the Arab Bureau's approach, how genuine cultural understanding creates possibilities for authentic connection, but also how easily such understanding can be subordinated to strategic objectives, how the empathetic insight of a cultural specialist is frequently overruled by political imperatives. Even so, it is still worthwhile to try when we can to recreate something essential that the Arab Bureau—despite its imperial constraints—occasionally achieved, which is to say moments of authentic cross-cultural connection where people recognise each other's humanity across profound differences.

The Arab Bureau's members weren't simply collecting information. They were engaged in the complex human work of building bridges across cultural divides at a time of violent conflict. Their legacy challenges us to navigate our own divided world with greater imagination, humility, and respect for human complexity. After years of following the footprints left behind by the Arab Bureau's ghost, I've come to believe its most enduring wisdom lies not in intelligence techniques, but in the recognition that true understanding begins with a willingness to listen to voices different from our own. This work does not set out to celebrate or condemn, but to shine a light and in doing so invites you to consider this story, and come to a clearer understanding of your own.

The past informs the present. Differences matter. Change is a constant.

INTRODUCTION

The 2009 annual lecture of the British Society for Middle Eastern Studies was delivered by my friend and mentor, the late Professor Roger Owen. His speech dealt with British and French military intelligence in Syria and Palestine during the First World War. What particularly caught my attention was his observation that Intelligence Studies experts, both military and civilian, and Middle Eastern scholars seemed to exist in separate worlds. They "not only do not talk to each other but do not attend the same conferences, read the same journals, or in some cases, know of each other's existence".[1]

Such a divide struck me as particularly relevant in the context of one of the most fascinating yet little known, and subsequently misunderstood, intelligence organisations of the modern era: the Arab Bureau. The vast majority of people who have heard of this intelligence agency at all will have done so thanks solely to T.E. Lawrence, a.k.a. Lawrence of Arabia, whose outsized legend has paradoxically obscured many of the most interesting aspects of what was a truly remarkable intelligence unit. The Arab Bureau existed for just a little over four years, from its unheralded establishment to its unannounced dissolution. Yet in that brief span of time, it revolutionised the way in which intelligence operations were conducted in complex cultural environments, and pioneered methods that would influence approaches to intelligence work on the part of both British and foreign agencies for decades, indeed, in certain aspects even up to the present day. To begin at the beginning, we need to start by asking what was the existing need that led to such a unique intelligence unit being established. To do that, we have to see and understand the strategic crisis that faced Britain at the moment of the Arab Bureau's birth.

The Arab Bureau emerged at a crucial moment in Middle Eastern and world history. The decision by the Ottoman Empire to enter the First World War on Germany's side had transformed the MENA region into a vital theatre in what had by then become a world-wide war. The Suez Canal was Britain's lifeline to India, and its protection was paramount. Yet British policy towards the Middle East was initially characterised not just by widespread uncertainty and confusion, but also by competing interests between the ruling authorities in London and Delhi, and this in spite of the fact that both were British. The different visions these powers held were so stark that, in spite of the fact that they were two arms of the same British Empire, at times they appeared to be diametrically opposed to one another.

Among other things, the Ottoman entry into the First World War made it obvious that a new approach to intelligence operations was needed, whether in gathering information, creating and circulating intelligence reports, or working with Allies to fend off anti-British propaganda, and perhaps even creating propaganda of its own. In order to take on such a challenge, it would be necessary to create an altogether new type of intelligence unit, one that could not only traverse physical or geographical terrain, from desert plains to urban landscapes, but also navigate a way through the region's intricate cultural and political landscape. It was into this space that the Arab Bureau would step.

Among other things, the uniqueness of the Arab Bureau resulted from its unorthodox composition. Unlike more traditional military intelligence units, it brought together an extraordinary collection of scholars, archaeologists, linguists, and regional experts, many of whom had spent years travelling and studying the MENA region long before the outbreak of war. Many were not military men—or women—at all but, rather, civilian specialists, thrust into uniform by the exigencies of war, and whose approach to intelligence work would prove quite different from that taken by most career military officers. As we shall see, they combined deep cultural knowledge with innovative methods of intelligence gathering and information analysis, and would also demonstrate unique skill when it came to crafting sophisticated Arabic-language propaganda, both in-house and through trusted local Arab allies. All of this demonstrated a more nuanced understanding of local circumstances and audiences than one would expect from an imperial armed force. Indeed, this unique combination of diverse individuals and expertise enabled approaches that would have been unthinkable in traditional military intelligence units.

The Arab Bureau operated as both an intelligence-gathering organisation and a producer of information and propaganda, working to influence

INTRODUCTION

events as much as understand them. Its members moved between the worlds of British military administration and Arab society, building relationships with local leaders and intellectuals while trying to shape the course of the war in Britain's favour. This dual role—as both observers and actors in the region's transformation—makes the story of the Arab Bureau particularly relevant if we want to understand how intelligence operations can successfully operate in culturally complex environments.

Yet despite its significance, the Arab Bureau remains surprisingly understudied. Its actual activities and innovations have been overshadowed by the mythology around Lawrence of Arabia, while the divide noted by Professor Owen—between scholars of the Middle East and those concerned with intelligence history and operations—has likewise prevented a full appreciation of the Arab Bureau's unique contribution in this arena. This book moves some way to bridging that gap, offering the first comprehensive look at how this remarkable organisation actually worked, what it achieved, and why its approaches to intelligence and cultural engagement remain relevant today.

Drawing on previously overlooked documents in both English and Arabic, including intelligence reports, private papers, and propaganda materials, this book reveals how the Arab Bureau pioneered what might be seen as a distinctly British approach to intelligence, one that combined traditional information gathering with a high degree of cultural engagement and strategic communication. Its story offers valuable insights not just into a fascinating chapter of First World War history, but into the broader challenges of operating effectively across cultural boundaries during periods of rapid change, whether in war or peace.

The single most important factor leading to the creation of the Arab Bureau was the Ottoman Empire's decision to enter the war on Germany's side, even though this event took place fully eighteen months before the Bureau's eventual establishment. Long before the Ottoman entry into the war, the Middle East was strategically vital for the Allies. It is, for instance, impossible to overstate the importance of the Suez Canal as a lifeline to British India. A major supply route for troops and goods, the loss of the Suez Canal, and consequent disruption of ties between British colonial interests and global communications, would have presented an insurmountable obstacle to an Allied military victory.

Given the region's strategic importance, it is incredible to realise that at the start of the war British policy towards the Middle East lay somewhere along a spectrum from ambivalence to disorder. While this is not the place to discuss in detail the numerous reasons for this, we will note in passing a few important points. First, before the disastrous Allied military campaign at Gallipoli, which ran from February 1915 to January 1916, the British High Command underestimated the Ottomans. This was due in large part to a lack of thorough and timely intelligence. Second, during the various Sinai operations, which included attacks against and the defence of the Suez Canal, from early 1915 to August 1916, British military authorities switched course, typically overestimating Ottoman strength. This equally misguided approach was compounded by insufficient intelligence and a shortage of forces to guarantee an effective advance across Sinai. Third, the fear of Muslim unrest in India, which might strike readers as a distant threat, was nevertheless a constant and terrifying prospect for British military planners.

The political situation was also complicated by the fact the two British administrations in London and Delhi had responsibilities for different Turkish, Arab, and Persian portions of the greater MENA, and these duties were often held hostage by competing policy goals. As such, a single Middle East policy considered acceptable by both Britain and India was always going to be a remote possibility. Once the war got underway it was perhaps inevitable that divergent policies towards the region would lead to the emergence of separate sets of intelligence goals, if not needs. Realising these different, sometimes even competing, interests, the Arab Bureau stated that one of its founding principles was "to harmonise British political activity in the Near East"[2] between departments. We will see in due course how that turned out.

From the start, critics of the Arab Bureau, with India leading the charge, accused the new intelligence organisation of failing at every turn. That said, the government in India had long coveted even more administrative control over the Middle East than it already held. As such criticism from that quarter was far from disinterested. Consequently, the government in India actively resented and worked against the Arab Bureau from the start.[3] Setting aside for now the success or failure of the Arab Bureau in coordinating British intelligence activities, our sole concern here is to make clear the British government's belief in the necessity of creating an intelligence unit that would achieve the goal of harmonising British political activity in the Middle East. In this complex geopolitical landscape, the Arab Bureau emerged as a novel approach

INTRODUCTION

to intelligence gathering and analysis. Its establishment reflected British recognition of the need for specialised knowledge and cultural understanding in navigating the intricacies of Middle Eastern politics and society in wartime, and possibly beyond.[4]

The challenges of coordinating these competing interests would shape the development of the Arab Bureau, and yet our understanding of its attempts to steer a path through these complexities has long been overshadowed by one compelling but distorting narrative.

My first literary contact with the Arab Bureau occurred at some unknown date decades ago, when I first read *Seven Pillars of Wisdom* by T.E. Lawrence.[5] This was prompted by an earlier encounter with David Lean's even less historically rigorous but cinematically peerless *Lawrence of Arabia*.[6] Unfortunately, it is in no small part thanks to Lawrence's semi-mythic status that serious academic research into the Arab Bureau as a military intelligence unit was largely absent for many years. Scholars set out either to write another study of that individual man, or to avoid him entirely. In the process, his colleagues and unit were too often completely overlooked.

The Lawrentian spectre continues to haunt the Arab Bureau, so that even today some writers shy away from looking too closely at this branch of British military intelligence. It was only in existence for four and a half years, from January 1916[7] until its closure when, as one of its fiercest contemporary critics later wrote: "The Arab Bureau in Cairo died unregretted in 1920."[8] Setting to one side this unduly harsh critique, the Arab Bureau remains one of the most fascinating branches of military intelligence from the First World War, or indeed from any other period of modern history, and an area worthy of closer academic investigation.

The Arab Bureau occupies a unique position in intelligence history, simultaneously renowned yet understudied. Its innovative approaches to intelligence gathering and analysis in a complex cultural environment set it apart from traditional intelligence units of its time. Although we may be justifiably anxious about encountering the ghost of Lawrence at every turn, it is also obvious that there remain significant gaps in our appreciation of the intelligence work done by the Arab Bureau. As such, this book fills a void in the historiography of wartime and post-war British military intelligence and imperial strategy in the Arab Middle East and North Africa during this period. In moving beyond Lawrence, it is possible to reveal a deeper story of innovation in intelligence gathering, report writing, propaganda production, and cultural engagement. What's more, it is a story we are able to trace through an almost forensic examination of the extensive archival records, some well known, others overlooked until now, both written by and about the Arab Bureau.

The story of the Arab Bureau also offers us lessons about innovation and institutional memory that remain highly relevant for contemporary intelligence operations. By examining how the Arab Bureau adapted to a complex cultural environment, developing pioneering intelligence methods along the way, it is possible for us to glean insights relevant to modern intelligence agencies that find themselves likewise operating in culturally diverse settings while also facing rapid technological and social changes.

In arguing for the innovative nature of the Arab Bureau, this study pays particular attention to their written outputs, both in English and Arabic, and highlights the procedures adopted and outcomes realised in two of the Bureau's primary professional duties: one, gathering intelligence and producing reports based on this; and, two, producing and disseminating Arabic-language propaganda. I chose to focus specifically on the Arab Bureau's written outputs for a number of important reasons. For one thing, these documents provide a direct window into the thought processes, analyses, and priorities of British intelligence agents operating in the Middle East and North Africa at this time.

For another, these written outputs, reports, memoranda, correspondence, and propaganda played a key role not only in informing but also shaping British policy decisions. As such, they are a fascinating resource that allows us to develop a much stronger understanding of the link between intelligence gathering and policy formation. Third, concentrating on these written outputs helps trace the evolution of British perceptions, and misperceptions, of Arab nationalism during this transformational period of the history of the modern MENA region, revealing how intelligence assessments both reflected and influenced broader cultural and political assumptions.

One of my central arguments throughout this book is that it was precisely because of the Arab Bureau's inherently unorthodox makeup and constitution that it was able to demonstrate such ingenuity. This in turn made it possible for it to go beyond practices one might reasonably expect to find in the comparable, rigidly hierarchical, even hidebound, military units of the time. Although they were in uniform for the dura-

INTRODUCTION

tion of their military service, the majority of Arab Bureau members were not career soldiers, and thus generally not inculcated with a formal military mindset.

Given the academic backgrounds many Arab Bureau members came from, it is entirely appropriate to think of them as scholars before soldiers. As we will see, in order to build the sorts of relationships necessary to make them more professionally viable, able to more effectively gather information from local sources, members of the Arab Bureau needed to be particularly attuned to subtle nonverbal cues, and to understand social hierarchies and contextual nuances. In short, their success depended on their capacity to navigate regional cultural terrain as much as the physical geography of deserts and cities.

This innovative approach of gathering together individuals from diverse scholarly backgrounds—including many with some degree of cultural familiarity with the region—was, therefore, integral to the Arab Bureau's achievements. Moreover, the Bureau fostered the emergence of groundbreaking approaches not only to intelligence gathering and reporting but also to propaganda production and dissemination, which deserve much greater recognition than has been the case. This innovative approach to both intelligence and propaganda set the Arab Bureau apart from its contemporaries. The documentary record incontrovertibly reveals an organisation that pioneered new approaches to understanding the region, as well as attempting to influence events there.

The Arab Bureau stands as a compelling if understudied nexus, a meeting point of information, intelligence, and propaganda in the service of imperial strategy. Its actual intelligence activities remain somewhat obscured by incomplete historical narratives. What this means is that, as alluded to above, the Arab Bureau maintains a particular position among the complex tapestry of intelligence units active at this time, in that, while its name is almost universally recognised, many details of its actual intelligence work are not. To clarify this apparent contradiction, the fame (or notoriety) of the Arab Bureau—its reputation—is too often attached to, or overshadowed by, Lawrence. Consequently, its relative obscurity stems from a dearth of scholarly studies providing considered, evidence-based appraisals of the operational activities of the unit as a whole.

In producing an enhanced study of the Arab Bureau and its activities, this book fills a notable gap in the academic record. Not only does it rectify historical omissions, but it also offers new perspectives on the complex interplay between intelligence, cultural understanding, and imperial power during a transformative period in global history. The Arab Bureau's unusual nature was evident not just in its structure but in its day-to-day operations. Its innovative ground-level activity had implications that reached far beyond Cairo, affecting how Britain approached intelligence gathering throughout the empire.

The Arab Bureau's methods were as unconventional as the organisation's composition. Whereas traditional military intelligence focused on enemy troop movements, fortifications, and the like, the Arab Bureau took a decidedly broader view. As well as matters of more traditional military intelligence, it also analysed tribal politics, religious sentiments, and economic conditions. It monitored the emerging Arab press and produced its own Arabic language publications. It tracked the complex web of relationships between local leaders. Most importantly, it worked to understand and influence the currents of Arab nationalism that were beginning to reshape the region.

The comprehensiveness of this approach represented something new in the history of intelligence operations. The Arab Bureau wasn't just gathering information. It was helping to create a new understanding of how intelligence work could operate in culturally complex environments. Its members recognised that in the Middle East success depended not just on knowing the enemy's military capabilities, but on understanding and engaging with the social, cultural, and political dynamics that shaped the region. The significance of such innovative thinking extended far beyond their immediate wartime context.

In summary, the Arab Bureau was a more original and innovative unit of military intelligence than has been previously understood. Where intelligence work is widely understood to include such tasks as collection, collation, and analysis, the Arab Bureau was also an effector, proactively disseminating information and propaganda. This element, which supports the argument about the Arab Bureau's originality, will be considered in full in due course. For now, it is worth mentioning in passing that the Arab Bureau's approach clearly foreshadows the development of later British intelligence units, including the Political Warfare Executive (PWE)[9] in the Second World War and the Information Research Department (IRD)[10] in the Cold War era, and that this deserves to be recognised. As such, it is reasonable to think of the Arab Bureau as the progenitor of a distinctly 'British way' of intelligence, a double-edged approach combining intelligence and propaganda.

INTRODUCTION

The transformation of British intelligence in the Middle East began at dawn one morning in May 1916, with a series of public executions in Damascus and Beirut. As the sun rose on that morning in those two cities, the gallows erected by the Ottoman authorities would cast a far longer shadow than anyone could have imagined. Intending to crush Arab nationalist aspirations through a calculated display of mass hangings, the Ottomans instead created a slew of martyrs whose deaths would transform individual tragedy into collective resistance. Rather than crushing rumblings of Arab nationalist discontent, which had been largely harmless until that point, the hangings instead provided the spark for changes that would reshape both intelligence gathering and the future of the region. No one present that morning could have known they were witnessing not just executions, but the birth of a revolution.

PART I

CRISIS

1

THE GALLOWS AT DAWN

DAMASCUS AND BEIRUT

In which the Ottoman authorities hold public mass hangings of Arab intellectuals in Damascus and Beirut, which events instead of crushing Arab unrest become a transformative moment in Arab nationalist consciousness, turning individual deaths into a collective story of emerging national identity and challenging imperial attempts to suppress intellectual networks. The executions also expose critical failures in British intelligence, while creating a powerful narrative of resistance that would catalyse the Arab Revolt, which begins less than a month later.

"Under the tension, slip, slide, perish"[1]

The story of the Arab Bureau begins not with its creation, but with a failure—a devastating intelligence blind spot that would dramatically alter the course of the war in the Middle East. On a May morning in 1916, as Ottoman authorities erected gallows in Damascus and Beirut, Britain's intelligence apparatus remained unaware of the impending executions that would fundamentally reshape Arab–Ottoman relations and catalyse the Arab Revolt. These public hangings, and Britain's inability to anticipate or prevent them, exposed critical weaknesses in traditional British intelligence methods and set in motion events that would necessitate an entirely new approach to understanding and operating in the region.

Dawn, 6 May 1916. In Marjeh Square, Damascus, Ottoman authorities have erected a gallows large enough to accommodate numerous victims at once. By sunrise, crowds have gathered to witness the public execution of seven prominent Arab intellectuals and nationalist figures. Among them is Abdul-Hamid al-Zahrawi, former Ottoman parliamentarian and president of the First Arab Congress, which had been held in Paris just three years earlier. Also hanged that morning was Abd al-Ghani al-Uraysi, editor of the influential Arabic newspaper *al-Mufid*, and Shafiq Muayyad al-Azm, scion of one of Damascus' most prominent families.

In Beirut on the same morning, another gallows stood ready in Sahat al-Burj ('Tower Square' in English, also known in French as 'Place des Cannons').[2] Another fourteen men faced the gallows, including journalists, poets, and political activists. Ottoman authorities had charged them with treason, specifically with plotting to establish an independent Arab state with British support. While some of the accused had indeed been in contact with foreign powers, others were guilty of nothing more than expressing Arab nationalist sympathies in their writings or private conversations.

The executions were carried out with calculated public brutality. The condemned men were forced to walk to the gallows wearing placards detailing their supposed crimes. Officials had ordered local notables to attend, ensuring the cities' elites would witness the price of disloyalty. Yet the crowds that gathered went far beyond the officially summoned witnesses. In Damascus, thousands filled Marjeh Square and the surrounding streets. The executions lasted through the morning, each death met with a mix of horror and angry murmurs from the onlookers.

News of the executions reached Cairo through multiple channels. The official Ottoman announcement portrayed the deaths as a necessary response to sedition, but private letters and telegrams told a different story. Arab merchants arriving from Syria brought eyewitness accounts. British intelligence networks, fragmented as they were, picked up reports of growing anger throughout the Levant. What was meant to be a demonstration of Ottoman power instead became a rallying cry for Arab independence. These coordinated executions, which the Ottomans had designed as a show of strength, meant to finally crush Arab nationalist aspirations, would instead turn out to be the catalyst for a revolution.

The path to the gallows had been years in the making. In a sense, these executions could be seen as the culmination of rising tensions between Ottoman authorities and Arab reformers. In the preceding years, Arab delegates and political figures had begun advocating for what were, at first, modest reforms. These included calls for the widespread use of Arabic in schools teaching Arab children, for changes in military

THE GALLOWS AT DAWN

conscription that would allow Arab soldiers to serve closer to home, and in some cases increased, if still limited, administrative autonomy for Arabs within the Ottoman Empire. While these demands had originated primarily among Christian Arab intellectuals, they had also gradually, inexorably, gained support from Muslim reformers.

The condemned men represented this emerging coalition, embodying as they did a cross-section of Arab intellectual and political life. In Damascus, al-Zahrawi's journey from Ottoman parliamentarian to accused traitor illustrated the narrowing space for reform. As president of the 1913 Arab Congress in Paris, he had advocated for greater Arab autonomy while carefully maintaining loyalty to the Ottoman state. The Azm family's involvement was particularly significant: they had served the Ottoman state for generations, with Shafiq's grandfather having been *wali*, or governor, of both Damascus and Egypt. The presence of these men among those condemned to die sent a clear message: not even the most established Arab families should imagine themselves immune from Ottoman wrath.

In Beirut, the victims included some of the city's most prominent cultural figures, deliberately spanning religious and social divides. Among their number was Petro Poli, a Catholic journalist whose writings had previously helped bridge sectarian divides. Another was Ahmad Tabbara, whose poetry celebrated Arab cultural heritage while carefully avoiding explicit political statements (although apparently not carefully enough). The Khazen brothers, Philippe and Farid, came from one of Lebanon's most prominent Maronite families. Further, Muslim reformers such as the Mahmassani brothers stood alongside Christian activists, their shared fate demonstrating how Ottoman authorities had come to view, and fear, any expression of Arab identity. For the Ottomans, Arab nationalism had come to be seen as a threat that transcended religious boundaries. The authorities made no distinction between those who had actively sought foreign support and those who had merely expressed sympathy with Arab cultural aspirations. But were these mass hangings a display of strength or weakness? Was this the result of Ottoman anger, or paranoia?

Beyond the Gallows: Crafting a Narrative of Resistance

The executions represented far more than a moment of Ottoman repression. They were a transformative event in the emergence of Arab nationalist consciousness. In deliberately targeting a diverse cross-section of Arab intellectual life, the Ottoman authorities had inadvertently created a powerful narrative of shared identity that transcended sectarian and social divisions. The victims—Muslim and Christian, urban intellectuals and traditional nobles, journalists and politicians—together became symbolic representatives of a nascent political imagination that challenged imperial boundaries. This carefully composed list transformed the deaths of individual men into a collective narrative of emerging Arab identity. The method of execution too was a crucial factor in this transformation. By forcing the condemned men to walk to the gallows wearing placards detailing their 'crimes', the authorities created a humiliating public spectacle that turned individual punishment into a narrative of resistance that would resonate through time.

Commander-in-chief of Ottoman Turkish forces, and Governor of Greater Syria, with discretionary powers, Djemal Pasha[3] was the living embodiment of the Ottoman's hardening stance towards all forms of Arab nationalist aspiration. To the local Arab population, he was known as—indeed, had earned the moniker—*as-Saffah*, 'the Bloodletter' or 'Butcher'. This nickname would follow him for the rest of his life, and it features prominently in later Arab nationalist literature, including in the pages of *Thawrat al-Arab*, or *The Arab Revolt* (literally *The Arabs' Revolt*), a book-length work of propaganda produced by the Arab Bureau in conjunction with the Arab nationalist journalist and author, As'ad Daghir, and which we will discuss in Chapter 9.

Djemal Pasha's path which ultimately led to setting up the gallows in Damascus and Beirut began the previous year with a military humiliation. Appointed commander of the Fourth Army, in February 1915 Djemal failed in his attempts to dislodge British forces that were protecting the Suez Canal. As a result, Djemal initiated a blockade of the entire eastern Mediterranean coast. Ostensibly aimed at preventing supplies from reaching enemy forces, the wartime blockade resulted in a devastating famine coming to Lebanon and parts of Syria. When swarms of locusts descended on the region's crops, this natural disaster with its Biblical undertones would compound the man-made crisis caused by Djemal's blockade. The result was the death, from both hunger and disease, of a quarter or more of the population of Lebanon, a tragedy that Arab writers would later cite as evidence of the Ottoman's inhumane disregard for Arab lives.

THE GALLOWS AT DAWN

Deadly Sympathies: Arab Nationalism in Wartime

Returning to the condemned men on the gallows, the charges against them revealed both the scope of Ottoman fears and the nature of their response to Arab nationalism. Official indictments painted a picture of widespread conspiracy, including allegations that the accused had been corresponding with French and British representatives in order to plot an anti-Ottoman, Arab revolt. Some of these charges had a basis in fact. Several of the condemned had indeed sought foreign support for greater Arab autonomy. However, others were sentenced merely for expressing sympathy with the call for cultural and linguistic rights.

Specific charges varied by individual. For instance, Abdul-Hamid al-Zahrawi was accused of using the 1913 Arab Congress in Paris as a cover, allowing him to negotiate with foreign powers. In Beirut, under Abd al-Ghani al-Uraysi's editorship, the newspaper *al-Mufid* published articles that advocated for Arab cultural rights, even while maintaining formal loyalty to the Sultan. In spite of these public avowals of loyalty to Ottoman rule, the authorities presented such newspaper articles as evidence of sedition. Meanwhile, the Khazen brothers were charged with using their journalistic positions to spread 'separatist ideas'. The Ottoman authorities were making a very public example of these men, albeit for diverse reasons. For one thing, their social and intellectual prominence meant their executions were guaranteed to have maximum impact. Moreover, the diversity of the men's backgrounds—Muslims and Christians, traditional nobles and emerging intellectuals, journalists and politicians—allowed the authorities to present Arab nationalism as a broad conspiracy rather than a limited movement.

The Precipice of Revolt: Hussein's Calculated Rebellion

The mass executions were, however, more than a symbolic moment of Ottoman repression. In fact, they would very quickly be seen as the immediate catalyst that pushed one of the empire's more discontented local rulers from sitting on the fence into open rebellion. Hussein bin Ali al-Hashimi (1854–1931) had been appointed Sharif of Mecca by the Ottomans as recently as 1908, but his relationship with the Ottoman government had been deteriorating more or less since that time. Sharif Hussein's association with the ruling Ottoman power, the Committee of

Union and Progress (CUP),[4] was marked by increasing tensions due to the empire's centralising initiatives and a policy of Turkification, both of which increasingly threatened Hussein's autonomous position in the Hijaz region of western Arabia. In order to guarantee Hussein's compliance with Ottoman orders, various members of his family, including at times one or more of his sons, were required to reside in the Ottoman capital as honoured 'guests' of the Sultan. Coupled with Hussein's wish for ever greater personal autonomy from his ostensible masters, relations with the authorities in distant, although never entirely absent, Constantinople grew increasingly strained over time. The strain only accelerated after the start of the war.

In the spring of 1916, two critical events convinced Hussein that his position under the Ottomans was untenable. First, on 2 April, he received a telegram from Djemal Pasha announcing the dispatch of a 3,500-strong Turkish force travelling to Yemen, but which would be passing through Hussein's domains. Hussein was convinced this was a ruse, a pretext to empty the Hijaz of Arab forces and replace them with Turkish troops, mirroring an Ottoman tactic previously used in Syria. There, local Arab soldiers had been sent to fight in Gallipoli and in their absence had been replaced by Turkish units. The second, more decisive event opening Hussein's eyes to the precariousness of his position were the mass executions in Damascus and Beirut.

Despite personal mediation efforts by Hussein's son, Emir Faisal,[5] the Ottoman authorities went ahead with the mass killings. These should be seen both as an attempt to crush any and all nascent Arab nationalist claims, as well as an utterly unambiguous sign that, even had they previously been indulged, from this point forth there would be no tolerance for any calls for Arab cultural or linguistic recognition, autonomy, or independence. As such, the executions represented more than just a response to a potential political threat, they were a direct assault on the intellectual and cultural foundations of Arab identity that Hussein represented, or which he at least avowed in public. Before 1916, there is little or no evidence of Hussein having any particular interest in Arab nationalism beyond the possibility of his accruing greater territorial or financial gain for himself and his own line. But now, feeling personally threatened, he saw the benefit of acknowledging his Arab-ness and signing up to the cause, perhaps gaining support from Arabs beyond his own tribe and territories.

THE GALLOWS AT DAWN

Faisal's reaction to the news of the hangings was immediate and dramatic. Upon first hearing about the executions, he cried out, "Oh Arabs, death is sweet!" More than a mere rhetorical flourish, his exclamation was a declaration of resistance. This was followed almost immediately by his despatch of a message to his father in Mecca, a message that contained a pre-arranged coded signal. "Send the blonde horse." This cryptic phrase signalled the decision to launch the Arab Revolt.

The timing was carefully calculated. For some months now, Hussein had been in negotiations with the British, particularly through correspondence with the Cairo-based High Commissioner in Egypt, Sir Arthur Henry McMahon. The noted—or notorious—McMahon–Hussein Correspondence was a series of ten letters exchanged between the two men, in which McMahon promised British support for an independent Arab state. As is often the case in matters that would later assume even greater importance, the devil was in the details. In truth, the promises McMahon made in his letters were couched in terms so deliberately vague as to be almost meaningless, or so the British hoped. Regardless of the final status of any post-war territorial arrangements, the executions both angered and terrified Hussein. Convinced that his demise at the hands of the Ottomans was only a matter of time, Hussein took the opportunity provided by the executions as the final impetus for an official, and very public, change of stance as he moved from secret diplomatic negotiations to open rebellion.

Hussein's calculations were complex and multi-layered. His Hashemite dynasty had long been a critical intermediary between local Arab populations and Ottoman central authority. For generations, they had negotiated a delicate balance of autonomy and loyalty, maintaining significant regional influence while nominally accepting Ottoman sovereignty. The executions represented a fundamental breach of this traditional relationship, a signal that the CUP no longer saw local Arab leaders as partners, but as potential threats.

For Hussein, the revolt was both a personal and political calculation. As head of the Hashemite dynasty, which claimed to trace its lineage directly to the Prophet Muhammad, he saw himself as the legitimate ruler of the holy cities of Mecca and Medina. The CUP's increasingly aggressive centralisation policies had already strained Hussein's position. Its efforts to standardise the empire under Turkish cultural and linguistic norms directly challenged the traditional role of Arab elites like the

Hashemites. As alluded to above, with the execution of the Arab nationalist sympathisers, jurists, writers, journalists, intellectuals, and other notables—men who until this point had sought reforms within the Ottoman system—the message was clear: the ground had shifted. Where once there had been an understanding that a space existed for conciliation, perhaps even negotiation or pro-Arab shifts in imperial policy, now there was no room for any degree of cultural autonomy, let alone political opposition. In wartime, the Ottomans now saw the Arabs more like the Armenians, as another enemy within.

The first Arab declaration of independence from the Ottoman Turks came on 5 June 1916. On that day, Hussein's sons Ali and Faisal broke from Turkish rule when they led an attack against Ottoman troops stationed in a camp in Medina, sabotaging the Hijaz Railway that connected the city to the north. Less than a week later, on 10 June, Hussein himself officially launched the revolt with a symbolic rifle shot in Mecca, followed by attacks against Ottoman forces there and against the city's water supply.

Far from a spontaneous uprising, the Arab Revolt should instead be seen as a carefully orchestrated political manoeuvre. Hussein had spent months cultivating relationships with secret Arab nationalist societies, particularly al-Fatat and al-'Ahd in Damascus. The Damascus Protocol[6] of 1915 had already laid the groundwork, affirming these societies' support for a revolt that would establish an independent Arab territory recognised by Britain. Given to Hussein's son Faisal in May 1915 when he was in Damascus en route to Constantinople to consult Ottoman officials, the Damascus Protocol was drawn up by the leadership of al-Fatat and al-'Ahd. In it, they declared that their secret societies would support any anti-Ottoman rebellion led by Sharif Hussein, if the demands in the protocol were also submitted to the British. Those demands effectively defined their territorial aspirations for an independent, post-Ottoman Arab state in the Middle East, which state would encompass Western Asia south of the 37th parallel north. This territorial demand would become the basis of the Arab understanding of the Hussein–McMahon Correspondence. The May 1916 executions shifted the ground, so that their theoretical plan was now seen as an urgent necessity.

Strategically, Hussein understood the geopolitical landscape. The British were eager for a diversion that could disrupt Ottoman military successes, particularly after British defeats at Gallipoli and Kut al-Amara, which will be discussed presently. But Hussein's ambitions extended beyond being a mere British proxy. He sought to position himself as the legitimate leader of an independent Arab state, using the revolt to challenge both Ottoman authority and potential British imperial designs. His lineage provided crucial legitimacy. As a descendant of the Prophet Muhammad, and controlling the holy cities of Mecca and Medina, Hussein could frame the revolt in religious as well as nationalist terms. The executions had demonstrated that the Ottomans were not just a political threat, but a force actively destroying Arab cultural and intellectual life. In launching the Arab Revolt, Hussein would present himself as a protector of both Arab identity and Islamic tradition.

As such, the revolt has to be understood simultaneously as an act of survival, ambition, and cultural preservation, arguably in that order of importance for Hussein. Understanding the important political shift that the executions had effected, by launching the revolt, Hussein was taking a practical and unequivocal step to turn the narrative into political reality, at the same time positioning himself as the leader of this nascent Arab nationalist movement.

British support was crucial, but Hussein's motivations went far beyond simple collaboration with colonial powers. He envisioned an independent Arab kingdom—certainly not a republic or other similar form of 'democratic' state—under his leadership, with the executions serving as the final proof that Ottoman rule was incompatible with Arab aspirations for cultural and political autonomy. As such, it is important to see the hangings as not just a moment of Ottoman brutality, but the precise historical pivot that transformed latent Arab nationalist sentiment into an active revolt. Hussein's decision to rebel was both a strategic calculation and a profound cultural statement, a rejection of Ottoman attempts to suppress Arab identity and political agency.

Bloodstained Networks: Stop the Presses

In practical terms, the executions also succeeded in severing complex networks of intellectual exchange, disrupting entire ecosystems of knowledge exchange and political discourse, knowledge grids that had developed across the Levant's major cities. Coffee houses and literary salons in Damascus, Beirut, and Cairo had fostered a vibrant culture of political and literary discourse, where ideas about Arab cultural revival circulated among educators, journalists, and reform-minded officials. The dead men, each in their own way, had been key nodes in these networks, and their deaths created a series of ruptures in both formal and informal channels of communication and debate.

Their networks, both formal and informal, had been particularly effective in connecting different social spheres. A single evening's salon might see military officers discussing poetry with newspaper editors, or religious scholars debating modern education with secular intellectuals, with merchants perhaps sharing commercial intelligence with political reformers. The impact was especially severe on the Arab press, which had emerged as an ever-stronger vehicle for cultural and political discussion, and was thus a particular target for Ottoman repression and condemnation. Beyond better-known publications, such as *al-Mufid*, dozens of smaller journals and literary reviews had created space for careful exploration of Arab identity and aspiration. The executions sent an unmistakable message to editors and writers across the region about the dangers of such intellectual inquiries.

Deadly Documents: Bloodied French

The evidence of the treachery of the pro-Arab nationalist elites, as Ottoman authorities characterised it, came partly through what many viewed as French betrayal. Shortly after the Ottoman entry into the war, the French authorities evacuated their offices in Beirut in haste. In the process of doing so, they were less than rigorous in destroying sensitive papers, leaving behind numerous documents that implicated several of the accused in correspondence with foreign powers. These letters included one to the French consul requesting French assistance to liberate Syria and Lebanon from Ottoman rule. Despite the American consul, Stanley Hollis—who represented a country that was still neutral at this stage in the war—urging the destruction of any secret or otherwise incriminating papers, his French counterpart refused to do so.[7] As such, the same powers that had encouraged Arab nationalism had failed to protect its advocates. Whether deliberate, as many Arabs still believe, or merely due to incompetence remains a subject of debate. That said, judging the case on its merits, a disinterested observer would almost unequivocally support the theory of it being a cock-up over a conspiracy.

THE GALLOWS AT DAWN

Djemal Pasha's decision to conduct the executions simultaneously in Damascus and Beirut was calculated for maximum psychological impact. By staging such terrible public spectacles in two of the region's most important cities, he sought to demonstrate Ottoman power throughout Greater Syria. Choosing the two public squares, central gathering places where the executions would be witnessed by the largest possible audience, was no mistake. The method of execution was also deliberately archaic. While the Ottoman Empire had modernised many of its institutions, for these executions they chose the traditional gallows in order to stage a macabre show designed to humiliate the condemned and terrify observers. Rather than achieving Arab quiescence, as he had hoped, Djemal Pasha's brutality soon proved counterproductive as, in the weeks that followed, informal networks carried accounts of the killings across Syria and Lebanon, and abroad. Passed from person to person in hushed conversations and smuggled letters, these repeated accounts turned the dawn deaths into a *cri de guerre*. Each retelling emphasised the brutality of the authorities and the courage of the victims. In the markets and coffee houses of Damascus, Beirut, and beyond, the executions became the subject of poems and stories that would circulate for generations.

Rather than crushing nascent Arab nationalism, the executions gave it a raft of martyrs around which opposition to Ottoman rule crystallised. The victims—lauded and mythologised for their dignity in the face of death, their final words proclaiming their innocence of treason while affirming their Arab identity—became powerful symbols that would be evoked repeatedly in nationalist literature and propaganda, including in the pages of *Thawrat al-Arab*.

Martyrs and Memories: From 1916 to 2011

Longer term, not only did the executions transform Damascus' Marjeh and Beirut's al-Burj Squares into powerful symbols of repression and resistance, but both continued to serve as gathering points for political protest in the century that followed. Martyrs' Day is observed on 6 May annually, and has become a central part of both Syrian and Lebanese national identity. In early 2011, as the uprisings of the so-called Arab Spring, which had started in Tunisia the previous December, swept the region, protesters filled these same squares, both of which had been renamed 'Martyrs' Square' in memory of the events of 1916. In 2011, the historical resonance and the symbolism was lost on no one. Many protesters carried banners bearing the names of the victims of 1916 alongside more recent victims of state violence. The spaces that had witnessed the birth pangs of Arab nationalism now hosted its modern inheritors. The historical parallel was explicit. Just as their predecessors had challenged Ottoman authority, a new generation gathered to demand political change, and so, as the 1916 executions exposed the Ottoman Empire's inability to accommodate Arab nationalist aspirations, protestors in 2011 challenged modern governments' resistance to reform. From the executions during the First World War to later movements for Arab political reform and independence, these spaces have maintained significance as sites of both repression and resistance for over a century.

Intelligence Failures: Bloody Ignorance; Battlefield Humiliations

In the spring of 1916, such future resonances were, obviously, impossible to foresee. The executions exposed not only Ottoman brutality but also Britain's strategic blindness in the Middle East. For the British in Cairo, the executions represented more than just the loss of potential allies. They exposed fundamental weaknesses in Britain's intelligence capabilities, and a fundamental lack of cultural understanding that hampered intelligence gathering throughout the region. While British officials maintained networks of informants, they often failed to grasp the complex web of relationships and loyalties that defined Arab political life. The impact of the executions on Arab society likewise caught British intelligence by surprise, revealing how poorly they understood the cultural dynamics they were attempting to influence. At least there was some recognition of this failure in intelligence gathering, which would help drive the creation of a new approach to regional intelligence, one that understood the importance of deep cultural knowledge alongside traditional military information.

With the British unable to prevent the deaths of potential allies, these events would at least play a role in precipitating the Arab Revolt, after months of to-ing and fro-ing on the part of both Hussein and the British authorities in Cairo. More immediately, the executions demonstrated Britain's urgent need for better intelligence about events in the Ottoman Empire. In this light, the timing of the executions was particularly significant. British intelligence failures in the war in the Middle

THE GALLOWS AT DAWN

East would prove calamitous. By mid-1916, two years into the First World War, British efforts against the Ottomans had twice been marked by disaster, so that systemic intelligence weaknesses had resulted in two catastrophic outcomes in a matter of months.

First, at Gallipoli, between February 1915 and January 1916, when British and Allied forces—including Australian, New Zealand (the latter two commonly known as ANZACs), Irish, Indian, and French forces—had suffered over 300,000 causalities, including injured, sick, and other evacuated. Almost 57,000 troops died from combat, disease, exposure to the cold, and other causes in the failed attempt to force the Dardanelles. That Ottoman forces suffered 77,000 fatalities cannot be seen as consolation on either side. The Allies' successful moonlit retreat on the night of 7–8 January, after nearly a year of strategic failure, was possibly the only Allied action that could be seen as a cause for celebration in an otherwise long, costly, bloody, and embarrassing campaign.

Second, in Mesopotamia (modern-day Iraq), an even more humiliating setback had unfolded. On 29 April 1916, following a five-month seige, and just days before the mass hangings in Damascus and Beirut, Major General Charles Townshend surrendered 13,000 British and Indian troops to Ottoman forces at Kut al-Amara, before they were marched into captivity. Nearly seventy per cent would not survive, either dying over the course of the forced march or during their captivity. British officers were given accommodations thought more fitting to their rank, and they sat out the rest of the war without undue suffering, albeit with bruised pride and humiliation. Given sixty years to consider events, Jan Morris described the surrender at Kut al-Amara as "the most abject capitulation in Britain's military history".[8] Morris was ar from being a lone Jeremiah: a century after these events, another reputable historian described this particular military disaster as "the worst defeat of the Allies in World War I".[9]

Both failures stemmed from a fundamental misunderstanding of Ottoman military capabilities, at the root of which lay an outdated approach to military intelligence. The executions highlighted how traditional military intelligence practices, designed for European battlefields, were inadequate for the complex cultural and political landscape of the Middle East. Before the war, the British Army's primary doctrine manual, *Field Service Regulations of 1909*, had not even included an index entry for 'intelligence', instead featuring a chapter entitled 'Information'.

Such a limited conceptualisation of intelligence work, which almost exclusively prioritised maps and formal reports over human intelligence sources, had left Britain ill-equipped to operate in a region where personal relationships and cultural understanding were crucial for gathering reliable information. This rigid adherence to traditional military methods proved particularly costly in the Middle East, where understanding local dynamics was crucial.

Before Gallipoli, British intelligence had dramatically underestimated Ottoman strength and resolve. By contrast, during the advance on Baghdad that led to the disaster at Kut al-Amara, British commanders had overcompensated, attributing to the Ottomans capacities they did not possess and concurrently failing to understand those competences they did. In both cases, Britain's intelligence apparatus had proved inadequate. This was due in no small part to the fragmented nature of British military intelligence at that time, divided as it was between competing departments and lacking deep regional understanding.

Lacking Intelligence, British Weakness Exposed

That the hangings in Damascus and Beirut took place just days after the surrender at Kut al-Amara could be seen as demonstrating Ottoman strength, albeit in a rather limited sense of the word, and British weakness in the region, however one chose to see it. The Ottomans could strike at will, while British intelligence could neither warn nor protect the victims. As reports of the executions filtered through to Cairo, it became increasingly clear that Britain's existing intelligence apparatus was not fit for purpose. The gallows stood as a symbol of British impotence in a region they had long considered their sphere of influence. This impotence was the result of long-standing structural weaknesses in British intelligence gathering. The question was no longer whether change was needed, but what form that change should take.

Before the war, Britain's intelligence gathering in the Ottoman Empire had been largely conducted through consular staff and the diplomatic corps, a system that proved woefully inadequate for wartime needs. Intelligence gathering in peacetime was an imperial activity, one that focused primarily on 'internal' security, which is to say in places under British control, such as Egypt and, beyond Ottoman realms, India. When war came, this limited approach left Britain strategically blind in crucial areas and showed up the traditional reliance on diplomatic channels which were wholly absent following the recall and/or expulsion of one's diplomats from their foreign missions.

The War Office in London, the Government of India, and the Residency in Cairo each maintained their own separate intelligence networks, jealously guarding information while pursuing often contradictory policies. The results were evident not just in military defeats but in missed political opportunities. Before the May 1916 hangings took place, not a single British agency had been able to warn the condemned men, nor intervene on their behalf. More broadly, Britain lacked a single, coherent strategy for engaging with Arab nationalist sentiments that were increasingly turning against Ottoman rule.

It should also be noted that, while the hangings obviously generated tremendous anger among the Arabs, they also caused concern among a number of Ottoman officials in Constantinople. Internal memoranda, later captured by British intelligence, revealed debates about the wisdom of such harsh measures. There were those who saw Djemal's executions as unnecessarily brutal, and who argued that executing respected community leaders would only inflame anti-Ottoman sentiment, even possibly leading to precisely what did take place, an Arab Revolt, albeit not one that spread as far and wide as either the Arab opposition or the British wanted. Other Ottoman officials worried that the public nature of the executions would damage the empire's image among neutral powers, such as the United States. But the hardliners prevailed, convinced that only severe measures could prevent the empire's Arab provinces from following the Balkans into nationalist-inspired separation.

This was not the war anyone had expected in 1914. The Ottoman Empire's entry on Germany's side had transformed what might have been a purely European conflict into one that threatened Britain's imperial lifeline through the Suez Canal to India. But, two years into the war, Britain had failed to adapt either its military approach or its intelligence gathering to the realities of this new front. The need for change was obvious, the form it should take less so. Meanwhile, in Cairo, the British-controlled Egyptian press reported the events in Damascus and Beirut in graphic detail, leaving readers in no doubt about their significance. *Al-Ahram*'s coverage placed the executions in the context of growing Ottoman repression. In Alexandria, where many Syrian intellectuals had found refuge, the executions sparked both numerous private meetings and public demonstrations of solidarity.

THE ARAB BUREAU

Technologies of Resistance: Information Transforms Political Consciousness

It might also be noted here that the executions occurred at a pivotal moment of technological transformation, where traditional and emerging communication technologies collided to reshape political consciousness. This technological landscape would become the precise terrain that the Arab Bureau would later map and manipulate with unprecedented sophistication. News of the executions travelled through a complex ecosystem of communication technologies. Merchant networks, operating much as they had for centuries, carried the news both through oral accounts and in handwritten letters. Now, however, the telegraph allowed for more rapid dissemination of basic information, while newspapers, both local and those published in exile, began to transform these fragmented accounts into coherent political narratives. Each technological layer added depth and complexity to the story of resistance.

The Ottoman authorities had inadvertently created a perfect case study in how information technology could transform political experience. By making the executions a public spectacle, they created a media event that transcended its immediate geographical boundaries. The placards detailing supposed crimes, the carefully staged public nature of the hangings, had themselves become a form of communicative technology designed to send a message of state power. Yet the technologies of resistance were already emerging. Arabic-language newspapers published in Cairo and other centres of Arab intellectual life began to reframe the executions. Journalists and intellectuals understood something crucial. Information was not just a medium of communication, but it might also be a technology of political resistance.

As we shall see, these insights would become central to the Arab Bureau's later innovations. Where the Ottoman authorities saw communication as a tool of control, the Arab Bureau developed a more nuanced understanding of information as a dynamic, networked technology capable of reshaping political consciousness. The Arab Bureau's technological approach was revolutionary for its time. They understood that modern political movements required more than traditional intelligence gathering. Wireless communication, aerial reconnaissance, and pioneering publication strategies became tools for creating what we might now call an information ecosystem.

Both the newspapers the Arab Bureau fostered,[10] as well as flagship productions like *Thawrat al-Arab* (*The Arab Revolt*), exemplified this approach.[11] These were not merely periodicals or formal books, but a form of information technology designed to build a networked political consciousness. Arab Bureau publications integrated multiple information sources—intelligence reports, cultural analysis, propaganda, and direct communication with Arab intellectuals—into a single technological platform.

The Arab Bureau's recruitment of "wandering scholars"[12] was itself a technological innovation. These were not traditional intelligence officers, but communicators who understood how information moved through social networks. They saw communication as a complex system, not a simple transmission of messages. Wireless communication became particularly crucial, with the Arab Bureau swiftly pioneering the use of wireless intelligence, understanding how this technology could simultaneously gather and disseminate information. The Bureau created what we might now call an adaptive information network, capable of rapidly transforming raw intelligence into political narrative. Visual technologies played a crucial role as well. Aerial photography, a cutting-edge technology at the time, allowed for unprecedented methods of intelligence gathering, while maps, photographs, and carefully designed visual propaganda became technologies of political communication as sophisticated as any textual medium.

To reiterate the point, the executions of 1916 can be understood as a critical moment in this technological transformation, demonstrating as they did how political consciousness could be mediated, shaped, and ultimately transformed through emerging communication technologies. While it was clearly inadvertent on the Ottomans' part, they provided the very technological conditions for this consciousness' most powerful articulation. The Arab Bureau took these lessons and transformed them into a revolutionary approach to intelligence and propaganda. Information was no longer just a tool of imperial control; it had become a technology of resistance, a means of creating political consciousness across vast geographical and social distances.

Scholarly Shadows: Reframing the Arab Bureau's Story

Even before my initial approach towards the Arab Bureau as a researcher, the Lawrentian spectre loomed large. However, something else was becoming clear, something long recognised by other scholars in this field. There was surprisingly little research into those Arab Bureau activities that didn't involve blowing up trains and railway lines. In other words, thanks in no small part to David Lean, those most dramatic and explosive elements of the Arab Revolt, had almost entirely overshadowed the Arab Bureau's actual intelligence practices and its broader role in shaping British wartime policy. This was a significant gap in our understanding, and an opportunity to tell a different story.

The oversight is particularly striking given the Arab Bureau's unique position in First World War intelligence history. Bruce Westrate's seminal work, *The Arab Bureau*,[13] illuminated an intelligence agency that had previously been known more by reputation than through its actual day-to-day activities. Yet even Westrate's focus on institutional structure and bureaucracy left significant gaps in our understanding of the unit's practices and effectiveness. More recent scholarship has begun to expand this picture.

For instance, in *Spies in Arabia*,[14] Priya Satia employed a cultural approach to intelligence history, thereby providing a fascinating cultural context that shaped Arab Bureau innovations and operations. In the same year, Polly Mohs' *Military Intelligence and the Arab Revolt*[15] broke new ground in analysing the Arab Bureau's intelligence work, particularly its groundbreaking use of signals and imagery intelligence, while Philip Walker's wonderful *Behind the Lawrence Legend*[16] revealed the contributions of previously overlooked Arab Bureau members, and James Barr's *Setting the Desert on Fire*[17] explored the complex relationship between intelligence gathering, propaganda creation, and military operations during the Arab Revolt.

This study operates within established debates about imperial knowledge production and orientalist discourse, particularly following Said's influential framework and subsequent scholarship by Satia and others.[18] However, rather than rehearsing these well-established theoretical discussions, this analysis takes a different approach, focusing on operational intelligence practices and institutional innovation. While acknowledging the imperial context and cultural assumptions that shaped Arab Bureau activities, the emphasis here is on what they actually did—their methods, sources, and outputs—rather than primarily on imperial discourse or postcolonial critique.

This said, major gaps remain in our understanding of the Arab Bureau's work. Most notably, there has not been any serious evaluation of its Arabic-language propaganda, in spite of this being central to its stated mission. The book-length propaganda project *Thawrat al-Arab*, for instance, has never—until now—been properly studied, and even the Arab Bureau's day-to-day intelligence practices have received insufficient attention, overshadowed by a focus on policy and bureaucracy. For these reasons and more, the connection between its intelligence work and the broader development of Arab nationalism has remained largely unexplored.

This book addresses these gaps by drawing on previously underutilised Arabic sources, including the Arab Bureau's own Arabic-language propaganda materials: newspapers, leaflets, and pamphlets, as well as better-known archives already pored over for decades by scholars, but which can now been seen in a new light when laid out alongside the Arabic materials. Altogether, these sources—the old, newly uncovered, and rediscovered—reveal a complex operation that went far beyond conventional military intelligence. As we shall see, far from simply gathering information, the Arab Bureau actively shaped narratives, built networks, and developed new approaches to understanding and influencing the region.

By examining these materials, we sketch a new picture of a century-old organisation, one that can be seen afresh as more innovative, more original, and more influential than was previously recognised. The chapters that follow trace how the Arab Bureau adapted traditional intelligence methods to meet unique regional challenges, developed new approaches to propaganda and information gathering, and ultimately helped reshape both British intelligence practices and Middle Eastern politics.

This reframing of the Arab Bureau's work sits at the intersection of two evolving scholarly fields. Middle East Studies has moved well beyond its orientalist origins to embrace more nuanced approaches to regional history and politics. While foundational works by the likes of Antonius[19] or Hourani[20] provide essential context about the ideological landscape in which the Arab Bureau operated, recent scholarship by Rogan,[21] Khalidi,[22] Gelvin,[23] and others has illuminated the complex interplay between imperial powers and local actors during the First World War period. Rogan's study situates the events of 1916 within the broader context of Ottoman decline and regional transformation, while Khalidi examines how events such as the mass executions contributed to emergent Arab nationalism. In a not dissimilar vein, Gelvin analyses the complex political loyalties in wartime Syria.

Similarly, Intelligence Studies has emerged as a distinct interdisciplinary field with involved theoretical frameworks for analysing historical operations. Andrew provides essential context on intelligence practices during this period but has also noted that intelligence services often suffer from "historical amnesia",[24] particularly regarding operations before the Second World War. This has resulted in limited integration between intelligence history and regional studies, a gap this research seeks to begin to address, in part by developing the concept of the 'imperial epistemic community', which will be expanded on soon.

The Arabic materials central to this study are critical in revealing the sophistication of the Arab Bureau's approach. Documents in the Foreign Office records, held in the National Archives, Kew, show how the Arab Bureau crafted propaganda narratives combining nationalist themes with anti-Ottoman messaging. Period newspapers from Egypt and the Hijaz—including *al-Qibla*, the official newspaper of the Arab Revolt, and major Egyptian dailies like *al-Ahram* and *al-Muqattam*—provide crucial context for understanding the media landscape in which the Arab Bureau operated. Arabic-language correspondence and intelligence reports found in both British and Middle Eastern archives offer further vital insights into how the Arab Bureau built and maintained its networks of local informants and allies.

By integrating these Arabic sources with English-language materials, we are able to develop a more nuanced understanding of how the Arab Bureau operated as well as, to a limited extent, how its activities were perceived by and influenced local populations, both during and after the war. This dual perspective is particularly valuable in analysing Arab Bureau propaganda efforts and their effectiveness in shaping Arab nationalist narratives.

Methodological Approach and Source Criticism

The Arab Bureau's novel approaches went far beyond traditional intelligence gathering. They developed new reporting formats, pioneered the integration of cultural and political analysis with military intelligence, and created clever propaganda operations that worked with, rather than merely speaking to, Arab audiences. Their methods of cultivating local sources and networks represented a significant departure from conventional military intelligence practices of the period.

THE GALLOWS AT DAWN

Through a close and detailed examination of these innovations, this study demonstrates that the Arab Bureau was more pioneering in its approach to intelligence gathering, analysis, and propaganda than has previously been recognised. In offering this new perspective, we are able to not only enhance our understanding of First World War intelligence operations, but also to gain new insights relevant to contemporary intelligence practices and Middle Eastern politics. But first, we must understand how this unusual organisation began its work. And so, while outrage over the executions continued to spread across the Arab world, the recently established Arab Bureau was settling into its Cairo headquarters, a suite of rooms in the Savoy Hotel.

Before going any further, I need to include here a note about my methodological approach and source criticism. This note is essential, but so is keeping it short so as not to alienate readers. As I have already stated, this work draws on extensive archival materials, while treating Arab Bureau sources as constructed institutional narratives, which is to say that we must keep in mind the fact that documents and records produced by the Arab Bureau—or, indeed, any comparable institution—are not, nor should they be read as, objective, factual accounts of what happened. Rather, they are purposefully shaped stories that reflect the institution's perspective, interests, and biases, wittingly or otherwise.

As such, it is important for the reader to understand, and for me to state explicitly, that the archival materials have been subjected to close critical interrogation rather than simply accepted at face value as objective historical records. Intelligence reports, memoirs, and administrative correspondence served multiple functions, such as conveying information while justifying the Arab Bureau's existence to sceptical superiors. Claims of innovation, cultural understanding, and analytical sophistication are therefore examined against external evidence rather than uncritically taken at their word.

This study builds on but diverges from Satia's cultural analysis in *Spies in Arabia*, which book emphasised how orientalist attitudes shaped British intelligence practices. While acknowledging these cultural dynamics, the focus of this work is very much on operational intelligence innovations rather than imperial discourse, which is to say examining what the Arab Bureau actually did rather than primarily how it perceived its subjects. Satia's work on cultural attitudes provides context but underestimates the Arab Bureau's genuine operational innovations in intelligence gathering and propaganda dissemination.

THE ARAB BUREAU

The Unintended Revolution: Brutality Breeds Resistance

As noted above, by 1916, the inadequacies of traditional British intelligence approaches in the Middle East had become starkly apparent. The mass hangings demonstrated not only the human cost of these failures but also the urgent need for new approaches to intelligence gathering and analysis. As the Arab Bureau got to work in Cairo, and reached out to agents and allies across the region, its members faced the challenge of developing methods that could bridge the gap between academic expertise and operational intelligence requirements, while navigating the complex cultural and political landscapes of the region.

The transformation of a group of academics, archaeologists, linguists, and unconventional military officers into a revolutionary intelligence unit would represent a significant departure from traditional British military practices. Their task was to create new frameworks for understanding and engaging with the Middle East at a moment when the region's strategic importance to Britain had never been greater, and when British intelligence capabilities had hardly ever seemed more inadequate.

In order to understand how Britain found itself so unprepared for this moment, we must first examine how the Ottoman Empire's entry into the war caught Britain off guard, and how the entry of an empire which had long been derided as the 'sick man of Europe' transformed what might conceivably have remained a European conflict into one that threatened British global imperial interests.

The gallows of Damascus and Beirut thus marked both an ending and a beginning; the brutal conclusion of one phase of Arab nationalist activity and the catalyst for new approaches to resistance and intelligence work. The fundamental question now facing British authorities was: How had they been so utterly unprepared for these pivotal events? To understand this failure, we must examine how Britain's traditional imperial intelligence system had proven catastrophically inadequate when confronted with the complexities of the Ottoman Empire at war.

2

UNPREPARED FOR WAR

BLACK SEA, CONSTANTINOPLE, EGYPT, INDIA

In which Britain's unpreparedness for war with the Ottoman Empire is revealed through a series of intelligence failures, from the escape of two German warships to military disasters at Gallipoli and Kut al-Amara. We also see how these setbacks exposed fundamental weaknesses in British military intelligence—including fragmented administration, inadequate cultural understanding, and poor coordination between departments—which resulted in a push for new approaches, and how these led to significant innovations in intelligence practices, notably combining military requirements with cultural expertise, and the formation of the Arab Bureau.

Opening Shots

On 29 October 1914, Ottoman warships slipped into the Black Sea and, without warning, opened fire on Russian ports. The SMS[1] *Goeben* and SMS *Breslau*—German battlecruisers that had sought refuge in Constantinople and been nominally transferred to Ottoman control—bombarded Odessa, Sevastopol, and other Russian installations along the coast. This surprise attack announced the entry of the Ottoman Empire into the First World War on Germany's side, a development that would ultimately transform the conflict and reshape the modern Middle East.

The presence of these German ships in Ottoman waters was itself a telling sign of British intelligence failures. In August 1914, after the start of the war in Europe, the Royal Navy, despite having superior forces in position to intercept them, had allowed the *Goeben* and *Breslau* to escape across the Mediterranean and ultimately to reach Constantinople.[2]

THE ARAB BUREAU

This was more than a minor naval blunder. The SMS *Goeben* was one of Germany's most modern battle cruisers, faster than any British warship in the Mediterranean, and armed with ten 11-inch guns. Its arrival in Constantinople immediately altered the regional balance of power, giving the Ottomans a warship more powerful than the entire Russian Black Sea fleet. The ships' crews remained German, their officers kept their German ranks, and they continued to take orders from Berlin, all facts that British intelligence was slow to confirm and analyse. The fact that the Royal Navy failed to halt the escape of these two prize ships highlighted a broader unpreparedness that would characterise British operations in the region. More than this, the arrival of the ships in Constantinople also had much further-reaching consequences, as together they effectively doubled Ottoman naval power overnight and gave Germany a powerful tool to draw the somewhat reluctant Ottomans into the war.

The Latin adage *Si vis pacem, para bellum* can be translated as "If you want peace, prepare for war." In October 1914, following the Ottomans' entry to the fight, the situation might be better seen as a case of *Male paratum ad bellum*: being ill-prepared for war. For Britain, the Ottoman entry into the war represented a catastrophic intelligence failure on multiple levels. Despite maintaining an extensive diplomatic presence in Constantinople and commercial ties throughout the Ottoman domains, British intelligence had almost entirely failed to anticipate this pivotal turn of events. The Foreign Office and India Office had relied on outdated assumptions about Ottoman weakness and internal divisions, while too many military planners had focused all their attention on Europe, leaving Britain woefully unprepared for a new front in the Middle East.

The implications were immediately apparent and far-reaching. Within hours of the Black Sea attacks, Russia had declared war on the Ottoman Empire, and Britain and France quickly followed suit. Overnight, the global strategic map was redrawn. The Suez Canal, Britain's umbilical cord to India, was now potentially threatened. The Dardanelles, also known as the Strait of Gallipoli, after an adjacent peninsula—or for those whose thoughts might hark back to classical antiquity, the Hellespont—had now become a crucial military objective. In addition, it was possible that the Ottomans' decision to pick a side might result in millions of Muslim subjects across the British Empire doing the same, forcing them to choose between religious loyalty to the Ottoman Caliphate and political allegiance to Britain and its empire.

The threat of an empire-wide anti-British uprising among Muslim subjects from Egypt to India was a fear that had been circulating for a number of years in London, New Delhi, and in the pages of sensationalist popular fiction, most brilliantly in John Buchan's geopolitical thriller *Greenmantle*. The Ottomans' entry into the war was a moment of crisis that more than any other exposed deep flaws in Britain's regional intelligence capabilities. Traditional diplomatic reporting had failed to grasp the extent of German influence in Constantinople. On the other hand, it had been shown that military intelligence had focused too narrowly on the size, make-up, morale, and movement of foreign forces, at the expense of missing broader political and social developments. Perhaps most critically in the Middle East and North Africa, British authorities lacked sufficient cultural understanding and general Arabic language skills to gauge broad political and social sentiments at play within local Arab populations. These shortcomings would have dire consequences in the months ahead.

The Black Sea raid ended British complacency regarding its approach to understanding Ottoman affairs. In spite of years of British diplomatic efforts to maintain good relations with Constantinople, here was incontrovertible evidence of just how thoroughly German influence had penetrated Ottoman military and political circles. More fundamentally, it revealed how little British intelligence understood about decision-making processes within the Ottoman government, the extent of German influence, or the complex relationships between Turks and Arabs within the empire.[3] Such a lack of basic understanding would hamper British operations throughout the early years of the war, leading to costly mistakes and missed opportunities before new approaches to intelligence were finally developed.

Pre-War Intelligence Failures

Before 1914, British intelligence gathering in the Ottoman Empire was fragmented and uncoordinated. The Foreign Office relied primarily on diplomatic reporting from embassies and consulates, while the India Office maintained its own network of political agents focused on protecting routes to India. Military intelligence officers collected basic information about Ottoman forces but rarely went any deeper, typically overlooking broader social and political conditions. Nor was there any centralised analysis that might have allowed for comparisons to be made between these different streams of intelligence, nor any mechanism for sharing crucial information between departments.

Such a disconnected approach reflected broader problems in British intelligence at the time. Despite maintaining the world's largest empire, Britain entered the First World War without any truly coordinated intelligence service. The War Office had a small intelligence branch, but this focused narrowly on military matters, whereas the fledgling Secret Service Bureau, established in 1909, concentrated almost entirely on counter-espionage at home. No agency had responsibility for anything like comprehensive analysis of intelligence from abroad, nor was there any real appreciation for the need to understand cultural and social dynamics in potential conflict zones.

The roots of this intelligence failure ran deep. As early as 1863, a Chief Justice in Bombay had written that "the chief administrators of our vast Indian Empire ... are often, if not habitually, in complete ignorance of the most patent facts ... around them".[4] This damning assessment, made in the wake of the Indian Rebellion,[5] had led to some changes in how intelligence was gathered in India, but similar blind spots persisted in other parts of the empire. In Ottoman territories, British officials consistently underestimated the empire's military capabilities, informed it should be said by a number of notable Ottoman military defeats and poor political cohesion. Officials often dismissed reports of growing German influence in Constantinople as alarmist. Most significantly, too few officials understood the complex interplay between Islamic religious authority, Arab nationalist aspirations, and Ottoman political control that would shape the region's response to war.

This intelligence failure stemmed partly from cultural limitations. Few British officials spoke Arabic or Turkish, while fewer still understood the religious and social structures that shaped local politics. The handful of non-local Arabic speakers that were on hand were scattered across different departments with little coordination, while those in possession of valuable cultural insights tended to be academics or explorers with no formal intelligence roles. As such, their expertise remained largely untapped until the pressures of war forced the authorities to try new approaches.

UNPREPARED FOR WAR

The pre-war period also saw persistent rivalry between different branches of British administration. The India Office, which had long had the Persian Gulf and much of Arabia under its sphere of influence, was reluctant to cede any bureaucratic power it held in the region and often seemed to be deliberately working at cross-purposes with the Foreign Office. Elsewhere on and off Whitehall, the War Office maintained its own limited intelligence operations with little reference to diplomatic reporting, and the Admiralty, despite its crucial role in protecting imperial communications, operated largely independently of all other departments.

Such institutional divisions were, perhaps inevitably, only exacerbated by competing strategic visions. Like a hammer seeing every problem as a nail, the India Office upheld a tight focus on two primary areas of concern: protecting sea routes to India and maintaining stability among Muslim populations on the Indian subcontinent.[6] For its part, the Foreign Office had a not unreasonable desire to preserve the Ottoman Empire as a buffer against Russian expansion, although here again this was too narrow an approach with regard to wider geopolitical trends, risks, and even opportunities. For military planners, the Middle East was viewed very much as a peripheral concern, and they preferred to concentrate their planning on European scenarios. In each case, one might say that there existed reasonable grounds for each agency to adopt the view they did, but one might also state that in each case it is also clear—if only with the gift of hindsight—that each single agency had too narrow a view of its task, which meant not being fully aware of the interconnected nature of the forces ranged against them. As such, no single department had the capability, nor the authority, to reconcile these different perspectives into something approaching a coherent strategic assessment.[7]

The result was a dangerous blindness to developing threats. British intelligence failed to recognise the extent of German military influence in the Ottoman army, despite clear signs of their increasing cooperation. They misread the political dynamics within the CUP, the dominant force in Ottoman politics. They underestimated Ottoman military prowess, based on a series of pre-war defeats. Most crucially, they failed to develop any substantial understanding of Arab political aspirations or the potential for nationalist movements to reshape the region. Such gaps in their understanding proved costly once war in the Middle East broke out, forcing Britain to develop new intelligence capabilities as a result of several bitter experiences.

War Comes to Egypt: From Veiled Protectorate to Occupation

When war erupted in Europe at the end of July, Egypt occupied a peculiar position in Britain's imperial framework. Though effectively under British control since 1882 through what was dubbed the 'veiled protectorate', Egypt technically remained under Ottoman sovereignty. This legal fiction had allowed Britain to maintain its stance as a defender of Ottoman territorial integrity while exercising de facto control via 'advisers' embedded throughout the Egyptian government. The outbreak of war forced Britain to abandon this careful diplomatic balance.

The initial crisis came in the form of an absent ruler, Khedive Abbas Hilmi II.[8] Recuperating in Constantinople following an assassination attempt, Abbas Hilmi Pasha found himself caught between his technical allegiance to the Ottoman sultan and his practical subordination to British authority. In Cairo, Prime Minister Hussein Rushdi, following directives handed to him by Sir Milne Cheetham,[9] the British consul general, moved swiftly to demonstrate Egypt's alignment with British interests by expelling German and Austro-Hungarian diplomats and seizing Central Power assets. This action, taken while the nominal ruler was abroad, highlighted the reality of where true power lay in Egypt.

With the Ottoman empire's de facto entry into the war, what had been an awkward situation for Britian in Egypt became untenable. Abbas Hilmi II, still enjoying his convalescence in Constantinople, called upon Egyptians to fulfil their duties as subjects of the Ottoman sultan and take up arms against the British. Such a demand forced Britain's hand. General John Maxwell,[10] commander of British forces in Egypt, quickly declared martial law while simultaneously attempting to reassure the Egyptian population with a remarkable, or perhaps unbelievable, promise. In a public address on 5 November, Maxwell announced that Egypt would remain officially neutral in the conflict and that "Great Britain takes upon herself the solemn burden of the present war without calling upon the Egyptian people for aid".[11] Maxwell's promise would ring hollow.

The declaration of the formal protectorate in December 1914 marked the final abandonment of the pre-war diplomatic fiction, which was topped off with the deposition of Abbas Hilmi and the installation of his altogether more pro-British uncle, Hussein Kemal,[12] as sultan. By these means, Britain signalled both its permanent intentions towards Egypt and a willingness to reshape the regional political landscape. The new high commissioner would replace the consul general, making explicit what had long been implicit: Egypt was firmly under British control. Unsurprisingly, Egypt became a crucial military staging ground, with British and imperial forces swelling from an initial 30,000 in the summer of 1914 to over 450,000 by the end of the war.

The declaration of the protectorate also transformed Cairo itself. The streets were utterly transformed as military operations took over all major hotels and public spaces, while a supporting economy—from bars to brothels, and everything besides—sprang up to service the troops. Cairo's belle époque elegance acquired a more martial aspect as hotels were requisitioned for military use, hospitals expanded, and camps sprung up on the outskirts. Shepheard's Hotel, long a symbol of European privilege in Egypt, became a military headquarters, while the Savoy would soon house the Arab Bureau itself. These physical changes reflected deeper transformations in the relationship between British authorities and Egyptian society, setting the stage for the complex dynamics that would characterise the war years.

The transformation of Egypt's status from the so-called 'veiled protectorate' to the new, more formal arrangement, also triggered complex reactions across Egyptian society itself. Urban intellectuals, who had been developing nationalist ideas since the 1870s, found their political aspirations suddenly curtailed. The professional classes, particularly lawyers and journalists, faced new restrictions on their activities. Meanwhile, the poorest of the poor—the rural *fellaheen*,[13] farmers and other agricultural labourers—would soon feel the weight of wartime demands for labour and resources. Although Egyptians were barred from military service, more than 300,000 would be forcibly conscripted as manual labour to support the British war effort. Even those Egyptians who had prospered under British influence found themselves navigating an increasingly complicated political landscape.

British Responses: Control and Contradiction

The war forced upon Britain an immediate and paradoxical shift in imperial policies towards different kinds of nationalism in the region.

THE ARAB BUREAU

For instance, while British authorities would soon begin actively cultivating Arab nationalist sentiment against Ottoman rule across much of the Middle East, in Egypt the more immediate priority was the suppression of Egyptian nationalist activities. Now that Egypt was officially occupied by a foreign power, Egyptian nationalist activities had a more obvious tendency to being de facto anti-British, and so might threaten Britain's control over this strategically crucial territory. By contrast, an anti-Ottoman, Arab nationalist uprising in the Hijaz, over which Britain had no desire to lay territorial claim, was fully in line with British war aims. This contradiction would shape British policy throughout the war years and beyond.

The swift implementation of martial law in November 1914 marked the beginning of this new phase. British authorities moved quickly to silence Egyptian nationalist voices, particularly those who might sympathise with Ottoman calls for pan-Islamic unity. The press, already under heavy censorship, found itself further restricted. Egyptian nationalist leaders faced arrest for activities such as distributing pamphlets critical of British rule—an ironic preview of one of the propaganda tactics soon to be employed by the Arab Bureau in support of Arab nationalism beyond Egypt's borders.

The British response to Ottoman entry into the war culminated, in December 1914, with the formal declaration of the protectorate and the installation of Hussein Kamel as Sultan of Egypt. This carefully orchestrated transition revealed both the strengths and limitations of British intelligence and influence operations at this early stage of the war. While British authorities successfully managed the immediate political transition, they struggled to shape Egyptian public opinion. Moreover, their attempts to ingratiate the new sultan with the Egyptian public through carefully placed press reports demonstrated a rather blunt, if traditional, approach to imperial propaganda, one that would soon be refined by the Arab Bureau.

The Egyptian nationalist response to these developments proved more complex than British authorities had anticipated. Beyond the drama of two failed assassination attempts against Hussein Kamel in 1915, Egyptian activists developed networks for distributing anti-British literature that would later be studied and adapted by the Arab Bureau for its own purposes. Law students staged silent protests, while underground nationalist societies proliferated despite British surveillance efforts. Such activities represented exactly the kind of grassroots nationalist organising that British authorities would later want to encourage among Arab populations still under Ottoman rule.

This period of contradiction—suppressing nationalism in Egypt while preparing to foment it elsewhere—highlighted the need for more nuanced approaches to intelligence and propaganda in the region. The heavy-handed implementation of martial law and censorship achieved immediate control but generated resentment that would have long-term consequences. Meanwhile, Egyptian nationalists' successful development of underground information networks demonstrated the kind of refined propaganda and intelligence-gathering capabilities that British authorities themselves lacked. The lessons learned from this period would directly influence the later development of the Arab Bureau's more subtle and culturally informed approaches to both intelligence gathering and propaganda distribution.

Key Departments, Competing Interests

In 1914, there were no fewer than eighteen different British officials with authority to make or influence one or more aspects of Middle East policy. Such an administrative tangle virtually guaranteed confusion and contradiction, with each department viewing any domestic or regional developments through its own narrow lens, which thus meant often working at cross-purposes with other branches of government. As was noted by Mark Sykes, one of the most famous (or notorious) British officials among that number with responsibility for the region noted, the result was an "administrative morass" in British Middle Eastern operations. As Sykes was to minute, this meant there was in place a system that stumbled "from crisis to inertia, and from coma to panic, watching assets frittered away and opportunities missed".[14]

The situation was made worse by personal and institutional rivalries. Officials jealously guarded their spheres of influence, viewing other departments as competitors rather than collaborators. Complex reporting chains meant that information often had to pass through multiple offices before reaching decision-makers, losing clarity and urgency in the process. As one contemporary observer noted, the system seemed designed to prevent rather than promote coordinated action. Such administrative chaos clearly demonstrated an urgent need for new British policy.

The India Office, historically the most powerful voice in regional affairs, understandably viewed everything through the prism of Indian security so that any development that might stir up religious sentiment among Britain's Indian Muslim subjects was viewed with alarm.[15] As such, the India Office's approach to the Ottoman Empire was, and would remain, deeply conservative, preferring to maintain the status quo at almost any cost rather than run the risk of upheaval.

Meanwhile, in the immediate pre-war years, the Foreign Office in London had pursued its own agenda through its embassy in Constantinople and a network of consuls throughout the Ottoman domains. Foreign Office officials tended to focus on maintaining diplomatic relations with the Ottomans and balancing European interests in the region. While they often viewed India Office concerns about Muslim sentiment as exaggerated, which frequently led to policy clashes between London and Delhi, they also saw value in maintaining the status quo, not least to stop Russia from moving on Persia, and from there into India: here was an opinion on which both London and New Delhi could agree. As Lord Salisbury had allegedly opined in the previous century, when asked why he refused to advocate for forcing greater changes in the Ottoman Empire: "Change? Why would you want things to change? Surely they are bad enough already?!"

As already noted, the War Office and the Admiralty both maintained other, different perspectives, which also meant layers of complexity, focusing here on narrow military considerations and there on intelligence networks solely concerned with shipping routes and coaling stations. The different strategic priorities held by each agency were real enough, but so too was the resultant dysfunctional state of intelligence gathering, interpretation, and reporting. Meanwhile, in Egypt, colonial administrators not only represented yet another centre of British influence—arguably with the best, if still imperfect, understanding of intra-regional actors—but they often found themselves caught between the competing demands from London, Delhi, and local Egyptian interests.

It will come as no surprise that such fragmentation had serious consequences, with information crucial to understanding region-wide developments often remaining locked in one or more departmental silos. These organisational weaknesses and administrative chaos contributed directly to Britain's early failures in the Middle East theatre. No single department had the authority or capability to develop a comprehensive strategy. No mechanism existed for sharing intelligence across institutional boundaries. No one was responsible for understanding the complex interplay of military, political, and cultural factors that would shape events. Reports warning of growing German influence in Constantinople, for instance, might reach one department but not be shared with others, while informed assessments of Arab political sentiment that might have made a real, practical difference were rarely circulated beyond the tightknit circle of officials who collected them. Consequently, news of, say, Ottoman military preparations often failed to reach those who could act on it. In short, there was plenty of intelligence, but almost no common sense.

Disaster at Gallipoli: Resistance and Retreat

The Gallipoli campaign of 1915 starkly revealed the consequences of Britain's intelligence failures. What began as an ambitious plan to force the Dardanelles and capture Constantinople became a costly demonstration of how thoroughly British forces had underestimated their wartime foe. The campaign's failure would force a fundamental reassessment of British intelligence practices in the region.

From the start, the operation suffered from inadequate intelligence. British planners relied heavily on outdated maps and pre-war reports that failed to capture recent Ottoman defensive preparations. Naval intelligence had little information about modernised coastal defences or newly laid minefields. Most critically, military intelligence had severely underestimated both the fighting capability of Ottoman forces and their determination to resist. The initial naval attempt to force the straits in February 1915 revealed these intelligence gaps in devastating clarity. Allied ships found themselves facing more numerous and better-placed guns than they had expected. Minefields proved far more extensive than intelligence had indicated. The loss of three capital ships in a single day forced the British to undertake a fundamental change in approach, leading to the decision to launch a land campaign that would prove even more costly.

The subsequent amphibious landings in April exposed further intelligence failures. British forces had little detailed information about the terrain they would be fighting over. Maps were inadequate, showing major features but missing crucial tactical details of the terrain, which is to say plans of cliffs, gullies, and other potential obstacles or defensive positions. As well as that, intelligence about Ottoman troop dispositions, the operational area upon which British military intelligence had supposedly focused, was often vague or inaccurate.

Most significantly, British intelligence had failed to understand the quality of Ottoman troops and leadership. Mustafa Kemal, the Ottoman commander later known to the world as Atatürk,[16] proved more tactically adept than British planners had assumed possible. Ottoman soldiers, fighting to defend their homeland, displayed levels of determination and combat effectiveness that British intelligence assessments had dismissed as unlikely. Notably, three pre-First World War defeats suffered by the Ottomans—in Libya against invading Italian forces in 1911, and in two Balkan wars in 1912 and 1913—were an important factor in the negative perception of Ottoman fighting ability held by its enemies, Britain and France—and even by its German and Austro-Hungarian allies—at the start of the First World War. However, one important if overlooked element in this equation was that, in those three wars, defeat did not come at the cost of territorial losses to the Turkish homeland, whereas at Gallipoli the motivation for Turkish troops was far stronger.[17]

The human cost of the intelligence failures at Gallipoli was enormous. Allied forces found themselves fighting uphill against well-prepared positions, suffering casualties that far exceeded pre-operation estimates. What had been planned as a bold stroke to knock the Ottomans out of the war instead became a grinding campaign of attrition that would last eight months before ending in humiliating evacuation. The failure of the campaign forced Britain to confront serious deficiencies in its intelligence capabilities. Traditional methods of intelligence gathering had proven entirely inadequate for modern warfare. The need for better maps, more accurate information about enemy capabilities, and deeper understanding of Ottoman military effectiveness became painfully clear.

As such, one can say that, among other intelligence matters, the disaster that was Gallipoli highlighted the importance of cultural understanding in military operations. British planners had dismissed Ottoman fighting capabilities, based partly on racial and cultural prejudices common in the pre-war period, but also on those pre-1914 Ottoman defeats already mentioned. These assumptions proved not just wrong but dangerous, leading to costly tactical and strategic miscalculations. The evacuation from Gallipoli, while brilliantly executed, marked a turning point in British military intelligence. It demonstrated the need for smarter approaches to gathering and analysing information about potential opponents. The lessons learned would influence the development of new intelligence capabilities, including the creation of specialised units with deeper regional expertise.

Catastrophe at Kut al-Amara: Siege, Surrender, Death March

If Gallipoli exposed weaknesses in British intelligence and planning, the siege and surrender of Kut al-Amara revealed them in even starker terms. The surrender of Major General Charles Townshend's[18] roughly 13,000-strong force in April 1916, after a 147-day siege, marked what many historians reckon to be the British Army's worst defeat since the American Revolutionary War—or the American War of Independence,[19] as the reader prefers—and the surrender at Yorktown, in 1781, of approximately 8,000 British and Allied troops under Cornwallis.[20] Like Gallipoli, the surrender at Kut al-Amara stemmed in large part from profound intelligence failures and cultural misunderstandings.

The campaign began optimistically enough, with British forces advancing up the River Tigris from Basra, initially meeting limited resistance. Townshend's 6th Indian Division—which consisted mainly of fresh, fit, newly-recruited soldiers from Western India—captured Kut al-Amara in September 1915. The town of Kut, which name is said to derive from a Hindi word for fort, sits in eastern Iraq (or Mesopotamia as it then was) on the left bank of the Tigris, roughly 100 miles (160 kilometres) south-east of Baghdad. Ambitious planners in India, far from the action, urged a continued advance on Baghdad, a plan that was encouraged by limited and erroneous military intelligence that suggested Ottoman forces in Mesopotamia were weak and demoralised. Further demonstrating a distinct lack of insight or cultural awareness, political officers in the employ of the Government of India predicted local Arabs would welcome British troops as liberators. Such assessments proved catastrophically wrong.

In November, as Townshend pushed towards Baghdad, he encountered unexpectedly strong Ottoman resistance at Ctesiphon, which had served for more than 800 years as the capital of various Persian empires, including the Parthians—of the Parthian, or 'parting shot' fame—and Sasanians. Only about 22 miles (35 kilometres) south-east of Baghdad, the frustration of the British/Indian forces must have been palpable. Here, military intelligence had underestimated both the size of the Ottoman forces and their fighting quality. The battle ended in British retreat, with Townshend's exhausted troops forced back to positions at Kut, where they soon found themselves besieged by a reinvigorated Ottoman army.

The intelligence failures that led to this situation were comprehensive, from inadequate maps of the region to spotty and thus inadequate information about Ottoman troop dispositions. Further, British understanding of local tribal politics proved superficial at best, while, perhaps most crucially, military planners had failed to grasp the logistical challenges of operating in Mesopotamia, which led to serious deficiencies in medical support and supply arrangements. All of these shortcomings were mercilessly exposed over the course of the ensuing siege. Relief attempts failed repeatedly, partly due to poor intelligence about Ottoman defensive positions and local terrain and climate. For instance, British forces had little to no understanding of local seasonal flooding patterns and how these would affect military operations. Medical arrangements too proved woefully inadequate, with thousands of troops suffering from disease and malnutrition. By the time Townshend surrendered on 29 April 1916, more than half his Indian troops were dead or incapacitated. Thousands more would perish on what amounted to a death march into captivity, although notably not the senior British leadership. To be the officer responsible for what has been called the worst British military defeat in more than 130 years is one thing, but to enjoy a comfortable captivity—as Townshend did—while one's men endured terrible conditions, dying in droves, might be likened to having shame heaped upon ignominy.

The disaster had profound implications for British military intelligence, and the 1917 Mesopotamia Commission[21] that followed highlighted serious flaws in intelligence gathering and assessment. Information that might have prevented the disaster had existed but remained trapped in departmental silos, while reports warning about logistical challenges had been ignored. Also, as elsewhere in the Middle East during the First World War, intelligence assessments were coloured by racial prejudices that consistently underestimated Ottoman capabilities. Most damningly, the Commission revealed that different branches of British administration had worked at cross-purposes throughout the campaign. The India

Office, which controlled operations in Mesopotamia, had pushed for an advance on Baghdad despite warnings from other departments about the risks, whereas military intelligence, with its narrower focus on the enemy's order of battle, had missed crucial political and logistical factors that would determine the campaign's outcome.

The human cost of the defeat was staggering. Of the close to 13,000 troops who surrendered at Kut, more than 4,000 died in or en route to captivity. Most of this number were Indian soldiers, their suffering exacerbated by racially motivated abuse and deliberately inhumane treatment on the part of their captors. Kut al-Amara demonstrated, even more clearly than Gallipoli, the need for fundamental changes in British intelligence practices. Traditional methods of intelligence gathering and analysis had yet again proved inadequate for modern warfare in culturally distinct environments. This latest disaster only added to the urgency of those calling for new approaches and operational methods that might be able to combine military expertise with deeper cultural and regional understanding.

Searching for a Novel Approach

By early 1916, thanks to the successive defeats at Gallipoli and Kut al-Amara, Britain was forced to confront its serious deficiencies in its regional intelligence capabilities. Traditional methods had clearly failed to provide anything approaching the comprehensive understanding needed for effective operations in the Middle East. Although the push for new approaches would ultimately lead to significant innovations in intelligence gathering and analysis, at this stage any such positive outcome, from the perspective of British intelligence requirements, was far from certain.

Perhaps the most obvious need was for better coordination between different branches of intelligence, to overhaul—or better still remove altogether—the "administrative morass" that Mark Sykes had already noted, where eighteen separate departments were ostensibly working for the same goal, but without knowing this was the case and rarely if ever speaking to one another. Sykes, already involved in Middle Eastern affairs and more widely travelled than most of his peers, emerged as a strong advocate for a more focused approach to Arab affairs. The first forum for discussions of this nature was the de Bunsen Committee, on which Mark

Sykes sat, representing the secretary of state for war, Lord Kitchener.[22] Kitchener was appointed secretary of state for war within a week of the start of the conflict in Europe. An exception among cabinet ministers in that he foresaw a long war—of at least 3 years' duration, by his reckoning—he also had the power to start planning for this, and as such set about organising the largest volunteer army ever assembled in Britain. Before the war, as consul general in Egypt, the country's de facto administrator, from 1911 until August 1914, Kitchener was also uniquely placed to understand the need for a radically new restructuring of, and approach to, intelligence operations in the Arab world.

At the same time, the de Bunsen Committee, named after its chair, Sir Maurice de Bunsen,[23] was the first committee established by the British government to determine its policy towards the Ottoman Empire. Contrary to the widely held view of perfidious Albion ceaselessly plotting to seize ever greater imperial holdings, in the case of what might happen in the event of the collapse of the Ottoman Empire, Britain was actually quite late in coming up with an imperial wish list. Indeed, although the de Bunsen Committee was formed to try and rationalise British desiderata in the region, it was only established on 8 April 1915—nearly nine months after the start of the war—and then only in response to French and Russian territorial demands in the event of an Allied victory and the subsequent collapse of the Ottoman Empire. Confronted with the territorial wish lists of its two main wartime allies, the British were in a sense—albeit an imperial sense—forced to come up with with their own list of demands by way of response.

As such, the fact that Mark Sykes had a seat on the committee was significant. Further, the fact that he had previously travelled across many of the foreign parts being discussed by the de Bunsen Committee allowed him, justly or otherwise, to claim to have superior insight, and thus authority, compared to the majority of fellow committee members. With Kitchener's ear, Sykes used his position on the committee to push for the creation of what he initially called an "Islamic Bureau",[24] in order to coordinate British intelligence activities in the region. While his understanding of the region would later be questioned, he was right in identifying the need for specialised intelligence capabilities. Questions around why he should be seen as a Middle East expert would arise mainly because he lacked any substantive knowledge of Arabic, Persian, or other regional languages; he had no academic background in Islamic studies or regional history, nor did he have any formal diplomatic preparation or experience in the region of any serious duration. His short, five-star jaunts, for which he travelled in an official capacity, hardly justified the claims made by friends and himself alike.[25]

The push for new approaches gained particular urgency from a growing awareness of German propaganda efforts in the Muslim world. The Germans had launched a number of campaigns aimed at stirring religious sentiment against Britain and its allies. At the start of the war, the noted Middle Eastern scholar Max von Oppenheim[26] was asked by the German Foreign Office to summarise the various strategic ideas for taking on Britain in the region. The result was his *Memorandum on Revolutionising the Islamic Territories of Our Enemies*.[27] The memo argued for enlisting the Ottoman Sultan to call on the world's Muslims to engage in a holy war, or jihad, against Germany's and Ottoman Turkey's European colonial enemies, France and Great Britain. Given the task of creating culturally aware, pro-Arab, anti-Allied propaganda, the Intelligence Bureau for the East (*Nachrichtenstelle für den Orient*) was established in Berlin, with von Oppenheim appointed to lead it. This propaganda bureau was soon producing materials targeted at Muslim populations throughout British territories.[28] Traditional intelligence methods employed by the British provided little or no insight into the effectiveness of these efforts or how to counter them, only further highlighting Britain's need for a better understanding of cultural and religious dynamics.[29]

It should be pointed out that the push for new approaches in British intelligence occurred against a backdrop of similar challenges facing other Allied powers. The French, drawing on a somewhat longer, and arguably deeper, tradition of Oriental scholarship and experience in North Africa, had developed some sophisticated regional intelligence capabilities. One of the most fascinating characters in this arena was Père Antonin Jaussen,[30] a French Dominican priest and archaeologist, who supplied the French with a great deal of useful intelligence through his personal networks active in Palestine and Syria. However, like the British, the French struggled to effectively integrate academic expertise with military requirements.[31]

The Russians, despite their extensive experience from the Great Game—a territorial rivalry with Britain which ranged across Central Asia and the north-west frontier and other approaches to British India, and dominated relations between the two empires for much of the nineteenth century—found their intelligence operations in the Ottoman territories hampered by poor coordination between military and diplomatic channels.[32] The Ottomans themselves, while possessing obvious advantages in local knowledge and linguistic capabilities, also often failed to effectively systematise this information for military purposes, although their counter-intelligence proved remarkably effective at identifying and disrupting enemy networks.

Institutional resistance to change remained strong, particularly from the India Office. Officials in Delhi viewed any new intelligence organisation as a potential threat to the purview they enjoyed in much of the Middle East, notably the Persian Gulf and Arabian Peninsula. While it is true that they had long experience with Muslim populations, and believed their traditional approaches to intelligence gathering were adequate, their resistance to change was particularly informed by memories of the particular events around the Indian Rebellion of 1857. Still fresh in the institutional memory, those events continued to inform the opinions and outlook of the Government of India, making it especially sensitive to anything that might affect Muslim opinion on the subcontinent. But 1857 was not 1916, and the gulf that lay between the reality of imperial rule in India and a nascent Arab revolt in the Hijaz was large.

The India Office's concerns about the proposed new bureau were evident in their successful insistence that its name be changed from 'Islamic' to 'Arab'. This seemingly minor detail reflected its deep anxiety about potential interference with India's Muslim population, which comprised approximately twenty per cent of the country's total population. At the start of the First World War, this number also represented roughly thirty-five per cent of the Indian Army. Given that the Indian Army was one of the two largest volunteer armies in the world, with a total strength of 240,000 men in 1914, the India Office's sensitivity to anything that might affect Muslim loyalty was far from mere bureaucratic paranoia.

Nevertheless, the pressure for change proved irresistible. The combination of military setbacks, intelligence failures, and new strategic challenges forced Britain to reconsider its approach. The result of this was the creation of the Arab Bureau in January 1916, which marked a significant departure from past approaches to intelligence practices. The Arab Bureau's founding document explicitly stated its dual mission to "harmonise British political activity in the Near East ... [and] keep the Foreign Office, the India Office, the Committee of Defence, the War Office, the Admiralty, and Government of India simultaneously informed of the general tendency of Germano-Turkish Policy". The report goes on to state: "The second function will be to co-ordinate propaganda in favour of Great Britain and the *Entente* among non-Indian Moslems [sic] without clashing with the susceptibilities of Indian Moslems and the *Entente* Powers."[33]

The new organisation would represent several key innovations in British intelligence practice, starting with what might be seen as the most original—some would say most risky—step of all, namely bringing together experts from different backgrounds, combining academic knowledge with military and political experience.[34] First, the Arab Bureau's recruitment of archaeologists, scholars, and others with regional experience and expertise, such as the Oxford-based archaeologist David Hogarth[35] and the well-travelled and highly regarded author and explorer Gertrude Bell,[36] represented a genuinely radical departure from traditional military intelligence staffing, as we will explore later.[37] Second, the Arab Bureau would focus on understanding cultural and social dynamics alongside and in addition to traditional military intelligence, recognising that effective operations in the Middle East required both deep cultural knowledge as well as military expertise, not just one or the other.

The establishment of the Arab Bureau in Cairo, rather than say London or Delhi, and in spite of strenuous objections from the India Office, reflected both practical and strategic considerations. Cairo's importance as a hub of British operations in the region made it the logical choice, particularly given Egypt's proximity to events on the ground at the start of 1916, as did its geographical position more or less midway between Britain and India. Being based in Cairo would prove especially valuable after the start of the Arab Revolt in June of that year.

The push for new approaches also reflected a growing recognition that the war in the Middle East was taking place in a distinct geographical, historical, and political context, and thus required different knowledge and novel methods from those employed in the conflict in Europe. Where traditional military intelligence focused on troop dispositions and tactical details, these on their own would prove hopelessly insufficient in an environment where political, religious, and cultural factors often had an outsized role in determining outcomes. This emerging understanding would help shape the development not only of the Arab Bureau's new intelligence capabilities, but would also ultimately influence British approaches to regional intelligence gathering for decades to come.

Better Late Than Never: Seeing the Cultural Gaps

The growing awareness of the importance of better understanding the complex socio-political and cultural landscape that was the Ottoman Empire meant recognising many gaps in the knowledge currently held by those engaged in military intelligence work across the region. Of these, one of the most obvious and most serious deficiencies was linguistic. Despite maintaining extensive interests across the Ottoman Empire, Britain had remarkably few officials who spoke Arabic or Turkish to the standard required for this to be an asset in a professional setting. Even in Egypt, then under British administration, most officials relied on interpreters for routine business. Such a language gap meant that critical intelligence often passed through multiple translations, losing nuance and sometimes accuracy in the process. More fundamentally, it limited British ability to understand local perspectives or gather intelligence directly from Arab sources, and so their ability to evaluate whether particular items of news or other information were useful or useless.

But cultural misunderstandings extended far beyond language. Before the establishment of the Arab Bureau, too many British officials had little chance of grasping, or indeed even being aware of, the complex religious dynamics that shaped regional politics. The role of the Ottoman Sultan as Caliph, spiritual leader of Sunni Muslims, had implications that military intelligence as traditionally constituted simply failed to appreciate. Similarly, the intricate relationships between different religious and ethnic communities—Arabs, Turks, Kurds, Christians, Jews, and various Muslim sects—created political dynamics that conventional intelligence methods struggled to analyse. The limited numbers and non-specialist nature of British intelligence personnel in the region before the war were almost inevitably going to result in a failure to understand how religious authority might eclipse, or at least inform, political loyalty, or how sectarian differences could play a part in influencing military and political decisions.

UNPREPARED FOR WAR

The tribal structure of many Arab societies presented particular challenges. British officials, accustomed to dealing with centralised state authorities, often misunderstood the potentially more fluid nature of tribal allegiances, as well as the importance of personal relationships in Arab political culture. Intelligence assessments frequently oversimplified tribal politics, missing crucial nuances that might determine the success or failure of military and political initiatives. Any worthwhile understanding of tribal dynamics required an intimate knowledge of genealogies, historical relationships, and complex—not to say liable to shift—patterns of alliances and rivalries, which few British officials possessed. Even basic concepts like the difference between settled and nomadic tribes, or the seasonal patterns of tribal movement, were often overlooked in exercises ostensibly involved with intelligence planning.

Perhaps most significantly, British intelligence failed to understand the complex attitudes of Arab populations toward Ottoman rule. Pre-war assessments overwhelmingly tended towards an assumption that Turkish dominance was universally resented by the region's Arabs, and that they would welcome any alternative, even that of a European colonial power. Such a gross oversimplification ignored the fact that a clear majority of Arabs remained loyal to the Ottoman state for the entire duration of the First World War, whether out of religious conviction, political pragmatism, or simple inertia. It also missed the emergence of Arab nationalist sentiments that would prove crucial during the war. Yet, as we will see later, the expertise Britain needed did exist, albeit outside traditional military and diplomatic circles.[38]

As we saw with the serious British military defeats at Gallipoli and Kut al-Amara, such cultural gaps had direct military consequences. At Gallipoli, British forces not only faced stronger resistance than expected but also failed to understand the religious and nationalist motivation of Ottoman troops defending Muslim territory against nominally Christian invaders. In Mesopotamia, similarly inadequate understanding of local tribal politics and religious sensitivities complicated military operations and occupation duties alike. Even routine interactions with local populations were hampered by cultural misunderstandings that could have serious strategic implications: the British, and other European colonial powers, tended to essentialise the local populations, treating all Arabs alike, thereby missing crucial regional and tribal distinctions, which could lead to causing offence at best, and at worst diplomatic blunders with consequent negative (which is to say deadly) military consequences. There were lessons learned, for sure, but at an enormous cost. Thousands of British and imperial troops died at Gallipoli and Kut due partly to intelligence failures. The suffering endured by Indian troops in Ottoman captivity after Kut highlighted the human consequences of such cultural misunderstanding. These sacrifices underscored the vital importance of developing better approaches to intelligence in culturally complex environments.

Better late than never, recognition of these cultural gaps did eventually produce significant changes in British approaches to intelligence. Traditional military intelligence officers, trained to focus on order of battle information and tactical details, would soon be supplemented by individuals from the Arab Bureau who had some greater degree of cultural insight, language skills, and other relevant regional expertise. The creation of the Arab Bureau, which would bridge many of these cultural gaps, resulted in one of the most original experiments in British military intelligence and the emergence of a new kind of intelligence unit, one that was happy to combine scholarly expertise with military nous, or archaeological knowledge with strategic intelligence, with religious and cultural understanding pressed into the service of greater operational effectiveness. This unconventional approach would prove crucial to British operations in the later years of the war, even while the path to developing these new capabilities was far from straightforward.

Even after the need for better cultural intelligence was seen and understood at the highest levels of British military and political leadership, questions around whether to develop new approaches to intelligence melted away, replaced with questions of how best to achieve this new goal. The answer was to bring together an extraordinary group of individuals whose unconventional skills and experiences would transform British intelligence operations in the Middle East.

The experience of 1914–16 demonstrated conclusively that traditional military intelligence alone was insufficient for operations in culturally distinct environments: success needed knowledge of, even a degree of empathy towards, local languages, customs, religious beliefs, and social structures. This shift towards more culturally informed intelligence gathering would influence British operations throughout the remainder of the war.[39] Going further, it would not just shape the development of British intelligence capabilities for the remainder of the war, but also influence approaches to regional operations for decades to come. Indeed, many of the innovations that were developed in response to the failures of the first two years of the war would help establish new paradigms for intelligence operations that remain relevant even today.

The creation of the Arab Bureau marked a decisive break with traditional intelligence-gathering methods, representing an ambitious attempt to address the previously mentioned failures via unprecedented methods, such as introducing new ways of combining military intelligence with cultural expertise. Bringing together academics, archaeologists, and regional experts alongside military officers, the Arab Bureau pioneered new approaches to intelligence gathering and analysis. Its story reveals not just how British intelligence adapted to the challenges of war in the Middle East, but also how original organisational structures could emerge from military crisis. The following examination of the Arab Bureau's formation, composition, and methods demonstrates how necessity drove innovation in ways that would influence British intelligence practices for decades to come.

PART II

RESPONSE

3

"BRITISH DESIDERATA IN TURKEY AND ASIA"

FOREIGN OFFICE, WHITEHALL, LONDON

In which we see the fundamental strategic confusion in British imperial policy towards the Middle East and a bureaucratic system unable to comprehend the complex regional dynamics emerging during the First World War. The belated response sees the de Bunsen Committee established, meeting, deliberating, and delivering their findings: an uncertain fudge of four possible policy options. Here we dissect how competing departmental interests, a deeply Eurocentric diplomatic mindset, and a profound lack of regional understanding led to a series of compromised and ultimately ineffective policy recommendations.

Britain's Belated Response: de Bunsen Committee

While British forces struggled on Middle Eastern battlefields, a small group of officials gathered in London to confront an even more fundamental question: What exactly did Britain want from the Middle East? The de Bunsen Committee represented a belated attempt to articulate coherent British objectives in the region. Yet the Committee's deliberations would expose the profound strategic confusion and bureaucratic disarray that had undermined British policy and intelligence from the war's outset. The de Bunsen Committee's failure to provide clear direction would further demonstrate the need for new approaches to understanding and engaging with the Ottoman territories.

The timing of the Committee's formation revealed much about British priorities—or, rather, the lack thereof. Indeed, the establishment of this committee was not the result of British strategic foresight at all, but rather a belated response to diplomatic initiatives, or proposed postwar land grabs, from its European allies.[1]

The formation of the de Bunsen Committee came at a critical moment in Britain's Middle Eastern campaign. Britian's initial optimism that greeted the Ottoman entry into the war, not to say its disdain for the Ottomans as an adversary, evaporated in the face of military setbacks. The Gallipoli campaign, launched just weeks earlier, was already showing signs of the difficulties that would lead to its eventual failure. In Mesopotamia, British forces had advanced beyond Basra but faced growing resistance. These military challenges highlighted the urgent need for clear strategic objectives, yet Britain's approach to the region remained remarkably uncoordinated.

While Britain had long maintained significant interests across the Middle East, from the Persian Gulf to Egypt, it had shown remarkable hesitation in articulating its specific post-war aims for the region. This reluctance stood in stark contrast to its allies' more proactive approach. France had already developed detailed plans for its desired sphere of influence, centred on Syria and Lebanon where it claimed historical interests dating back to the Crusades. French diplomats had been quietly but persistently advancing these claims since the war's outbreak, drawing on a long-established cultural and educational presence in the Levant to justify their ambitions. Their proposals for a post-Ottoman reality went far beyond mere influence, outlining specific territorial demands and governance structures for the post-war settlement.

Correspondingly, Russia had made no secret of its own extensive ambitions. The Tsarist government, continuing its centuries-old quest for warm-water ports, saw the Ottoman entry into the war as an opportunity to finally secure its long-sought prizes: Constantinople and the Straits. Russian diplomats had presented detailed memoranda to support its claims, which extended beyond the Dardanelles Strait to include significant portions of eastern Anatolia. These Russian desiderata were particularly concerning to British officials in India, who feared their implications for Britain's strategic position in Asia beyond the historical Near East and connected Ottoman domains.

Britain's pre-war position in the Middle East had been built on a complex web of informal influence rather than direct control. In the Persian Gulf, a series of treaties with local rulers had established what amounted to a British protectorate, managed through the Government of India. In Egypt, at least until the start of the war, British influence had been exercised through financial control and military occupation,

"BRITISH DESIDERATA IN TURKEY AND ASIA"

maintaining the fiction of Ottoman sovereignty while wielding effective power. This indirect approach, known as the 'veiled protectorate', had served British peacetime interests well but was ill-suited to either wartime conditions or post-war planning.

The committee tasked with coming up with a possible solution to this puzzle was chaired by Sir Maurice de Bunsen, although the Committee's composition and methodology perfectly exemplified these longstanding patterns. A career diplomat with extensive European experience—de Bunsen had served in Paris, very briefly in Constantinople, and in Vienna—but without any particular expertise in Middle Eastern affairs, the chairman embodied the problem.[2] His appointment to chair a committee determining Britain's Middle Eastern policy reflected what can be seen as the persistent confusion of European diplomatic expertise with actual regional understanding. This choice of chairman was telling: Britain's approach to the region remained oddly disconnected from its realities. De Bunsen's background in European diplomacy reflected a tendency to view Middle Eastern questions primarily through the lens of European power politics, an approach that would prove increasingly inadequate as the war progressed.

The Committee's other members, while representing different departmental interests, largely shared this European diplomatic background, while the broader membership reflected the competing interests at stake: Sir Arthur Hirtzel spoke for the India Office, zealously guarding its traditional domains; Sir Hubert Young provided the Foreign Office perspective; Admiral Sir Henry Jackson ensured the Admiralty's interests weren't forgotten; moreover, while Sir Mark Sykes was the personal representative of Field Marshall Lord Kitchener, secretary of state for war, he brought his own characteristic confidence and regional experience,[3] which, though limited, still surpassed that of certain fellow committee members. Notably absent was any representative with deep understanding of Arab affairs or Ottoman internal politics, a gap that had a significant negative impact on the Committee's deliberations and conclusions.

European Diplomatic Mindset: A Pattern of Misunderstanding

The formation and conduct of the de Bunsen Committee reflected more than just wartime improvisation. It also revealed fundamental flaws in Britain's entire approach to Middle Eastern affairs. The Committee's

European diplomatic orientation, far from being an accident of wartime expediency, represented the culmination of decades of British policy, an approach that had profound negative implications for both the Committee's work and Britain's broader strategic position there.

The Committee's make-up reflected deep-rooted methodologies in British diplomatic culture. Throughout the late nineteenth and early twentieth centuries, key diplomatic posts in the Middle East had been systematically filled by officials whose expertise lay in European, rather than regional, affairs. Constantinople, despite its critical importance as the capital of the Ottoman Empire, was typically staffed by diplomats whose careers had been built in European capitals. As Foreign Office officials might have noted, they sent to the Porte men who could navigate the waters of European diplomacy but could not fathom the depths of Ottoman politics. Such staffing patterns reflected an implicit assumption that the management of relations with other European powers was always going to be more important than understanding wider regional dynamics.

In Constantinople, British ambassadors often focused more on maintaining diplomatic balance among European powers than on understanding internal Ottoman developments. This tendency was exemplified by Sir Gerard Lowther's tenure as ambassador (1908–13), during which Britain failed to develop meaningful relationships with the Young Turk movement, despite its growing importance in Ottoman politics. As one contemporary observer noted, "We were so busy watching the European game that we missed the Ottoman revolution happening under our noses."[4] To some degree, such a narrowly western and central European focus was understandable. On the other hand, the narrowness of this approach, which effectively eliminated any serious consideration of the Ottomans, their interests, political culture, and possible vulnerabilities, can now be seen as a failure that would have serious consequences for British policy.

The de Bunsen Committee's methodology was likewise profoundly shaped by this European orientation. Rather than seeking direct input from regional experts, or from others with deep knowledge of Ottoman affairs, the Committee preferred to rely heavily on diplomatic correspondence and departmental memoranda, which likewise reflected European preoccupations. As one member later admitted, "We approached the question as if we were redrawing the map of Europe, not understanding the fundamentally different nature of political organisation in the East."[5]

No more telling example of the Committee's failings can be found than its treatment of the various threads of Arab nationalism that had been emerging across the region for a decade and more: here again a purely European diplomatic mindset created strategic blindness. Despite clear evidence of growing Arab political consciousness—most obviously the 1913 Arab Congress, held in Paris[6]—and increasing nationalist activity in Syria, the Committee largely viewed such developments through the lens of European considerations. When Arab nationalism was discussed at all, it was primarily in terms of how it might affect relations with France or Russia, rather than as a significant political force in its own right.

This failure to engage seriously with Arab political developments was particularly striking given Britain's extensive presence in Egypt and the Gulf. As one official noted in a prescient memorandum written shortly after the Committee's report: "We have confused proximity with understanding, presence with insight. Years of administration in Egypt have taught us the mechanics of rule but not the dynamics of Arab society."[7] This observation highlighted a crucial distinction between administrative experience and genuine political understanding, which distinction became increasingly important as the war progressed.

When the de Bunsen Committee reported on its findings, in a wonderful example of a bureaucratic fudge, it actually came up with four answers, as we shall see shortly. However, in each case the proposed solutions revealed this same European diplomatic mindset. Options were framed primarily in terms of their implications for European power relationships, rather than their feasibility within the regional context: for instance, discussing matters in terms of satisfying French and or Russian ambitions, rather than with any serious consideration for the implications for local governance or political stability. Likewise, the 'decentralisation' option, discussed below, drew more on European federal models than on any deep understanding of Ottoman administrative realities.

This persistent European orientation had practical consequences beyond mere analytical failures. It affected how Britain gathered and interpreted intelligence, structured its administrative arrangements, and conceptualised its strategic objectives. Most importantly, it created what one official described as "a kind of institutional myopia—we could see clearly to Vienna or Paris but were blind to developments in our own backyard."[8] The recognition of these shortcomings, and the creation of the Arab Bureau—staffed with regional specialists rather than career diplomats, and focused on local political dynamics and cultural and linguistic expertise—in response to this need marked the shift from a European to a regional orientation that would prove crucial for Britain's wartime operations in the Middle East.

Emerging Recognition: Towards an Imperial Epistemic Community

Further, the recognition of these systemic failures in British policy and intelligence marked the beginning of a fundamental shift in how Britain conceptualised expertise in Middle Eastern affairs. Clearly such a transformation went beyond mere administrative reorganisation. Instead, it represented the emergence of what I am calling an imperial epistemic community.[9] Such a community would challenge traditional diplomatic assumptions about how knowledge of the region should be gathered, analysed, and operationalised.

A novel concept, the model of an imperial epistemic community helps explain how Britain began to move beyond the limitations of its European diplomatic mindset towards a new community comprised of individuals who shared not just knowledge of the region, but a fundamentally different approach to understanding it. Unlike the traditional diplomatic corps, with its focus on European power politics, members of this nascent community emphasised direct engagement with local languages, cultures, and political dynamics. They represented a new breed of imperial expert—men who could read Arabic newspapers as easily as French diplomatic notes, who understood tribal politics as well as they did European diplomacy.

This evolution was evident in the changing nature of official discourse about regional expertise. Traditional diplomatic experience, once considered the primary qualification for Middle Eastern assignments, began to be seen as potentially limiting rather than enabling. The need was for people who understood the region as it really was, and not as it appeared to be when seen from this or that European chancellery. This shift in thinking was particularly evident in discussions about intelligence gathering, where traditional diplomatic reporting was increasingly seen as inadequate for understanding regional dynamics.[10]

"BRITISH DESIDERATA IN TURKEY AND ASIA"

The emerging imperial epistemic community drew from diverse sources, including academics and military officers—as well as political officers from India—and less formally qualified individuals who brought with them some useful regional experience. What united these sources was not just their knowledge of the region but their shared conviction that understanding the Middle East required moving beyond traditional diplomatic frameworks. Embodied in the Arab Bureau, this community began to develop its own distinctive approaches to gathering and analysing intelligence, emphasising the need to see the region through its own eyes rather than through a European lens.

The creation of the Arab Bureau would represent the institutional embodiment of this new approach. Unlike traditional diplomatic or military institutions, the Arab Bureau was explicitly designed to integrate different forms of expertise—linguistic, cultural, political, and military. Its staffing reflected this new understanding of regional expertise. Rather than career diplomats, it would recruit individuals who could demonstrate deep engagement with regional languages, cultures, and politics. This marked a significant departure from the European diplomatic model that had dominated the de Bunsen Committee. Perhaps most significantly, the creation of the Arab Bureau represented an implicit acknowledgement that traditional imperial institutions were inadequate for understanding and operating in the Middle East. Now, the newly recognised goal was to establish an intelligence organisation that could essentially think in Arabic while reporting in English, that understood both tribal politics and military strategy, and that could integrate political intelligence with military operations. This re-conceptualisation of expertise—redefined as integrative, culturally informed, and operationally focused—marked a sharp break from previous diplomatic and intelligence approaches.

The Committee's Context and Challenges

Another important point of context around the formation of the de Bunsen Committee was the declaration by the Ottoman Sultan-Caliph, in November 1914, of a jihad,[11] the term here meaning a religiously sanctioned armed conflict: the idea of any war being 'holy' is too conceptually problematic to allow for the term to be used loosely or unthinkingly. As such, we are perhaps here better served if we focus on appreciating that the issuance of a *fatwa*, or religious ruling, by the Sultan carried sufficient authority that it raised serious concerns about Muslim opinion throughout the British Empire, particularly in India. How would Britain's Muslim subjects respond to the call? Obviously, there was not going to be a single unified response, but the threat of an uprising by significant numbers of Muslims in India, Egypt, and elsewhere was enough to trouble the British (and French where they held sway) authorities. At the same time, adding an additional layer of political complexity—and the potential for both opportunities and complications for British policy—were the newly emergent Arab nationalist movements.

As such, it is important to realise that the Committee's deliberations were shaped by several immediate, and at times competing, concerns. The first was the need to respond to French[12] and Russian[13] territorial claims without compromising British interests. The second was the challenge of balancing strategic requirements, particularly regarding communications with India, against diplomatic commitments to allies.[14] The third was the question of how to maintain stability in the Muslim world while pursuing policies that might lead to the dismemberment of the Ottoman Empire.

These competing imperatives significantly complicated the Committee's work, as its members struggled in a real sense to reconcile the irreconcilable: How was it possible to maintain Ottoman integrity while planning its partition? Could they support Arab aspirations while simultaneously acknowledging French claims? How might they also protect Indian interests while accepting Russian ambitions? This fundamental tension would be reflected, but not satisfactorily solved, in the Committee's final recommendations.

Four Options, No Solution

Before looking at the conclusions reached by the de Bunsen Committee, it is important to note that for many decades before the outbreak of war, it had been Britain's explicit policy in Europe to support the Ottoman Empire's territorial integrity, even maintaining it in the face of objections or competing interests from other European powers.[15] Now, suddenly at war with the Ottomans, the Committee was forced to come up with a policy to reflect the new, radically altered geopolitical reality.

"BRITISH DESIDERATA IN TURKEY AND ASIA"

After two months—an admirably quick turnaround time by the standards of many other committees—these men produced what should be seen as one of the First World War's most remarkable documents of bureaucratic indecision. Rather than make clear choices about British priorities, the committee instead offered four distinct possible approaches, each carefully hedged with caveats and qualifications: a masterpiece of departmental compromise.[16]

The first option was to maintain Ottoman territorial integrity while establishing spheres of influence, essentially a proposal to preserve the pre-war status quo but with enhanced British control. This approach appealed particularly to India Office officials, who were worried about Muslim opinion in India, which contained the British empire's largest Muslim population, and preferred evolutionary rather than revolutionary change in the region. Any supporters of this approach could rightly note that this option aligned with Britain's traditional approach of informal empire,[17] exercising influence without direct administrative responsibility. The appeal of this option lay in its apparent simplicity, i.e. it would maintain existing administrative structures while gradually expanding British influence through economic and political means.

However, this conservative approach faced significant practical challenges, foremost among them the fact that the Ottoman Empire had, in casting its lot with Germany and Austria-Hungary, clearly already abandoned neutrality between European powers. More fundamentally, the very concept of maintaining Ottoman integrity while establishing European spheres of influence contained an inherent contradiction. Moreover, it would be impossible to implement, as it would be akin to preserving the empire while concurrently seeing it dismembered.

The second option advocated for a limited partition focused on Mesopotamia and the Persian Gulf, which reflected long-standing British strategic interests in those regions. Since the 1870s, Britain had gradually increased its presence in the Gulf, signing treaties of protection with local rulers and effectively turning the waters of the Persian Gulf into what has been characterised as a British lake. Mesopotamia's potential importance had grown with the conversion of the Royal Navy to oil fuel before the war, thus making access to the region's suspected oil reserves a strategic imperative. This approach had several apparent advantages. For one thing, it would secure these vital interests while minimising direct administrative commitments elsewhere. It would also secure British strategic interests in the Gulf, and potential oil resources yet to be found there, while also limiting administrative commitments. Further, it would avoid direct confrontation with French ambitions in Syria, or Russian claims to Constantinople. However, it also raised serious questions about the viability of a truncated Ottoman state and the potential impact on Muslim opinion. The India Office in particular worried that even limited partition might spark religious unrest across the Muslim world.

The third option proposed a complete partition of all Ottoman territories among the Allies, representing the most radical departure from pre-war arrangements. Under this scheme, Britain would claim direct control over Mesopotamia and Palestine, while France would receive Syria and Cilicia in southern Anatolia (extending inland from the northeastern coasts of the Mediterranean Sea, and today partly marking the border between the Republic of Turkey and Syria), and Russia would gain Constantinople and eastern Anatolia. This option acknowledged the likely dissolution of Ottoman power but raised thorny questions about the future governance of the so-called holy places and the potential reaction in the Muslim world.

The partition option reflected a growing belief among increasing numbers of officials that the Ottoman Empire's days were numbered. As such, if the dissolution of an empire that had been present for more than six hundred years was inevitable, it was only in Britain's interests to be involved in shaping whatever state or states were to succeed it. This approach would at least allow for clear spheres of influence, and direct control, over strategically important regions. On the other hand, it would also require significant administrative commitments, which no European power was likely to want by the war's end, and it also risked serious religious and political backlash.

The fourth option was for the creation of a decentralised Ottoman Empire, with autonomous provinces under various European protections. This last suggestion was a brave, but flawed, attempt on the part of the Committee members to square the circle of maintaining Ottoman sovereignty while also satisfying Allied territorial ambitions. This most complex of the four proposals would mean preserving the Sultan's nominal authority, which given his status and role as Caliph was seen as particularly important at this stage of the war, with the threat of religiously inspired, anti-Allied uprisings still troubling officials from New

"BRITISH DESIDERATA IN TURKEY AND ASIA"

Delhi to London, and most places in between. At the same time, option four would also allow Britain and its allies to exercise effective control over their areas of interest.

This 'decentralisation' option appealed to those seeking a middle ground between preservation and partition, maintaining as it did the fiction of Ottoman integrity while also allowing for effective European control in areas of interest. The scheme had the added advantage, in the eyes of its backers, of drawing on pre-war Ottoman reform proposals, and it also seemed to offer a way to simultaneously satisfy both European ambitions and various local demands for autonomy. However, its very complexity would have made implementation problematic, to say the least. Furthermore, it almost entirely failed to address any of the practical details of how such a system would function in practice.

As is clear from the above, each of the four options reflected different departmental priorities and concerns. The India Office, mindful of both its responsibilities in the Gulf and its concerns about Muslim opinion, favoured approaches that maintained at least nominal Ottoman sovereignty. The Foreign Office was more concerned with balancing European diplomatic considerations, especially those of the French, but also Russian ambitions, while protecting British interests. The Admiralty, focused on securing naval routes and potential oil supplies, continued to prioritise control of the Gulf and southern Mesopotamia.

The inability of the Committee to choose decisively between these options reflected deeper uncertainties about Britain's regional objectives, which at times were easier to state in terms of what Britain did not want: in spite of being foremost wartime allies, Britain wanted to prevent French dominance in Syria; they were keen to halt Russian control of the Dardanelles; and they were set against any German influence in Mesopotamia.[18] As to what they wished to achieve, not even the de Bunsen Committee, which was established in order to settle the matter, seemed able to answer this question.

With regards to the story of the Arab Bureau, it was most telling of all that the de Bunsen Committee almost entirely overlooked what would soon become one of the most significant factors shaping regional developments: the emergence of Arab nationalism. This oversight was particularly striking given that the First Arab Congress had been held just two years earlier, in 1913, in Paris, over the course of which the delegates had openly discussed questions of Ottoman reform and Arab autonomy. The Committee's silence on this crucial development suggested either a failure to recognise its importance or, perhaps more troublingly, an unwillingness to engage with political currents that might complicate Britain's imperial ambitions.

Administrative Tangle

"We have eighteen different people empowered to make policy in the Middle East—not including Persia—creating a system that stumbles from crisis to inertia, and from coma to panic, watching assets frittered away and opportunities missed."[19] In a coincidence too glorious to ignore, the United States today has the same number of intelligence agencies—eighteen—at work, oftentimes on the same questions, as frustrated British policy and intelligence in the Middle East before the Arab Bureau! This frustrated observation from Mark Sykes in a contemporary memorandum captured the essence of Britain's administrative paralysis in the region. The proliferation of policymakers reflected a deeper institutional problem: the absence of any coherent strategic vision for British interests in the Middle East.

The administrative complexity was staggering in its scope. In Egypt alone, authority was divided between the Foreign Office, which technically oversaw the British Agency in Cairo; the War Office, which controlled military forces; and the India Office, which maintained its own intelligence networks and political connections.[20] Similar overlapping jurisdictions existed in Mesopotamia, where the Indian Army operated under nominal War Office direction while the Foreign Office managed diplomatic implications. Even in the Persian Gulf, long considered an Indian preserve, lines of authority had become increasingly blurred as the war's demands complicated traditional arrangements.[21]

The India Office's perspective, viewing the Middle East primarily through the lens of Indian security, dominated much of Britain's regional policymaking. This viewpoint was deeply rooted in historical experience, particularly the traumatic memory of the Indian Rebellion of 1857, which had made officials in Delhi hypersensitive to any developments that might affect Muslim opinion in India.[22] The spectre of pan-Islamic sentiment, potentially uniting Muslims across Asia against British rule, created a persistent anxiety that often constrained policy options.

"BRITISH DESIDERATA IN TURKEY AND ASIA"

The Foreign Office faced different challenges, balancing European diplomatic considerations with regional realities. Its perspective was complicated by the need to maintain relationships with both France and Russia, whose ambitions in the region often conflicted with British interests. The Baghdad Railway question had already demonstrated how Middle Eastern issues could become entangled with broader European diplomatic concerns.[23] Foreign Office officials often found themselves trying to reconcile incompatible promises and commitments made to different allies.

This balancing act was particularly evident in Syria, where French claims to future control conflicted with emerging British military and strategic interests.[24] Foreign Office attempts to mediate these competing interests were further complicated by a limited understanding of local political dynamics. Foreign Office officials often found themselves in the impossible position of making commitments regarding territories they barely understood to people whose motives they could only guess at.

The War Office, focused on immediate military objectives, frequently found itself at odds with both departments.[25] Military planners viewed the Middle Eastern theatre primarily through strategic and logistical lenses, often failing to appreciate the political and cultural complexities that could affect military operations. This narrow focus would contribute to disasters like Gallipoli and Kut al-Amara, where inadequate understanding of local conditions proved as dangerous as enemy action.[26] The Admiralty maintained its own distinct priorities, focused on securing naval routes and access to oil supplies for the newly converted Royal Navy fleet.[27] Their requirements often conflicted with both military strategic planning and diplomatic considerations, further complicating efforts to develop coherent regional policy.

These competing jurisdictions created a maze of overlapping authority and conflicting priorities. In Constantinople, for instance, the British Embassy answered to the Foreign Office, while military attachés reported to the War Office, and intelligence officers might be responsible to either the India Office or the Admiralty. This administrative tangle meant that crucial information often remained trapped in departmental silos, failing to reach those who needed it most.[28]

The situation was exacerbated by institutional provincialism—the tendency of each department to view regional developments solely through the lens of its particular interests and responsibilities. The India

Office's preoccupation with Muslim opinion in India often blinded it to the emergence of Arab nationalism as a distinct political force. Similarly, the Foreign Office's focus on European diplomatic balances sometimes led it to underestimate the importance of local political developments.

Most problematically, this administrative complexity created what might best be described as strategic paralysis masked by administrative hyperactivity. Multiple departments produced volumes of analysis and recommendations, yet the fundamental questions about Britain's regional objectives remained unanswered. Each department jealously guarded its traditional spheres of influence while resisting any attempts at coordination that might diminish its authority. This institutional morass proved particularly ill-suited for understanding and responding to the complex dynamics of a rapidly changing Middle East. The traditional separation between military and political matters, already problematic in peacetime, proved especially dangerous during wartime. Political developments might have immediate military implications, while military actions might have far-reaching political consequences; yet, Britain's fragmented administrative structure made it difficult to appreciate these interconnections.

Intelligence Crisis

As we have by now established, the inadequacies of British intelligence in the region were, by the end 1915, all too painfully clear. The Ottoman's successful defence at Gallipoli had shattered illusions of quick victory, while in Mesopotamia the siege of Kut al-Amara was unfolding as a slow-motion disaster.[29] The scope of Britain's intelligence failure was comprehensive, given their pre-war dismissal of the Ottoman empire with the already somewhat clichéd label the 'sick man of Europe', in spite of clear evidence of German-led modernisation efforts. Once fighting began, the same intelligence apparatus proved unable to grasp the complex political dynamics unfolding across the region. By 1916, the pendulum had swung to the opposite extreme of overestimating Ottoman strength, again the result of inadequate intelligence.

One of the particular flaws of Britain's regional intelligence gathering was that it comprised three main efforts, each operating in virtual isolation from the others. The War Office relied primarily on military attachés, whose formal status often limited their access to sensitive information. These officers, trained in European military traditions, struggled to understand Ottoman military organisation and capabilities, and their reports frequently missed crucial developments, particularly in understanding how German military advisers were actively transforming Ottoman forces.

The Foreign Office maintained networks of consular officials who provided detailed but often slow-moving political reports. These diplomats, while often possessing excellent language skills and local contacts, were constrained by their official positions and traditional diplomatic practices, and their reporting structure, designed for peacetime diplomacy, proved too slow and formal for wartime. Moreover, the closure of consulates across Ottoman territory following the outbreak of war had severely restricted their information-gathering capabilities.

The third major intelligence strand with remit in the region was from the Government of India. This operated its own parallel intelligence system, focused primarily on Persian Gulf security and potential threats to India, and its networks, while impressive in their extensive reach, had an all too narrow focus on Indian security concerns.[30] This meant that it often missed or misinterpreted important political and social changes occurring across the Arab provinces of the Ottoman Empire. Also, its preoccupation (albeit not in itself unwarranted) with potential Muslim unrest in India did colour its analysis of regional developments, leading it to overemphasise religious factors while underestimating nationalist sentiments.

This tripartite structure created significant gaps in coverage. The intelligence failures manifested in different ways across the region. For instance, in Constantinople the focus of pre-war intelligence on diplomatic reporting meant Britain had limited understanding of Ottoman military modernisation efforts, which extended to both the army and navy, while in Arabia the emphasis on tribal politics often overlooked broader social and religious developments. The limitations of existing structures were particularly evident in three critical areas. The first was language capability: few British officers could speak Arabic, and fewer still could understand the subtle dialectal variations that might reveal a source's origins or reliability. A review conducted in late 1915 revealed that fewer than twenty British military officers in the Middle Eastern theatre possessed what might be termed operational Arabic language skills. Of these, only a handful could engage effectively with written Arabic sources, particularly newspapers and political tracts that were becoming increasingly important for understanding regional developments.[31]

The second was cultural knowledge: the ability to understand tribal politics, religious sensitivities, and social structures that shaped regional dynamics. Traditional military intelligence training provided no framework for understanding these crucial factors. In effect, such a limited approach meant that while the British (sometimes) had the ability to enumerate enemy materiel and record troop movements along the railways, they were wholly ill-prepared when it came to understanding the motivations of the foes they faced, or to assessing their morale. Such cultural blindness proved particularly costly in dealing with tribal leaders, whose political allegiances could shift based on complex social and religious factors that British intelligence struggled to comprehend.[32]

The third was the capacity to synthesise various forms of intelligence into actionable analysis. The traditional military intelligence report proved inadequate for capturing the complex interplay of military, political, and cultural factors that characterised the Middle Eastern theatre. Even when accurate intelligence was collected, the existing analytical framework proved inadequate for understanding its significance. Traditional intelligence categories struggled to capture the complexity of regional dynamics, in which tribal politics, religious affiliations, and emerging nationalist sentiments intertwined with military considerations. The net result of this was that intelligence officers frequently gathered together a great number of pieces of information, but lacking the overall picture had no idea how to arrange them, or what form the final image might take.

Recognising Systemic Failures

The very complexity of the Middle Eastern theatre demanded innovation in intelligence gathering and analysis. What was needed was a sophisticated approach to intelligence gathering and analysis that could integrate multiple sources of information while maintaining cultural sensitivity. By the start of 1916, it was clear that such an approach went beyond traditional military intelligence to encompass what might be thought of as operational cultural intelligence, i.e. the ability to understand not just surface events but their underlying causes and implications.³³ On an institutional level, the process of recognising this emerged gradually, driven by successive military setbacks and political miscalculations that highlighted the inadequacies of existing approaches. The traditional separation between military and political intelligence had become increasingly artificial in a theatre where tribal politics could have strategic implications, and where understanding cultural nuances could be as important as tracking troop movements. Yet recognition of this need faced significant institutional resistance. Traditional military authorities viewed cultural and political intelligence as secondary concerns, while diplomatic services often failed to appreciate the military implications of their political reporting.

The first serious attempts to address these systemic failures came from various quarters simultaneously. Mark Sykes, despite his limitations, deserves credit for being among the first people with a voice in government to recognise the need for such a new approach, and to also push to bring it into effect. In a late 1915 memorandum, he argued for the creation of what he imagined as an "Islamic Bureau", an organisation that would coordinate intelligence and help harmonise British policy across the region.³⁴ As noted, the name itself would prove contentious, with the India Office eternally worried about Muslim opinion on the subcontinent, and so it was ultimately changed to the "Arab Bureau", while in essence the concept remained the same. Setting aside the question of names, the idea behind the Bureau, and Sykes' core insight about the need for coordinated regional intelligence, was a sound one.

Within the military establishment, some officers began pushing for comprehensive regional understanding. This concept went beyond traditional military intelligence to include detailed knowledge of local political structures, tribal relationships, and cultural dynamics. These officers, often drawing on colonial experience in India or Sudan, recognised that effective military operations in the Middle East required a different kind of expertise than European warfare. The Foreign Office, too, was beginning to recognise the limitations of its traditional diplomatic reporting. The closure of consulates across Ottoman territory had severely restricted its information-gathering capabilities, forcing consideration of alternative intelligence sources. Some officials began advocating for 'unofficial channels', including utilising academic, commercial, and religious networks that had previously been considered outside the scope of diplomatic intelligence.

Meanwhile, the India Office's perspective underwent its own evolution, with some officials arguing for a broader imperial vision, one that could balance Indian concerns with wider strategic necessities. This shift, while gradual and incomplete, represented a significant departure from previous institutional orthodoxy. The recognition of earlier, pre-existing systemic failures pointed to the need for fundamental innovation rather than mere adjustment of existing structures. Several specific requirements emerged from the growing awareness of existing inadequacies.

One of the most obvious needs was for improved language capabilities, and not just in book-learnt, classical Arabic and Ottoman Turkish, but also in real language used in everyday settings. This would have to include knowledge of the numerous regional dialects and colloquial variations that existed throughout the region.[35] Such linguistic knowledge naturally meant going beyond simple translation work if it was to measure up to what we might now call cultural literacy, which includes the ability to understand nuances, implications, and unstated meanings in both written and spoken communication.

Another apparent need was a more general requirement for deeper cultural knowledge, which in this context meant understanding, among other things, tribal politics, religious sensitivities, and social structures, all of which played a role in forming regional dynamics. Combined with this, there also existed a need for new analytical frameworks that could successfully integrate military, political, and cultural intelligence. Those now engaged in this brave new intelligence work in the region would be required to use such frameworks if they were to have any hope of overcoming the traditional separation between these different types of intelligence, which had up to now created such dangerous gaps in understanding. What was ultimately needed was not only the ability to collect but also to synthesise, the aptitude to see patterns and connections across a range of different information domains.

Taken together, this led to the realisation that, from this point on, effective intelligence in the Middle East required individuals who could bring to bear a new set of skills, or at least additional types of expertise which were not typically found in traditional intelligence practices. This led in turn to discussions about recruitment. Knowing what skills such an original intelligence approach required was one thing; finding suitable people was another. Where to find staff with the requisite academic, commercial, or other civilian experience in the region?

"BRITISH DESIDERATA IN TURKEY AND ASIA"

The implementation of these goals was always likely to prove challenging, not least because of the conservative tendencies that exist in most entrenched bureaucracies, both military and civilian. Unsurprisingly, resistance was actively encountered from all sides. Traditional military hierarchies struggled to accommodate what sceptical voices would dismiss as 'amateur orientalists', while the equally hidebound Foreign Office worried about maintaining the niceties of diplomatic propriety while also engaging in such unorthodox intelligence activities as were now proposed. Meanwhile, in far-flung corners of the empire, as we have already mentioned, the India Office was always going to remain protective of its traditional spheres of influence and put up resistance wherever possible.

In fairness to the sceptics and naysayers, these discussions around what novel sorts of intelligence requirements and individuals were now needed were revolutionary at the time. What was being proposed was not just a wholly original form of intelligence unit but also a brand-new type of intelligence officer, one who combined scholarly knowledge with practical military intelligence requirements, while also maintaining military effectiveness.

Stumbling Towards a New Approach

As 1915 came to a close, Britain's position in the Middle East reflected a profound institutional crisis. The de Bunsen Committee's inability to articulate clear strategic objectives, the operational paralysis created by competing administrative jurisdictions, and a number of catastrophic intelligence failures had combined to create strategic drift masked by administrative hyperactivity.

As 1916 dawned, the groundwork was being laid for an unprecedented experiment in intelligence gathering and analysis. The solution meant breaking free from traditional military and administrative constraints, and the creation of a new organisational structure that could overcome the systemic failures discussed so far. As such, the establishment of the Arab Bureau in Cairo represented not just an administrative innovation, but an attempt to fundamentally reimagine how Britain understood and operated in the Middle East.

The lessons of the de Bunsen Committee's failure to reach any decisive agreement would directly influence the formation of the Arab

THE ARAB BUREAU

Bureau. As the man commissioned to start recruitment for the new Arab Bureau got to work, he would be actively looking for the sorts of individuals who represented everything the Committee had lacked. Instead of career diplomats whose expertise lay in European affairs, David Hogarth—who held the glorious title of Keeper of Antiquities at the Ashmolean Museum, the University of Oxford's own collection—was looking for what he termed 'wandering scholars',[36] men and women, many of whom had spent years immersed in the region's languages, cultures, and politics. In contrast to the de Bunsen Committee, which relied on formal diplomatic channels and official memoranda, Hogarth wanted to secure the services of those whose qualification was direct, ideally deep, experience of Arab society, from archaeologists who had worked alongside local communities to travellers who had ventured beyond the usual diplomatic circuits.

As we shall see in the next chapter, the Arab Bureau would attempt to overcome the limitations of traditional approaches. Their efforts also reveal both the possibilities and constraints of institutional innovation in wartime, not to mention tackling the enduring challenge of reconciling imperial ambitions with regional realities. The lessons learned from Britain's stumbling response to the Middle Eastern crisis of 1915 would shape not only the remainder of the war effort but the entire future of British engagement with the region.

What was needed was not simply better intelligence, but a fundamentally different approach to producing and applying knowledge about the region. This realisation would lead to the creation of a unique organisation designed to bridge the gap between academic expertise and operational intelligence, the Arab Bureau.

4

THE SCHOLAR SPIES

OXFORD

In which we trace the Arab Bureau's innovative remit and recruitment style, and how it brought together a core membership of unique personnel, enabling the emergence of a groundbreaking intelligence unit that stood to challenge traditional imperial intelligence practices. Gathering a diverse, even motley, assemblage of scholars, linguists, and regional experts—rather than the more predictable collection of conventional military officers—the Arab Bureau starts developing a unique and highly sophisticated approach to understanding the Middle East and North Africa, in the process adopting transformative methods that would reshape British intelligence gathering in the region.

Hogarth's Call for "Wandering Scholars"

The formation of the Arab Bureau didn't arise from a single dramatic decision but through an intricate web of personal and professional connections centred around Whitehall, the University of Oxford, and a series of other, informal, networks. Under David Hogarth's leadership, the search was on to create a band of 'wandering scholars'[1]—archaeologists, linguists, and seasoned travellers—who would represent a new paradigm in intelligence work, recruited for the methodological rigour their academic training afforded them, skills that previous military intelligence leadership had often overlooked.

Hogarth himself embodied this new approach. As Keeper of Antiquities at the Ashmolean Museum from 1909,[2] he brought academic credentials that may traditionally have been dismissed as largely irrelevant to intelligence work. His decades of archaeological work across the Ottoman Empire had given him not only technical skills but, crucially, an extensive network of contacts throughout the region. Having directed excavations at sites including Ephesus, Cyprus, and Alexandria, Hogarth had acquired an intimate knowledge of local communities, political environments, and geographical terrains. This practical field experience gave him insights that conventional intelligence officers simply could not match.[3]

When tasked with assembling the Arab Bureau, Hogarth applied scholarly networking methods to intelligence recruitment. He sought individuals who possessed what he termed "unconventional expertise", knowledge acquired not through military training but through immersive engagement with the region. His criteria for recruitment went beyond language skills to encompass what one might describe as cultural fluency, i.e. the ability to read between the lines of social interactions, understand unstated assumptions, and navigate complex cultural landscapes.[4] Of the initial group of five officers who arrived in Cairo 11–22 December 1914, only Captain Stewart F. Newcombe was a professional military man, while the others, including then 26-year-old Second Lieutenant T.E. Lawrence, represented Hogarth's vision of scholar–recruits.

Hogarth's strategy grew from Britain's recognition of prior intelligence failures. Traditional approaches often treated the Middle East as a collection of strategic positions rather than a region defined by its intricate social, political, and cultural landscapes. What Hogarth and others recognised, even if they didn't articulate it in quite these terms, was that British intelligence had maps (albeit incomplete) of the region's deserts and mountains, but not of the minds of those they would be working with, or indeed against.[5]

This reimagining of expertise necessitated structural changes in how intelligence was gathered, processed, and communicated. Traditional military intelligence relied on standardised reporting formats designed for European battlefield conditions, focusing on quantifiable metrics like troop strengths, armament types, and supply lines.[6] The Arab Bureau, by contrast, developed what would today be called contextual intelligence formats, which integrated cultural, historical, and political analysis with military observations. Their reports might include sections on tribal alliances, religious sensitivities, and historical grievances alongside traditional military information.[7]

A memorandum from Colonel Gilbert Clayton[8] to the Foreign Office articulated this shift, as he explained that intelligence requirements in the Middle East theatre differed fundamentally from those in European operations: "A comprehensive understanding of tribal relationships may prove more strategically valuable than precise enemy positions. A thorough knowledge of religious festivals might better predict enemy movements than conventional scouting. We are developing reporting protocols that reflect these realities."[9]

The Foreign Office's initial response revealed their struggle to adapt to this new approach, with Arab Bureau reports seen as too academic: too much sociology, and not enough soldiering.[10] Yet as conventional military intelligence repeatedly failed to anticipate regional developments, the value of the Arab Bureau's approach became increasingly apparent. By late 1916, General Archibald Murray, initially sceptical, had begun requesting that traditional military intelligence be supplemented by the Arab Bureau's assessments, acknowledging that "understanding the Arab mind" had become a strategic necessity.[11]

Academic Expertise Transformed

The Arab Bureau's recruitment of scholars transformed academic skills into practical intelligence assets in ways that conventional military training could not replicate. This transformation is evident in how specific scholarly disciplines were applied to intelligence challenges in the field. Archaeological expertise proved unexpectedly valuable. The methodical documentation skills honed through archaeological fieldwork enabled detailed cataloguing of local information. Just as archaeologists meticulously recorded artefacts and their contexts, so too Arab Bureau officers systematically documented political relationships, tribal hierarchies, and cultural practices.[12]

Lawrence's pre-war mapping of Crusader castles across Ottoman Syria exemplifies this transformation. His journeys, covering nearly a thousand miles on foot, did more than contribute to his academic credentials. They allowed him to develop an intimate understanding of regional geography, tribal politics, and local cultures that would later underpin his wartime successes. Lawrence's undergraduate thesis, *The Influence of the Crusades on European Military Architecture to the End of the XII Century*, required meticulous field research across Ottoman territories. During the summer of 1909, he embarked on an ambitious three-month walking tour through Palestine, Syria, and parts of southern Turkey, documenting Crusader fortifications.[13]

THE ARAB BUREAU

What might once have seemed purely academic research now proved invaluable pre-war training. Lawrence's journey forced him to negotiate with local officials, navigate tribal territories, hire local guides, and develop an eye for strategic terrain, skills directly applicable to intelligence work. As he later recounted, his academic expedition also taught him about "the politics of small places", the complex web of local power dynamics that shaped daily life.[14] He observed how tribal affiliations trumped nominal Ottoman authority in many areas, noting regional variations in attitudes toward central Ottoman rule, insights that would inform his later strategic recommendations during the Arab Revolt. "My college requirement to identify minor variations in battlement construction," he once remarked, "trained me to notice differences invisible to the casual observer, whether in stonework or tribal alliances."[15]

Contrary to Satia's depiction of the Arab Bureau as largely an exercise in orientalist fantasy, the evidence suggests a more complex reality. While members certainly carried imperial assumptions, their operational effectiveness often required adapting to local realities in ways that challenged rather than reinforced their preconceptions. Lawrence's very real evolution from archaeological romantic to pragmatic intelligence officer well illustrates this tension between orientalist expectations and operational demands.

Similarly, the archaeological expeditions at Carchemish, led by Hogarth from 1911 to 1914 and later by Leonard Woolley with Lawrence as his assistant, exemplified how academic relationships could be transformed into intelligence networks.[16] Located near the Turkish–Syrian border, the Carchemish excavations brought British scholars into daily contact with local workers, regional officials, and visiting dignitaries. Nearby German archaeological work also provided unexpected insights into their interests in the region. The mundane logistics of supporting such an expedition—arranging supplies, negotiating labour contracts, securing permits—created relationships with local merchants, tribal leaders, and Ottoman officials that would later serve as intelligence channels.[17]

Woolley described this transformation in a post-war memoir:

> Our archaeological contacts proved more valuable than any purpose-built spy network. We had spent years developing relationships based on mutual respect and intellectual exchange, relationships that survived the rupture of diplomatic ties. Where a newly-deployed intelligence officer might be immediately identified and isolated, we had

locals who would bring information to us unbidden, often not realizing its military significance.[18]

Also before the war, Lawrence, Woolley, and Newcombe had collaborated on what was ostensibly an archaeological survey of the Sinai Peninsula and Negev border in 1913, but was in fact an intelligence mission mapping potential Ottoman routes for an attack on the Suez Canal.

Linguistic abilities represented another scholarly asset repurposed for intelligence work. The Arab Bureau recognised that language mastery went beyond mere communication to encompass cultural understanding. The ability to think in Arabic while reporting in English[19] was paramount for the Arab Bureau's ideal of an intelligence officer who could move fluidly between cultural contexts, interpreting one world for another.[20] This linguistic dexterity allowed Arab Bureau agents to detect nuances and implications in communications that might escape those with merely functional language skills.[21]

The Arab Bureau's grasp on local languages was often far from perfect. What Lawrence and his colleagues did possess, however, was the ability to function effectively within Arab cultural contexts. This functional, if flawed, command proved sufficient for operational needs. Lawrence could identify regional accents and dialects, determine a speaker's likely origin, and navigate complex social interactions—skills far more valuable than perfect grammar.

This pragmatic approach to language reflected the Arab Bureau's broader understanding that effective intelligence work required cultural fluency rather than linguistic purity. Where traditional colonial approaches viewed unfamiliar languages with a degree of misgiving, the Arab Bureau recognised language as one component of broader cultural intelligence. Its success in developing local networks despite limited language skills demonstrated that what mattered most was not linguistic mastery but the ability to build meaningful relationships across cultural boundaries.

Perhaps most significantly, the Arab Bureau repurposed the academic habit of intellectual networking. Scholars' professional practice of building relationships with international colleagues became an intelligence-gathering framework. Connections established through archaeological expeditions, linguistic research, and academic exchanges yielded valuable intelligence networks. As one memorandum noted, these connections, "built on mutual intellectual curiosity rather than military objectives",²² often proved more valuable than conventional intelligence-gathering approaches.

The transformation of archaeological methodology into intelligence practice was far more systematic than mere coincidence. Hogarth's archaeological background provided not just subject knowledge but a distinctive methodological framework that reshaped intelligence gathering. At excavation sites like Carchemish, archaeologists developed rigorous systems for documenting spatial relationships, cataloguing artefacts, and reconstructing historical narratives from fragmentary evidence—skills perfectly suited to intelligence work.

Hogarth brought an archaeologist's eye to intelligence operations, applying stratigraphic thinking to understand how tribal territories overlapped and intersected through historical migrations. His meticulousness was legendary, and he was said to take the same care and precision in recording the position of pottery shards as he would later apply to tribal boundaries. This archaeological mindset transformed intelligence from mere data collection into systematic knowledge production.²³

A New Kind of Imperial Expert

The Arab Bureau's radical composition brought together a disparate group of scholars whose pre-war activities unexpectedly prepared them for wartime intelligence. This unorthodox assemblage represented a striking departure from traditional military intelligence units, which typically comprised career officers with conventional military training but limited regional knowledge.

The unit's roster read like an academic directory rather than a military unit. Alongside Hogarth, Clayton,²⁴ Lawrence, Bell, and Woolley were figures like Philip Graves,²⁵ a correspondent for *The Times* with extensive Middle Eastern experience, who had exposed the *Protocols of the Elders of Zion* as a forgery; Alfred Guillaume, an Islamic scholar who could cite the Quran from memory; Herbert Garland, metallurgist, later Superintendent of Laboratories at the Cairo Citadel, and linguist fluent in multiple Arabic dialects; and Kinahan Cornwallis, diplomat, administrator, and veteran of the Sudan Civil Service with connections throughout the region.

This diversity reflected Clayton's principle that effective regional intelligence required multiple perspectives. As he wrote to the Foreign

Office: "The complexities of this region cannot be grasped through any single disciplinary lens. We require the archaeologist's historical perspective, the linguist's communication skills, the anthropologist's cultural insights, and the politician's strategic understanding—all working in concert." This multidisciplinary approach represented a revolutionary departure from compartmentalised intelligence structures that typically separated political, military, and cultural analysis.[26]

Gertrude Bell's contributions were particularly distinctive, providing unique insights that military officers struggled to grasp. She bridged cultural divides, accessing networks closed to male agents, and documented genealogies and political alliances critical to understanding the region's complexities.[27] Her networks extended the Arab Bureau's reach.[28] For instance, her relationships with influential tribal leaders in Mesopotamia often opened doors that military officers could not approach directly, providing access to tribal leaders, women's quarters, and social spaces inaccessible to male operatives.[29]

Bell's transformation from traveller to intelligence officer illustrates the Arab Bureau's genuine expertise—that of its individual members as well as the organisation collectively—as well as its tendency towards self-mythology. While her pre-war journeys provided valuable regional knowledge, her wartime reports often portrayed cultural insights that reflected as much orientalist assumption as empirical observation. As such, Arab Bureau claims of cultural sensitivity must be weighed against evidence of actual local engagement rather than educational credentials alone.

In 1916, conventional military intelligence had failed to anticipate tribal responses to British advances north of Basra. Bell, drawing on her pre-war research into tribal structures, produced a remarkable analysis correlating tribal territories with likely political alignments. She integrated historical grievances, genealogical relationships, and economic factors in order to predict which tribes might support British forces and which would likely remain loyal to Ottoman authorities. Colonel Percy Cox, Chief Political Officer in Mesopotamia, described her analysis as "more valuable than a regiment of cavalry scouts" for operational planning.

Garland's mastery of Arabic dialects and Ottoman Turkish allowed him to detect subtle linguistic clues and coded messages. During the war, his ability to identify regional specificity in intercepted communications proved instrumental in uncovering Ottoman troop movements. Woolley's archaeological experience gave him the expertise to manage complex social environments, while Graves's journalistic background equipped him to synthesise diverse sources of information into actionable intelligence.

These individuals represented a new kind of imperial expert, and their approach contrasted sharply with traditional intelligence practices, emphasising as they did cultural nuance, historical context, and interdisciplinary analysis.[30] Archaeologists read landscapes for strategic value; linguists decoded regional loyalties; and anthropologists contextualised tribal politics. Arab Bureau intelligence reports reflected this depth of knowledge, often combining tactical insights with broader cultural analysis.[31]

The Arab Bureau's training methods were equally unconventional. Rather than imposing military protocols, they focused on teaching intelligence techniques to scholars already adept in regional knowledge.[32] This reverse training emphasised secure communication and analytical methods, leveraging their existing expertise.[33]

Intelligence Networks in Practice: The Case of Hussein Ruhi

The practical application of the Arab Bureau's scholarly approach to intelligence gathering is perhaps best exemplified by Hussein Ruhi,[34] a Persian of the Baha'i faith who operated in Jeddah, his cover being his role of Arabic interpreter for the head of the mission, Colonel Cyril Edward (C.E.) Wilson. Unlike conventional military intelligence officers, Ruhi leveraged his cultural knowledge, linguistic abilities, and academic background as a former schoolteacher to penetrate networks that remained impervious to traditional British intelligence methods.

Ruhi cuts a fascinating and somewhat enigmatic figure in the Arab Bureau's history. Physically unimposing, described by one British officer as "more like a mandrake than a man" with his small stature and disproportionately large head, he nevertheless wielded outsized influence through his extraordinary intellectual and cultural capabilities. His background was itself unusual: Persian by birth, Baha'i by faith, he had served as a schoolteacher in Cairo before the war. His background in education proved crucial to his effectiveness, giving him the cultural authority to move in scholarly and religious circles closed to European agents.

Ruhi's effectiveness stemmed from his ability to move seamlessly between worlds, delivering lectures in mosques while cultivating an image as a Muslim theologian, despite being a Baha'i. His unconventional background made him exactly the kind of asset Hogarth's Arab

THE SCHOLAR SPIES

Bureau sought: individuals whose scholarly or cultural expertise could be applied to intelligence gathering in ways military training simply could not replicate.[35]

Colonel Wilson detailed Ruhi's operations in his correspondence with Cairo, writing, "Ruhi has established himself as a respected theological authority, delivering regular lectures at the Jeddah Great Mosque on Islamic jurisprudence that attract local scholars and officials. These scholarly gatherings provide unparalleled intelligence opportunities—conversations after prayers yield information no amount of conventional surveillance could secure."[36] Ruhi's scholarly activities were not mere cover but integral to his intelligence work, creating trust networks that were valuable resources for information.

His academic credentials opened doors throughout Hijazi society. In one remarkable instance, Ruhi gained access to two underground pan-Islamic secret societies operating in Jeddah, groups actively working against British interests. Rather than infiltrating them through deception, he joined as a genuine participant in their intellectual discussions, gradually steering them towards positions less hostile to the Allies. As Wilson noted: "Ruhi has not simply gathered information from these societies but has influenced their thinking through scholarly debate, demonstrating that intelligence work at its most sophisticated involves not merely collection but active engagement."[37]

What makes Ruhi's case particularly illuminating is his dual role, i.e. serving both the Arab Bureau and, unbeknownst to many of his handlers, the Government of India simultaneously. This duplicity, rather than compromising his effectiveness, enhanced it, allowing him to gather intelligence that served multiple British interests while navigating the complex factional politics of wartime Arabia. As Captain Norman Bray noted, Ruhi had "devoted a great deal of his time and energies on work in [the Government of India's] interests ... I cannot speak too highly of his work in this respect".[38]

Scholarly Methods in Intelligence Work

The Arab Bureau's scholarly orientation transformed how intelligence was collected and analysed. Captain John Young, late of the Egyptian Survey Department and seconded to the Arab Bureau, who kept a meticulous compilation of character sketches of Jeddah and Mecca's leading figures exemplifies this approach.[39] Rather than focusing solely on military capabilities or troop movements, Young produced detailed studies of local power structures, social dynamics, and cultural contexts—compiling what one might recognise as anthropological field notes rather than traditional military intelligence.

Young's methodology demonstrates how academic approaches transformed intelligence practice. Trained at Cambridge before the war, Young brought ethnographic techniques to his intelligence work in the Hijaz. Rather than relying on formal questioning or surface-level observation, he developed what he called "deep documentation", a process of building comprehensive profiles of key individuals that included not just their official positions but their educational background, family connections, religious affiliations, economic interests, personal habits, and even literary preferences.

These character studies went far beyond conventional intelligence dossiers. A typical entry, such as his profile of Sheikh Abdullah al-Sulayman,[40] included details that traditional intelligence officers might have considered irrelevant: "Reads Persian poetry, particularly fond of Omar Khayyam; collects mechanical watches; suffered from malaria as a child which has left him with occasional fevers; maintains close correspondence with scholars at al-Azhar University; has a reputation for scrupulous honesty in financial matters." Yet such seemingly extraneous details provided crucial context for understanding motivations and predicting behaviour.

Young's exercise books, filled with "detailed and pithy comments on the leading personalities in Jeddah and Mecca", represented exactly the kind of deep contextual understanding the Bureau valued. His work, "aided by Hussein Ruhi's ferreting", formed an important contribution to the second edition of the *Hijaz Handbook*, an intelligence manual that approached the region through cultural and historical lenses rather than purely strategic ones.

This application of scholarly methodology to intelligence work extended beyond individual characters to mapping physical spaces. Ruhi drew a number of accurate, detailed maps of Mecca, identifying the town's thirteen districts with the names of their sheikhs, combining geographical knowledge with social and political information. This integration of multiple knowledge domains reflects the interdisciplinary nature of the Arab Bureau's approach, where the boundaries between archaeology, anthropology, linguistics, and military intelligence blurred in productive ways.

The Arab Bureau developed systems to adapt academic expertise to wartime technological constraints. They pioneered what might now be called 'human terrain mapping'—detailed documentation of cultural, linguistic, and social environments. Arab Bureau officers established card indexes of key regional personalities, compiled linguistic dictionaries of local dialects, and created annotated maps showing tribal territories, religious affiliations, and historical conflict zones. These physical knowledge systems compensated for technological limitations, creating an original intelligence infrastructure from academic methodologies.

Institutional Tensions: Scholarly Approach versus Military Convention

The methods employed by the Arab Bureau generated significant friction with traditional military institutions. General Headquarters of the Egyptian Expeditionary Force viewed the Bureau with undisguised contempt, with General Lynden-Bell dismissing it as "an infernal thing called the Arab Bureau. It is run by civilians and is totally unbusinesslike and un-military".[41]

This institutional tension went beyond mere bureaucratic rivalry—it represented a fundamental clash of epistemologies, different ways of knowing and understanding the world. Traditional military intelligence operated within what might be called a positivist framework, valuing quantifiable data, standardised reporting, and hierarchical information flow. By contrast, the Arab Bureau embraced what Hogarth termed a contextual intelligence model that emphasised qualitative understanding, cultural interpretation, and networked information sharing.

The practical manifestations of this epistemological divide were numerous and often contentious. Military headquarters expected standardised intelligence reports focusing on enemy troop strengths, weapons capabilities, and tactical dispositions. Arab Bureau reports, however, might devote pages to the historical grievances between particular tribes, the significance of specific religious celebrations for military operations, or the complex political implications of familial relationships among regional leaders. Where traditional military intelligence sought certainty and definitive assessments, the Arab Bureau often presented multiple interpretations, acknowledging the ambiguities inherent in cultural and political analysis.

Colonel Wilson, though himself a military man of conventional background, became caught in this institutional crossfire. At a conference in Cairo, he found himself ambushed when General Murray "criticised my telegrams, reports, requests, in fact every blessed thing I have done". The military establishment's scepticism extended to specific Bureau personnel. Lynden-Bell launched a personal attack on Wilson, calling him "a wild man" who "seems to be an extraordinary fellow without any military instincts of any sort or kind. His sole qualification for his present position appears to be a knowledge of Arabic". This dismissal of linguistic and cultural expertise as being secondary to military experience encapsulates precisely the conventional thinking the Arab Bureau was established to challenge.

The tension between Wilson and Lawrence further illustrates this institutional conflict. Wilson's exasperation with Lawrence (he once told Clayton that Lawrence "wants kicking and kicking hard at that then he would improve"[42]) reflected a fundamental clash between different approaches to intelligence gathering and analysis.[43]

These tensions played out daily in the Arab Bureau's operations. Military officers assigned to the Arab Bureau often chafed at what one called "the archaeologists' pace"[44] of intelligence analysis. Major Hubert Young, a long-standing critic of the Arab Bureau, despite his own scholarly background, complained in his diary about "endless debates over the proper translation of a single Arabic phrase"[45] in cases where he believed immediate action was necessary. Conversely, academic members bristled at what they perceived as military oversimplification. Hogarth once wrote scathingly about a general's request for a "one-page summary of Arab tribal politics", noting that "one might as well request a one-page summary of European history".[46]

Clayton's management approach mitigated these conflicts.[47] By fostering 'structured flexibility', he enabled the Arab Bureau to harness the strengths of both perspectives. Scholars brought analytical depth, while military officers ensured actionable outcomes. This synthesis allowed the Arab Bureau to develop intelligence methods that were both original and effective.

This reassessment of Arab Bureau capabilities challenges Westrate's earlier influential evaluation,[48] which institutional focus illuminated the Bureau's bureaucratic struggles but underestimated its methodological innovations. His emphasis on administrative conflicts with the India

THE SCHOLAR SPIES

Office, though accurate, overshadowed the Arab Bureau's revolutionary approach to cultural intelligence, meaning that where he saw institutional dysfunction, this study reveals systematic innovation in cross-cultural engagement. Further, Westrate's assessment that the Arab Bureau failed to develop coherent regional policy reflects his focus on formal diplomatic outcomes rather than intelligence methodology. While he correctly identified the Arab Bureau's institutional vulnerabilities, he missed its transformation of intelligence practice from data collection to cultural interpretation. The Arabic propaganda materials examined in this study—absent from Westrate's analysis—reveal capabilities that his institutional framework could not capture.

The Scholar–Spies Legacy

The Arab Bureau's establishment marked a transformative moment in British intelligence history. By integrating academic expertise with military operations, it challenged traditional paradigms and demonstrated the strategic value of cultural understanding. The Arab Bureau's success lay in its ability to synthesise diverse perspectives, fostering innovation in a complex geopolitical landscape.

This transformation had profound implications for intelligence practices beyond the immediate war context. The Arab Bureau pioneered what might be called culturally informed intelligence, a systematic approach that elevated the status of contextual understanding from supplementary information to essential strategic knowledge.[49] The Bureau's methods demonstrated that effective intelligence in culturally distinct environments required more than translated reports or local informants; it demanded a fundamental reorientation of how intelligence questions were formulated, how information was gathered and assessed, and how analysis was integrated into strategic planning.

Perhaps most significantly, the Arab Bureau demonstrated that effective intelligence required what anthropologists now call 'thick description', contextually rich analysis that interprets actions within their cultural frameworks. Where traditional intelligence sought factual reporting, the Arab Bureau recognised that facts without cultural context could lead to dangerous misinterpretations. Their emphasis on understanding motivations, historical grievances, and cultural values reflected an insight articulated years later by anthropologist Clifford

Geertz: that human behaviour becomes meaningful only within its cultural context.[50]

The Arab Bureau's legacy extended into institutional developments as well. The creation of the Middle East Department within the Colonial Office in 1921 incorporated many Arab Bureau methodologies. The Department's extensive documentation—particularly its handbooks on regional tribes, political figures, and cultural practices—formed the foundation of British administrative knowledge in newly acquired territories. Its emphasis on linguistic and cultural expertise influenced recruitment and training patterns for colonial administrators throughout the interwar period.

What made the Arab Bureau truly revolutionary was not just its personnel but the way it functioned as as an imperial epistemic community, a network of knowledge producers whose expertise served strategic imperial objectives while reshaping how knowledge about the region was created and understood. Unlike traditional intelligence units that merely collected information, the Arab Bureau actively constructed frameworks for interpreting the Middle East that would influence British policy for decades.

This imperial epistemic community operated at the intersection of academic knowledge and operational intelligence, transforming scholarly understanding into strategic capability. Members shared not just information but interpretive frameworks, methodological approaches, and conceptual models that bridged traditional divisions between military and academic knowledge. Bell's tribal mapping, for instance, represented more than useful data; it created a new conceptual approach to understanding tribal politics that became foundational to British regional engagement.

The transformative power of this imperial epistemic community lay in its ability to reshape how the empire itself understood the regions it sought to influence. By integrating archaeological, linguistic, and anthropological perspectives with military and political concerns, the Arab Bureau created knowledge systems that were better, and thus more useful, than conventional intelligence. Its approach anticipated by decades what intelligence theorists would later identify as the fundamental challenge of intelligence work: not just gathering facts, but creating frameworks for understanding complex cultural and political landscapes.

As we turn to the Arab Bureau's operational challenges in Cairo, the next chapter will explore how these innovations were tested in the field. The transformation of scholarly expertise into actionable intelligence

THE SCHOLAR SPIES

offers lessons not only for historians but for contemporary practitioners of cross-cultural engagement and intelligence work. The Arab Bureau's story reminds us that understanding foreign societies requires more than gathering facts: it demands immersion in cultural contexts, historical perspectives, and linguistic nuances that transform raw information into meaningful intelligence.

5

ROOMS AT THE SAVOY

CAIRO

In which we follow the Arab Bureau's remarkable transformation from an innovative concept to a functioning intelligence unit headquartered in wartime Cairo. The Arab Bureau starts formal operations from rooms in the Savoy Hotel, struggles with institutional resistance from jealous rivals at the India Office, but continues with its development of a set of revolutionary intelligence-gathering methods that challenged and changed traditional imperial practices.

The Arab Bureau Takes Shape

The Arab Bureau's establishment in Cairo's Savoy Hotel marked a significant departure from traditional British military intelligence practices.[1] Located in spacious rooms overlooking the bustling city, this unique intelligence unit found itself at the intersection of British imperial administration and the complex political landscape of wartime Egypt. The choice of Cairo, while operationally logical, given Egypt's strategic position controlling both the Suez Canal and communications between London and India, created its own set of challenges and opportunities.[2]

The Savoy's downtown location on Midan Suleiman Pasha, known locally as Midan Qasr al-Nil (today's Midan Talaat Harb), meant that the Arab Bureau was at the crossroads of wartime activity.[3] The streets around the hotel teemed with British military personnel, Egyptian civil servants, and a constant flow of visitors from across the Arab world, creating an ideal environment for gathering intelligence. However, this very visibility posed operational security challenges that required careful management.

THE ARAB BUREAU

The decision to house the Arab Bureau in a hotel rather than a military facility was both practical necessity and strategic choice. Cairo's existing military installations were already strained by wartime operations, while the Savoy's location offered unique advantages. Its position allowed the Arab Bureau to maintain a civilian façade while conducting sensitive intelligence work, though this arrangement demanded careful management of security protocols and document handling.

The Arab Bureau's physical environment reflected the tensions inherent in its work: it had a map room[4] with tactical displays and military situation boards, as well as a room that Lawrence called 'the scriptorium', a library-like space where the scholar–spies analysed texts, cross-referenced historical sources, and debated interpretations of intelligence. Moving between these spaces required not just physical but conceptual transitions, shifting between different modes of understanding and analysis. While Arab Bureau staff worked at the Savoy, many, including Lawrence, were billeted at the nearby Grand Continental Hotel, facing Opera Square and the Ezbekiyya Gardens.

The Arab Bureau's timing proved critical. Its establishment coincided with a watershed period in the war effort. The failures at Gallipoli and Kut had demonstrated the costly consequences of inadequate intelligence, while growing tensions in the Arab provinces demanded a better understanding of regional dynamics. Arab Bureau staff worked to develop new methods for gathering and analysing intelligence that could help prevent similar strategic miscalculations.

From the start, they faced stiff operational hurdles. The existing intelligence infrastructure in Cairo was notably fragmented. The Residency maintained its own political intelligence department, while the British-controlled Egyptian Army intelligence branch operated separately. The War Office also had its own representatives, as did the Government of India. Each of these agencies zealously guarded its sources and information, even as wartime demands called for greater cooperation.

Operational Infrastructure and Communication Networks

Communications posed a significant early challenge, given the Arab Bureau's declared remit and newly acquired responsibility for coordinating intelligence across multiple departments and jurisdictions. The Bureau needed to establish secure channels for transmitting and receiving intelligence, whether across Cairo, between agents in the field and headquarters, or as the hub of what was effectively a tri-continental operation, linking London to North Africa and coordinating with Delhi, Simla, and other British agencies in various African and Asian sites.[5]

The physical infrastructure for this network had to be built largely from scratch, working around existing military and civilian systems that were often already strained by wartime demands.[6] Staffing presented its own distinct challenges. Beyond the core team of Clayton, Hogarth, Bell, and others, the Arab Bureau needed to recruit and train support staff capable of handling sensitive materials while maintaining strict security protocols. Local Egyptian employees, a necessity in any establishment for certain menial but essential, non-intelligence tasks, required careful vetting and supervision. The challenge of maintaining operational security while leveraging local expertise became a constant balancing act.

The technological context is crucial for understanding Arab Bureau innovations.[7] In an age before satellite imagery, electronic surveillance, or instant communications, human intelligence remained paramount. The Arab Bureau operated in a technological environment where information travelled at the speed of a camel caravan across much of their operational area.[8] Wireless telegraphy existed but remained limited, unreliable in desert conditions, and vulnerable to interception, a fact which the Arab Bureau would shortly be taking advantage of themselves. In this environment, the ability to predict behaviour based on cultural understanding became a technological advantage in itself.

Financial and administrative matters posed additional early challenges. The Arab Bureau's unique position, neither purely military nor entirely civilian, created complications in everything from procurement to personnel management. Standard military procedures often proved inadequate for their specialised needs, thus requiring the development of new administrative approaches that could accommodate both military requirements and the flexibility needed for effective intelligence operations. These administrative challenges were further complicated by the need for coordination between departments that had previously operated independently.

Coordination Between Departments

The challenge of coordinating between departments proved one of the Arab Bureau's most complex early tasks. Cairo's existing intelligence infrastructure was a study in fragmentation, with multiple agencies operating independently and often at cross-purposes.[9] Each of these entities had developed its own methods and networks of informants over years or decades, with little incentive to share resources or intelligence. Colonel Clayton himself embodied this complexity, simultaneously heading both military and civilian intelligence units while also serving as a representative of the Governor General of the Sudan in Cairo.

The Arab Bureau's mandate to coordinate these various intelligence efforts met with immediate resistance. Existing departments viewed the new organisation with suspicion, seeing it as a potential threat to their autonomy and established practices.[10] The India Office proved particularly resistant, viewing any new intelligence organisation in its sphere of influence as an intrusion into its domain.[11] The India Office's extensive network of political agents and informants across the region represented decades of careful cultivation, and it showed little enthusiasm for sharing these resources with the newcomers.[12]

Clayton's approach to this challenge demonstrated both diplomatic skill and practical innovation.[13] Rather than attempting to exert immediate authority over existing intelligence operations, the Arab Bureau initially focused on establishing itself as a clearing house for information. This approach allowed other departments to maintain their autonomy while gradually building trust through the sharing of analysed intelligence that proved valuable to all parties. As Lawrence would later observe, "Clayton made the perfect leader for such a band of wild men as we were ... He was like water, or permeating oil, creeping silently and insistently through everything."[14]

Regular meetings between department representatives became a crucial mechanism for coordination, which sessions provided opportunities for sharing intelligence and discussing regional developments. However, the process of establishing these meetings revealed deep-seated institutional rivalries. Representatives often arrived with instructions to observe but not share, creating situations where multiple departments held pieces of crucial intelligence that remained unconnected. Arab Bureau efforts to coordinate military and political intelligence proved particularly challenging. Military intelligence officers, trained in conventional warfare, often struggled to appreciate the importance of the political and cultural intelligence that the Arab Bureau valued, while political officers sometimes failed to recognise the military significance of their own intelligence, which led to gaps in reporting that the Arab Bureau worked to bridge.

The complexity of coordinating with field agents from different departments required particular attention. The Arab Bureau developed protocols for managing potentially overlapping intelligence gathering efforts, and it worked to prevent different departments from inadvertently compromising each other's operations. This required careful diplomatic handling, as established intelligence officers often resented what they saw as interference in their traditional domains.

These coordination challenges were further complicated by the different reporting structures and priorities of each organisation. The Residency's political intelligence department, for instance, focused primarily on Egyptian internal affairs and reported directly to the High Commissioner. Their intelligence gathering methods, developed over decades of managing Britain's 'veiled protectorate' in Egypt, were geared towards monitoring local political developments rather than the broader regional intelligence that the Arab Bureau sought to collect and analyse.

War Office representatives in Cairo presented another layer of complexity. Their focus on conventional military intelligence—troop movements, fortifications, and order of battle—sometimes seemed at odds with the Arab Bureau's broader approach to regional intelligence. However, the Bureau's early successes in providing valuable cultural and political context for military operations gradually helped bridge this divide. Its analysis of tribal politics, for instance, proved crucial for military planning, demonstrating the value of a more comprehensive approach to intelligence gathering. The general officer commanding (GOC) was a British general commanding British and Empire troops in Egypt, while the Sirdar[15] was a British general commanding the Egyptian Army,[16] which was not a formal belligerent, a distinction that created further coordination challenges.

The Arab Bureau's solution to these coordination challenges evolved gradually. Rather than attempting to impose immediate centralised control, it developed what might be called a hub-and-spoke model of intelligence sharing. Each department maintained its autonomous operations while the Arab Bureau served as a central point for collating and analysing intelligence from multiple sources. This approach allowed the Arab Bureau to identify gaps in intelligence coverage and areas where departments' efforts overlapped, while respecting established institutional boundaries.[17]

THE ARAB BUREAU

Intelligence Network Management

The Arab Bureau's innovative approach to intelligence gathering was particularly evident in its handling of complex information networks.[18] Rather than relying solely on traditional military channels, the Bureau developed ground-breaking methods for gathering and verifying intelligence from multiple sources. From the rooms in the Savoy, Arab Bureau officers coordinated a web of informants that included local scouts, urban merchants, religious scholars, and political figures. Each source was carefully evaluated not just for reliability but for their position within local social and cultural networks.[19]

The verification process for sources demonstrated remarkable sophistication for the time.[20] Information from field agents would be cross-referenced against wireless intercepts, verified through local contacts, and analysed in light of cultural and political contexts that their academic members understood intimately. This multifaceted approach to intelligence gathering went far beyond contemporary military practice. For instance, when receiving reports about Ottoman troop movements, the Arab Bureau would ideally seek to confirm these through at least three independent sources—perhaps a Bedouin scout's observation, an intercepted wireless message, and information from local merchants or religious figures who had travelled through the area.

Arab Bureau technological adaptations revealed a remarkable willingness to embrace innovation despite operating in an era of limited communications technology.[21] While technological limitations were real, the Arab Bureau also developed methods of integrating emerging technologies with traditional intelligence methods. The technological constraints meant that Lawrence, as the Arab Bureau's mapmaker, was frequently going back and forth between the Savoy and the Survey of Egypt, across the Nile in Giza, for which he had the unusual privilege of a car, despite being only a newly commissioned second lieutenant.

The Arab Bureau's approach to wireless intelligence proved particularly advanced. It made extensive use of signals intelligence, primarily through wireless intercepts that had only recently become possible due to increased reliance on radio communications during the war. However, the Bureau's innovation in this aspect lay not in the technology itself but in its developing new methods for combining SIGINT (signals intelligence) with HUMINT (human intelligence) and other sources, creating a more comprehensive intelligence picture than conventional methods allowed.

The Arab Bureau also pioneered early approaches to aerial reconnaissance, integrating this nascent technology with ground-level intelligence.[22] Though still in its infancy, aerial observation provided unprecedented views of Ottoman positions and troop movements. Arab Bureau analysts developed methods for correlating aerial observations with tribal informant reports and wireless intercepts, creating complex intelligence assessments that anticipated modern all-source analysis. This adaptive approach to technology—neither rejecting traditional methods nor fetishising new ones—created a flexible intelligence capability that could respond to the unique challenges of desert warfare in ways conventional military units could not match. These operations at Arab Bureau headquarters allowed what Lawrence described as "a band of wild men" to develop unorthodox approaches that would have been impossible within traditional military structures.

The effectiveness of these approaches was particularly evident in the Bureau's handling of tribal intelligence. Rather than treating tribal leaders as simple informants, the Arab Bureau developed nuanced frameworks for understanding how tribal politics, economic interests, and traditional alliances influenced the information it received. This level of understanding allowed them to build more reliable intelligence networks than conventional military units could maintain. Even when information proved incorrect, Arab Bureau officers' deep cultural knowledge often allowed them to understand why a source might have provided inaccurate information—whether due to tribal rivalries, political aspirations, or simple misunderstandings—which in turn helped them refine their intelligence-gathering methods.

Translation and language work required particular attention. The Arab Bureau established protocols for handling Arabic-language materials that went beyond simple translation.[23] Staff were trained to note dialectal variations that might indicate a document's origin, while cultural references and idioms were carefully analysed for additional context. This linguistic sophistication allowed the Arab Bureau to better assess the authenticity of documents and understand subtle nuances in communications.

Field operations developed their own distinctive methods. The Arab Bureau created guidelines for officers operating in Ottoman territories, including protocols for emergency communication and procedures for protecting local sources. These guidelines evolved with practical experience, and as field personnel shared successful techniques among themselves. The Arab Bureau's approach to field operations emphasised flexibility and adaptation to local conditions while maintaining consistent standards for intelligence gathering.

Regular assessment meetings became another aspect of Arab Bureau working methods. These sessions brought together staff with different areas of expertise to evaluate current intelligence, identify emerging patterns, and present and discuss new intelligence and its implications, a collaborative approach towards analysis that helped ensure that any evaluations considered different perspectives. Likewise, the Bureau's approach to source verification evolved and improved over time, developing what might be called a triangulation method, where intelligence from human sources was cross-referenced against wireless intercepts and any field observations. Staff maintained detailed records of source reliability, noting both successful and failed intelligence to build a comprehensive picture of source credibility over time.

The India Office Rivalry

The conflict between the Arab Bureau and the India Office represents far more than a mere bureaucratic dispute. It embodied a fundamental tension within British imperial intelligence structures, revealing the complex dynamics of institutional knowledge, power, and innovation during a critical period of imperial transformation.[24]

Historically, the India Office's resistance to the Arab Bureau was deeply rooted in the traumatic legacy of the Indian Rebellion of 1857. This watershed moment had exposed catastrophic intelligence failures that fundamentally reshaped British colonial administrative practices.[25] This historic failure led to the development of an extraordinarily rigid approach to intelligence gathering, characterised by centralised control and deep suspicion of external interference.

The Arab Bureau's very conception challenged these established practices. Where traditional intelligence units viewed knowledge as something to be segmented and controlled, the Bureau proposed a more integrated approach. This reflected what intelligence theorists would later describe as a shift from viewing intelligence as a set of discrete information streams to understanding it as a holistic, contextual form of knowledge production.

The theoretical implications of this conflict are profound. The resistance encountered by the Arab Bureau exemplifies what organisational theorists describe as the "institutional resistance to innovative intelligence structures".[26] The India Office's response was not merely bureaucratic obstruction but a deep-seated institutional defence mechanism. Its approach reflected what scholars of imperial administration call the 'cultural inertia' of colonial bureaucracies—a tendency to resist changes that might destabilise established power structures.

Practically, this resistance manifested in multiple, carefully orchestrated limitations. The India Office successfully restricted the Arab Bureau's involvement in all matters pertaining to Indian Muslims, both within India and abroad. Moreover, the India Office limited the Arab Bureau's ability to produce or disseminate propaganda materials for Indian audiences, creating explicit geographical and thematic boundaries around the new intelligence unit.

The numerical context of these restrictions is revealing. By 1914, the Indian Army comprised approximately 240,000 men, with Muslims representing around 35 per cent of its total strength. Any potential disruption to this delicate demographic balance was viewed with extreme caution. The India Office's concerns went beyond mere administrative territorialism; they represented a complex calculus of imperial control and potential instability.

This institutional conflict reveals the tensions inherent in what this research conceptualises as an imperial epistemic community, a network of experts sharing a common worldview about colonial knowledge and administration.[27] The Arab Bureau represented a radical challenge to this established epistemic community. Its interdisciplinary approach, which brought together academics, linguists, and military personnel, fundamentally questioned the traditional boundaries of imperial intelligence work.

The most innovative aspect of the Arab Bureau's response was its ability to transform institutional constraints into opportunities for innovation. Unable to operate within traditional imperial frameworks, the Bureau developed new approaches to intelligence gathering and analysis that were decades ahead of their time. This mirrors contemporary theoretical understanding of organisational adaptation, where limitations can become catalysts for transformative change.

Paradoxically, the very resistance the Arab Bureau encountered from the India Office became a crucible for its most significant innovations. The need to work around institutional barriers forced a level of creativity and adaptability that might not have emerged in a more supportive environment. This speaks to a broader principle in innovation theory: truly transformative approaches often emerge not despite institutional constraints, but because of them.

The Imperial Epistemic Community

Understanding the Arab Bureau requires moving beyond traditional approaches to institutional history. At the heart of this analysis lies a novel theoretical concept: the imperial epistemic community. To comprehend this framework, we must first unpack the broader idea of an epistemic community and then explore its transformation in the imperial context. An epistemic community, in its most fundamental sense, represents a network of professionals with recognised expertise and competence in a particular domain. The term, formally coined in 1992 by international relations scholars, describes a group of experts who share a set of normative and principled beliefs, causal understanding, notions of validity, and a common policy enterprise. Traditionally applied to understand international policy coordination, this concept provides a powerful lens for analysing how specialised knowledge is created, shared, and applied.

The classic model of an epistemic community identifies four key characteristics: a shared set of normative and principled beliefs; commonly held causal beliefs about members' domain of expertise; shared notions of validity; and a common policy-driven enterprise. While initially developed to analyse international policy networks, this framework offers remarkable insight into more complex knowledge-producing groups. The Arab Bureau represents a particularly fascinating case study, as it embodies many of these characteristics while simultaneously challenging and expanding the original concept.

My own contribution—the concept of the imperial epistemic community—extends and reimagines this framework within the specific context of colonial knowledge production. Unlike traditional epistemic communities that operate in relatively horizontal networks, the imperial variant exists within a fundamentally hierarchical structure. This introduces a critical dimension: the power dynamics inherent in colonial knowledge creation.

The imperial epistemic community is characterised by several distinctive features: members possess a shared commitment to imperial objectives, despite potentially having nuanced or conflicting interpretations of what this might mean; the active production of knowledge that serves imperial strategic interests; a complex interplay between scholarly expertise and operational requirements; and the ability to shape understanding of colonised regions through specialised knowledge.

In the case of the Arab Bureau, this manifested in a remarkable synthesis of academic expertise and intelligence operations. Members brought diverse backgrounds—archaeology, linguistics, geography—but were united by a common enterprise of understanding and influencing the Middle Eastern region. Their expertise was not merely academic but deeply practical, aimed at supporting British imperial interests.

This approach challenges traditional divisions between scholarly knowledge and intelligence work. The Arab Bureau members were scholars before they were soldiers, applying academic methodologies to intelligence gathering. An archaeologist's understanding of historical trade routes could inform military strategy; a linguist's cultural insights could reshape diplomatic approaches. Thus, knowledge became a form of operational capital.

This imperial epistemic community framework reveals how such groups actively construct knowledge about colonised regions. They are not passive collectors of information but dynamic producers of understanding that fundamentally shapes imperial policy. The Arab Bureau did not simply report on the Middle East; they created the very intellectual frameworks through which British decision-makers understood the region.

Critically, this model recognises both the sophistication and the limitations of such knowledge production. Arab Bureau members were genuinely committed to understanding the Middle East, yet they remained constrained by imperial perspectives. Their cultural expertise was profound, but never entirely free from orientalist assumptions. They sought to understand, but always with the ultimate goal of imperial control. This theoretical approach provides insight into the complex mechanisms of colonial knowledge production, revealing how specialised expertise becomes a form of power. The imperial epistemic community is not just a group of experts, but an active agent in shaping imperial understanding and policy.[28]

The Arab Bureau represents a particularly sophisticated instantiation of this concept. Its members existed in a unique intellectual space: they were simultaneously scholars, intelligence operatives, and imperial agents. They developed methods of knowledge production that were decades ahead of their time, creating frameworks for understanding regions that would influence British engagement for generations.

By applying the imperial epistemic community framework, we can move beyond simplistic narratives of colonial expertise. We see instead a complex, dynamic process of knowledge creation: innovative, deeply flawed, but ultimately transformative. The Arab Bureau was not just gathering intelligence; it was actively constructing the very intellectual landscape through which the British Empire would understand and engage with the Middle East.

Transforming Intelligence Practice

The Arab Bureau's operational innovations represented more than tactical adaptations to wartime conditions; they embodied a fundamental re-conceptualisation of imperial intelligence gathering.[29] From their rooms at the Savoy, this unusual assemblage of scholars and specialists developed approaches to intelligence that would influence British policy throughout the Middle East for decades to come.

The Arab Bureau's most significant achievement lay in its integration of cultural, historical, and political knowledge into operational intelligence. It demonstrated that effective intelligence in culturally distinct environments required more than translated reports or casual observations; it demanded systematic engagement with local contexts, careful attention to cultural nuances, and rigorous analysis that went beyond surface-level information gathering.

The Arab Bureau's handling of inter-departmental coordination was also original. Developing a hub-and-spoke model of intelligence sharing rather than attempting to exert centralised control, the Bureau created a system that could accommodate institutional rivalries while still improving overall intelligence effectiveness. This approach, respecting established boundaries while creating new pathways for information sharing, offered a pragmatic solution to the fragmented nature of British imperial intelligence structures.

Perhaps most significantly, the Arab Bureau established new standards for verification and analysis. Their multi-source approach to intelligence verification, systematic documentation of source reliability, and collaborative analytical methods represented significant advances over contemporary practice. These innovations reflected the Arab Bureau's unique composition, bringing together academic rigour, cultural expertise, and operational requirements in ways that transformed how intelligence was gathered, analysed, and applied.

As such, the Bureau's legacy extended beyond its immediate wartime operations, not least for its handbooks, analytical frameworks, and operational methods that formed the foundation for British engagement with the Middle East in the post-war period. The Middle East Department, established within the Colonial Office in 1921, drew heavily on Arab Bureau personnel and methodologies. Former Arab Bureau members played key roles in shaping British policy throughout the region, bringing their distinctive approach to intelligence and administration into the structures of post-war imperial governance.

Yet the story of the Arab Bureau also reveals the inherent tensions of colonial knowledge production. Even as they developed these new approaches to understanding the Middle East, their ultimate purpose remained the advancement of British imperial interests. The very expertise that allowed them to understand local contexts was intimately tied to projects of imperial control. This paradox—profound cultural understanding in service of imperial domination—lies at the heart of the imperial epistemic community concept.

As the war progressed, the Arab Bureau would face new challenges that tested its novel approaches to intelligence. The shift from gathering information to actively shaping events would require even greater integration of cultural knowledge and strategic action. The Arab Bureau's ability to navigate these challenges while maintaining its distinctive approach to intelligence would prove crucial to its effectiveness in the complex landscape of wartime Middle East politics.

In tracing Arab Bureau operations from Hogarth's conception of the 'wandering scholar' recruitment model to the practical realities of intelligence coordination in Cairo, we see the emergence of a new paradigm in colonial intelligence gathering, one that recognised the essential importance of cultural knowledge, historical context, and interdisciplinary analysis. This paradigm, however imperfectly realised in practice, represented a significant departure from traditional approaches and offered new ways of understanding the relationship between knowledge and power in imperial contexts. As the Arab Bureau's operational infrastructure took shape in Cairo, its most revolutionary innovation would emerge through the transformation of pre-existing scholarly networks into new intelligence ecosystems that bridged academic expertise with wartime strategic imperatives, as we will see in the next chapter.

PART III

INTELLIGENCE AND INNOVATION

6

NETWORKS OF KNOWLEDGE

MIDDLE EAST, NORTH AFRICA, INDIA

In which the Arab Bureau's hidden world of scholarly intelligence networks is revealed, and we explore how the expertise of scholarly networks was transformed into powerful intelligence ecosystems, creating innovative information webs that bridged academic expertise with wartime strategic needs. By examining how intellectual connections evolved into sophisticated intelligence channels, we see how cultural knowledge morphed into new forms of operational capability that created an unprecedented approach to gathering and understanding intelligence across the complex cultural landscape of the Middle East in the First World War.

Transforming Scholarly Connections into Intelligence

In the summer of 1914, Philip Graves,[1] then Constantinople correspondent for *The Times*, understood something fundamental about intelligence that most military strategists did not: knowledge flows through human relationships, not just official channels.

Graves' extensive network of contacts across Ottoman territories—journalists, merchants, scholars, and local intellectuals—represented a more evolved information ecosystem that would become crucial to the Arab Bureau's intelligence operations. These weren't just casual connections but intricate webs of trust and mutual understanding built through years of professional engagement. The intelligence value of these networks was recognised even before the Arab Bureau's formation. In 1913, Newcombe, Woolley, and Lawrence conducted the Wilderness of Zin survey under the cover of the Palestine Exploration

THE ARAB BUREAU

Fund, mapping the Negev and Sinai for potential Turkish invasion routes towards the Suez Canal.[2]

When the war broke out, these pre-existing scholarly and professional networks became unexpected intelligence assets.[3] An archaeological expedition's local workers, a linguist's academic contacts, a journalist's source network—these human connections proved more valuable than any conventional military intelligence gathering method.

At the same time, the Arab Bureau's claims of superior cultural understanding, while central to their institutional identity, also demand careful scrutiny. Members frequently described themselves as uniquely qualified cultural intermediaries, yet this narrative—unsurprisingly constructed in part for institutional legitimacy—must be distinguished from demonstrated cross-cultural competence. When Hogarth boasted of recruiting 'wandering scholars' with regional expertise, he was simultaneously marketing the Arab Bureau's value to suspicious authorities in London and Delhi.

Coupled with this, the Arab Bureau's collaboration with Arab intellectuals, though genuine, was often portrayed in terms that served British institutional interests. For instance, reports emphasised willing cooperation and shared objectives with such individuals while downplaying the transactional nature of many of these relationships and the limited scope of actual cultural exchange. Also, while postcolonial scholarship rightly emphasises the power dynamics inherent in imperial knowledge production, focusing solely on discourse can obscure the practical operational innovations that emerged from cross-cultural intelligence work.

As such, our central argument remains valid, viz. the Arab Bureau understood what traditional intelligence services did not: in a complex regional landscape like the Middle East, intelligence was not about collecting data but about comprehending the nuanced human networks that shaped political and social dynamics.[4] This chapter explores how these scholarly networks were transformed into sophisticated intelligence ecosystems that would revolutionise British understanding of the Middle East during the First World War.

Archaeological Expeditions as Network Builders

Archaeological expeditions represented far more than academic pursuits in the years before the First World War. They were platforms for building complex regional networks that would prove invaluable to intelligence operations.

The Carchemish excavation epitomised this phenomenon. Led by David Hogarth[5] and later involving Lawrence, the site became a crucial nexus of scholarly and regional connections. Located near the Turkish–Syrian border, the Carchemish excavations brought British scholars into daily contact with local workers, regional officials, and visiting dignitaries. The expedition's German colleagues—archaeological work being nothing if not international—inadvertently provided Britain with insights into German interests in the region.[6]

Woolley's approach at Carchemish demonstrated how scholarly work could generate intelligence infrastructure.[7] By meticulously documenting site operations, managing local workers, and navigating complex regional politics, Woolley was simultaneously conducting archaeological research and building an information network.[8] Workers who helped map ancient fortifications could provide insights into contemporary terrain. Conversations about historical trade routes could reveal contemporary logistical information.

These expeditions required significant linguistic and cultural skills. Researchers had to develop deep local relationships, understand complex social hierarchies, and navigate intricate cultural dynamics. A single archaeological expedition might involve negotiations with local tribal leaders, government officials, and regional powerbrokers, each interaction potentially generating valuable intelligence.

In looking at the Arab Bureau's accomplishments, Satia sees primarily imperial knowledge production serving orientalist assumptions, while the archival evidence reveals more genuine intellectual exchange with Arab partners. The Arab Bureau's collaboration with figures like As'ad Daghir and Faris Nimr to be discussed presently, while certainly serving British interests, also required acknowledging Arab intellectual agency in ways that complicate simplistic narratives of imperial domination.

The networks developed through these expeditions were deliberately cultivated. Researchers understood that their work depended on maintaining positive relationships with local communities. This required genuine intellectual respect, cultural sensitivity, and a commitment to understanding regional complexities that went far beyond traditional colonial approaches.

Importantly, these networks existed independently of immediate military objectives. They were built through years of patient scholarship, intellectual curiosity, and genuine cross-cultural engagement.[9] When war broke out, these pre-existing relationships became unexpected strategic assets—information channels that military intelligence would never be able to quickly or easily develop.

Linguistic Research and Cultural Translation

Linguistic abilities represented another scholarly asset repurposed for intelligence work. The Arab Bureau recognised that language mastery went beyond mere communication to encompass cultural understanding. The ability to think in Arabic while reporting in English exemplified the Arab Bureau's ideal of intelligence officers who could move fluidly between cultural contexts, interpreting one world for another. Herbert Garland's[10] linguistic work exemplified this approach.[11] His expertise in Arabic dialects went far beyond academic classification. By meticulously documenting linguistic variations, Garland was simultaneously conducting scholarly research and developing a nuanced understanding of regional social dynamics. His ability to detect a speaker's precise origin from dialectal variations transformed linguistic study into a form of intelligence gathering. During the war, his ability to identify regional accents in intercepted communications proved instrumental in uncovering Ottoman troop movements.

Linguistic researchers developed networks that crossed traditional imperial boundaries. Their work required deep engagement with local communities, where researchers built relationships with scholars, religious leaders, and everyday speakers.[12] The complexity of these networks went beyond simple language study; linguists understand that language is not just a communication tool but a window into another culture. As such, their work required not just grammatical expertise but immersion in that culture.[13] A conversation about linguistic nuances could reveal profound insights about regional social structures, political sentiments, and cultural dynamics.

The linguistic reality of the Arab Bureau's operations reveals a crucial insight often obscured by romanticised accounts: perfect language mastery was less important than cultural and contextual understanding. Lawrence's Arabic, far from the native-level fluency often attributed to him, was what he himself characterised as "a perpetual adventure" for his listeners.[14] Before the war, he had received just two months of formal Arabic instruction at the American Mission School in Lebanon under

NETWORKS OF KNOWLEDGE

Miss Fareedah al-Akle. By his own admission, Lawrence "never heard an Englishman speak Arabic well enough to be taken for a native of any part of the Arabic-speaking world, for five minutes".

What Lawrence and his colleagues did possess, however, was the ability to function effectively within Arab cultural contexts. Lawrence reckoned he had control of approximately 12,000 words and cognates— "a good vocabulary for English, but not enough for Arabic"—which he combined with what he called "a grammar and syntax of my own invention". Yet this functional, if imperfect, command proved sufficient for operational needs. Lawrence could identify regional accents and dialects, determine a speaker's likely origin, and navigate complex social interactions, skills far more valuable than grammatical perfection.

This pragmatic approach to language reflected the Arab Bureau's broader understanding that effective intelligence work requires cultural fluency more than simple linguistic purity. Where traditional colonial approaches viewed unfamiliar languages with "deep suspicion, bordering on paranoia",[15] the Arab Bureau valued the ability to speak multiple languages as conducive to a more holistic cultural intelligence.

From Academic Pursuits to Operational Intelligence

The transition from scholarly expertise to intelligence operations was not a linear process but a complex transformation driven by individual scholars' unique experiences and the unprecedented challenges of the First World War. Lawrence perhaps embodied this transformation most dramatically. His undergraduate research on Crusader castles saw him travel extensively through Ottoman territories, which was far more than a mere academic exercise. Lawrence was systematically mapping fortifications, developing an intimate understanding of regional geography, and building networks of local contacts that would prove invaluable for intelligence work.[16]

At Carchemish, Lawrence had already developed crucial skills that would directly translate to intelligence operations. Organising supplies, managing local workers, documenting site locations—these were not just archaeological techniques but methods of network management and information gathering. His ability to navigate complex social environments, negotiate with local authorities, and maintain detailed, nuanced records would become critical intelligence capabilities.

Bell's transformation was equally profound. Her extensive travels through Syria and Mesopotamia had given her an unparalleled understanding of tribal politics and social dynamics. Where traditional military intelligence saw only abstract geographical spaces, Bell saw intricate networks of relationships, genealogies, and political interconnections.[17] Her linguistic abilities and cultural understanding allowed her to access social spaces completely closed to male agents, creating intelligence capabilities that went far beyond traditional approaches.

These scholars understood something fundamental that earlier military intelligence did not: effective regional understanding required more than tactical information. It demanded a comprehensive grasp of cultural, social, and political dynamics. An archaeological excavation was not just about uncovering artefacts but about understanding complex human networks. A linguistic study was not merely about language but about comprehending the intricate social structures that language reflected.

The outbreak of war created an urgent need for this type of expertise. Traditional military intelligence had proven catastrophically inadequate in understanding the complexities of the Middle Eastern theatre. The failures at Gallipoli and Kut al-Amara demonstrated the devastating consequences of cultural ignorance. Suddenly, the scholars' deep regional knowledge became not just academic but strategically critical.

Academic Skills as Operational Capabilities

The skills developed through scholarly research proved remarkably adaptable to intelligence work. Archaeological methodologies, in particular, provided a complex framework for intelligence gathering and analysis that military training could never replicate.[18]

The Arab Bureau's approach to field reconnaissance similarly borrowed from archaeological practice. When Arab Bureau officers sketched route maps, they incorporated survey techniques developed for archaeological expeditions. Their field notes combined military observations with detailed documentation of water sources, settlement patterns, and terrain features to create intelligence conventional military scouts simply could not produce.[19] This methodological transference represents one of the Arab Bureau's most significant yet overlooked innovations: the application of scientific field methodologies to intelligence gathering.[20]

Archaeologists had developed unique capabilities for reading landscapes that went far beyond military topographical understanding.

Where a conventional military officer might see only terrain, an archaeologist like Hogarth or Woolley saw a complex landscape of human relationships, historical movements, and strategic possibilities. Ancient trade routes became potential military supply lines. Traditional water sources could determine troop movement strategies. The scholars' approach to source criticism—a skill honed through years of academic research—became a revolutionary intelligence methodology. Where military intelligence might accept information at face value, these scholar–spies developed more educated verification processes.[21] They understood how to cross-reference sources, detect potential biases, and construct comprehensive understanding from fragmentary information.

Anthropological training provided crucial insights into tribal structures and political allegiances that military intelligence had never achieved. Understanding local social dynamics, recognising complex networks of obligation and relationship, became as important as traditional tactical intelligence. A tribal genealogy could predict potential military alliances. Cultural understanding became a strategic asset.

The Arab Bureau recognised that effective intelligence required more than collecting information: it demanded the comprehension of the complex cultural contexts that shaped regional behaviour. Its operatives' academic backgrounds allowed them to see patterns in seemingly unrelated information, understand the significance of subtle cultural indicators, and place current events within deeper historical contexts.

This was not simply about applying academic skills to military objectives. It represented a fundamental reimagining of intelligence work. What these scholars brought to intelligence gathering was academic rigour, almost infinite patience, and attention to detail, an approach that prioritised deep understanding over quick conclusions.

Arab Intellectual Partnerships

The depth of the Arab Bureau's collaboration with local intellectuals represented a more developed approach to information gathering, which transcended traditional colonial intelligence methods. These relationships were not simply about extracting information but about creating genuine intellectual partnerships that could reshape regional understanding.

Faris Nimr,[22] publisher of *al-Muqattam*, exemplified this approach. His relationship with the Arab Bureau went far beyond a simple informant network. Nimr was a key collaborator in creating information ecosystems that could simultaneously serve multiple strategic objectives. His newspaper became a critical platform for cultural and political communication, bridging Arab intellectual circles and British strategic interests.

Similarly, the Arab Bureau's work with Ya'qub Sarruf[23] demonstrated the complexity of these intellectual networks. Sarruf, a prominent journalist and intellectual, represented a nuanced channel of communication that went beyond traditional propaganda efforts. These collaborations were not about simple messaging but about creating sophisticated platforms for cultural dialogue and strategic influence.

Sheikh Rashid Rida's[24] involvement provided another critical example. His writings in *al-Manar* became a carefully negotiated space for intellectual exchange. The Arab Bureau understood that effective communication required more than direct messaging: it demanded engagement with existing intellectual traditions and the creation of culturally authentic narratives.[25]

These relationships challenged traditional colonial communication models. Where previous imperial information operations saw local intellectuals as passive recipients of messaging, the Arab Bureau approached them as active collaborators in knowledge production. Each interaction was a complex negotiation of cultural understanding, political objectives, and intellectual respect.

The Arab Bureau's approach recognised that effective influence required deep cultural engagement. It wasn't simply trying to transmit information but to create meaningful dialogues that could reshape regional political understanding. This meant working with intellectuals who had already established credibility within their own cultural contexts. Crucially, these relationships existed in a complex moral and political space. The intellectuals were not simple agents of British imperial interests but autonomous actors navigating their own complex political landscapes. The Arab Bureau's success depended on understanding and respecting these intricate dynamics.

The collaboration extended beyond individual relationships. The Arab Bureau created sophisticated ecosystems of intellectual exchange that simultaneously served multiple strategic objectives. A newspaper article, a scholarly exchange, a carefully placed piece of information, these became tools of a nuanced form of cultural and political communication.

NETWORKS OF KNOWLEDGE

The Nahda Movement and Intelligence Networks

The intellectual networks of Arab nationalists and scholars proved far more complex than simple informant relationships. Jurji Zaydan,[26] founder of *al-Hilal*[27] magazine, represented a particularly interesting collaborator. His pan-Arab intellectual project aligned in fascinating ways with the Arab Bureau's strategic objectives, creating a nuanced information ecosystem that went beyond traditional propaganda.

Zaydan's work in historical writing became an unexpected intelligence channel. His historical novels and scholarly publications created narratives about Arab identity that subtly intersected with British strategic interests. By documenting Arab cultural continuity and intellectual achievements, Zaydan was building Arab nationalist consciousness while simultaneously providing the Arab Bureau with deep cultural insights.[28]

The Bureau's collaboration with Arab Christian intellectuals was particularly noteworthy. Many, like Faris Nimr and Ya'qub Sarruf, occupied unique positions within Ottoman social structures. Their newspapers—*al-Muqattam* and *al-Ahram*—became critical platforms for nuanced political communication. These weren't simply information channels but complex negotiation spaces where cultural and political narratives could be carefully constructed.

The Arab intellectual landscape of the early twentieth century was far more nuanced than colonial narratives suggest. Many Arab Christian and Muslim intellectuals saw potential strategic alignments that could advance their own nationalist aspirations while navigating complex imperial relationships. Intellectuals of the Nahda Movement, an Arab cultural renaissance that began in the 1800s, like Butrus al-Bustani[29] played crucial roles in these networks. Their vision of Arab cultural renaissance lived on after them, and often found unexpected resonance with certain British strategic objectives. Likewise, their relationships with the Arab Bureau weren't straightforward collaborations but rather intricate negotiations of cultural and political identity.

The role of Syrian and Lebanese émigré intellectuals in expanding the Arab Bureau's information networks was particularly important.[30] Many had established significant publishing networks in Egypt, creating platforms that could simultaneously serve intellectual and strategic communication purposes.

Religious diversity added another layer of complexity to the environment. Christian Arab intellectuals like Faris Nimr often occupied unique intermediary positions. Their publications could navigate sensitive political territories, providing channels of communication that more overtly positioned actors could not. The intellectual exchanges that took place in these periodicals went beyond simple information transmission. They represented complex negotiations of cultural authenticity, political aspiration, and strategic positioning. An article in *al-Hilal* might simultaneously serve nationalist intellectual goals, provide cultural insight for British strategists, and create nuanced political narratives.

These networks challenged fundamental assumptions about colonial information operations. The Arab intellectuals were independent agents actively shaping their own political narratives, not passive recipients of imperial messaging. Each collaboration was a delicate intellectual dance, balancing personal political commitments with strategic possibilities.

Building Information Ecosystems

Information verification represented a technical innovation in the Arab Bureau's intelligence approach. Unlike traditional intelligence that evaluated reports in isolation, these scholar–spies developed systematic frameworks for cross-referencing multiple sources. They created a structured process where information from diverse origins—wireless intercepts, field observations, economic reports, cultural insights—could be methodically integrated and assessed, creating intelligence products of unprecedented depth.[31]

The verification process was itself a form of intelligence gathering. A single piece of information would be meticulously examined through multiple lenses: a wireless intercept might be validated against a merchant's economic report, an aerial photograph, and a local informant's observations. Such an approach created a multidimensional intelligence picture far more comprehensive than conventional methods of verification. Garland exemplified this approach in so far as where a traditional translator might simply render a message's literal meaning, Garland would analyse linguistic nuances, detect coded references, and understand the broader political and cultural context embedded in the communication. A seemingly innocuous message could reveal complex layers of political sentiment, internal tensions, or strategic intentions.

The Arab Bureau developed a schema of verification architecture, their 'web of verification' where each source was assessed not merely for factual reliability but for its specific position within local networks.[32] This represented a significant technical advancement in intelligence methodology from the standard of the time. The Bureau's system recognised that a merchant might provide accurate economic information but less reliable political insights, or that a tribal leader might offer detailed local knowledge but limited perspective on broader regional dynamics.

This approach required extraordinary cultural sophistication. The scholars understood that information was never purely objective but always contextualised by cultural, historical, and personal perspectives. They developed methods for understanding how different sources might interpret the same event through different lenses.

Most noteworthy was the Arab Bureau's approach to seemingly contradictory intelligence. Rather than discarding inconsistent reports as unreliable, standard practice in conventional intelligence, Arab Bureau analysts developed methods to extract meaningful insights from these very contradictions.[33] Competing tribal accounts, for instance, were analysed as indicators of underlying political tensions, alliance negotiations, or strategic ambiguities that more simplistic approaches would entirely miss.

The physical infrastructure of this verification system was equally complex. Carefully filed documents, cross-referenced reports, and detailed source evaluations created a comprehensive intelligence ecosystem. Each piece of information was not just collected but meticulously analysed, contextualised, and integrated into a broader understanding of regional dynamics.

The Arab Bureau's approach to information networks represented a radical departure from traditional intelligence gathering.[34] These were living, adaptive systems that prioritised interconnection over isolated data points. Unlike rigid military intelligence structures, the Bureau's networks could rapidly reconfigure, integrating diverse sources of knowledge in real-time.[35] The power of these ecosystems lay in their flexibility. A single piece of information could be simultaneously validated, contextualised, and reinterpreted through multiple perspectives: a report from a Bedouin scout might be cross-referenced with a merchant's economic insights, a linguistic analysis of regional communications, and broader historical understanding.

This approach required extraordinary intellectual infrastructure, and so Arab Bureau members maintained complex relationship maps that tracked not just individual sources but the intricate connections between them. For instance, a tribal leader's testimony wasn't evaluated in isolation but understood within broader networks of familial, economic, and political relationships. Thus it was that the Bureau's networks extended far beyond simple information collection, instead becoming platforms for cultural translation, where each piece of information was carefully situated within its broader social and political context. A seemingly mundane communication could reveal complex layers of regional dynamics when properly contextualised.

Challenges and Limitations

The information networks of the Arab Bureau were not without significant challenges. Geographic limitations created profound constraints on intelligence gathering. Much of the Arabian Peninsula remained effectively *terra incognita*, with vast territories that were difficult or impossible to access directly. Communication infrastructure posed another critical challenge. Vast distances, limited technological capabilities, and the complex terrain of the Middle East meant that information transmission was inherently unreliable.[36] The Arab Bureau had to develop multiple communication channels, including traditional messenger networks alongside emerging wireless technologies.[37]

Source reliability remained a constant concern. The Arab Bureau developed intricate frameworks for evaluating information sources, recognising that local informants might have complex motivations. A tribal leader's report might be influenced by inter-tribal rivalries, economic interests, or personal political aspirations. Understanding these underlying dynamics became as important as the information itself. Language complexity added another layer of difficulty, where rich dialectal variations across the Middle East meant that linguistic interpretation was far from straightforward, in spite of the skills of the assembled members of the Arab Bureau. A seemingly straightforward communication could contain multiple layers of meaning that would be invisible to less informed analysts. Security concerns created additional complications. The need to protect information sources while maintaining the integrity of its networks required constant careful negotiation. Each new connection potentially exposed existing networks to risk, meaning the Bureau had to exercise extraordinary care and strategic thinking.

NETWORKS OF KNOWLEDGE

The very breadth of the Arab Bureau's approach created operational challenges. Its comprehensive method of intelligence gathering meant that tactical information could become outdated by the time it was fully analysed and distributed. The rapidly evolving nature of regional politics required constant network reconfiguration.

The Imperial Epistemic Community in Practice

The Arab Bureau's network operations represent the perfect exemplification of the imperial epistemic community concept introduced in the previous chapter. Its approach to intelligence gathering went beyond mere information collection to become a fascinating means of knowledge production that would shape British understanding of the Middle East for generations. This approach challenged traditional colonial intelligence by emphasising cultural understanding, contextual knowledge, and interdisciplinary analysis.[38]

This imperial epistemic community operated at the intersection of academic knowledge and operational intelligence, transforming scholarly understanding into strategic capability. Members shared not just information but interpretive frameworks, methodological approaches, and conceptual models that bridged traditional divisions between military and academic knowledge. Bell's tribal mapping, for instance, represented more than just useful data; it created a new conceptual approach to understanding tribal politics that became foundational to British regional engagement.[39]

The transformative power of this epistemic community lay in its ability to reshape how the empire itself understood the regions it sought to influence. By integrating archaeological, linguistic, and anthropological perspectives with military and political concerns, the Arab Bureau created knowledge systems that were simultaneously more refined and more useful than conventional intelligence. Its approach anticipated by decades what intelligence theorists would later identify as the fundamental challenge of intelligence work: not just gathering facts but creating frameworks for understanding complex cultural and political landscapes.

The practical application of this concept is evident in how the Arab Bureau's networks operated. Rather than simply collecting information, they were actively constructing interpretive frameworks that would shape British understanding of the region. Their intelligence reports did not merely present facts but created useful analytical models for understanding regional dynamics.

This epistemic community developed what might be called 'cultural intelligence methodologies', approaches to information gathering and analysis that went far beyond traditional military intelligence. They recognised that understanding a region required more than collecting facts; it demanded comprehending the complex cultural, social, and political dynamics that shaped behaviour and perception.

The Arab Bureau's approach to recruitment reflected this epistemic function. It sought individuals who could not only gather information but also interpret and contextualise it within broader cultural frameworks. Their preference for scholars, linguists, and regional experts reflected an understanding that intelligence required interpretive skills as much as information-gathering capabilities.

The Bureau's information-verification methods similarly reflected this epistemic approach. Information was not simply checked for accuracy but evaluated for its place within broader cultural and historical contexts. This represented a fundamental shift in how intelligence was understood and practised, moving from a collection-centred model to a knowledge-production framework.

Legacy of Scholarly Networks

The Arab Bureau's transformation of scholarly networks into intelligence ecosystems represented a revolutionary approach to understanding complex regions. By integrating academic expertise with operational intelligence, it created information networks that were more effective than traditional military intelligence.[40]

The legacy of these networks extended far beyond their immediate wartime utility. The knowledge frameworks, analytical approaches, and cultural understanding they developed would influence British engagement with the Middle East for generations. The Middle East Department, established within the Colonial Office in 1921, drew heavily on Arab Bureau personnel and methodologies, representing a direct institutional continuation of its approach to the region.

The Arab Bureau's network operations anticipated modern approaches to intelligence by decades. Current intelligence theory increasingly recognises that effective understanding requires more than collecting information; it demands comprehending the complex human systems that shape behaviour and perception. The Arab Bureau's approach to cultural intelligence, network analysis, and information verification prefigured developments that would not become standard practice until the late twentieth century.

The theoretical implications of the Bureau's work extend beyond specific intelligence practices to broader questions about knowledge production in colonial contexts. The Arab Bureau's role as an imperial epistemic community reveals how intelligence operations could simultaneously serve immediate strategic objectives while creating enduring frameworks for understanding regions. This dual function—both operational and epistemic—represents a crucial insight for understanding how intelligence shapes policy and perception.

As we turn to the technological innovations explored in the next chapter, we see how these scholarly networks provided the foundation for revolutionary approaches to signals intelligence, aerial reconnaissance, and other emerging technologies. The Arab Bureau's ability to integrate cultural expertise with technological innovation created an unprecedented approach to intelligence that would influence operations throughout the First World War and beyond.[41]

The scholarly networks that had begun as academic connections transformed into brilliant intelligence ecosystems that fundamentally changed how information was gathered, analysed, and understood. This transformation represented not just an operational innovation but a conceptual revolution in how intelligence could function in complex cultural environments.

7

"READING THE ENEMY'S MAIL"

INTELLIGENCE BREAKTHROUGHS: HIJAZ

In which the Arab Bureau demonstrates how cultural understanding, technological innovation, and clever network analysis could transform intelligence gathering, creating unprecedented capabilities for understanding and influencing complex regional dynamics during the First World War. Through innovative integration of wireless intercepts, aerial reconnaissance, human intelligence networks, and deep cultural expertise, the Arab Bureau developed methods that would influence intelligence operations for generations to come, establishing new models for how information could be collected, verified, and transformed into strategic understanding across the complex landscape of the Middle East.

The Intelligence Revolution

In the summer of 1916, an intelligence officer from the Arab Bureau bent over a wireless set in a makeshift station near Jeddah, carefully transcribing the dots and dashes of an intercepted Ottoman transmission. This was not intelligence gathering as it had previously been understood: this was a revolution in the making. The Arab Bureau's approach to intelligence represented a fundamental reimagining of how information could be collected, analysed, and transformed into strategic understanding. Where traditional military intelligence saw information as a series of discrete facts to be collected and reported, these scholars-turned-spies understood intelligence as a complex, living system of knowledge.

At the heart of this revolution was a simple yet radical insight: understanding a region required more than just collecting information. It demanded a deep, nuanced comprehension of cultural, social, and political dynamics that traditional intelligence methods had never even attempted to capture. The First World War had exposed the catastrophic limitations of conventional intelligence practices. The disastrous campaigns at Gallipoli and Kut al-Amara had demonstrated how a failure to understand local conditions could transform military operations into humanitarian catastrophes. Traditional military intelligence, with its focus on troop movements and enemy capabilities, had proven woefully inadequate in the complex landscape of the Middle East.

The Arab Bureau emerged as a response to this intelligence crisis. It was not just a new department but a fundamentally different approach to understanding regions. Where other intelligence units saw themselves as collectors of information, the Arab Bureau saw itself as an interpreter of complex cultural dynamics. As has already been discussed, the unit's very composition was revolutionary, where typical military intelligence officers were less numerous than academics of many stripes: archaeologists, linguists, journalists, travellers, and popular authors. Gertrude Bell, with her extensive travels and linguistic abilities; Lawrence, with his deep engagement with Arab culture; and Hogarth, the museum curator who brought scholarly rigour to intelligence analysis. Each brought a perspective that, before the Arab Revolt, traditional military intelligence might well have dismissed as irrelevant.

This chapter explores how the Arab Bureau's innovative approach to intelligence transformed British understanding of the Middle East, particularly in the Hijaz region during the Arab Revolt. By integrating cultural expertise with emerging technologies and complex human intelligence networks, the Bureau developed methods that would influence intelligence operations for generations to come.

Signals and Wireless Intelligence Development and Innovation

The Arab Bureau's approach to wireless communication represented far more than the mere adoption of a new technology. The Bureau saw this nascent form of communication as a complex information ecosystem that could transform intelligence gathering. Where traditional military intelligence viewed intercepted messages as simple tactical data, the Arab Bureau understood these transmissions as intricate texts revealing complex regional dynamics.

Wireless communication became the Bureau's most reliable, and arguably most important, intelligence platform. Given the limitations of

"READING THE ENEMY'S MAIL"

wireless telegraphy in desert conditions and its vulnerability to interception, the ability to predict behaviour through cultural understanding emerged as a significant technological advantage.[1]

The Arab Bureau's signals intelligence methods were revolutionary. Wireless interception was still in its technological infancy, but the Arab Bureau developed remarkably erudite approaches to analysis. It didn't simply decode messages but constructed elaborate frameworks for understanding the context, implications, and broader significance of each transmission. Take, for instance, its handling of a wireless message about Ottoman troop deployments in the Hijaz. Where a traditional intelligence unit might simply note the number of troops and their potential destination, the Arab Bureau's analysts would examine multiple layers of meaning: What did a message's tone reveal about Ottoman morale? How did specific language choices reflect internal political tensions? What could be inferred about command structures from the communication's structure?[2]

The integration of wireless intelligence into the Bureau's broader operational framework emerged most clearly in 1916–17, during the early Arab Revolt operations. The Arab Bureau established wireless intercept stations at strategic locations, including Jeddah and later Aqaba, creating a monitoring network that provided unprecedented insight into Ottoman communications. These stations, often operating with minimal equipment under challenging desert conditions, nonetheless yielded intelligence of exceptional strategic value when combined with the Arab Bureau's cultural and linguistic expertise.

A key breakthrough came in the summer of 1916 when the Arab Bureau established a wireless intercept station near Jeddah. This station, operating with limited technical resources, became a crucial node in its intelligence network. The Arab Bureau developed systematic approaches to gathering, translating, and analysing Ottoman wireless communications. Its effectiveness stemmed not from technological sophistication but from its ability to integrate technical intercepts with deep cultural understanding.

The Bureau's approach to wireless intelligence was fundamentally different from contemporary military practices. Where other intelligence units saw technology as a replacement for human intelligence, the Arab Bureau understood these tools as complementary components of a complex information ecosystem. A wireless intercept might be cross-referenced with a local merchant's economic report, an aerial photograph, and a tribal leader's observations, creating a multidimensional understanding that transcended traditional intelligence boundaries.[3]

Codebreaking and Linguistic Analysis

The linguistic dimension of signals intelligence includes the Arab Bureau's most interesting innovations. The Bureau's approach to intercepted communications went far beyond simple translation to encompass deep cultural and linguistic analysis. This was intelligence not just as information gathering but as cultural interpretation.

Garland's contributions were particularly significant, as his expertise in Arabic dialects and Ottoman Turkish offered the possibility of transforming wireless intelligence from simple message interception to nuanced cultural analysis. Where a conventional translator might render only the literal meaning of intercepted communications, Garland could detect subtle dialectal variations that revealed a message's origin, understand cultural references that carried hidden meanings, and recognise coded language that might escape less informed analysts.[4]

As this example shows, the Arab Bureau developed what might be called 'linguistic intelligence', using language analysis not just to understand the content of communications but to extract deeper insights about Ottoman command structures, internal political tensions, and regional alliances. A single word choice in an intercepted message might reveal valuable intelligence about the sender's origins, education, or political affiliations. Building on these linguistic insights, the Bureau's approach to encrypted communications moved beyond conventional techniques. Rather than relying solely on mathematical codebreaking methods, its operatives applied their cultural and contextual understanding to the decryption process.[5] Knowledge of Ottoman administrative structures, military terminology, and cultural reference points provided crucial advantages when interpreting coded messages.

A particularly valuable breakthrough came from the Bureau's analysis of Ottoman military communication patterns. By studying the timing, frequency, and style of wireless transmissions, Arab Bureau analysts could detect changes in Ottoman command structures, identify communication breakdowns, and anticipate military operations. This pattern analysis, combined with content interpretation, created a multidimensional understanding of Ottoman military operations that went far beyond traditional intelligence capabilities.

The Arab Bureau's linguistic methods extended to message authentication. Its deep language expertise allowed it to detect forgeries, identify inconsistencies, and validate the authenticity of intercepted communications. Such an approach to message verification represented a significant innovation in signals intelligence, anticipating modern methods by decades.[6]

Perhaps most importantly, the Arab Bureau recognised that effective signals intelligence required more than just technical interception capabilities. It demanded a deep understanding of the cultural, political, and social contexts that shaped communication. The Bureau's approach integrated wireless intercepts into a broader intelligence framework, creating a comprehensive understanding that technical methods alone could never achieve.

Aerial Reconnaissance and Visual Intelligence

Aerial reconnaissance represented another frontier of technological innovation in the Arab Bureau's intelligence operations. Early photographic intelligence was crude by modern standards, but the Arab Bureau saw these emerging technologies as more than mere mapping tools. A photograph of a landscape was not just a geographical record but a potential source of insights about trade routes, tribal movements, economic patterns, and regional infrastructure.

The Arab Bureau's most significant innovation lay in its integration of aerial observations with ground-level cultural knowledge. Where conventional military intelligence might use aerial photographs simply to identify enemy positions, the Arab Bureau developed methods for contextualising these images within broader cultural and geographical understanding. Its archaeological expertise proved surprisingly valuable in this process. Scholars accustomed to analysing ancient settlement patterns and historical trade routes could apply these same analytical skills to interpreting modern landscape photographs.[7]

Hogarth's archaeological experience provided a methodological framework for aerial intelligence analysis. His training in interpreting landscape features, identifying settlement patterns, and analysing spatial relationships translated directly to aerial reconnaissance interpretation. Where military officers might see only terrain features, Hogarth could recognise traditional water sources, ancient trade routes repurposed for modern transportation, and settlement patterns that revealed important social and economic information.

The Arab Bureau pioneered early approaches to aerial reconnaissance, integrating this nascent technology with ground-level intelligence. Though still in its infancy, aerial observation provided unprecedented views of Ottoman positions and troop movements, and Arab Bureau analysts developed methods for correlating aerial observations with tribal informant reports and wireless intercepts, creating multi-layered intelligence assessments that anticipated modern all-source analysis.

The Arab Bureau's approach to aerial intelligence was particularly evident in its coverage of the Hijaz Railway operations. The Bureau developed methods for integrating aerial observations of railway infrastructure with human intelligence about Ottoman transportation activities. This comprehensive approach allowed the Bureau to identify vulnerabilities in Ottoman logistics systems and develop effective strategies for disrupting supply lines. Its analysis went beyond simple identification of targets to encompass broader understanding of how railway operations affected Ottoman military capabilities, economic systems, and political control.

The Arab Bureau's visual intelligence methods extended beyond aerial photography to include map-making, terrain analysis, and infrastructure assessment, as it developed original approaches to cartography that integrated traditional military mapping with cultural and historical knowledge. Arab Bureau maps included not just geographical features but tribal territories, historical trade routes, water sources, and other culturally significant landmarks that proved valuable for military operations.[8]

This integration of visual data with cultural knowledge represented a significant innovation in intelligence methodology. The Arab Bureau recognised that effective visual intelligence required more than just observation; it demanded interpretation within cultural and historical contexts. This approach anticipated modern visual intelligence methods by decades, demonstrating the value of integrating technical capabilities with deep regional expertise.[9]

Human Intelligence Networks, Tribal Intelligence Operations

Intelligence, for the Arab Bureau, was fundamentally about human relationships. Where traditional military intelligence saw local popula-

"READING THE ENEMY'S MAIL"

tions as potential sources of tactical information, these scholars-turned-spies understood human networks as complex, living ecosystems of knowledge and influence. The Bureau's recruitment and management of human intelligence sources was particularly novel. Arab Bureau personnel didn't simply gather information; they cultivated long-term relationships built on mutual understanding and respect. Their informants were not just sources but collaborators in a complex process of regional understanding.

Tribal intelligence exemplified this intelligent approach. While conventional military intelligence viewed tribal leaders as potential allies or obstacles to be managed, the Arab Bureau saw them as nuanced political actors operating within complex networks of obligation, historical relationship, and economic interdependence. Take, for instance, its analysis of tribal movements in the central Arabian Nejd region. Where a traditional intelligence report might simply list troop movements or potential alliances, the Arab Bureau's documentation explored the historical context, economic motivations, familial connections, and cultural dynamics that shaped these decisions.[10]

The Bureau's source evaluation methods were equally urbane. Rather than simply categorising sources as reliable or unreliable, the Bureau developed nuanced frameworks for understanding how different sources might provide accurate information in specific contexts. A tribal leader might offer exquisite detail about local movements but less reliable information about broader political developments, and a religious scholar might provide profound insights into cultural dynamics but be less helpful on matters of tactical military intelligence.

A notable intelligence breakthrough came through the Arab Bureau's work with the Harb tribe in the Hijaz region. Through careful cultivation of relationships with Harb leaders, the Arab Bureau developed detailed understanding of Ottoman troop movements, supply lines, and defensive positions that proved crucial for the Arab Revolt's early military operations. These relationships went far beyond simple information gathering to encompass complex political negotiations, cultural understanding, and mutual strategic interests. The Arab Bureau's assessment of Harb tribal dynamics in early 1917 directly influenced the strategic decision to expand Arab Revolt operations northward, demonstrating how insight around tribal intelligence could shape major campaign decisions.

THE ARAB BUREAU

Sharif Hussein's own network of informants provided another critical intelligence resource. His extensive connections throughout the Arabian Peninsula created an information network that the Arab Bureau was able to access through careful collaboration. So, by combining Hussein's regional contacts with its own analytical capabilities, the Bureau developed a comprehensive understanding of regional dynamics that would have been impossible using conventional intelligence methods. The effectiveness of these tribal intelligence operations was demonstrated during the Arab Revolt's military campaigns.[11] Arab Bureau officers integrated tribal intelligence into tactical operations with remarkable success. Their ability to anticipate Ottoman movements, identify vulnerabilities, and coordinate operations across diverse tribal groups demonstrated the strategic value of their highly evolved human intelligence capabilities.

Urban Networks and Ottoman Intelligence

The Arab Bureau's human intelligence networks extended beyond tribal connections to also encompass urban operations. In cities like Jeddah, Cairo, and Damascus, Arab Bureau officers developed complex information ecosystems that integrated diverse sources into comprehensive intelligence pictures. These urban networks operated according to different principles than tribal connections, requiring the Bureau to use distinct approaches to source recruitment, management, and verification.

Merchant networks proved particularly valuable in urban intelligence operations. Commercial connections across the Ottoman Empire created natural information channels that the Arab Bureau could access through careful collaboration. Merchants' economic insights, travel observations, and professional connections provided valuable intelligence about Ottoman supply systems, economic conditions, and regional trade patterns. The Arab Bureau recognised that economic information was not separate from military intelligence but an integral component of comprehensive regional understanding.

Religious and intellectual networks offered another crucial dimension of urban intelligence. Through careful cultivation of relationships with religious scholars, educational institutions, and intellectual circles, the Arab Bureau gained access to information about political sentiments, cultural dynamics, and social developments that would have remained invisible to conventional military intelligence. These relationships required extraordinary cultural sensitivity and intellectual engagement, drawing on the academic backgrounds of Arab Bureau members like Hogarth and Bell.

The Arab Bureau's integration of urban and tribal intelligence represented another significant innovation. The Bureau recognised that these distinct information ecosystems were not separate but were interconnected components of a complex regional landscape. Urban merchants maintained connections with tribal territories; religious scholars influenced rural communities; and political developments in cities affected tribal decisions. By developing methods for integrating these diverse intelligence streams, the Arab Bureau created comprehensive regional understanding that transcended the boundaries of traditional intelligence.

Multi-Source Approach, or Intelligence Fusion

One of the Arab Bureau's most revolutionary contributions to intelligence methodology lay in its integration of diverse information sources into cohesive, multidimensional understanding. Where conventional military intelligence treated different sources as separate information streams, the Arab Bureau developed methods for combining wireless intercepts, aerial observations, human intelligence, and cultural analysis into comprehensive intelligence pictures. This integration process represented a fundamental reimagining of how intelligence could be gathered, analysed, and applied. In part, the Arab Bureau's unique position within Cairo's complex intelligence landscape—with separate military, diplomatic, and political intelligence units operating across the city—forced it to develop innovative methods for integrating these diverse intelligence streams into comprehensive analysis.[12]

At the heart of this approach was what might be called intelligence fusion, the systematic combination of diverse sources to create an understanding greater than the sum of its parts. A wireless intercept about Ottoman troop movements might be combined with aerial observations of logistics infrastructure, tribal reports about local sentiment, and cultural analysis of regional political dynamics. This multi-source approach created a comprehensive picture that single-source intelligence could never achieve.

THE ARAB BUREAU

The verification process was itself a form of intelligence integration. The Arab Bureau developed methods for cross-referencing information across multiple sources, recognising that verification was not simply about confirming facts but about contextualising information within broader understanding. A tribal informant's report might be validated through wireless intercepts, aerial observations, and economic intelligence, creating a multidimensional verification process that went far beyond simple confirmation.

The Arab Bureau's approach to intelligence analysis was equally novel, so that, rather than treating analysis as a separate stage following information collection, it integrated analytical thinking throughout the intelligence process. Collection, verification, contextualisation, and analysis became not sequential steps but integrated components of a comprehensive approach to understanding. This methodological innovation transformed intelligence from a product to a process, an ongoing, adaptive effort to comprehend complex regional dynamics.

The Arab Bureau's analytical framework drew on academic methodologies rarely applied to military intelligence. Archaeological approaches to piecing together fragmentary evidence, anthropological methods for understanding cultural dynamics, linguistic techniques for textual analysis, these scholarly practices were transformed into practical intelligence methodologies. This integration of academic and operational approaches created analytical capabilities far beyond what had been possible with conventional military intelligence.

The physical manifestation of this integration was evident in the Arab Bureau's operations centre in Cairo. Maps, charts, and intelligence reports covered the walls, creating a visual representation of the Bureau's multidimensional understanding. This wasn't merely decorative but functional—a physical system for integrating diverse information sources into comprehensive regional pictures. Arab Bureau officers could literally see connections between different information streams, identifying patterns and relationships that might otherwise remain hidden.

The Arab Bureau's most significant analytical innovation lay in its temporal integration of intelligence. Where conventional military intelligence focused primarily on current information, the Bureau systematically incorporated historical context, current developments, and future projections into their analysis. This temporal integration, understanding present events within historical contexts while anticipating future developments, created a dynamic intelligence capability that conventional approaches could never match.

Hijaz Railway Operations

The Arab Bureau's intelligence operations against the Hijaz Railway provide a compelling case study of their integrated approach. The railway, a vital Ottoman supply line stretching from Damascus to Medina, represented a critical strategic target during the Arab Revolt. The Arab Bureau's comprehensive intelligence operations against this infrastructure demonstrated its original approach to information gathering, analysis, and operational application. This intelligence campaign began with systematic mapping of the entire railway system. This wasn't simply geographical documentation but a comprehensive understanding of how the railway functioned within broader Ottoman military, economic, and political systems. Arab Bureau analysis integrated technical information about infrastructure vulnerabilities with operational knowledge of Ottoman logistics systems and strategic understanding of the railway's political and economic significance.[13]

Wireless intelligence played a crucial role in these operations, with Arab Bureau intercept stations monitoring Ottoman communications about railway operations, providing invaluable insights into scheduling, supply movements, and security arrangements. Officers' linguistic expertise allowed them to extract maximum intelligence value from these intercepts, identifying patterns and anomalies that revealed important operational information.[14]

Aerial reconnaissance complemented wireless intelligence, providing visual documentation of railway infrastructure, Ottoman defensive positions, and logistical activities. The Arab Bureau integrated these aerial observations with ground-level intelligence, creating detailed understanding of railway operations that proved invaluable for targeting decisions.

Human intelligence networks provided the third critical component of the Bureau's railway operations. Tribal informants reported on Ottoman troop movements, security arrangements, and repair activities. Urban sources provided information about supply shipments, personnel movements, and administrative decisions. These human sources offered contextual understanding that technical intelligence alone could never provide.

139

Another of the Arab Bureau's more innovative contributions lay in its integration of these diverse intelligence streams. The Bureau developed a comprehensive picture of the railway's operations, vulnerabilities, and strategic significance that guided Arab Revolt military operations with remarkable effectiveness. Its analysis went beyond simple identification of targets to encompass a more informed understanding of how railway operations affected Ottoman military capabilities, economic systems, and political control.

This integrated approach to railway intelligence directly influenced operational effectiveness. The Arab Revolt's campaign against the railway, immortalised in accounts of Lawrence's operations but actually representing a broader Arab Bureau effort, demonstrated how intelligence could transform military effectiveness. By targeting not just infrastructure but key nodes in Ottoman logistical systems, these operations achieved strategic impact far beyond tactical destruction.[15]

The Hijaz Railway operations also demonstrated an original approach to measuring intelligence effectiveness. Rather than simply counting destroyed infrastructure, the Arab Bureau developed methods for assessing how railway disruptions affected Ottoman military capabilities, economic systems, and political control. This outcomes-focused evaluation represented another significant innovation in intelligence methodology.[16]

Technical Constraints and Cultural Limitations

For all its sophistication, the Arab Bureau's intelligence gathering was not without profound challenges. The very qualities that made its approach revolutionary—its interdisciplinary nature, reliance on cultural expertise, and complex network of sources—also created significant operational limitations.

The Arab Bureau operated within an intelligence environment already strained by wartime demands, where standard communication channels were overloaded and secure information transfer remained a constant challenge. Technological constraints presented immediate challenges. Wireless communication, though revolutionary, remained primitive by modern standards. Atmospheric conditions, equipment limitations, and power constraints meant that signal reception was often unreliable. Intercept stations frequently captured fragmentary messages, requiring thoughtful analytical approaches to extract meaningful intelligence from incomplete information.[17] The Arab Bureau developed methods for working within these constraints, using cultural and linguistic knowledge to reconstruct meaning from partial intercepts.[18]

Aerial reconnaissance faced similar technological limitations. Early aircraft had limited range and payload capacity, restricting the scope and quality of photographic intelligence. Camera technology was still developing, often producing images of limited clarity and detail. Weather conditions and geographical challenges further complicated aerial operations in the Middle East environment. Despite these constraints, the Arab Bureau developed effective methods for maximising the intelligence value of available aerial resources.

As discussed previously, numerous factors meant that available communication infrastructure remained a serious challenge for the Arab Bureau. The enormous distances encompassed by the region as well as the severe constrictions of the available technology meant that transmitting information was fundamentally unstable. As such, delays to intelligence transmission were inevitable, and required analytical approaches that could account for information latency. Communication infrastructure posed another critical challenge. Vast distances, limited technological capabilities, and the complex terrain of the Middle East meant that information transmission was inherently unreliable. The Arab Bureau had to develop multiple concurrent communication channels, including traditional messenger networks alongside emerging wireless technologies. This created inevitable delays in intelligence transmission, creating the need for analytical approaches that could account for information latency.[19]

Geographic challenges were perhaps the most immediate constraint. The vast expanses of the Arabian Peninsula remained largely unknown. Even with the knowledge gathered by Arab Bureau members during their pre-war travels, significant areas of the region remained mysterious and inaccessible. Mapping was imprecise, communication was difficult, and verification of information became exponentially more complex in remote regions.[20]

The Arab Bureau's approach to these technological constraints was itself innovative. Rather than allowing technical limitations to define their capabilities, it adapted to and worked within these constraints. Its integration of multiple intelligence sources compensated for individual technical limitations. Its officers' deep cultural knowledge allowed them to extract maximum value from limited technical information. And their academic training in working with fragmentary evidence—a skill honed through archaeological and historical research—proved invaluable for reconstructing meaning from incomplete technical intelligence.[21]

Cultural and Operational Challenges

Beyond technical constraints, the Arab Bureau faced significant cultural and operational challenges that complicated its intelligence operations. These challenges were not peripheral but central to its work, requiring constant adaptation and innovation in its methodological approaches.

Language presented a critical limitation, because in spite of the Arab Bureau's linguistic capabilities, the variety of regional dialects and the complexity of tribal nomenclature inevitably led to frequent misunderstandings. Technical military terms were particularly challenging to translate accurately, and many political and tribal concepts simply had no direct English equivalents.[22] The Arab Bureau developed approaches to managing these linguistic challenges, including contextual translation methods that went beyond literal meaning to capture conceptual significance.[23]

Cultural bias presented a more subtle but persistent challenge. Like any intelligence product of its time, the *Arab Bulletin* was not immune to the cultural assumptions that influenced its reporting and analysis. While often sophisticated in its cultural understanding, the publication sometimes viewed Arab motivations through a distinctly Western lens, leading to oversimplified interpretations of complex tribal dynamics and religious sentiments. As such, the Arab Bureau's source verification methods, while better than most others, remained imperfect. The Bureau recognised that information from remote areas was inherently unreliable, and it developed nuanced approaches to managing this uncertainty. A report from a distant tribal region might be carefully contextualised, with analysts explicitly noting the limitations of their sources.

Security concerns created additional complications. The *Arab Bulletin*'s restricted circulation list, initially limited to just twenty-five carefully selected officials, was curated to maintain strict control over sensitive intelligence. However, this security was repeatedly compromised, creating diplomatic challenges that forced Arab Bureau officials to make significant modifications to their reporting methods. Staffing limitations were another significant constraint. The Arab Bureau relied on a small circle of orientalists and regional experts, many of whom were simultaneously engaged in operational roles. When key personnel were away on extended assignments, the depth and quality of analysis could suffer dramatically.

There were also inherent tensions in the Arab Bureau's approach. As the Arab Revolt progressed, the Arab Bureau found itself balancing multiple, sometimes conflicting objectives.[24] Its desire to provide objective intelligence sometimes conflicted with its strategic goal of supporting the revolt. This created a delicate analytical challenge: How to maintain analytical rigour while supporting a specific political outcome? The most profound limitation, perhaps, was institutional. The Arab Bureau existed in a complex bureaucratic landscape where traditional military intelligence services viewed its methods with deep scepticism.

These challenges were not weaknesses but integral to the Arab Bureau's ground-breaking approach. Its officials understood that intelligence is never perfect, that uncertainty is inherent in understanding complex human systems.[25] The Bureau's sophistication lay not in eliminating these limitations, but in developing methods to work productively within them.[26]

Intelligence Innovations and Strategic Influence

The Arab Bureau's intelligence innovations had a direct and profound impact on British strategy during the Arab Revolt. The Bureau's comprehensive approach to regional understanding influenced military operations, political decisions, and strategic planning throughout the campaign, demonstrating the practical value of its methodological innovations.

The Arab Bureau's intelligence directly shaped the early stages of the Arab Revolt.[27] Its comprehensive analysis of regional political dynamics, Ottoman military vulnerabilities, and tribal alignments provided crucial strategic context for British support of Sharif Hussein's movement. The Bureau's assessments of potential tribal support, likely Ottoman responses, and regional political implications informed critical decisions about the timing, scope, and nature of British involvement.

The Arab Bureau's intelligence assessments provided the foundation for Lawrence's famous guerrilla campaign against Ottoman forces.[28] Its detailed understanding of tribal dynamics, regional geography, and Ottoman vulnerabilities shaped Lawrence's innovative approach to irregular warfare.[29] His operations against the Hijaz Railway, successful raids on Ottoman positions, and effective mobilisation of tribal forces all drew directly from Arab Bureau intelligence about regional conditions and opportunities.[30]

Arab Bureau intelligence made significant operational contributions to conventional military campaigns as well. The Bureau's comprehensive understanding of how Ottoman forces operated within the unique Middle Eastern environment provided crucial context for General Edmund Allenby as he developed his Palestine campaign. Here, Allenby relied heavily on Arab Bureau intelligence about Ottoman positions, defensive capabilities, and regional dynamics.[31]

Perhaps most significantly, the Arab Bureau's intelligence also directly influenced British political strategy throughout the Middle East. The Bureau's detailed understanding of regional political dynamics, tribal relationships, and sectarian tensions informed diplomatic initiatives, alliance-building efforts, and post-war planning. This strategic influence extended far beyond immediate military operations to encompass broader geopolitical considerations that would shape the region for generations.[32]

The effectiveness of Arab Bureau intelligence was demonstrated in specific operational successes. The capture of Aqaba in July 1917, a crucial victory for the Arab Revolt, drew directly from Arab Bureau intelligence about Ottoman defensive positions, tribal dynamics, and regional geography.[33] Its comprehensive understanding of local conditions enabled a bold approach that achieved strategic surprise, demonstrating how practical intelligence could drive operational innovation.[34]

The Arab Bureau's influence extended to resource allocation decisions as well. Its detailed assessments of regional opportunities and constraints helped British leadership make difficult decisions about allocating limited wartime resources. By providing comprehensive analysis of how specific investments might yield strategic returns, the Bureau helped maximise the effectiveness of British support for the Arab Revolt.[35]

Long-Term Legacies

The true measure of the Arab Bureau's intelligence work extends far beyond its immediate wartime utility. Its innovations would reshape how intelligence organisations understood the fundamental nature of information gathering, creating precedents that would influence intelligence practices for generations to come.

"READING THE ENEMY'S MAIL"

The Bureau's approach to cultural intelligence was decades ahead of its time. While contemporary intelligence units saw culture as a peripheral concern, the Arab Bureau understood it as a fundamental dimension of strategic understanding. They demonstrated that effective intelligence work required more than collecting facts, it demanded deep, nuanced comprehension of cultural, social, and political dynamics.

The legacy of the Arab Bureau is evident in subsequent British intelligence operations.[36] Its approach to tribal politics influenced how British administrators engaged with local populations throughout the mandate period. Percy Cox's handling of tribal politics in Iraq during the early 1920s drew directly from Arab Bureau methodologies, showing how its insights continued to shape regional engagement long after the war's end.[37] The IRD's Middle East operations in the 1950s consciously or unconsciously drew on methods pioneered by the Arab Bureau.[38] Its approach to propaganda, cultural analysis, and a nuanced understanding of regional dynamics all bore the hallmarks of Arab Bureau methods.[39]

The Arab Bureau's integration of academic expertise with operational intelligence challenged conventional boundaries between scholarly knowledge and intelligence practice. It established a precedent for how multidisciplinary expertise could enhance intelligence capabilities that would later become fundamental to modern intelligence methodologies.[40] Its integration of academic expertise with operational intelligence challenged the traditional division between scholarly knowledge and intelligence work, and it demonstrated that cultural understanding could be a strategic asset rather than a peripheral concern.

The Arab Bureau's influence extended to the development of area studies as an academic discipline. Its combination of archaeological, linguistic, and cultural knowledge provided a model for comprehensive regional analysis that would shape academic approaches to understanding the Middle East. It demonstrated how interdisciplinary expertise could create more profound understanding of complex regions.

The Arab Bureau's innovations had significant theoretical implications that continue to influence both Intelligence Studies and Middle East Studies. Its integration of cultural understanding with operational intelligence challenged traditional theoretical approaches that treated culture as merely context rather than a fundamental component of intelligence work. This demonstrated what Simon Willmetts terms "culturally integrated intelligence frameworks",[41] establishing new paradigms for understanding how cultural knowledge enhances operational effectiveness.

The Arab Bureau's approach to knowledge networks in intelligence operations was particularly thoughtful. Rather than seeing intelligence gathering as a simple process of information collection, it developed frameworks for understanding how knowledge flows through complex social and political networks.[42] This anticipated modern theoretical approaches to network analysis in intelligence operations, demonstrating what Wagner identifies as "integrated knowledge networks",[43] decades before such concepts became standard in intelligence theory.

The Arab Bureau's experience also offers important insights regarding institutional learning in intelligence organisations. Its success in developing new approaches while operating within traditional military structures provides a model for understanding how intelligence organisations can innovate effectively. However, the subsequent loss of many of its methods demonstrates what Christopher Andrew terms 'HASDD (Historical Attention Span Deficit Disorder)',[44] whereby valuable innovations are forgotten only to be painfully rediscovered later.

The Arab Bureau's contribution to understanding cultural intelligence was particularly significant. It demonstrated that effective intelligence requires more than just linguistic capability or superficial cultural knowledge. Rather, it developed frameworks for analysing how cultural factors influence both intelligence gathering and strategic planning. This anticipated modern theoretical approaches that recognise cultural understanding as fundamental to intelligence effectiveness.

The theoretical implications of the Arab Bureau's work extend beyond specific intelligence practices to broader questions about knowledge production and regional understanding. Its role as what this study terms an 'imperial epistemic community' provides a framework for understanding how intelligence organisations contribute to broader knowledge production about regions. This theoretical insight remains relevant for understanding how intelligence services shape regional knowledge and policy formation.

However, the challenges of retaining institutional knowledge plagued the Arab Bureau's legacy. Despite its innovations, numerous of their more creative and successful methods were forgotten in the immediate post-war period. It would take decades for intelligence organisations to rediscover and appreciate the full extent of the Bureau's contributions.

"READING THE ENEMY'S MAIL"

Theoretical frameworks in both Intelligence Studies and Middle East Studies continue to draw insights from the Arab Bureau's work. Its demonstration of how different forms of expertise could be integrated into intelligence operations challenged traditional disciplinary boundaries and suggested new approaches to understanding complex regions.

The Arab Bureau's legacy is not just about specific intelligence techniques but about a fundamental approach to understanding human complexity. It demonstrated that effective intelligence work requires more than collecting information: it demands comprehending the intricate human networks that shape regional behaviour, perception, and decision-making.

A New Intelligence Paradigm

The Arab Bureau's approach to intelligence gathering represented more than a wartime innovation. It was a fundamental reimagining of how human knowledge could be collected, understood, and applied in complex cultural environments. Its success emerged from a simple yet revolutionary insight: intelligence is not about collecting information but about understanding context. Where traditional military intelligence saw facts as discrete data points, the Arab Bureau saw them as interconnected elements of a complex human ecosystem.

This approach challenged fundamental assumptions about intelligence work. Intelligence was no longer a purely military function but an essential form of cultural translation. By integrating academic expertise, technological innovation, and deep cultural understanding, the Bureau demonstrated that effective intelligence required seeing beyond surface-level information to comprehend the deeper dynamics shaping human behaviour.

The Arab Bureau's innovations were multifaceted. Its approach to human intelligence networks transformed how information could be gathered, showing that relationships were as important as raw data. Its technological methods anticipated modern signals intelligence by decades. Its verification and analytical techniques introduced levels of nuance and sophistication that would not become standard practice for generations.

More than its specific methods, the Arab Bureau offered a new philosophical approach to intelligence. It understood that effective understanding requires embracing complexity rather than seeking simplistic certainties. Its willingness to acknowledge uncertainty, to present multiple interpretations, and to see intelligence as a dynamic process was revolutionary for its time.

The tensions the Arab Bureau navigated remain relevant today. How can intelligence organisations balance cultural understanding with operational effectiveness? How can diverse expertise be integrated into coherent strategic insights? How can intelligence work acknowledge complexity without losing actionable clarity? These are not just historical questions but continuing challenges for intelligence organisations confronting increasingly complex global environments.[45]

The Arab Bureau's most enduring contribution was a fundamental shift in perspective. Intelligence is not about predicting the future with certainty but about developing frameworks for understanding complex human dynamics.[46] The Arab Bureau showed that true intelligence requires empathy, intellectual flexibility, and a willingness to embrace nuance. In a world increasingly characterised by cultural complexity and interconnected challenges, the Arab Bureau's approach remains as relevant now as it was a century ago. Its work is a continuing invitation to reimagine how we gather, understand, and use knowledge about human societies.

As we turn to examining the *Arab Bulletin* in the next chapter, we will see how these intelligence approaches were codified and distributed through a revolutionary publication that would influence British strategic thinking throughout the war and beyond. The *Arab Bulletin* represented not just an intelligence product but a sophisticated knowledge system that embodied the Arab Bureau's innovative approach to understanding the complex landscape of the Middle East.

8

THE *ARAB BULLETIN* AS INTELLIGENCE INNOVATION

CAIRO

In which the Arab Bulletin *emerges as a revolutionary intelligence publication that transformed how Britain gathered, analysed, and understood information about the Middle East, and which represented an unprecedented integration of academic expertise, cultural understanding, and military intelligence. This chapter explores how this innovative publication developed from a simple supplement to a comprehensive analytical tool that combined tactical reporting with urbane strategic insight, ultimately reshaping British intelligence practices and setting new standards for regional analysis.*

The Arab Bulletin: *A Literary Tinge*

Standing in the Arab Bureau's offices in Cairo, David Hogarth faced an unusual challenge. It was 6 June 1916, and the archaeologist-turned-intelligence officer was examining issue number one of what would become one of the most innovative intelligence products of the First World War. Before him lay the inaugural edition of the *Arab Bulletin*, a classified publication that would revolutionise how Britain gathered, analysed, and understood intelligence about the Middle East.

As previously noted, even the Arab Bureau's place of work, a set of rooms in the Savoy Hotel, that grand edifice in the heart of Cairo, spoke volumes about the unconventional nature of this new intelligence unit. Like virtually every other hotel in Cairo, the Savoy had been requisitioned for military use, effectively becoming a military installation since the tail end of 1914. Instead of housing paying guests, the luxurious rooms, stripped of many of their opulent furnishings, now served as offices for that unusual collection of people working for the duration of the war as officers of British military intelligence: mainly pre-war scholars with particular specialist knowledge of this or that aspect of the region's history, languages, or peoples. They may have traded academic gowns for military uniforms, but they still brought their intellects and their insights to the task at hand.

While military intelligence reports were of course nothing new, the idea for the *Arab Bulletin* as it was now constituted had originally come from Lawrence. As Hogarth wrote in a retrospective, in the one-hundredth issue of the *Arab Bulletin*, "The Headquarters of the General Staff, then at Ismailia, issued an Intelligence Bulletin, and to this 'Arab Bureau Summaries' were originally intended to be a supplement, the first suggestion of them having been made by Captain, now Lieut.-Colonel T.E. Lawrence."[1]

Hogarth's reflections on Lawrence's suggestion to create the *Arab Bulletin* may, of course, reveal as much about institutional memory-making as historical fact. Like many intelligence retrospectives, these accounts naturally emphasised innovation and foresight while obscuring the uncertainties, false starts, and bureaucratic compromises that characterised actual Arab Bureau operations. The creation of the *Arab Bulletin* was less the product of strategic genius than a pragmatic response to immediate pressures.

Nonetheless, as the publication's primary editor, Hogarth would shape what remained an ambitious experiment in intelligence reporting. His vision went far beyond the conventional military reports of the time. Where traditional, standard intelligence summaries maintained a somewhat narrow focus on troop movements and battle outcomes, the *Arab Bulletin* would attempt something far more comprehensive, which was, as far as possible, to understand the Middle East in its entirety: its peoples, histories, cultures, economics, and politics.

This approach reflected a radical departure from military intelligence practices of the time. Before the First World War, most intelligence officers were regular military men temporarily assigned to intelligence duties, often with little specific knowledge of their area of operations. The Arab Bureau, by stark contrast, brought together experts who had spent years studying the region, and whose combined expertise would prove invaluable in creating an intelligence product that went far beyond traditional military reporting, of which they had no previous experience.

The first issue of the *Arab Bulletin* established the template for the publication's subject matter. Alongside crucial updates on military developments came detailed analysis of tribal politics, careful consideration of religious sentiments, and examination of economic conditions across the region. This comprehensive approach was unprecedented in military intelligence of the time. More remarkably, this wasn't just an academic exercise. Insights from its pages would directly influence British strategy and operations throughout the war.

The *Arab Bulletin*'s restricted circulation list read like a who's who of British leadership in the Middle East, limited to twenty-five carefully selected officials who would shape policy and strategy in the region.[2] Each copy was marked 'Secret', though this designation would prove difficult to maintain. When an Italian attaché discovered a copy at the intelligence section in Ismailia and informed his French counterpart, Hogarth faced a delicate diplomatic challenge. His solution, granting controlled access rather than risking unauthorised circulation, would influence the future contents of the publication, but it would also arguably extend its influence.[3]

The publication's very name reflected its non-traditional status. This was not a 'report' or 'summary' but a bulletin, a term that suggested something more substantive, more analytical. Hogarth insisted on high literary standards, noting that "Since it was as easy to write in decent English as in bad, and much more agreeable, the *Arab Bulletin* had from the first a literary tinge not always present in Intelligence Summaries."[4] This understated observation belied a radical departure from standard military intelligence reports of the time, which often sacrificed clarity for technical jargon.

To pick a random edition, Issue 48, released on 21 April, 1917, consisted of fifteen pages, over which spread its exclusive readership was treated to four main articles: a sweeping history of Arab–Turkish relations from the seventh century to possible post-war outcomes; current intelligence on the Arab Revolt, including detailed information about tribal defections to the Allies, to join Emir Feisal's forces in the field; an analysis of Turkish war debt drawn from Ottoman speeches and budget projections; plus a comprehensive, seven-page report on economic conditions in Syria and Palestine. This last piece detailed everything from the impact of the Allied blockade on imports to the latest issuance of Turkish paper notes, from the consequent hoarding of coins by the local population to prospects for the upcoming harvest, and even the spread of diseases since the war's start, covering all the usual suspects: cholera, typhus, smallpox, and—an altogether different pox—syphilis.[5]

Such breadth in a publication's subject matter was unprecedented in military intelligence of the time. More remarkably, this comprehensive approach proved invaluable for British officials across different departments—from Colonial to Foreign to War Office—providing them with a holistic view of the military situation while educating them about historical, political, and socio-economic trends. This meant that policymakers were better informed than any of their predecessors could possibly have been.

The *Arab Bulletin* emerged at a crucial moment in British intelligence operations in the First World War. Thanks to the Arab Bureau, Britain finally had in place a single intelligence unit tasked with operating as a clearing house for any and all information about Ottoman activities, where previously rival intelligence departments had fought on multiple fronts, with insufficient information being exchanged between them. This moment marked a welcome, and long overdue, transformation in British intelligence activities in the region, moving away from an ad hoc approach towards a more formal, centralised, and region-wide strategy, demonstrating procedural and operational shifts that were identifiably modern.

The timing was critical, coming relatively quickly after intelligence failures had contributed to the dual military disasters of bloody stalemate and retreat at Gallipoli and the bloody, embarrassing, and for thousands of servicemen ultimately deadly surrender at Kut al-Amara. In both cases, these were demonstrably intelligence-led fiascos. More than that, both failures stemmed not just from lack of information but also from a distinct lack of understanding, or any broader insight, of the physical terrain, or Ottoman fighting capabilities, or local political dynamics, morale, and other psychological elements that would prove to be mission critical. With the *Arab Bulletin*, the Arab Bureau had created a publication that would attempt to address these gaps, in the process providing not just military intelligence as it was understood, but a vision of things as they were, which was equally important to the successful outcome of operations in the region. In short, the *Arab Bulletin* was providing planners with previously inaccessible insight. This was not just information but understanding.

What made the *Arab Bulletin* truly revolutionary was not just the scope of its contents but its atypical approach to intelligence gathering and analysis. Its contributors drew on an unprecedented range of sources, including field reports from British officers, networks of local informants, early wireless intercepts, nascent aerial reconnaissance, and systematic analysis of Arabic- and Turkish-language press. In doing so, this integration of multiple intelligence streams, coupled with deep cultural understanding, set new standards for comprehensive regional analysis that would influence generations of intelligence practitioners.

Spies, Scouts, and Storytellers: Mapping Invisible Networks

The savviness of the Arab Bureau's approach to intelligence gathering is immediately apparent in the pages of the *Arab Bulletin*. Unlike traditional military intelligence reports, with their heavy reliance on field observations and prisoner interrogations, this publication wove together information from such a remarkable variety of sources that the integration of materials wasn't merely comprehensive, it was transformative.

To take one example, let us consider how the *Arab Bulletin* handled intelligence about Ottoman troop movements. A typical report might combine first-hand observations from Bedouin scouts with intercepted wireless messages and aerial reconnaissance photographs. Arab Bureau analysts, however, went very much further, drawing, for instance from local newspaper reports elements that could provide general context, adding market rumours where these may have had a bearing on the news, and supplementing this already rich blend, without even stopping to think, with their own personal knowledge and deep understanding of everything from regional geography to tribal politics. The result was intelligence that was not just more complete, but more nuanced and definitely more useful.

The sophistication of this approach is evident in a report in Issue 54, circulated on 22 June 1917, and a report discussing Ottoman forces' activities in Syria, which the *Arab Bulletin* contributor freely acknowledges draws extensively on another foreign intelligence report.[6] The original report was written and supplied to French intelligence's Syria desk in November 1916 by Père Jaussen, the Dominican priest and French intelligence agent. Rather than simply accepting estimates of troop numbers supplied by Jaussen, the *Arab Bulletin* article draws on and presents multiple accounts, collating and carefully analysing the implications of each, ultimately delivering a report that does not have all the answers. Such willingness to acknowledge uncertainty and explore competing interpretations was revolutionary for its time. When dealing with sensitive sources, *Arab Bulletin* reports and editorial procedures meant striking a careful balance between transparency and security, in spite of the avowedly very limited readership for whom these pages were prepared. For example, while some sources were specifically cited, particularly those referencing official reports or public statements, numerous others were protected behind phrases like 'a reliable source in Damascus', a practice that later became standard in modern intelligence work. At times, the Arab Bureau's use of such a seemingly innocuous phrase was actually done to conceal an altogether more complex situation and source origin.

Another example of Arab Bureau innovation was its adoption of new technologies, which was done willingly and with alacrity. Although both wireless interception and aerial reconnaissance were in their infancy, the *Arab Bulletin* eagerly incorporated these new sources of intelligence. A January 1917 issue matter-of-factly referenced "information gleaned from enemy wireless traffic" about Ottoman reinforcements heading to the Hijaz.[7] This casual mention belied the significance of signals intelligence in modern warfare. At other times, the Arab Bureau was equally careful not to reveal their capabilities when it came to the use of signals intelligence, and replaced mention of 'wireless traffic' with 'a reliable source' or similar wording, sometimes followed by a mention of Damascus or another place, but just as often deciding to let further detail of the source location hang in the air, so to speak. Given Hogarth's comments about copies of the *Arab Bulletin* found circulating outside the official list, such caution was undoubtedly prudent.

Similarly, reports based on or supported by aerial reconnaissance also began appearing, offering unprecedented views of Ottoman defences and troop dispositions. Like wireless capabilities, though still in its infancy aerial reconnaissance provided another groundbreaking source of intelligence which the Arab Bureau eagerly jumped on. The *Arab Bulletin* frequently referenced intelligence derived from aerial photographs, including, for example, detailed descriptions of Ottoman defences near Aqaba based on 'recent aerial reconnaissance'. While this nascent technology obviously had severe limitations, the fact that the Arab Bureau was willing to embrace it demonstrated its forward-thinking approach to intelligence gathering in its recognition of the advantages aerial observation provided, which were impossible to obtain via traditional, ground-based means.

On the ground, the Arab Bureau maintained more traditional but equally vital intelligence-gathering methods. All Arab Bureau officers were capable of drawing rough sketch maps of terrain, routes, and enemy positions—skills that were customary among intelligence officers at the time but whose widespread absence today represents a significant loss. These hand-drawn maps, combined with detailed route reports, provided essential intelligence for military operations. Garland's survey from Yambo to Abu Markha, for instance, combined tactical observations with crucial details about water sources and terrain: "The water at Nakhl Mubarak is clear and good and may be drunk without boiling ... the road lies between and over very stony foothills for about fourteen miles."[8]

Perhaps most forward-thinking was the *Arab Bulletin*'s systematic and highly advanced use of open-source intelligence. Long before it became standard practice, the publication's analysts carefully monitored Arabic- and Turkish-language newspapers, public statements, and even market rumours to build a comprehensive intelligence picture, and their analysis of public sentiment through Constantinople's press clearly demonstrated a deep understanding of how open sources could complement secret intelligence. For instance, their systematic analysis of reports from *Mokattam* and other Cairo newspapers about mass hangings of Syrian intellectuals and systematic starvation of the civilian populations demonstrated an acute ability to rapidly contextualise developments through diverse sources.

The integration of these diverse sources reached new levels of sophistication as the war progressed. When reporting on an Ottoman communiqué issued in Berne to the German-Swiss press in September 1916, for instance, the analysts noted how it failed to acknowledge the loss of Mecca two months previously, using the fact of this omission to assess Ottoman propaganda strategies and internal political pressures.[9] By 1918, a single issue might combine information from field agents in Damascus, intercepted Turkish communications, aerial reconnaissance, and open-source analysis, providing a comprehensive picture of Ottoman troop movements.

The summary offered in Issue 98 provides another good example of the Arab Bureau's novel multi-source approach, which allowed for more accurate and nuanced reporting. This issue offered a detailed report from the Commander-in-Chief of the Mesopotamian Expeditionary Force on 'Enemy Intelligence on the Euphrates', which was reported to consist of two distinct branches—the Muntefiq Mission (known as Missmont), and the Euphrates Group Intelligence Organisation—as well as an account from "an intelligent and trustworthy Armenian ... of what he saw and learned of the internal troubles of the Turks".[10] This included a fascinating report about public buildings in Damascus "placarded" with proclamations to the Turkish Government—"Why do you not open your eyes? You must not follow in the footsteps of Germany. Germany's policy and her Government's attitude towards her subjects, are contrary to the principles of Islam"—and another addressed directly "To Enver, Talaat, and Jemal [sic]" the CUP triumvirate, a.k.a. the Three Pashas, otherwise the Young Turk triumvirate:

> You, who have co-operated with Germany, have ruined, devastated and outraged the country. You have behaved most cruelly towards your nation and the whole responsibility falls upon you and your Government. This is the first warning that has been given you: should you not change your policy, serious consequences will result.

The Arab Bureau's network analysis techniques were also innovative. By mapping sources and informants across multiple issues of the *Arab Bulletin*, it was able to create a complex network spanning military, political, and tribal spheres. This grasp of information networks anticipated modern social network analysis (SNA) in intelligence work. The Bureau's approach included identifying key influencers within tribal and political structures, mapping communication channels between various actors, and analysing relationships between different groups and their impact on regional dynamics.

Such a layered methodology protected both human sources and technical capabilities while enabling comprehensive analysis. While the practice of anonymising sources while maintaining analytical transparency reflects what contemporary scholars would likely refer to as the interplay between formal and informal intelligence gathering, the more important point is that this enabled the Arab Bureau to balance source

THE *ARAB BULLETIN* AS INTELLIGENCE INNOVATION

protection with analytical rigour, in the process demonstrating a very modern understanding of intelligence tradecraft.

The Arab Bureau's integration of human intelligence was likewise notably well developed, with networks that extended far beyond traditional military channels, incorporating merchants, religious figures, and tribal leaders. Such a diverse selection of sources not only allowed for cross-verification and enhanced validation, but also provided insights into aspects of Ottoman society from a range of perspectives, many of which were simply beyond the wit of conventional military intelligence. Moreover, it made the pages of the *Arab Bulletin* really come alive.

For instance, considering the coverage of developments in Damascus in late 1917, a report in a single issue was able to combine reports from local merchants about food prices and shortages, information from religious figures about growing dissatisfaction with Ottoman religious policies, and intelligence from tribal leaders about shifting allegiances. Such a multi-layered approach provided a far richer understanding of conditions in the city that would have been impossible using more conventional means.

The Arab Bureau's approach to human intelligence wasn't just innovative in its comprehensiveness, but also in its systematic evaluation of source reliability. As far as possible, each source was carefully categorised and evaluated, with clear distinctions made between first-hand observations, second-hand reports, and general rumours. This systematic approach to source evaluation anticipated modern intelligence practices by decades and is a prime illustration of how, for many of the Arab Bureau's members, the employment of careful academic methods was their professional instinct. Perhaps most remarkably, again thinking about Bureau officers' typically non-military training, they clearly understood the value of maintaining intelligence sources beyond their ability to provide immediate tactical information. Through the careful cultivation of long-term relationships with key informants, protection of source identities, and systematic evaluation of source reliability, officers set new, higher standards for human intelligence operations.

An Intellectual Journey: From Tactical Reports to Strategic Vision

The *Arab Bulletin*'s analytical sophistication grew markedly over its multi-year run. From June 1916 to August 1919, through 114 meticulously crafted issues, the publication evolved from primarily reporting events to offering complex strategic analysis that would help shape the post-war Middle East. Its life was extended somewhat, albeit in another guise, with the additional publication of four issues of *Notes on the Middle East* between 7 December 1919 and 24 May 1920. This evolution reveals both the growing expertise of the Arab Bureau and its approach to intelligence analysis.

The earliest editions of the *Arab Bulletin* were relatively brief and focused largely on immediate military concerns, for instance opening with a summary of recent events, followed by detailed reports on specific topics. It was Issue 5, released 18 June 1916, that provided the earliest reporting on the Arab Revolt,[11] largely confining itself to straightforward reporting of military developments, with the analysis largely tactical and the writing clear and precise. Even here, though, the Arab Bureau's commitment to accuracy was evident in its careful verification of sources.[12] As the publication matured, so its readership would come to see each issue becoming more tightly structured and comprehensive or broad in its coverage.

By late 1916, just months after first being published, the *Arab Bulletin* was showing clear signs of growing analytical sophistication. For example, Issue 25, which was published in October, demonstrated this evolution by not just presenting Ottoman statements but analysing their significance. In this issue, when examining a Turkish delegation's announcement in Berne, *Arab Bulletin* analysts highlight crucial omissions and inconsistencies in the public statement, using these to assess both Ottoman military difficulties and internal political pressures.[13]

In order to avoid presenting what might be seen as an uncritical assessment of the *Arab Bulletin*, it is noted here that these intelligence assessments, while presented as objective analysis, inevitably also reflect the Arab Bureau's need to justify its methods and continued existence to increasingly sceptical authorities. Throughout its publication history, the *Arab Bulletin* functioned simultaneously as intelligence product and institutional advertisement, with editorial choices shaped as much by the need to demonstrate value as by analytical rigour.

The *Arab Bulletin*'s transition to greater erudition and more complex analysis accelerated through 1917, alongside coverage of a broader range of topics, and increasing integration of military, political, and economic intelligence. An example of this maturation can be seen in Issue 50.[14] Over twenty-four pages, it combines an incredibly detailed eleven-page

THE *ARAB BULLETIN* AS INTELLIGENCE INNOVATION

report by way of an update on the Arab Revolt, three pages of notes on various tribes in the Aden Protectorate, analysis of developments in Libya, and an assessment of diplomatic missions as far afield as Abyssinia.

The Arab Revolt update from the field was written by Lawrence and offers a fascinating sample of the sorts of areas which a single *Arab Bulletin* report might cover. Entitled "Raids on the Railway" and covering events from 15 March to 7 April, the report encompasses far more than the title suggests. Lawrence includes plentiful notes on route marches undertaken, of obvious utility to any who followed in his wake, as well as more descriptive passages covering meteorological observations and notes on natural history: "Wadi Aid proved almost luxuriant with its thorn trees and grass. There was a cool east wind, and the valley was full of white butterflies and the scents of flowers." He also included military-orientated reporting on the raids themselves:

> We fired altogether fifty rounds (shrapnel) from 2,200 and 900 yards and about ten belts of machine-gun ammunition. Deserters reported about thirty dead (I saw nine only) and forty-two wounded. We captured the pedigree mare of Ali Nasr (the Egyptian "Bab Arab" in Medina) and a couple of camels from the well-house, and destroyed many rails. Our causalities were one man wounded.[15]

Although not precisely as rendered by Lean in *Lawrence of Arabia*, it is interesting to note Lawrence's direct reference to the capture of the horse, and the humiliation this was meant to cause its owner.

The Arab Revolt: Guerrilla War and Intelligence Revolution

Sticking for now with *Arab Bulletin*'s coverage of the Arab Revolt, this is an area that offers perhaps the clearest demonstration of the publication's original approach to intelligence reports. From the first reports of mounting tensions in Mecca to detailed analysis of the revolt's aftermath, the publication's treatment of this crucial campaign shows how far military intelligence had evolved under the Arab Bureau's guidance. The outbreak of the revolt was confirmed initially with characteristic caution, stating, in June 1916, "We have as yet no information on the strength of the forces of the Sherif of Mecca ...]They are all untrained and have no artillery or machine guns."[16] Such careful language, neither over- nor understating the situation, would set the tone for subsequent coverage of the Arab Revolt.

THE ARAB BUREAU

By July, the Arab Bureau was able to demonstrate its sophisticated intelligence gathering capabilities, and an ability to integrate multiple intelligence streams. One issue, from July 1917,[17] wove together firsthand reports from an Arab officer who had visited Mecca ("Sherif's forces will attack furiously, are wildly excited, waste a lot of ammunition, but contain many good shots"), intercepted German wireless messages denying any rebellion ("We are in a position to deny absolutely that there has been any rebellion in the Hedjaz at all"),[18] and analysis of reports from Cairo newspapers about mass hangings of Syrian intellectuals. This integration of multiple sources to build a comprehensive picture would become one of the publication's hallmarks.

The Arab Bureau commitment to honest reporting, even when the news was unfavourable, also stands out across the *Arab Bulletin*'s publication history. "At Medina things are not going well," stated one blunt assessment: "The Arabs have retired a good way from the Town, which cannot therefore be described as besieged."[19] Such frankness was rare in military reporting of the time, where there was often pressure to present events in the most positive light possible, but the *Arab Bulletin*'s willingness to acknowledge setbacks helped commanders maintain a realistic view of the situation and plan accordingly. Its authors were, no doubt, also cognisant that it was faulty intelligence that had contributed in so deadly a manner to the failures of earlier campaigns against the Ottomans, and that, while mistakes had been made, they need not be repeated.

Coverage of operations against the Hijaz Railway also shows growing sophistication in the *Arab Bulletin*'s military analysis. By early 1917, reports moved beyond simple accounts of raids to examine their broader strategic impact. Issues 37 and 38 analysed how guerrilla operations, while not resulting in permanent occupation of enemy positions, succeeded in disrupting Ottoman communications and forcing them to disperse their forces,[20] an understanding of asymmetrical warfare well ahead of its time.

As the revolt progressed, Arab Bureau analysis grew increasingly refined. By summer 1917, coverage had evolved from simple battle reports to complex assessments of how events like the capture of Aqaba might affect the deployment of Ottoman forces in Palestine. For example, analysis connected local developments to broader strategy, outlining how the port's capture might necessitate a redeployment of Turkish forces, potentially weakening their positions elsewhere. Such strategic analysis helped shape British military planning.[21]

THE *ARAB BULLETIN* AS INTELLIGENCE INNOVATION

The Arab Bureau's coverage of specific operations demonstrated its growing analytical sophistication. Take the raids on the Hijaz Railway in early 1918. Beyond reporting tactical details, the *Arab Bulletin* examined how these operations affected Ottoman logistics, morale, and strategic decision-making. When analysing a successful raid near Ma'an, for instance, the publication went beyond casualty figures to examine how the attack influenced Ottoman troop deployments and local tribal allegiances.

By war's end, the *Arab Bulletin*'s coverage of the revolt had evolved into something unprecedented in military intelligence: a new analytical framework for understanding and influencing complex regional dynamics. Its reports presciently noted how competing political aspirations among local leaders would likely shape the post-war landscape, anticipating many of the challenges that would emerge in the following decades. This evolution would influence how future generations of intelligence officers approached similar challenges in complex political and military environments.[22]

This approach extended to analysis of broader strategic implications. The *Arab Bulletin*'s coverage of the fall of Damascus in October 1918 exemplifies this evolution. Beyond reporting military details, it examined how the city's capture affected regional politics, local administration, and even economic conditions. Analysis explored everything from immediate challenges of maintaining order to longer-term implications for British policy in Syria.

Another area of coverage that allows us to witness the clear analytical evolution of the *Arab Bulletin* is its treatment of tribal politics, with early reports tending to rest on the presentation of straightforward accounts of tribal allegiances before shifting, by early 1917 and on through 1918, to far more nuanced analysis. For example, Issue 45, provides a detailed breakdown of relationships between various tribal leaders in the Nejd region, effectively creating what we would now recognise as a social network map.[23] Such analysis went beyond simple allegiances to examine historical relationships, economic ties, and religious influences that shaped tribal decisions. This proved invaluable for British officials trying to navigate the complex web of tribal politics.

The growing confidence of *Arab Bulletin* contributors and editorial staff is particularly evident in its handling of complex religious and political issues, such as the evolution of its analysis of Hussein's position as Sharif of Mecca. Early reports focused mainly on his military capabilities and tribal support, but by the spring of 1917, when the Arab Revolt had been in progress almost a year, the analysis had deepened considerably. In Issue 49, a report by Hogarth—"The Next Caliphate"—provided decision-makers and military planners with a nuanced examination of Hussein's caliphal ambitions, noting how religious legitimacy, political power, and Western support created both opportunities and constraints: "The general consent of the Arabs will not easily be accorded to any new Caliph unless and until he has proved himself conspicuously powerful without Christian help."[24]

Analysis of Hussein's position revealed remarkable nuance, noting how his control of the Holy Cities lent significant religious legitimacy to his cause while also placing him in a delicate position.[25] The *Arab Bulletin* tracked how Ottoman religious proclamations denouncing the revolt as un-Islamic created genuine tension among religious scholars—exactly the kind of insight that proved invaluable for British strategy.

By 1918, the *Arab Bulletin* was offering analysis of how military success interacted with political fragmentation. While noting the revolt's military achievements, a July issue of the publication also highlighted emerging tensions. "While the Sharif envisions a unified Arab state under his leadership," noted one report, "other local leaders are increasingly assertive about their own autonomy."[26] This recognition of the complex interplay between military and political factors anticipated many of the challenges that would emerge in the post-war period.

The *Arab Bulletin*'s understanding and treatment of economic intelligence showed similar development, with its earliest reports focusing mainly on basic information about food supplies and trade routes, which evolved into far more evidence-based economic analyses by the middle of 1917, one year into its publication run. Now the *Arab Bulletin* was producing analytical reports of genuine erudition, for instance describing how economic factors influenced both military operations and political allegiances. One seven-page report examined everything from the impact of the Allied blockade on imports and civilian populations to analysing the Ottoman Empire's monetary policy, the resulting currency inflation, and the civilian hoarding of gold coins in response to currency increases, as well as the broader implications for regional stability. Speaking of the Ottoman officials responsible for trying to manage the fallout from this wartime economy, an anonymous author writes, "It is characteristic that the Turkish official accepts no bribe in paper notes. He takes only gold, the Napoleon d'or being most favoured."[27]

Most remarkably, the publication even made attempts at predictive analysis, a practice well ahead of its time, so that rather than simply reporting what had happened *Arab Bulletin* reports increasingly tried to anticipate future developments. A number of issues in the summer of 1918 offered prescient analysis of how competing visions of Arab unity might shape the post-war political landscape. Across six issues of the *Arab Bulletin*, in the late summer of 1918, we find a series of discussions around the nascent and still evolving concept of Arab unity and different interpretations of Arab nationalism, and competing political aspirations. One writer, for example, confidently and accurately offered the view that "While the Sharif envisions a unified Arab state under his leadership, other local leaders are increasingly assertive about their own autonomy. These competing visions will likely shape the post-war political landscape of the region and present challenges for British policy."[28] The fact that Sharif Hussein would be ousted from all his Arabian domains by Ibn Saud before the end of 1924 speaks precisely to what this report alludes.

By this stage, these and other assessments were rarely limited to purely military matters, extending as a matter of course to cover political developments, tribal reactions, economic trends, and any other aspect of the local socio-economic and political situation, as contributors saw fit. For example, mid-1918 analysis regarding post-war challenges presciently noted the disruption caused to traditional trade routes by Britain's wartime financial support for the Arab Revolt, while also mentioning that the influx of funds and large quantities of small arms had fundamentally altered regional economic dynamics. Such insights proved valuable not just for wartime planning but for understanding the long-term implications of British policy in the region.

The editorial process, primarily overseen by Hogarth, was crucial to the evolution of the various topics covered by the *Arab Bulletin* discussed above. Hogarth's radical insistence on acknowledging uncertainties and presenting competing interpretations set new standards for intelligence analysis, and while it might not have been the news his paymasters wanted to hear, he was not afraid of honest reporting regardless of the message. When faced with conflicting reports about Ottoman troop strengths in Syria, for instance, the *Arab Bulletin* was quite happy to present multiple accounts along with careful analysis of their relative credibility.[29] Hogarth believed it better to present discrepancies and complex realities than to oversimplify for the sake of apparent certainty. This approach, revolutionary for its time, helped guard against confirmation bias and encouraged consideration of alternative scenarios.

In 1919, the final seven issues of the *Arab Bulletin* demonstrate how far the Bureau's analytical capabilities had developed. In these final issues, the publication had transformed into a sophisticated tool for post-conflict analysis.[30] Issue 110, a 22-page analysis devoted entirely to Medina, the lifting of the siege, and intelligence gathered from interrogating the Ottoman commander Fakhri Pasha,[31] showcases the evolving sophistication of the Arab Bureau's analysis.[32] The report doesn't just present facts but, rather, examines multiple possible political futures for the Hijaz, Arabia, and the wider Middle East, considering military, political, economic, and cultural factors.

Although the closure of the Arab Bureau would cut short this evolution, these last editions of the *Arab Bulletin* demonstrate how far the publication had come from its modest beginnings. What had started as a wartime intelligence bulletin had evolved into something far more ambitious, a comprehensive analytical tool for understanding and operating in the complex landscape of the Middle East. The analysis offered on the future of Syria across the final handful of editions usefully demonstrates this mature analytical approach where, rather than simply reporting on current conditions, *Arab Bulletin* contributors examine multiple possible futures, in the process considering how factors as diverse as French ambitions in the region to local Arab nationalist movements, might shape events. Taken together, this kind of predictive analysis, while common today, was years ahead of its time.

The *Arab Bulletin*'s final issues also show remarkable sangfroid when confronted by the uncertainty of what might follow in the post-war period, often favouring an exploration of multiple possibilities instead of presenting any single interpretation. Weighing evidence and examining implications, this is yet another example of the *Arab Bulletin*, and thus the Arab Bureau, anticipating modern analytical practices that emphasise the importance of considering alternative scenarios and explicitly acknowledging uncertainty. What had begun as a way to share tactical information had become a uniquely brilliant venue for understanding events and shaping policy in one of the world's most complex regions in the midst of unprecedented turmoil.

THE *ARAB BULLETIN* AS INTELLIGENCE INNOVATION

Another aspect of *Arab Bulletin* coverage of the Arab Revolt that undoubtedly deserves a mention here is its understanding of the potential power in asymmetrical warfare, a concept barely recognised in conventional military thinking of the time. Numerous reports examine how relatively small forces could achieve strategic effects through careful targeting of enemy vulnerabilities, with additional analysis going beyond mere tactical reporting to examie the psychological impacts, as well the broader economic disruption, and political implications of such guerrilla operations. In these pages, the Arab Bureau also developed new approaches to measuring operational effectiveness. Rather than focusing solely on traditional metrics like enemy casualties or material destruction, it examined how operations affected Ottoman force deployment, command decisions, and strategic planning, an approach to assessing military effectiveness that influenced both operational planning and strategic decision-making.

Impacting Strategy: The Pen Directing the Sword

The *Arab Bulletin*'s practical intelligence directly influenced British military planning and policy decisions throughout the war. From its earliest issues, *Arab Bulletin* reporting shaped British support for the Arab Revolt, and this impact can be traced through specific operational decisions and broader strategic shifts in British policy. Its careful assessment of Sharifian capabilities and limitations helped commanders make realistic decisions about the type and scale of support needed. Early reports of initial successes, tempered by honest acknowledgement of shortcomings, led to increased but carefully targeted British support, evidenced by the strategic deployment of liaison officers and the calibrated provision of military aid. Meanwhile, detailed analysis of guerrilla operations against the Hijaz Railway, championed by officers like Garland and Lawrence, also played a part in shaping British strategy in the region. These weren't just tactical reports, but comprehensive assessments of how railway attacks affected both military operations and civilian relations.

The *Arab Bulletin*'s influence on military operations is particularly evident in its coverage of guerrilla warfare against the Hijaz Railway, where Arab Bureau officers provided detailed analyses of raid tactics and their broader strategic impact. By 1917, such insights were directly influencing British strategy, leading to more coordinated and effective operations against Ottoman supply lines.

THE ARAB BUREAU

The *Arab Bulletin*'s impact on strategic planning reached its height in 1918. By early that year, the concentration of reports from north-west Arabia was clearly informing high-level decision-making. When General Allenby launched his Syrian offensive, he did so based partly on *Arab Bulletin* reports indicating weakening Ottoman positions, while the publication's integration of military, political, and economic intelligence provided commanders with a more complete picture than they had ever had before, allowing for better-coordinated operations between British forces and Arab allies. More importantly, its deep, which is not to say disinterested, understanding of local political dynamics helped commanders anticipate and exploit Ottoman weaknesses. By examining not just military factors but also economic pressures, political tensions, and logistical challenges, the Arab Bureau helped identify key pressure points where British operations could achieve maximum effect.

This operational influence extended to specific campaigns, such as discussions around the port of Aqaba, which drew on *Arab Bulletin* reporting, for instance analysis of not just the port's strategic significance but also Ottoman defences and, crucially, local tribal attitudes. The eventual success of the operation to capture Aqaba validated the Arab Bureau's comprehensive approach to intelligence gathering and analysis.

Also significant was the role the *Arab Bulletin* played in shaping British understanding of Arab nationalism, where its coverage moved from relatively simple assessments of pro- and anti-Ottoman sentiment to increasingly refined analysis of competing visions for an Arab political future. By comparing *Arab Bulletin* reporting on Hussein's claims with the actual evolution of his statements, we can see how it helped British officials navigate the complex political landscape of Arab nationalism. The *Arab Bulletin*'s influence is also evident in how it helped manage competing interests within the British establishment. Serving as a central clearing house for information from various sources, including the Cairo Residency, Sudan Intelligence, and Army Intelligence, it helped create a more coherent and comprehensive understanding of the region, a role that became especially important as Britain struggled to reconcile different departmental views on Arab policy.

Intelligence Challenges and Limitations: Breakthroughs and Blind Spots

Despite its innovations and successes, the *Arab Bulletin* faced significant challenges that reveal both the limitations of wartime intelligence and the persistent difficulties of understanding a complex region, challenges that offer useful insights into the development of modern intelligence practices. Among the most immediate challenges was verification of information.

Geographic challenges significantly constrained the *Arab Bulletin*'s effectiveness. The vast expanses of the Arabian Peninsula meant that much territory remained completely unknown to outsiders. Even with the pre-war travels of various Arab Bureau members, large areas remained unmapped. This lack of geographic knowledge affected both military planning and intelligence gathering. While the *Arab Bulletin* made remarkable efforts to map and describe unknown regions, its coverage necessarily remained incomplete.

While the *Arab Bulletin* drew on an unprecedented range of sources, confirming the accuracy of reports, particularly from remote areas—for example, in a report like "The Desert: 'Movements in the East and Centre'",[33] covering tribal movements in the central Arabian Nejd region—proved consistently difficult and especially acute due to British officers having only limited access to the terrain, and thus being forced to rely heavily on local informants. The Arab Bureau's solution was to present information with appropriate caveats, making clear distinctions between confirmed facts and unverified reports. Even while this approach was more advanced than contemporary practice, it should be said that it still fell short of modern standards for source evaluation.

These geographic limitations were further complicated by language barriers, because while the Arab Bureau counted numerous scholars and Arabic speakers among their number, the variety of regional dialects and the complexity of tribal nomenclature inevitably led to misunderstandings or partial access to facts on the ground. Technical military terms presented particular difficulties, as did the translation of tribal titles and political concepts that had no direct English equivalents. While the *Arab Bulletin* attempted to standardise transliteration and maintain glossaries, inconsistencies persisted throughout its run.

Operational and production challenges further affected the *Arab Bulletin*'s effectiveness. As Hogarth observed, maintaining a regular publication schedule proved difficult. As he wrote, "this rate [four numbers a month in 1916 and early 1917] proved for a time impossible to maintain, as the confidential work thrown by the General Staff and the Admiralty on the Government Press increased rapidly".[34] The rapidly evolving nature of desert warfare, combined with the *Arab Bulletin*'s publication schedule, meant that tactical intelligence could be outdated by the time it reached readers. This was particularly evident during the mobile campaigns of 1917–18, when tribal allegiances and force dispositions might shift dramatically within a matter of weeks. The *Arab Bulletin* attempted to address this by including retrospective analysis of military movements, but this risked reducing its utility for immediate operational planning.

Staffing limitations and organisational dynamics created additional complexities. The Arab Bureau comprised a small circle of Arabists, orientalists, and other regional experts, many of whom worked simultaneously in the field. This consequently affected the quality of the academic side of analysis. The specialised knowledge required for effective analysis of tribal politics and regional dynamics made it difficult to train new staff quickly, even when resources were available for expansion. While the *Arab Bulletin* maintained formal connections with the Egyptian Expeditionary Force's intelligence section and the Indian government's political officers, coordination was not always smooth, and different organisational cultures, not to mention competing priorities and bureaucratic interests, sometimes led to competing interpretations of the same intelligence. This was particularly evident in divergent assessments of Ottoman military capabilities and the strategic significance of various tribal alliances.

The *Arab Bulletin*'s content challenges Satia's characterisation of Arab Bureau intelligence as primarily orientalist projection. While cultural biases certainly appear, the reports demonstrate genuine analytical innovation in synthesising diverse sources and adapting intelligence methods to regional realities. This operational focus reveals aspects of Arab Bureau activities that purely cultural analysis misses.

Cultural bias presented a more subtle but persistent challenge. Like any intelligence product of its time, the *Arab Bulletin* was not immune to the cultural assumptions that influenced its reporting and analysis. As such, while it arguably had a highly evolved sense of local culture, it still frequently, perhaps unavoidably, viewed Arab motivations through a Western lens, leading to oversimplified interpretations of complex tribal dynamics and religious sentiments. Perhaps most damagingly for military planning purposes, its reports often included an implicit assumption that Arab tribes would naturally turn against the Ottomans,

THE *ARAB BULLETIN* AS INTELLIGENCE INNOVATION

underestimating the strength of Islamic ties between Arabs and Turks, as this general Arab uprising ultimately never occurred. This resulted in *Arab Bulletin* coverage of the potential for a wider Arab uprising reflecting overly optimistic assumptions about Arab desires for independence, or at least the potential for a mass, armed anti-Ottoman action.

This optimism may have been influenced by British strategic interests in fomenting rebellion, leading to potential confirmation bias in interpreting intelligence. Early predictions about widespread Arab support for the revolt proved somewhat exaggerated, reflecting both a reliance on pro-Sharifian sources and perhaps the hopes of Arab Bureau staff to see swift Sharifian success.

The *Arab Bulletin*'s role in shaping policy created its own complications. As its influence grew, there was increasing pressure to align analysis with strategic objectives, potentially compromising analytical objectivity. This tension became particularly acute during discussions of post-war arrangements, when the *Arab Bulletin*'s assessments of local political dynamics could have significant implications for British policy decisions. The need to maintain credibility while serving policy objectives created a delicate balance that wasn't always successfully maintained. The wide-ranging nature of *Arab Bulletin* reporting sometimes ran the risk of compromising sources or ongoing operations. The level of detail provided in some reports, such as Lawrence's activities in the field, could have seriously compromised operations had the information fallen into enemy hands. This struggle to balance the need to share information with the need to protect sources and methods is a challenge that remains central to intelligence work today.

Wartime Innovation and the Arab Bulletin's Long Shadow

The *Arab Bulletin*'s influence extended far beyond its immediate wartime utility. Looking back from our present vantage point, we can see how it shaped not only British Middle East policy but also the long-term evolution of intelligence practices. Hogarth recognised its potential historical significance when he wrote, "A complete file of the Bulletin since its beginning should be indispensable to anyone who hereafter may have to compile for official use a history of the Arabs."[35] His prediction proved prescient, as the publication's detailed accounts of tribal politics, its mapping of trade routes and resources, and its analysis of religious and cultural factors does indeed continue to provide modern researchers with insights into the period that are not readily available from other comparable contemporary sources.

More fundamentally, the *Arab Bulletin* established new standards for comprehensive regional analysis that would influence generations of intelligence practitioners and scholars. Its integration of diverse intelligence sources, emphasis on cultural understanding, and attempts at predictive analysis anticipated practices that would become standard decades later. The publication's approach to understanding and reporting on Arab nationalism, for instance, which moved from a starting point that offered relatively simple assessments to producing analysis of great insight, and which was able to present and evaluate numerous competing visions for an Arab political future, is a prime example of precisely the type of understanding of a complex and multifaceted situation which modern intelligence services strive to achieve.

The *Arab Bulletin*'s legacy is also evident in its influence on how intelligence services approach regional analysis, with the Arab Bureau adopting a holistic approach, one that combined cultural, political, economic, and military analysis, and which resulted in the provision of a model for understanding complex regional dynamics that remains relevant. The Arab Bureau's recognition that effective intelligence requires more than just collecting information, that it actually demands understanding context, appreciating nuance, and recognising the complex interplay of factors that shape events, was likewise to anticipate modern approaches to intelligence analysis.

The publication's handling of sources and verification processes, while imperfect, also left a lasting mark on intelligence practices. Its careful distinction between confirmed facts and unverified reports, its integration of multiple sources to build comprehensive assessments, and its willingness to present competing interpretations all anticipated modern analytical methods. Even its struggles with security and source protection, discussed above, helped establish principles that would become central to intelligence work.

Another area of significance was the way in which the *Arab Bulletin* demonstrated the value of having regional experts involved in intelligence work. The unique composition of its contributors—archaeologists, scholars, linguists, and travellers who brought deep regional knowledge to their wartime roles—showed how academic expertise could enhance intelligence gathering and analysis. It also served as a model that would later influence the development of academic area studies as well as the integration of academic expertise into intelligence work. The broader approach to cultural intelligence would also prove influential, particularly its recognition that understanding cultural and religious factors was crucial for both military operations and political strategy, another early approach that anticipated the modern emphasis on cultural intelligence. And while the *Arab Bulletin*'s attempts to understand and explain complex religious and tribal dynamics were certainly not always successful, they nevertheless set an important precedent for how intelligence services approach cultural analysis.

The *Arab Bulletin*'s influence on military doctrine and operational planning is also worth noting. As mentioned above, its sophisticated treatment of asymmetrical warfare, especially through providing coverage of railway raids and tribal operations, helped establish frameworks for understanding irregular warfare that influenced military thinking for decades. While much has been written about Lawrence's writings on the guerrilla tactics employed over the course of the Arab Revolt, his own ideas were reflected in numerous reports written by his colleagues. The publication regularly presented analysis of how small forces could achieve strategic effects through carefully targeted operations anticipating modern concepts of asymmetrical warfare and special operations, which recognition that military success in complex environments generally requires an approach beyond conventional force undoubtedly helped to shape British military doctrine in colonial and postcolonial contexts.

The *Arab Bulletin*'s impact on diplomatic practice was equally significant, with analyses of tribal politics and regional dynamics influencing how British diplomatic officers subsequently approached their work throughout the empire, not just in the MENA region. By demonstrating how detailed cultural and political intelligence could inform diplomatic engagement, the publication was able to offer a model for establishing patterns that would, where applied, influence British colonial administration well into the post-war period. Finally on this point, the Arab Bureau's broader recognition that effective diplomacy required deep understanding of local power structures and cultural dynamics also went some way towards establishing new standards for diplomatic reporting and analysis.

Institutionally, the *Arab Bulletin*'s legacy can be traced through various organisational innovations in British intelligence. The concept of having regional specialists working alongside military intelligence officers, which was first systematically implemented by the Arab Bureau, would influence the structure of British intelligence organisations for generations. Meanwhile, while not wholly original to the Arab Bureau, the integration of academic expertise with operational intelligence was refined and systematised through the *Arab Bulletin* into practices that would shape future institutional arrangements.

The publication's influence on intelligence tradecraft was particularly evident in its treatment of human intelligence sources. The Arab Bureau's approach to source cultivation and protection, its careful evaluation of source reliability, and its systematic integration of human intelligence with other sources helped establish practices that would become standard in intelligence work, while the recognition that effective human intelligence required long-term relationship building and deep cultural understanding influenced how future generations of intelligence officers approached source development.

Perhaps most remarkably, the *Arab Bulletin*'s legacy extended to how intelligence services approached the challenge of predicting and shaping political developments. Its attempts to understand and influence the complex political dynamics of the Arab world—while not always successful nor, one might argue, especially desirable—helped establish frameworks for political intelligence that would influence how intelligence services approached similar challenges in other regions. The publication's treatment of competing political movements, its analysis of religious and cultural factors in political development, and its attempts to anticipate future political trends all helped establish patterns for political intelligence that remain relevant today.

As for its influence on later intelligence writing and presentation, the *Arab Bulletin* also deserves recognition and praise. Its emphasis on clear, analytical writing, free from military jargon while maintaining technical precision, helped establish standards for intelligence reporting that would influence generations of practitioners. The careful balance between detail and accessibility, and the clear presentation of competing interpretations, alongside its integration of different types of intelligence all helped establish models for effective intelligence communication.

As is obvious from the many examples just cited, in the decades following the First World War, many of the *Arab Bulletin*'s innovative practices would become standard in intelligence work. Its emphasis on

THE *ARAB BULLETIN* AS INTELLIGENCE INNOVATION

integrating multiple sources, its attention to cultural factors, its attempts at predictive analysis, and its recognition of the importance of economic intelligence all anticipated developments that would shape modern intelligence practices. Further, and in keeping with the desire for intellectually honest yet rigorous approaches, even its shortcomings proved instructive, helping as they did to establish principles about source protection, bias awareness, and the importance of rigorous verification that remain relevant.

Complexity as Strategic Advantage: When Scholars Became Spies

The story of the *Arab Bulletin* is ultimately one of innovation born of necessity. Faced with the challenge of understanding and operating in the complex landscape of the Middle East during the First World War, the Arab Bureau created something entirely new: an intelligence product that combined academic rigour with operational relevance, cultural understanding with strategic insight. What began as an experiment in intelligence reporting evolved into a sophisticated written product that would help shape both British strategy and the future of intelligence work. Through the pages of the *Arab Bulletin* we see the emergence of practices that would become standard in modern intelligence, but perhaps most importantly we also see the recognition that effective intelligence requires more than just collecting information. It demands understanding context, appreciating nuance, and recognising the complex interplay of factors that shape events.

The *Arab Bulletin*'s innovations weren't just technical or methodological. They represented a fundamental shift in how intelligence could be gathered, analysed, and presented. By bringing together scholars, soldiers, and specialists, the publication demonstrated the value of combining different types of expertise. Its willingness to acknowledge uncertainty, present competing interpretations, and look beyond immediate military concerns set new standards for intelligence reporting. Yet the story of the *Arab Bulletin* also reveals the persistent challenges of intelligence work. The struggles with verification, the tension between sharing information and protecting sources, the influence of cultural bias—these challenges remain familiar to intelligence professionals today. In this sense, the *Arab Bulletin*'s limitations are as instructive as its innovations.

Its legacy extends beyond its immediate impact on British policy during the First World War. The *Arab Bulletin*'s approach to comprehensive regional analysis, its integration of cultural understanding with military intelligence, and its emphasis on clear, analytical writing influenced how future generations would approach the challenge of understanding complex regions.

Moreover, the *Arab Bulletin*'s success in bridging the gap between tactical intelligence and strategic understanding offers important lessons for contemporary intelligence organisations. At a time when intelligence services face increasingly complex challenges, from hybrid warfare to cyber threats, the *Arab Bulletin*'s ability to connect immediate operational needs with broader strategic implications remains instructive. Its demonstration that effective intelligence must operate simultaneously at multiple levels—tactical, operational, and strategic—anticipated the layered approach that characterises modern intelligence work.

The *Arab Bulletin*'s handling of uncertainty and complexity also deserves attention in any final assessment. Rather than following the fools' path of presenting simple answers to complex questions, it embraced ambiguity and nuance, and its willingness to present competing interpretations, acknowledge limitations, and explore alternative scenarios demonstrated a sophistication that many modern intelligence organisations still struggle to achieve. Such intellectual honesty—presenting the world as it is rather than as one might wish it to be—remains a crucial lesson for contemporary intelligence work.

Furthermore, the *Arab Bulletin*'s role in shaping institutional memory and organisational learning merits consideration. Through its detailed documentation of operations, analysis of successes and failures, and careful preservation of regional knowledge, the publication created an invaluable repository of experience and insight. This systematic approach to capturing and transmitting institutional knowledge, while admittedly not without its limitations, helped establish patterns for how intelligence organisations could learn from experience and build upon past insights.

In the final analysis, all these themes—innovation born of necessity, the integration of diverse expertise, the balance between tactical and strategic concerns, the honest treatment of complexity, and the importance of institutional learning—remain relevant for modern intelligence organisations, so that even as contemporary services grapple with evolving threats and emerging challenges, the example of the *Arab Bulletin*

THE *ARAB BULLETIN* AS INTELLIGENCE INNOVATION

suggests that solutions may lie not in revolutionary changes but in the careful integration of different types of expertise, the systematic development of analytical frameworks, and the willing embrace of complexity.

In the end, the *Arab Bulletin* stands as a testament to the broader innovative spirit of the Arab Bureau. It demonstrates how, in the crucible of war, necessity drove innovation in intelligence gathering and analysis. Its story reminds us that understanding a complex region requires more than just military intelligence: it demands a comprehensive approach that considers cultural, political, and economic factors alongside tactical information. This lesson, first demonstrated in the pages of the *Arab Bulletin*, remains relevant for anyone seeking to understand the complex dynamics of the Middle East or indeed any region of the world today.

PART IV

PROPAGANDA AND ARAB ALLIES

9

THAWRAT AL-ARAB

CREATING AN ARABIC-LANGUAGE PROPAGANDA MASTERPIECE: CAIRO

In which the creation of Thawrat al-Arab *reveals a brilliant and original approach to propaganda on the part of the Arab Bureau and demonstrates a unique and most innovative collaboration between British intelligence and Arab intellectuals that would challenge traditional understandings of wartime information operations. This chapter explores how this book-length item of British Arabic-language propaganda—created as a collaborative partnership with an Arab author—represented a groundbreaking approach to spreading Arab nationalist sentiment while advancing British strategic interests.*

Crafting an Arab Narrative: A Book Born of Resistance

While previous chapters have examined how the Arab Bureau revolutionised intelligence gathering and analysis, its most innovative work may have been in the realm of propaganda and information operations, where its revolutionary approach to cross-cultural communication would challenge traditional understandings of how intelligence agencies could operate in foreign cultural environments.

In Cairo, on 9 December 1916, a 250-page Arabic book entitled *Thawrat al-Arab* (*The Arabs' Revolt*),[1] rolled off the presses of al-Muqattam Printing House. With its modest print run of 500 copies and plain cover featuring only a title and attribution to "a member of the Arabian Associations", nothing about its appearance suggested any particular significance.

Yet this book represented something extraordinary. Not only was it commissioned, created, and distributed through the efforts of the Arab

Bureau, but at roughly 85,000 words it is arguably the longest single piece of British propaganda produced during the entire First World War.[2] Of greater technical and political significance, this work represents a sophisticated collaboration between British Military Intelligence and Arab intellectuals that challenges traditional understandings of how intelligence services operated in this period. From a scholarly perspective, more remarkably still, for decades this significant text has sat in plain sight in archives and libraries, overlooked by scholars of both British intelligence—receiving not a single mention in the three main scholarly works on the Arab Bureau[3]—and Arab nationalism.

Created with the full support of the Arab Bureau, *Thawrat al-Arab* exemplifies the intelligence agency's more original approach to intelligence and propaganda work. Behind the book's stated anonymous authorship there lay a complex web of relationships between British intelligence officers and Arab intellectuals, most importantly here As'ad Daghir,[4] a Lebanese Orthodox Christian journalist and editor who worked for Faris Nimr,[5] a fellow enthusiast for the Arab nationalist cause who owned both the newspaper *al-Muqattam* and the printing house of the same name that published *Thawrat al-Arab*. The anonymity on the frontispiece was also obviously a protective measure for the author and any of his extended family still living in Ottoman realms, a wise precaution given the dangerous political climate and recent mass hangings.

Rather than simply translating British propaganda into Arabic or imposing Western narratives, the Arab Bureau enabled Arab intellectuals to speak authentically to Arab audiences. This sophistication extended from the book's conception all the way through to its distribution, demonstrating an understanding of local cultural dynamics that was rare, to say the least, among Western intelligence services of the period.[6]

The contents of *Thawrat al-Arab* reflect this approach. The book is divided into twelve chapters, moving from distant history to urgent contemporary events. The first third of the text provides historical background, establishing a narrative of both Arab greatness and Ottoman decline; the middle portion covers the immediate pre-First World War period, roughly from the 1913 Arab Congress, via Ottoman persecution of Arab nationalists, to the eve of the Arab Revolt; while the final third deals with the revolt itself, and the author's vision, shared with many Arab nationalists of this period, of a great Arab future. This structure allowed Daghir to build a comprehensive case for Arab independence while maintaining scholarly credibility.[7]

THAWRAT AL-ARAB

Thawrat al-Arab was published just six months after the start of the eponymous Arab Revolt, demonstrating the urgency with which the Arab Bureau approached this propaganda project. Sharif Hussein launched the anti-Ottoman Arab Revolt just a month after Ottoman authorities had publicly hanged a large number of prominent Arab nationalist figures in Damascus and Beirut, including several friends of the book's anonymous (at the time of publication) author. These hangings played a significant part in helping precipitate Hussein's decision to launch the Arab Revolt when he did, and their shadow looms large over the pages of *Thawrat al-Arab*.[8]

At first glance, *Thawrat al-Arab* appears typical of this type of book from this period, which is to say a mix of history, political analysis, and manifesto. The frontispiece carries what one would expect in a text written for a highly literate, politically engaged readership, namely the title and subtitle in elaborate Arabic font. Perhaps the first hint of the book's unusual make-up is what follows immediately. Instead of the author's name there is instead a carefully worded, and anonymised, attribution of authorship to "a member of the Arabian Associations".

Below the title and authorial credentials appears the legend "The King among the Arabs", a clear reference to Sharif Hussein, titular head of the Arab Revolt. This was no mere honorific. Hussein had claimed this title, which is somewhat atypical for a traditional-minded Muslim ruler, for himself shortly after launching his revolt against Ottoman authority. In doing so, he was making an audacious triple declaration: independence from Ottoman control; rejection of the Sultan's claims to authority over the global *ummah*; and his own claim to be the rightful heir to more than 1,300 years of caliphal tradition.[9]

Between the title at the head and publication details at the foot, the frontispiece contains a list of roughly 100 words outlining the book's main themes, arranged in an inverted pyramid:

> The European War and the East – The Eastern Question and its Branches – The Arabian Question and its Role – Arabs and Turks in the Past – The Arabs and the Unionists – Forming the Arabian Associations and its Reasons – The First Arab Conference and its Outcomes – Intentions and Tools of the Unionists – Unionists, Islam and the Arabs – The Situation Escalates – The Volcano Erupts – Swearing to Reign over the Arabs – The Arabs' Future – A Martyr's Testament and a Mujahid's[10] Salute.[11]

THE ARAB BUREAU

The creation of pro-British and Allied propaganda had been explicitly identified as a central component of the Arab Bureau's mission from its founding. The Foreign Office report that outlined the key functions of this new intelligence unit stated that among these would be "to co-ordinate propaganda in favour of Great Britain and the Entente [France] among non-Indian [Arab] Moslems without clashing with the susceptibilities of Indian Moslems and the Entente Powers".[12] While propaganda may have been mentioned second in their mandate, this should not be taken to mean the task was of secondary importance. Indeed, the fact that it was singled out for particular mention meant that the creation of Arabic-language propaganda was of paramount importance.[13]

Thawrat al-Arab was conceived with two intertwined, perhaps inseparable, goals: to win broader Arab support for Hussein's anti-Ottoman uprising, and the cause of Arab nationalism more broadly, while simultaneously attacking Ottoman authorities and their policies in order to undermine support for their war effort.

The dedication page reveals much about the book's political context and emotional power. It is dedicated "To the souls of the nation's martyrs", followed by a list of fifteen dedicatees, "and others". Giving the names of the fifteen murdered dedicatees creates an immediate emotional connection with readers, linking the abstract cause of Arab nationalism to specific human losses. These men were victims of war, hanged by the Ottomans in a series of anti-Arab nationalist purges between 1914 and May 1916, when Ottoman authorities carried out almost simultaneous public hangings in Beirut and Damascus. These squares were subsequently renamed *Sāḥat ash-Shuhadā* (Martyrs' Square) in both cities, with the anniversary still commemorated every 6 May.[14]

Intellectual Collaboration: British Intelligence, Arab Authorship

Behind the anonymous authorship was Asʻad Daghir, a Lebanese Orthodox Christian journalist, editor, and author. Based in Cairo for much of the First World War, Daghir worked for, among others, Faris Nimr, a fellow enthusiast for the Arab nationalist cause and the owner of al-Muqattam Printing House.[15] The extent of this collaboration between British intelligence officers and Arab intellectuals represented something new in the conduct of propaganda operations, a much deeper partnership that was hoped to simultaneously advance the interests of these two otherwise seemingly disparate forces.

Some earlier writers, by focusing narrowly on imperial discourse, have occasionally overlooked the practical challenges of cross-cultural propaganda, challenges that complicate any simple orientalist reading of the Arab Bureau. The creation of *Thawrat al-Arab* involved not only advancing British interests but also engaging with Arab intellectual traditions and nationalist aspirations, thereby recognising Arab agency and cultural sophistication.

Daghir's personal connections to many of the executed nationalists gives the text its emotional urgency. The men named in the dedication were not random victims but prominent public figures, including two former elected members of the Ottoman parliament, a delegate to that same institution, along with distinguished lawyers, jurists, educators, poets, and journalists. The mass public execution of such well-known public figures was an event that marked a turning point in Arab–Ottoman relations and would precipitate the start of *The Arab Revolt*, to use the book's title in English.

The Arab Bureau's partnership with figures like As'ad Daghir represented genuine cross-cultural collaboration, yet their reports to London inevitably emphasised Arab enthusiasm and British cultural sensitivity while downplaying the limited scope of actual intellectual exchange. What the Arab Bureau readily characterised as 'authentic Arab voices' often reflected careful British editorial control and strategic messaging objectives.

Nevertheless, these men represented a spectrum of Arab nationalist thought, ranging from those who merely sought greater recognition for Arabic language and culture within the Ottoman Empire, to advocates for increased autonomy, to those demanding outright independence. Under normal conditions, none would have been considered dangerous extremists or revolutionaries, but war has a way of subverting routine calculations. As one author neatly put the case, "It was the misfortune of the Syrian nationalists that what had been mere dissent before 1914 became treason afterwards."[16] Further, it is also true that upon the outbreak of war some adopted more radical positions than they had during peacetime, though many continued arguing for reform rather than revolution until their deaths.[17] Most of the dedicatees were known to Daghir personally, and more than a few were close friends. His writing occasionally betrays hints of survivor's guilt for having arrived in Cairo before the purges, which he almost certainly would have been targeted by.

Hussein too was personally hit, and genuinely affected, by news of the executions, and if there was one factor more than any other that forced his hand to start the revolt, it was this.

For months, Hussein had been engaged in what would become known as the Hussein–McMahon Correspondence, a series of ten letters exchanged between July 1915 and March 1916 with Sir Henry McMahon, the British High Commissioner in Egypt. While these letters discussed British support for Arab independence in exchange for an Arab revolt against the Ottomans, the exact territorial boundaries of the proposed Arab state remained deliberately ambiguous, with crucial regions like Palestine subject to careful diplomatic hedging. Despite this lack of clarity, and without having secured firm British commitments to his vision of a unified, post-war Arab kingdom, Hussein made the fateful decision to throw in his lot with the Allies and launch the Arab Revolt. This hasty move into armed rebellion, before finalising terms with his British allies, would later become one of the greatest sources of post-war disappointment, when competing promises and imperial interests superseded the vague assurances given to Arab nationalists.

Thawrat al-Arab would not have been created if the Arab Bureau had not had a finely tuned understanding of how to work with local allies, setting to one side for now any inequality or lack of veracity that may well have underscored this relationship. The fact remains that this novel collaboration between British intelligence officers and Arab intellectuals represented a new approach to the conduct of propaganda operations. Rather than simply translating British propaganda into Arabic or imposing its own views, the Arab Bureau enabled a synergy that allowed Arab intellectuals to speak authentically to Arab audiences. Daghir brought not only his literary skills but also his personal, atavistic understanding of Arab culture and politics to this literary project. As a result of his work at Faris Nimr's *al-Muqattam* newspaper, Daghir was well-positioned to craft arguments that would resonate with educated Arab readers. At the same time, his personal connections to many of the Arab nationalist figures featured in the book gave the work an authenticity and emotional resonance that no British-authored text could have achieved.[18]

The challenges of producing authentic foreign-language materials are illustrated by a pertinent observation from one of C.S. Forester's[19] Napoleonic-era Hornblower novels. Addressing the claims of a group of

British naval officers, a master forger responds, "You gentlemen may pride yourselves on writing good French, grammatical French, but a Frenchman reading it would know it was not written by a Frenchman ... You must have your French composed *ab initio* by a Frenchman, contenting yourselves with merely outlining what is to be said."[20] This observation perfectly captures the Arab Bureau's experience with Arabic-language productions. Indeed, this understanding clearly informs the Bureau's approach to both major works like *Thawrat al-Arab* and other, smaller-scale works of propaganda in Arabic.

The relationship between the Arab Bureau and these intellectual collaborators was more nuanced than that of simply employer and employee. Beyond the important questions of imperial representation and cultural appropriation that postcolonial scholars have thoroughly examined lies the practical question of how cross-cultural propaganda actually functioned in wartime conditions. Daghir and Nimr were no mere tools of British propaganda but instead partners in a complex wartime alliance. They shared certain goals with the British, not least of which was the defeat of the Ottomans, while maintaining their own vision of Arab independence. If it does not obviously run through the pages of *Thawrat al-Arab*, this tension between British strategic aims and Arab nationalist aspirations lies somewhere at the back of the book project, making it a fascinating document of wartime collaboration.[21]

The speed with which the book was produced is remarkable. Its going from conception to distribution in just under six months, is an extraordinary achievement[22] given the book's length and the wartime conditions under which it was published. Such a rapid timeline suggests both the urgency the Arab Bureau attached to the project and the effectiveness of its working relationship with Daghir, as well as with Nimr's publishing house.[23] Signs of this haste are visible in the text. Alongside a dozen or so identifiable spelling mistakes, a number of other typographical errors crept in. The endpapers include an incomplete list of nine errata, with a page and line number for each, suggesting at least one post-printing proofing. The last line offers a plea for clemency that echoes down the centuries: "There are other printing mistakes which are obvious to the reader."

Regrettably, details of the meetings to agree on commission, fees, and deadlines have so far proved elusive. Also missing from the historical record are details of who on the Arab Bureau staff acted as the intermediary with the publisher, if not the author directly. These gaps in our knowledge make it difficult to fully understand the mechanics of this remarkable collaboration. That said, it is also safe to say that in terms of this fascinating, remarkable, and previously overlooked side of the Arab Bureau's professional outputs, the results speak for themselves.

Words as Weapons: Writing History, Fighting the Ottomans

By any standard, *Thawrat al-Arab* is a substantial literary effort, both in purely textual terms but also in the span of its purview, ranging as it does from long-distant history to urgent contemporary events, some of which occurred just weeks before publication. *Thawrat al-Arab* opens not with a declaration of revolt but with history, a short, 400-word preface setting its portentous literary tone: "Several centuries have passed during which the noble Arabs have clung to and endured the unfair decrees of time, with noble forbearance in spite of their wounded pride."

Daghir goes on to bemoan widespread ignorance among Arabs of both their past greatness and the causes of the current uprising. In response to this educational lacuna, he presents *Thawrat al-Arab* as an educational tool, where he hopes that by writing about their history and current situation he might inspire Arabs to show the world they are worthy of being considered among its great peoples, joining the Arab Revolt and throwing off the increasingly deadly mantle of Ottoman oppression.

The first two chapters lay groundwork essential for Arab readers to understand their own past and present situation. Chapter 1, "The European War and the East", traces Ottoman decline from their defeat in 1683 at the Battle of Kahlenberg, better known to English readers as the Battle of Vienna.[24] Daghir carefully outlines the empire's long, if slow, decline, weaving together what he calls various 'questions' that constituted the immediate background to Ottoman geopolitical decline. These are, in list order, the Eastern Question, the Macedonian Question, the Albanian Question, the Bosnian and Herzegovinian Question, the Serbian Question, and the Armenian Question. These issues had preoccupied European statesmen and newspaper editors for generations, and Daghir spends quite some time examining in forensic detail the numerous treaties, wars, and diplomatic manoeuvres that were gradually weakening Ottoman power.[25]

Chapter 2, "The Arabian Question", reaches further back, to pre-Islamic times, establishing Arabs as "a Semitic nation" descended from "Sam the son of Noah". Here Daghir makes audacious territorial claims, greater even than those made by Hussein in his negotiations with McMahon: "The Arabian countries are bordered by the Taurus Mountains in the north, Iran, the Persian Gulf and the Sea of Oman in the east, the Indian Ocean in the south, and the Red and Mediterranean Seas in the west, including Syria, Iraq and the Arabian Peninsula." This expansive vision would later cause great tension with British, and also French, plans for the post-war settlement.

But this was no mere history lesson. Daghir's narrative served multiple propaganda aims, which included numerous attempts, through the retelling of historical accounts, to demonstrate Ottoman weakness and decline, and to suggest the inevitability of imperial collapse, while concurrently doing his best to establish Arab greatness, both past and future, in his readers' eyes. Unsurprisingly, Daghir takes particular care to highlight the Arabs' special place in Islamic history, noting they were the people whose language was chosen by God for his final revelation.[26]

Chapters 3–5 reveal the complex dynamics between Arab nationalists and Ottoman authorities in the pre-war period. Chapter 3, "The Alleged Agreement between Arabs and Turks", provides a detailed examination of state-level Arab–Ottoman relations, including the outcomes of the 1913 Arab Congress. This chapter bears careful reading for anyone wishing to understand the manoeuvres and machinations unfolding at this time, particularly the CUP's apparent (or from Daghir's perspective blatant and demonstrable) duplicity towards the Arab representatives.[27]

Daghir quotes extensively from speeches delivered at official receptions and banquets in Constantinople, where Arab delegates were ostensibly welcomed with open arms. Many of these speeches were delivered by men who would later be hanged, in spite of their positive approach to their official relationship with the Ottoman Turks and the CUP in particular. As Abdul Karim al-Khalil, for instance, declared at that gathering, "these meetings have helped in dispelling all complicated matters dividing the Arabs and Turks", while another delegate, Sheikh Ahmad Tabbarah, opened his address with a characteristic flourish, saying, "I address your Highness by clear Arab tongue, the tongue of the Holy Quran and the great Arab prophet who said, 'I love whoever loves the Arabs.'"[28] Not the CUP, as it turned out.

The official record dutifully notes the audience's apparently enthusiastic response to such declarations of loyalty. When Tabbarah proclaimed, "We have declared with full mouths and state now and in every place and time that we grew up under the shadow of the Ottoman Crescent (applause) and we want to live and die under its shadow (applause)," the parenthetical notations of audience reaction serve to heighten the tragic irony, given that both speakers would later die at the hands of Ottoman hangmen.

Chapter 4, "The First Shocks", builds on the theme of Ottoman treachery, citing the ban on Arab associations and the arrest and trial of Egyptian-Circassian Ottoman officer Aziz Bey Ali al-Masri. This case proved particularly significant. Instead of an immediate post-trial execution, Daghir reports that "[in] the interest of Arab public opinion ... and after witnessing the increasing rage of the Arabs following the end of the trial, they decided to assassinate him in prison". Even this plan failed to materialise thanks to pressure from "the ambassadors of the Great Powers", i.e. Britain and France, and because "Great Britain had paid special attention to the matter". Chapter 4 also includes revealing complaints about the poor state of education and communications in Arab provinces. A speech by Salim Effendi Salam bemoans the condition of schools, particularly for girls, when he writes, "What do I say about them? Oh! deputies of the nation? They are in the lowest place. Women are the foundation of literary life and the cornerstone of the social body. And if it is degraded, then the nation remains degenerate as well." Well, quite.

Ottoman Oppression Versus Arab Dignity

Chapter 5, "The Arabs' Loyalty to the Unionists", demonstrates through speeches and letters how Arab nationalist figures seemingly maintained their loyalty to the empire right up to the outbreak of war. As Daghir puts it, "At no point in time have the acts and atrocities of the Unionists ever kept the Arab emirs from remaining loyal to them." The chapter includes extensive correspondence from figures who would later be executed, including a remarkable 4,000-word letter from al-Sayyid al-Idrīsī to Imam Yaḥyá that was published in the fourth issue of Rashid Rida's[29] journal *al-Manar*[30] in 1913.[31]

These three chapters mark a crucial transition in the text's narrative arc. They establish both the reasonableness of Arab nationalist demands and the apparent duplicity of Ottoman authorities in responding to them. Through careful selection and presentation of speeches and correspondence, Daghir builds his case that the Arab Revolt emerged not from long-standing separatist ambitions but from Ottoman persecution of even moderate Arab leaders who sought reform within the empire.

Daghir's selection and presentation of speeches and letters serves multiple propaganda aims. In Chapter 5, he reproduces a series of letters from Arab nationalists, carefully noting that he has omitted "nothing ... except for the names of individuals still living as well as any matters unrelated to the realm of politics". The letters include correspondence from "the deceased officer" Salīm Bey al-Jazāʾirī to a friend and political ally; "the deceased" Mukhtār Bayhum to a friend in Egypt, written just five days before the Ottoman Empire entered the First World War; and "the deceased" Muḥammad al-Maḥmaṣānī's response to friends who had urged him to remain safely in Egypt after the announcement of mass military mobilisation.[32]

The repeated use of "the deceased" before each name creates a powerful rhetorical effect, reminding readers of the ultimate cost of Ottoman treachery. Al-Maḥmaṣānī's letter proves particularly poignant. Refusing the chance to stay in Egypt where he was safe, he wrote, "The homeland is in need of every one of its sons during these trying times, so it would be treasonous for us not to carry out our duty towards it." His sense of duty would lead directly to his execution.

Perhaps most remarkable is what Daghir describes as "an extensive secret correspondence" from "the deceased" ʿAbd al-Ḥamīd al-Zahrāwī to Rashīd Riḍā. Running to about 3,000 words and marked "Top Secret", rather than plans for rebellion the letter instead expresses the author's continued faith in Ottoman reform. Daghir presents this as evidence of "the vast severity of the crime that the Unionists have committed by executing this well-intentioned, simple-hearted man, who had exposed himself to the criticism of his friends and the ire of his nation for his hope to achieve harmony between the Arabs and the Turks".

The speeches from the 1913 Arab Congress and subsequent delegation to Constantinople reveal similar themes. Alexander Bey Amoon of the Decentralization Party captured the mood when he told the assembly that "the Ottoman nation has reached the brink of a cliff, as it is between a painful past and a dark future while looking at yesterday with unhappiness and sorrow and looking at tomorrow with fear and worry".

The measured tone of such speeches, seeking reform rather than revolution, serves Daghir's argument that Arab nationalism was driven to revolt by Ottoman intransigence rather than inherent separatist aims.[33]

These documents also reveal the complex dynamics of Arab–Ottoman relations outside of the major cities. From the far south of Arabia, Daghir includes correspondence between al-Sayyid al-Idrīsī and Imam Yahyá, chosen to demonstrate how even "one of the Arab emirs who despises the Unionists the most" had initially sought compromise. Al-Idrīsī writes with evident frustration about failed negotiations, "We have undergone negotiations on this matter with the government three times—nay four times—after their messengers reached us. Whenever we replied in a way signalling agreement, they would turn their backs towards us in a show of haughtiness, arrogance, and contempt."

The cumulative effect of these carefully chosen documents is to present Arab nationalism as inherently moderate and loyal, driven to revolt only by Ottoman persecution. The letters and speeches serve as evidence not just of Arab loyalty but of Ottoman betrayal of that loyalty. By letting these documents speak largely for themselves, with minimal editorial intervention, Daghir creates an apparently objective case for revolt that would have resonated powerfully with educated Arab readers.

The careful selection and presentation of these documents connects to several broader themes that run throughout *Thawrat al-Arab*. First, they establish a pattern of Arab loyalty and Ottoman betrayal that undergirds the book's entire argument. The letters' authors repeatedly demonstrate their commitment to Ottoman unity even as they seek reforms, supporting Daghir's larger narrative that Arab nationalism was pushed towards revolt as opposed to being inherently separatist. This theme culminates in his assertion that "this great loyalty would only manifest itself most clearly after the Ottoman Empire entered the war. For at that time the Arabs put aside all of their disputes with the Turks and joined them in heart and soul to defend their shared homeland".

Second, the documents demonstrate what Daghir presents as the increasing paranoia and brutality of Ottoman rule. The progression from the hopeful speeches at the 1913 Arab Congress to the desperate letters written on the eve of war creates a narrative arc that makes the eventual revolt seem inevitable. By letting the documents tell this story, rather than simply stating it, Daghir achieves greater credibility with his readers.

The approach to propaganda seen in these chapters operates on multiple levels. First, authentication through documentation. Rather than making unsupported claims, Daghir grounds his arguments in verifiable documents and speeches. The Arab Bureau's willingness to let these authentic Arab voices speak, even when they sometimes express sentiments not entirely aligned with British interests, lends credibility to the larger propaganda effort.[34]

Second, authentication through personal connection. The repeated use, like a litany or mantra, of "the deceased" before names, and the inclusion of private correspondence, transforms political figures into human beings with whom readers could empathise. This personal element makes the propaganda more effective by engaging emotions as well as intellect.

A third means of authentication is via multiple perspectives. By including voices from different regions and backgrounds, including urban intellectuals, tribal leaders, and religious scholars, the text builds a case for Arab unity while acknowledging diversity. Such an approach would have resonated with educated Arab readers aware of their society's complexities.

Fourth, and finally here, authentication through strategic ambiguity. The text maintains certain useful ambiguities, particularly regarding the exact shape of post-war Arab independence. This reflects both the Arab Bureau's need to avoid contradicting other British commitments and its understanding that some ambiguity could be strategically useful in building support for the revolt.[35]

Perhaps most remarkably, these chapters demonstrate the great extent to which the Arab Bureau allowed its Arab collaborators autonomy in crafting the message. The extensive quotation from Arab sources, some of which express pan-Islamic sentiments that might have made British officials uncomfortable, shows remarkable sophistication in understanding how to build credibility with Arab audiences. Such willingness to work through authentic local voices, even when their message didn't perfectly align with British interests, marks a level of erudition in propaganda operations that wouldn't become standard practice until decades later.[36]

The text's tone shifts dramatically around the halfway point. From Chapter 6, "The Unionists' Tools to Erase Islam and Crush the Arabs", Daghir launches increasingly bitter attacks against Ottoman authorities.

He accuses them of offenses against Islam, Muhammad, his Companions, "and all that is sacred in Islam". His most potent allegations centre on claims that the CUP was actively working to eliminate Islam itself, perhaps an unlikely charge, but one calculated to inflame religious sentiment against Ottoman rule.[37]

Throughout the text, Daghir employs numerous literary devices to enhance his arguments, devices that also demonstrate deep understanding of his audience. He frequently uses the phrase "the language of the Ḍād" to signify Arabic, while "those who pronounce the Ḍād" stands for the Arabs themselves, both of which were commonly employed tropes among Arab nationalists of this period. He also intersperses his historical analysis with poetry, letters, and speeches from Arab nationalist figures, many written just before their executions, a mix of genres helping to maintain reader interest while also reinforcing the emotional impact of his arguments.[38]

The rhetorical power of *Thawrat al-Arab* rises markedly in its treatment of recent events. Chapter 7, "Aggravated Sermons", presents a scathing indictment of Djemal Pasha, whom Arab public opinion had already dubbed '*as-Saffah*' (the Blood-Shedder, or Butcher).[39] Chapter 7 is also home to one of the text's most remarkable pieces of propaganda: a completely fabricated account claiming Ottoman authorities had desecrated the tomb of Abd al-Qadir al-Jazairi,[40] the revered nineteenth-century Algerian emir who had led a resistance against French colonisation before eventually surrendering and living in exile in Damascus. Al-Jazairi was widely respected across the Arab world not only as a military leader who had fought European imperialism, but also as a devout scholar and Sufi mystic. In Daghir's fictional account, Ottoman forces allegedly destroyed al-Jazairi's shrine and scattered his remains, an act calculated to provoke maximum outrage among Arab readers regardless of their religious or political affiliations.

This fabrication was particularly potent because it accused the Ottomans of disrespecting a figure who embodied both Arab nationalism and Islamic piety, thereby attacking the Ottomans' legitimacy on multiple fronts. The story appears to have been crafted specifically to inflame Arab sentiment against the Ottoman leadership, presenting them as enemies not just of Arab political aspirations but of respected Arab cultural icons. The falsehood of this propaganda becomes even more evident when considering the actual reverence among Arabs for al-Jazairi's remains; his body remained intact and was eventually reinterred with great ceremony in Algeria after its independence in 1962, a national homecoming for a hero whose legacy continued to inspire Arab nationalist sentiment. Despite extensive research in Ottoman, British, and French archives, no evidence has emerged to suggest that any actual desecration occurred, confirming this to be a pure propaganda invention, though whether it was Daghir himself or his British sponsors who fabricated it remains unclear.[41]

Daghir employs various techniques to establish credibility with his readers. When relating particularly dramatic events, he often prefaces them with phrases such as "according to what trustworthy sources have reported who had seen with their own eyes". Sometimes he passes on messages from third parties, allowing other trusted sources, some known only by pen names familiar to readers, to deliver the news. For instance, "The esteemed writer known as 'The Traveller' reported to the newspaper *al-Muqattam* what an eyewitness told him who had arrived in Cairo in the middle of the month of October in the year 1916."

Martyrs and Manuscripts: The Language of Resistance

The book's most powerful passages deal with the recent atrocities, with the immediacy of those events mirrored by an urgency in the text. In Daghir's hands, the account of the May 1916 hangings in *Thawrat al-Arab* is a combination of eyewitness testimony and an opportunity to get across a political message. The accounts of the condemned men's final moments combine pathos with a despatch from the frontline of the struggle for Arab independence. Daghir writes, "They all proceeded to the gallows in a state of calm composure the likes of which are rarely seen," before going on to describe how one condemned man "gave an eloquent and brief speech in which he elucidated the noble aims for which the Arabs had striven".[42] Such descriptions in hopes of stirring his readers, and the choice to convey such eloquent last words in support of Arab political aspirations, are a clear attempt, through the use of highly charged and emotive language, to transform these deaths from something quotidian, mere executions, into martyrdom in pursuit of the nationalist cause.[43]

Daghir's account of the hangings takes on a grim inevitability, deeply personal and replete with tragedy. The pathos is emphatic in the stories he tells of final meetings between family members, or prisoners in chains on their way to the gallows. While his claim that all the condemned were equally composed facing death may be hyperbolic, such assertions about heroic postures served his propaganda aims better than the unvarnished truth, which was likely a more confused and tragic spectacle.

From these executions, Daghir turns to the devastating famine in Lebanon, employing similar techniques as above and additionally making use of American accounts of the starvation and other maladies caused by the hunger: [American] "Newspapers have estimated that 85,000 people have starved to death in Lebanon alone over the course of three months," Daghir writes. There's no doubt that American neutrality, at this point in the war, meant that Daghir's inclusion of eyewitness reports from such seemingly disinterested sources is meant to lend additional weight, as well as greater credibility and force to this testimony.[44]

Moving on to Chapter 8, "The Volcano Erupts", there is another shift in authorial tone as the focus moves from suffering to action. Here Daghir presents Sharif Hussein's decision to revolt as a reluctant but necessary response to relentless, and increasingly murderous, Ottoman oppression. According to this account, Hussein agreed to lead the revolt only after appeals from various Arab associations, most of whose members had escaped Ottoman persecution. Dahir's account relates how these associations approached Hussein because of his "noble heritage" and position as "Servant of the Two Noble Sanctuaries", viewing him as really the only suitable candidate to lead an anti-Ottoman uprising.

Nearly half of the chapter is taken up with a reproduction of a lengthy speech delivered by Hussein. Replete with both Quranic references and fiery diatribes, Hussein is particularly damning of those CUP rulings he considers to be in direct contradiction of Islamic law. For instance, he attacks their changes to inheritance law, saying, "they annulled the following statement of God—the most high—'For the male, what is equal to the share for two females' by dividing inheritance between the two sexes equally". Levelling an attack against the ruling CUP for introducing gender equality with regards to inheritance law would be unlikely to win many friends today, but it is instructive nevertheless, highlighting as it does both Hussein's avowedly rigid conservatism and a perhaps more modern approach to interpretation and implementation of this one aspect of *sharia* law on the part of the Ottoman leadership.

Chapter 9, "Europe and Arab Independence", presents what now appears as painfully optimistic assessments of European support for Arab independence. Without anticipating the perceived betrayals that would come after the war, Daghir quotes extensively from British and French statements of support for the Arab Revolt, statements that Britain and France would soon backtrack on. This chapter also makes sweeping claims about global Islamic backing for the revolt, assertions that were good propaganda but far from empirically accurate. As we have said elsewhere, the majority of Arabs would remain loyal to, or at least not rise up against, the Ottomans right through until the end of the war. As has also been stated elsewhere, but which bears repeating here, the reasons why certain groups or individuals chose not to join the Arab Revolt were numerous and varied, and therefore any perceived lack of resistance should not necessarily be seen as evidence that the majority of Ottoman subjects tacitly supported their overlords.

Thawrat al-Arab's last three chapters are relatively brief, together comprising only eleven pages and roughly 4,500 words, but they provide a powerful and emotionally resonant conclusion to the work. Chapter 10, "The King Among the Arabs", further develops the case for Hussein as the only possible choice to lead an independent, post-war Arab kingdom. The chapter reproduces in full a decree announcing "The first Arab Ministry in the new era", dated 7 Dhu al-Hijah 1334 (AH), which is 5 October 1916 (CE).[45]

This decree reveals both Hussein's ambitions and his limitations. Signed "Sharif of Mecca and its Prince, al-Hussein bin Ali", it appoints various officials to his nascent government. Most notable among these is Sheikh Abdullah Siraj, a prominent Islamic scholar elected to the Ottoman Parliament of 1908—although he never served in that capacity—as Chief Justice and Deputy Prime Minister. Siraj's standing as a respected Islamic authority lent additional credibility to Hussein's claims to leadership of the Arab world.[46]

However, the decree also betrays what must be seen as clear evidence of nepotism, as well as the limits to the 'democratic' (in any meaningful sense of the word) Arab state that others might have imagined would emerge after the war, with Hussein appointing "Our son, Abdullah bin al-Hussein for the Ministry of Foreign Affairs and Undersecretary of the Interior". Other appointments included Abd al-Aziz bin Ali as Chief of War and Undersecretary for the Commander of the Army; Sheikh Ali

Maliki as Minister of Education; Sheikh Yusuf Bin Salem as Minister of Public Affairs; Sheikh Muhammad Amin, a former director of the Holy Haram, as Minister of Endowments; and Sheikh Ahmed bin Abdul Rahman Banaga as Minister of Finance.

Chapter 11, "The Arabs' Future", employs powerful metaphors to contrast Arab ignorance before the revolt with their rediscovered wisdom. Daghir writes that the Ottomans had tried "to curb and wipe out the Arabs' nationalism. At best, all they could do was cast a thick veil of ignorance over the Arabs' eyes, shrouding their eyes from the light of guidance and leaving them to stumble about in utter darkness for a period of time". This imagery, deliberately echoing the Islamic concept of *jahiliyah*, or pre-Islamic ignorance, would be obvious to readers. This coupling of a standard Muslim trope with the depiction of Hussein raising a banner of Arab independence as representing the lifting of the veil of ignorance played directly into Hussein's hands: "Now that time has ended and the veil has been torn asunder, revealing behind it the Arab bride, more dazzling and beautiful than ever before." An "I was blind, now I see" moment.

The final chapter, "A Martyr's Will and a Mujahid's Greeting", provides an emotionally powerful conclusion through two carefully chosen texts. The first is a letter from "the deceased Abd al-Ghani al-Arisi," one of the dedicatees, writing his testament to the Arab nation. The second is a rousing poem by Fu'ad al-Khatib, described as "among the first people to give his congratulations to Arab independence in the Hijaz". The poem closes with a call to action that encapsulates the book's broader aims:

> O free Arabs! Verily, there is a dawn for you
> That looks down smiling onto the universe ...
> March on to Syria, to the land of Iraq,
> To the furthest reach of the Peninsula, and carry the flag.

Throughout these final chapters, Daghir employs an increasingly urgent and emotionally charged tone, weaving together religious imagery, nationalist sentiment, and calls for immediate action. At the same time, his employment of the last words and poetry of the hanged men—or martyrs, as they are inevitably characterised—demonstrates the author's understanding of how to move his Arab readership, either to action or to tears, while at the same time maintaining *Thawrat al-Arab*'s overall scholarly facade.

THAWRAT AL-ARAB

Distribution and Impact: From the Page to the People

The Arab Bureau's initial print run of *Thawrat al-Arab* was just 500 copies, and while this might seem an extremely modest number by modern standards, it requires contextualising within the realities of literacy and publishing in the wartime Middle East. In 1916, literacy in the MENA region remained extremely limited. The best estimates for literacy at this time are less than eight per cent in Egypt, and certainly no more than ten per cent across the Ottoman Empire as a whole.[47] As one scholar described it, illiteracy in the nineteenth century was "pervasive throughout Arab society", adding that "all assessments point to only a tiny, almost infinitesimal minority that was able to read. The percentage of literacy throughout the region was measurable in single-digit figures".[48]

Yet the Arab Bureau understood something crucial about how information spread in Arab society, including the continuing power of oral transmission. In a semi-literate society, portions of a text such as *Thawrat al-Arab* would almost certainly have been read aloud to groups, at least in urban centres, in cafes and comparable gathering places. As such, the Arab Bureau could be confident that each copy would reach far more people than its immediate readership, via public readings and word of mouth. Likewise, Arabic authors and publishers more generally could reasonably expect their published work to reach far wider audiences than direct readership alone would account for. As for *Thawrat al-Arab*, its mix of history, political analysis, poetry, and the emotional messages of the so-called martyrs' last words made it particularly suitable for such oral transmission. With this in mind, it should be clear that a print run of 500 copies in a semi-literate society represented a far more significant investment than it seems at face value.

With regards to the distribution of *Thawrat al-Arab*, this followed carefully planned networks, with the archival record showing copies were strategically distributed to Arab Bureau branch stations or contacts in "Basra, Jedda, Mecca, Khartoum, Tangier, etc.", the 'et cetera' no doubt taking in other locations where the British had allies through whom they anticipated further influencing Arab opinion.[49] This network of distribution points might suggest careful planning to reach key centres of Arab intellectual and political life or, on the other hand, possibly just a well-established network of locations through which all such propaganda materials—such as Arabic-language newspapers, leaflets, and other miscellanea—were regularly sent. As for *Thawrat al-Arab*, a contemporary Arab Bureau memorandum notes that "the book has been much appreciated in the Sudan, whence a demand for further copies has been received",[50] which clearly suggests the Bureau enjoyed a degree of success in reaching its intended audiences.

As discussed elsewhere, the Arab Bureau complemented this book distribution with the placement of articles in both their own sponsored Arabic publications as well as newspapers with sympathetic, pro-British, or at least anti-Ottoman editors. *Al-Muqattam* was the most obvious of these, what with it being owned by Faris Nimr, and being responsible for printing *Thawrat al-Arab*. In the days before mass communication, such texts relied heavily on circulation to lend them authority. The role of the Arab Bureau in both disseminating *Thawrat al-Arab* and placing announcements in *al-Muqattam* and other pro-British newspapers should not be underestimated. Such a multi-pronged approach to propaganda, combining book-length arguments with newspaper coverage, is yet another demonstration of the intricacy of the Arab Bureau's methods and approaches to propaganda in the region.[51]

The book's legacy continues, its influence obviously extending beyond its immediate wartime context. As the first extended written argument in support of Arab nationalism since the start of the First World War, and importantly one of the earliest pro-Arab nationalist works of comparable length, *Thawrat al-Arab* holds a significant, albeit previously unheralded, place in the development of Arab nationalist thought. Modern Arabic-language reissues in 1987 and 2016 suggest continuing interest in these early articulations of Arab independence.[52] That said, without being able to obtain sales figures for either of these more recent editions it is unclear whether these reissues were driven by interest in the text, and early Arab nationalist texts more broadly, or nothing more than the fact that technological advances make such reproductions cheap to produce.

Either way, and if for no other reason, *Thawrat al-Arab* has a degree of historical significance in that it is apparently the earliest Arabic-language work to contain lengthy, contemporaneous discussion of the Armenian genocide. This fact, combined with its detailed coverage of anti-Arab persecution and the Lebanese famine, makes it an important historical source for understanding how contemporaries viewed and wrote about these events.[53] More broadly, and in support of our overall

THAWRAT AL-ARAB

argument about the innovative nature of the Arab Bureau, it offers clear evidence of a more complex relationship between British intelligence and Arab intellectuals than is often acknowledged, one where collaboration could simultaneously serve both British imperial and Arab nationalist aims, however temporarily.

The approach developed through *Thawrat al-Arab* would influence British information operations for decades to come, suggesting as it does a model of cross-cultural communication that goes beyond simple propaganda, recognising the power of intellectual engagement and cultural authenticity. Even today, perhaps more than ever, in an era of increasing global complexity, the Arab Bureau's approach to this publication remains remarkably relevant, offering as it does a powerful reminder that effective communication requires genuine intellectual dialogue, cultural understanding, and a commitment to nuanced, authentic engagement.[54]

Measuring the effectiveness of propaganda is always challenging, and perhaps more so after a century has passed. In spite of this, the significance of *Thawrat al-Arab* clearly extends beyond any immediate impact it may have had on Arab public opinion. For one thing, such a lengthy item of propaganda provides an unarguable demonstration of the Arab Bureau's understanding of how to work with local allies to influence Arab opinion, and its ability to make a creditable attempt to achieve that goal. The text's very existence challenges traditional views of the Arab Bureau as amateurish or ineffective, revealing instead an organisation capable of strikingly original approaches to intelligence and propaganda work.[55]

Previous assessments of the Arab Bureau were inevitably limited by omitting consideration of their Arabic outputs. The rediscovery and translation of *Thawrat al-Arab* after decades of scholarly neglect allows us to see it as the important document it is, but also as a document that allows a far more nuanced appreciation of the Arab Bureau's work that has been either overshadowed by the mythology around Lawrence or simply never received attention due to widespread ignorance of its remarkable Arabic-language outputs.

Dual-Purpose Propaganda: Authentic Arab Voices and Imperial Designs

The story of *Thawrat al-Arab* forces us to fundamentally reassess our understanding of early intelligence organisations and their capabilities. Previous scholarly works on the Arab Bureau, lacking access to its Arabic-language propaganda efforts, were forced to overlook or otherwise ignore them, leading to incomplete and often dismissive evaluations of the Bureau's work. Yet here was a military intelligence unit in 1916 demonstrating deep understanding of cross-cultural communication, influence operations, and the complex dynamics of local political movements.

The Arab Bureau's approach to creating *Thawrat al-Arab* reveals an organisation far more complex than traditional accounts suggest. Working through trusted local intellectuals, allowing authentic Arab voices to shape the message, distributing through established cultural networks, the Bureau's methods demonstrate synergies between British intelligence and Arab nationalists beyond the general view of such relationships at this time. While other intelligence units focused on collecting and analysing information, the Arab Bureau understood the importance of shaping narratives and influencing opinion through culturally authentic means.

This remarkable collaboration between British intelligence and Arab intellectuals represents something more than simple propaganda. It shows the Arab Bureau's commitment to furthering British war efforts by spreading Arab nationalist sentiment, and that it attempted to do so to a much greater extent than has previously been argued. The fact that this project was conceived and supported by the Arab Bureau bolsters the view of that organisation as a highly professional intelligence unit, regardless of how unorthodox its membership and approaches were when compared to similar units.

The creation and distribution of *Thawrat al-Arab* challenges traditional views of the Arab Bureau as amateurish or ineffective. Rather, it reveals an organisation pioneering what we would now call information operations, in the process exemplifying several key innovations in how it approached intelligence and influence operations. Unlike other intelligence units of the period, the Arab Bureau recognised that effective propaganda required deep cultural understanding and authentic local voices. Rather than simply translating British materials into Arabic or imposing Western narrative frameworks, it enabled Arab intellectuals to craft messages that would resonate with Arab audiences.[56]

This was perhaps the most original of all the Arab Bureau's approaches, its readiness to allow Arab collaborators significant autonomy in crafting the message. While *Thawrat al-Arab* served British strategic interests by promoting the Arab Revolt, it also contained nationalist arguments that went well beyond what British authorities would ultimately support. This tolerance, or perhaps even embrace, of ambiguity, letting Arab voices speak authentically even when they didn't perfectly align with British aims, shows remarkable understanding of how to build influence in complex cultural environments. These were the sorts of approaches that wouldn't become mainstream in intelligence work until decades later.

The Bureau's collaboration with Daghir, and Nimr's publishing house, represented a refined understanding of the local intellectual landscape. Both men were known figures in Arab nationalist circles, with established reputations and networks. Daghir's position at *al-Muqattam*, and Nimr's ownership, gave them credibility that no British-produced propaganda could match. The Arab Bureau's willingness to work through these intermediaries, rather than trying to control every aspect of the message, shows remarkable flexibility for a military intelligence unit.

As we have explored, this approach extended beyond the book's publishing, encompassing the distribution network and utilising existing Arab cultural and commercial connections. By sending copies to key locations like Basra, Jeddah, Mecca, Khartoum, and Tangier, the Arab Bureau tapped into established patterns of how information and ideas spread through the Arab world. The timing of the book's release also showed strategic thinking, appearing just six months after the start of the Arab Revolt, when potential supporters would be weighing whether or not to join Hussein's cause.

The text itself demonstrates a clear understanding of how to layer different types of appeals, with historical arguments providing intellectual justification for Arab independence while the inclusion of contemporary accounts of Ottoman persecution helped to create emotional resonance. Its treatment of religious themes shows particular sophistication, with Daghir presenting Ottoman actions as offences not just against Arab nationalism but against Islam itself. The author is thus able to utilise religious themes to legitimise the Arab Revolt. Daghir's accusations that the CUP was working to 'eliminate Islam' might seem exaggerated to modern—and perhaps also to contemporary—readers, but they demonstrated a keen understanding of how to frame political messages for maximum impact in Arab society. Poetry and the last words of the hanged nationalist sympathisers add another layer of cultural authenticity to this propaganda masterpiece, a multi-layered approach that shows the Arab Bureau's clear grasp of how to craft messages that operated at multiple levels in Arab society.

Perhaps most remarkably, in the final judgement, this propaganda effort emerged from an intelligence unit that so often faced criticism from other British military and diplomatic services. Even while enduring the barbs of its ostensible allies, the Arab Bureau's willingness to invest significant resources in bringing to life such long-form propaganda, produced through genuine collaboration with local allies, marks it as an innovator in intelligence practice.

Often dismissed as amateurs by its contemporaries and some historians, the Arab Bureau's work with *Thawrat al-Arab* reveals it as a pioneer of what we would now call information operations, understanding that effective influence required working through authentic local voices, that propaganda needed cultural resonance to be effective, and that a degree of ambiguity in messaging could be strategically useful. This reassessment of the Arab Bureau's capabilities is fully supported by examining the broader context of its Arabic propaganda efforts. *Thawrat al-Arab* was the longest but not, as we have seen, the only demonstration of the Bureau's ability or willingness to work with Arab intellectuals and opinion leaders.[57]

Thawrat al-Arab stands as evidence of a more complex relationship between British intelligence and Arab intellectuals than previously acknowledged, one where collaboration served both imperial and nationalist aims, however temporarily. Rather than simply imposing British narratives translated into Arabic, the Arab Bureau enabled local voices to speak to local audiences, even when their message didn't perfectly align with British interests.[58]

The rediscovery and analysis of *Thawrat al-Arab* thus contributes to a necessary reassessment of early intelligence organisations. Its translation into English also allows it to be appreciated by a much wider audience than it has had since its creation in the imperial capital that was Cairo, more than a century ago in the midst of the First World War. The very existence of *Thawrat al-Arab* makes it abundantly clear that some of these units were far more advanced in terms of understanding cultural dynamics and influence operations than previously understood. In the case of the Arab Bureau, some were demonstrating capabilities that wouldn't become standard practice in intelligence work until well after the Second World War. This savvy handling of complicated intelligence in a complex and alien cultural environment marks the Bureau as pioneers in intelligence practice, worthy of renewed scholarly attention and respect.[59]

Thawrat al-Arab demonstrated the Arab Bureau's unique ability to work through authentic local voices, creating propaganda that resonated deeply with Arab cultural and intellectual traditions. This method went far beyond conventional propaganda efforts, revealing an organisation that understood propaganda not merely as persuasion but as a form of cultural dialogue. Yet *Thawrat al-Arab* was only one element of a much broader, multi-layered information strategy. To fully appreciate the Arab Bureau's revolutionary approach to propaganda, we must examine their diverse array of newspapers, visual materials, and targeted publications that together created a comprehensive information ecosystem spanning the Middle East.

Why Thawrat al-Arab *Remained Hidden*

The rediscovery of *Thawrat al-Arab* after decades of scholarly neglect raises an important methodological question: How did an 85,000-word propaganda masterpiece remain invisible to historians for over a century? This oversight reflects systematic barriers that have shaped our understanding of the Arab Bureau's capabilities.

The explanation lies in the intersection of linguistic constraints and disciplinary boundaries. Most historians of British intelligence lacked the Arabic skills necessary to engage with these sources directly, while the work's anonymity provided no obvious connection to British operations. Even when catalogued in major libraries, *Thawrat al-Arab* had the appearance of simply another wartime publication rather than a sophisticated intelligence collaboration.

More fundamentally, disciplinary silos reinforced this blindness. Intelligence historians focused on institutional records in British archives, while scholars of Arab nationalism examined indigenous intellectual movements without considering their interaction with British operations. *Thawrat al-Arab* fell between these domains: too embedded in British strategy for Arab intellectual historians, too culturally specific for Intelligence Studies.

The sparse British archival record compounded this problem. Unlike the extensively documented *Arab Bulletin*, British references to *Thawrat al-Arab* consist primarily of brief distribution notes, providing insufficient context for researchers to recognise its significance. This archival silence meant that even when scholars encountered the text, they lacked the framework to understand its intelligence origins or strategic importance.

This scholarly oversight has had profound implications for our understanding of early intelligence organisations and their capabilities, revealing how methodological limitations can obscure entire dimensions of historical experience. Yet, as the next chapter reveals, *Thawrat al-Arab* represents only the most substantial example of the Arab Bureau's Arabic propaganda efforts, the flagship of a vast fleet that included newspapers, stamps, postcards, maps, and targeted pamphlets. This 'paper war' created an unprecedented information ecosystem, constituting the first modern information warfare campaign of its kind in the Middle East.

10

THE PAPER WAR

LONDON–CAIRO–MECCA

In which the Arab Bureau's propaganda efforts are revealed to be more complex than even the pages of Thawrat al-Arab *might suggest, showing us a multi-layered information strategy which went far beyond simple messaging, utilising newspapers, stamps, postcards, and specially targeted pamphlets to engage diverse audiences across multiple cultural contexts. This chapter demonstrates how the Arab Bureau developed a wealth of fascinating and original materials, employing a range of cross-cultural communication techniques that anticipated later information operations and, in the process, showing an unprecedented ability to work through local voices and existing communication networks.*

Newspapers

If *Thawrat al-Arab* revealed the Arab Bureau's sophisticated approach to long-form propaganda, their broader information strategy demonstrated an even more remarkable understanding of how information circulated in Arab society. From Cairo to Mecca, from London to the remote corners of Ottoman domains, the Arab Bureau orchestrated a complex network of newspapers, visual materials, and targeted publications that together constituted what might be called the first modern information warfare campaign in the Middle East. This 'paper war' extended far beyond simple messaging, creating a multi-layered ecosystem of information that could simultaneously serve multiple strategic and intelligence objectives.

On an unremarkable Cairo morning in late 1916, a group of local merchants gathered at their usual spot near al-Azhar Mosque. As they drank tea and exchanged pleasantries, they also passed around the latest issues of various newspapers. Among these was *al-Qibla*, ostensibly the official publication of Sharif Hussein's nascent government in Mecca. What these merchants didn't know was that the paper they were discussing represented just one piece of an intricate propaganda network, carefully orchestrated by a small group of British intelligence officers working from a hotel just a few miles away.[1]

As was made clear from looking at the example of *Thawrat al-Arab*, the Arab Bureau's propaganda campaign represented one of the most remarkable information operations of its time, and from any theatre of the First World War. From its office in the Savoy, the Bureau orchestrated a complex network of newspapers, pamphlets, and other publications that reached across the Arab world and beyond. Its approach went far beyond simple propaganda, in the process demonstrating a remarkable degree of cultural sensitivity and understanding, as well as a range of new approaches in how it engaged with Arab audiences.

At the heart of the Arab Bureau's propaganda operations were three Arabic-language newspapers, each serving a distinct purpose and audience. *Al-Haqiqa*[2] (*The Truth*) represented perhaps the most direct form of British-backed propaganda. Produced in London but, after 1916, increasingly influenced by the Arab Bureau, it relied heavily on impressive production values, such as being printed in photogravure, in two colours, and in a broadsheet format, which is to say double the size of other illustrated papers of the time. Its very materiality conveyed British power and resources.[3]

Al-Qibla (*The Direction*), referring to the Muslim direction of prayer, i.e. towards the city of Mecca, took a more subtle approach. Published in Mecca, and occasionally in Jeddah, it maintained a convincing appearance of full independence while actually being entirely dependent on British support, which it received through the Arab Bureau's Jeddah office.

The third paper, *al-Kawkab* (*The Star*), produced in Cairo from November 1916, represented a middle ground between the openly pro-British *al-Haqiqa*[4] and the ostensibly independent *al-Qibla*. Its mission was to convince Arab readers that Britain and its allies were fighting to defend Islam and promote Arab freedom, while maintaining enough editorial distance to remain credible to sceptical urban readers.[5]

The content of these newspapers reveals a great deal about how the Arab Bureau understood and engaged with their audiences, *al-Qibla*'s pages arguably demonstrating the most nuanced and delicate editorial judgement. For example, a typical issue might lead with a scholarly discussion of Islamic law or theology, establishing its credentials as a serious religious publication. This might then be followed by some more straightforward items of news about the war, carefully curated to support Arab nationalist objectives without appearing overtly pro-British. This careful sequencing allowed the paper to present political criticism as a natural extension of religious duty rather than mere opposition politics. Its content strategically mixed scholarly arguments supporting Arab nationalism with traditional religious discussions alongside extracts from classical Arabic literary works, maintaining credibility with both traditional religious audiences and modernist nationalists.

Al-Qibla also regularly published articles about different Muslim-Arab contributions to Islamic civilisation and world culture, effectively linking current Arab nationalist aspirations to a reimagined, if at least partially idealised, glorious past. As an example of the paper's apparently even-handed approach, we can examine how it handled criticism of the Ottoman leadership, the CUP. Rather than attacking them purely on political grounds, *al-Qibla*'s editorial line tended instead to focus on the CUP's alleged religious transgressions. For example, it ran articles detailing Ottoman plans to translate the Quran into Turkish (which was not the common practice it is today), or discussing a proposal to replace the names of the Rightly Guided Caliphs—the first four successors to Muhammad—in the mosques of Constantinople, framing such threatened Ottoman actions as threats to Islamic tradition as a whole rather than mere political oppression. Such an astute, not to say wily, approach allowed the paper to advance anti-Ottoman messages while maintaining its religious credibility.

Al-Qibla's coverage of Arab contributions to Islamic civilisation was perhaps a very obvious means of building nationalist sentiment through historical narrative, but for all its blatancy also one likely to work. Regularly publishing detailed articles about Arab scholars, scientists, and philosophers who had shaped Islamic civilisation, *al-Qibla* carefully balanced religious and cultural pride, presenting historical achievements as evidence of Arab capacity for independent governance. Such an approach proved particularly effective because it grounded contemporary political aspirations in historical precedent, making Arab independence seem like a return to the natural order rather than a revolutionary change.

THE ARAB BUREAU

In the eyes of at least one American contemporary observer, *al-Qibla* exhibited an intelligent editorial strategy that balanced multiple audiences simultaneously, addressing both "the free Bedouin of the desert, and the cultured university student of the town".[6]

Al-Kawkab took a different approach, focusing more directly on political discourse or specific political issues while maintaining a carefully calibrated distance from obvious British influence. In the process, it demonstrated a particularly noteworthy approach: advancing British strategic interests while maintaining Arab nationalist credibility. The pages of *al-Kawkab* regularly exposed Turkish oppression of Arabs in Syria as well as Turkey's pan-Turanian ambitions.[7] The paper's writers, mostly Arabs themselves, crafted arguments that aligned British strategic interests with Arab nationalist sentiments without appearing to do so explicitly.

In doing so, *al-Kawkab* often drew upon the intellectual foundations laid by earlier Arab thinkers like 'Abd al-Rahman al-Kawakibi,[8] whose critiques of Ottoman despotism had helped shape the emerging discourse of Arab nationalism. Al-Kawakibi's work on the nature of tyranny provided a ready intellectual framework that *al-Kawkab*'s writers could adapt to wartime circumstances, making their criticism of Ottoman rule seem part of a natural intellectual progression rather than merely wartime propaganda.

When covering Turkish actions in Syria, the paper would pair reports of specific Ottoman actions with carefully chosen historical examples of Arab governance, implicitly contrasting current oppression with past glory. Coverage of pan-Turanian ambitions was especially clever, using Ottoman sources and statements to demonstrate how Turkish nationalism threatened all Arab peoples, regardless of their political views. The paper consistently framed the conflict not as Britain versus Turkey, but as Arab aspirations against Turkish dominance.

By way of yet another contrasting approach, *al-Haqiqa*'s content strategy relied heavily on visual impact, particularly the employment of photographs that demonstrated British military and industrial might. Images of artillery pieces, munitions factories, and battleships were "calculated to impress the Oriental and African mind", as Edward Long, the paper's sometime shadow, or hidden, editor, rather condescendingly put it.[9] Yet contemporary reports suggest this approach proved effective with its target audience. Not only that, but the paper's physical quality alone spoke to British power, using as it did expensive photogravure printing techniques and publishing in a large, broadsheet format conveying abundance and strength through its very materiality.

The photographic content of *al-Haqiqa* clearly demonstrates a shrewd understanding of the means and usefulness of conveying messages of power through imagery. Beyond military hardware, the paper featured carefully composed photographs showing British technological advancement, such as modern factories populated with Arab workers, new railway lines stretching across desert landscapes, and telegraph offices connecting remote regions. These images conveyed not just military might but the promise of modernisation, in other words a bright and exciting future. Particularly effective were photos showing Muslim soldiers in British uniforms being awarded medals, or engaged in prayer, visual evidence that service with Britain was compatible with Islamic practice.

Each publication employed different linguistic registers appropriate to its audience. For example, *al-Qibla* often used classical Arabic in its religious discussions while adopting a more modern journalistic style for news coverage, while *al-Kawkab* maintained a consistently cultured tone aimed at educated urban readers, whereas *al-Haqiqa* typically used much simpler language alongside its impressive visuals. This careful calibration of language and content is just one further demonstration of the Arab Bureau's understanding of how to reach different segments of Arab society.

In each case, whenever it was deemed appropriate to use it, Islamic religious terminology received especially careful handling. When discussing the Arab Revolt, publications needed to employ religious language that would resonate with traditional believers while advancing nationalist goals. Sharif Hussein's proclamations are perhaps the most obvious example of this careful balancing act, in which he uses classical religious formulae and Quranic references while at the same time introducing modern political concepts. This linguistic sophistication helped maintain credibility with both traditional religious audiences and modernist nationalists.

As well as the production side of the newspaper business, Arab Bureau distribution networks for these publications likewise showed a remarkable degree of cleverness in their use of existing commercial channels, thereby revealing another layer of intricacy to the Arab Bureau's overall strategic approach to propaganda operations in the region. Rather than relying solely on official channels, the Bureau developed complex distribution mechanisms that utilised existing commercial infrastructure. When concerns arose that free distribution was undermining the publications' credibility,[10] based on the belief that readers distrusted anything given away for free,[11] the Arab Bureau adapted by developing commercial distribution channels. The Cairo book trade, centred around the al-Azhar Mosque complex, proved particularly important, with booksellers often bundling Arab Bureau-supported publications with other popular materials, creating natural distribution patterns that entirely hid their propaganda nature. Such an approach allowed materials to reach audiences through familiar and trusted channels, thereby maintaining their appearance of independence and avoiding any possible taint of these articles being from, or associated with, official British sources.

Sometimes, unexpected opportunities emerged. For instance, when copies of *al-Haqiqa* were being purchased in Afghanistan as wrapping paper, this being cheaper than actual wastepaper, initial concerns gave way to recognition of a valuable opportunity. The papers were still being read as they moved through commercial networks, reaching remote areas while incurring none of the suspicion that might be attached to official distribution channels. Such lucky breaks, alongside attention paid to traditional patterns of information exchange, through the use of existing networks of bookshops and newspaper vendors around major mosques, allowed Arab Bureau-backed propaganda to hide in plain sight while circulating alongside religious and literary texts. All of these tactics proved especially effective in maintaining the credibility of their materials.[12]

Stamps

Arab Bureau paper-based propaganda efforts were by no means limited to newspapers. In addition to doing its best to harness the power of the press, the Bureau produced a range of other materials, perhaps none more inventive than a set of Hijaz postage stamps. Issued in September 1916, these stamps represented one of the Arab Bureau's most elaborate, ornate, not to say visually attractive propaganda efforts. Brilliantly conceived as a direct response to enemy denials of the Arab Revolt's existence—which is to say German telegrams saying that no such revolt had broken out—the plan was outlined by Ronald Storrs with characteristic waggishness, when he stated that "the best proof that it had taken place would be provided by an issue of Hijaz postage stamps, which would carry the Arab propaganda, self-paying and incontrovertible, to the four corners of the earth".[13]

The project's execution demonstrated remarkable cultural sensitivity and attention to detail. Storrs and Lawrence spent days at Cairo's Arab Museum studying Islamic decorative arts and, as Storrs later wrote in his memoir, *Orientations*, "collecting suitable motifs in order that the design in wording, spirit and ornament, might be as far as possible representative and reminiscent of a purely Arab source of inspiration".[14] One of their first conscious editorial decisions was to avoid pictorial elements and European lettering, as these were foreign to Arab artistic traditions and thus likely to arouse suspicion in the eyes of Arabs who encountered them. Instead, they incorporated authentic Islamic design elements from prayer niches, mosque doors, and Quranic manuscripts.

The stamps came in various denominations, each featuring a distinct Islamic geometric pattern and Arabic calligraphy. The one-piastre stamp, for example, displayed an eight-pointed star pattern common in mosque decoration, while more valuable denominations incorporated increasingly complex arabesque designs. The Arabic text was rendered in classical *thuluth* script, a calligraphic style traditionally used for mosque inscriptions and Quranic texts, which thus lent an element of religious gravitas to what was essentially a civil administrative tool. This careful integration of authentic Islamic design elements made the stamps effective not just as propaganda but as symbols of Arab political identity.

The actual design work was entrusted to two talented Cairo artists, Agami Effendi Ali and Mustafa Effendi Gozlan,[15] who created intricate arabesque patterns that captured the essence of Islamic decorative arts. The technical production was equally impressive, and was handled by the Survey of Egypt's printing department in Giza, just a couple of miles from the Arab Bureau's downtown Cairo headquarters. The stamps were produced using three-color reproduction techniques, advanced for the time, with the high production quality undoubtedly conveying a message about the resources and capabilities of the Arab cause, not to mention those backing it.

An ingenious idea, the stamps served multiple propaganda purposes simultaneously, starting with, as Storrs noted at the very start of the project, their very existence clearly and unarguably proclaiming the reality of Arab independence from Ottoman rule. In terms of their purely physical aspect, the beautiful designs and high production quality demonstrated not only the resources available to the Arab cause, but also, albeit hidden in plain sight, the care and attention the Arab Bureau was willing to invest in its propaganda efforts. The stamps' artistic elements showcased Arab cultural sophistication while their efficient postal service usage proved administrative competence. Perhaps most importantly, every letter carrying these stamps spread the message of Arab independence far beyond the reach of newspapers or leaflets.

While many stamps entered normal postal circulation, special presentation sets were prepared for influential figures, including King George V. The propaganda value of these stamps became immediately apparent as German and Ottoman authorities scrambled to deny their legitimacy, attempting to discredit the stamps by claiming they were merely British forgeries—which in a real sense they were—but these accusations only served to generate more publicity and interest. The impact the stamps made in the world of philately was equally swift. By November 1918, even before the war's end, dealers were already advertising to purchase used examples.[16] This unexpected development provided another avenue for spreading awareness of the Arab cause, as stamp collectors and dealers began writing articles about the new issues in their specialist publications. Such rapid appreciation among collectors served as further proof of the stamps' effectiveness as propaganda with global reach.

The success of the Hijaz stamps is an especially lively validation of the Arab Bureau's overall urbanity, wherein it was able to turn even a small, seemingly mundane administrative item to its purposes and see a set of stamps serving as a powerful propaganda tool. By paying careful attention to cultural authenticity in design while ensuring modern efficiency and quality in terms of production and distribution, the Arab Bureau created something that was simultaneously practical and powerfully symbolic. The stamps represented a perfect fusion of traditional Islamic artistic elements with modern administrative efficiency, effectively communicating the Arab Bureau's broader message about the compatibility of Arab independence with modern governance.

Map and Postcards

Two other remarkable, visually driven parts of the Arab Bureau's propaganda efforts took strikingly different approaches to demonstrating

British power. These took the form of a world map designed to showcase Allied dominance and a carefully crafted postcard featuring the British Union Flag, complemented with Arabic text. Both items, produced in collaboration with Wellington House in London, reveal much about how the Arab Bureau thought about visual propaganda for Arab audiences.

The world map was created in October 1916 and was referred to in Arab Bureau and other British Government correspondence as a "Map of the World with letterpress in Arabic". It presents, as perhaps only a map can, an immediate visual representation of British and Allied power, where more than two-thirds of the globe is coloured blue—representing Britain, the British Empire, and its wartime allies—as opposed to all enemy territories, which appear in yellow. The map's large size—roughly 85 x 60 centimetres, or 33 x 23 inches (paper size A1)—and production quality were themselves statements of power, as was the case with the stamps and *al-Haqiqa*, printed on high-quality paper using expensive colour processes at a time when most Arabic publications were black and white. The very simplicity of this visual message, which is to say the overwhelming dominance of Allied blue against diminishingly small patches of enemy yellow, was clearly meant to convey a stark and unmistakable message about the inevitability of Allied victory.

However, this apparently straightforward propaganda piece sparked a fascinating debate about its effectiveness among British officials. In Wellington House, T.C. Macnaghten offered a particularly waspish critique in one memo, writing, "With regard to the Arabic copy, I can only say that the obvious suggestion to my mind is that if all these vast countries coloured in blue cannot polish off the tiny little lot coloured yellow, they cannot be a very efficient crowd."[17] This observation highlighted a key challenge in visual propaganda, i.e. it runs the risk of images conveying unintended messages to different audiences. Despite such reservations, the Arab Bureau pushed forward with distribution across the Middle and Far East, with colonial officials from a large number of diverse territories participating in its dissemination even while some continued to express a degree of reluctance around the utility of such a tactic.

These debates around the map's effectiveness reveal something important about the Arab Bureau's approach to propaganda, which is to say they were willing to experiment with different visual approaches, even when faced with internal scepticism. Notably, they were keen in particular to target areas where Ottoman influence was strongest in an attempt to use the map to counter Turkish claims about the war's progress.

The Arabic text accompanying the map employed careful rhetorical strategies, whereby it consistently refers to Allied regions in terms that suggest permanence and legitimacy, while enemy territories were described using language implying temporary occupation. This linguistic framing complemented the visual message about the war's likely outcome. The Arab Bureau's distribution strategy showed a genuine understanding of how this visual propaganda might work differently across contexts. While the map's message might seem heavy-handed to more educated, urban audiences, the Bureau recognised that it could prove effective in areas where literacy was lower and visual impact more important.[18]

The Union Flag postcard represents a possibly even more interesting case of visual propaganda, combining one of the most dominant symbols of any nation, in this case also carrying the undeniable stamp of British authority and power, alongside a few words of carefully crafted Arabic.[19] As with the other propaganda materials already discussed, the postcard's material qualities were again of the highest standard, printed as it was on high-quality stock using vibrant colours that accurately reproduced the flag's familiar design, at a stroke conveying power, both in terms of arms and the visual symbol of Britain and its empire. Coming into first-hand contact with one of the postcards a little over a century since its creation, in the National Archives, in Kew, one will notice how it remains in remarkably fine condition.

Again, as with other all the examples of Arabic language propaganda we've been exploring, the postcard's design required a delicate balance to get across the desired message without being heavy-handed, presenting British power in such a way that it would appeal to Arab audiences without appearing domineering. This was arguably successfully achieved through the careful combination of visual elements and text, emphasising partnership rather than imperial might. The language treads carefully, trying to avoid any hint of colonial dominance, emphasising instead themes of partnership and mutual benefit. The title reads simply "The Flag of the State of Britain", or, more straightforwardly, "The British Flag".[20] Such an approach is another reflection of the Arab Bureau's understanding that effective propaganda needed to align with Arab political aspirations, rather than simply assert British power. The text, which is no doubt a little too flowery for some tastes, reads:

Oh! the flag of justice flutters over the necks [heads] of the heroes of England, their souls are insignificant to them. May the Lord of the Throne [God] have mercy on them bless them, as the first pain is prolonged for them. They do not seek death in battle, not to deter them from their majesty in majesty. May God have mercy, as it is able, to save them from torment.

As was also the case with the Arab Bureau-issued stamps, the text was rendered in *thuluth*, a centuries-old script that is closely, but not exclusively, associated with religious documents, thereby lending the item a degree of elegance and respectability that reflected Arab aesthetic traditions while also striking a delicate balance between asserting British military capability and expressing support for Arab political goals. Even the layout itself might be seen as offering a balance between Western and Arab design principles, where the flag is prominent but does not overwhelm the Arabic text.

In marked contrast to the newspapers, which were of course purporting to be independent Arab productions, the postcard and map at least had the advantage, if one chooses to see it in that light, of obviously having been created by the British. In this way the originators of these items didn't have to worry about their subterfuge being either detected or revealed.

What makes both of these items, the map of the world and the Union Flag postcard, particularly significant is how they demonstrate the Arab Bureau's willingness to experiment with different approaches to visual propaganda. While the map represents a more direct assertion of power through visual means, the postcard shows a more nuanced approach that combined visual impact with careful cultural consideration. The contrasting reception of these two items reveals much about the challenges of visual propaganda in cross-cultural contexts. While the map generated internal debate about its effectiveness, contemporary reports suggest the postcard achieved wider circulation and more positive reception. This difference might be attributed to the postcard's attempt to balance visual impact and cultural sensitivity. Although the archives did not reveal figures, the fact that the postcard was smaller and more portable presumably meant it was printed in far greater numbers than the map.

British diplomatic archives preserve detailed accounts of how these items were received in different regions. For instance, a series of memos from Mesopotamia-based military intelligence officers noted varying responses to the map. One officer in Baghdad reported, "The more educated view it with scepticism, but among the general population, the visual impact of Allied dominance proves compelling." From Basra came observations that while educated Arabs often dismissed the map as obvious propaganda, in the marketplace "groups gather to discuss it, with the vast blue expanse of Allied territory creating considerable impression".

The postcard generated even more extensive commentary in official correspondence from the period. One British contact in Damascus wrote, "The postcard circulates freely through commercial channels, carrying its message without the obvious taint of propaganda. Local merchants particularly appreciate its quality, seeing it as a sign of British commitment to the region." From Cairo came reports that copies were being collected and displayed in shops and cafes, with one intelligence officer noting favourably, "The combination of British power and Arabic script proves particularly effective—it suggests partnership rather than dominance."[21]

Additional insight comes from captured German intelligence reports, which expressed frustration at the items' impact, with reports noting that such popular productions, particularly the postcard, speaking as they did in a visual vernacular immediately accessible to the people, were difficult to counter. In the process, these items projected British power in the region in ways that were clearly sparking the enemy's notice, forcing from them a reaction of some jealous regard. Another German officer in Constantinople warned that the map, despite its simplicity, was encouraging defeatist attitudes among those who see the overwhelming blue expanse as proof of Allied victory.

The variety of the visual propaganda efforts used by the Arab Bureau, and its obvious understanding that different approaches work better with some audiences over others, shows not only that the Bureau was willing to try out a variety of schemes, but also that there was in place the institutional framework that meant such ideas were both welcomed and acted upon. While the map might be said to represent a more traditional approach to propaganda—simple, direct, and focused on power—the postcard shows perhaps a more enhanced, or subtler, understanding of how to combine visual impact with cultural sensitivity. Whatever interpretation we choose to place on these objects at this remove in time, they clearly reveal an organisation and a bureaucracy that was willing to experiment with different propaganda methods, while learning from experience about what proved most effective in reaching Arab audiences.

The Moshi Pamphlet: German East Africa

Yet another item of remarkable propaganda from the offices of the Arab Bureau was a truly original piece of work that became known in the archives simply as the Moshi Pamphlet.[22] Created entirely in response to a seized German memorandum produced for their officials in East Africa, the Moshi Pamphlet displays both reach and acuity, and also perhaps a growing closeness of different branches of British intelligence in the period after the creation of the Arab Bureau, which was after all central to their remit.

The original German memorandum, known to the Arab Bureau as the Moshi Document, is an important piece of evidence revealing German colonial attitudes towards Islam in East Africa in the immediate pre-war period.[23] The Moshi Document was a circular issued on 13 October 1913 by German Imperial Governor Heinrich Schnee, addressed to district offices, military stations, and the Residentur Urundi, now Burundi, in then German East Africa. The contents of the document represent a significant shift in German colonial policy towards Islam. The document outlines a strategy to counteract Islamic influence in the colony, asking officials to report on possible measures to prevent Islamic propagation by government employees, particularly teachers, with initial suggestions including the possibility of banning Muslim teachers from performing circumcisions, or from serving as prayer leaders in mosques.

The document was discovered by British forces when they captured Moshi in 1916. It was then passed on to the Arab Bureau to make of it such propaganda as it was able, in order to shine a light on German hypocrisy in their claiming to be allied with Muslims, fighting on the same side as the Ottoman Empire. The British response was a propaganda poster intended for Chinese Muslim audiences that featured a facsimile of the original German document, along with photos of Fort Moshi and a portrait of Governor Schnee, in an effort to expose Germany's anti-Islamic policies. This poster was just one part of British efforts to undermine German–Ottoman alliance messaging among Muslim populations in various colonial territories, but the only one that displays close Arab Bureau involvement.

THE ARAB BUREAU

With the Moshi Document in their possession, Arab Bureau staff in Cairo had valuable evidence of German hypocrisy: while publicly courting Muslims elsewhere, this internal memo revealed Berlin's attitude of contempt towards its own Muslim subjects in East Africa. The Arab Bureau's response would demonstrate just how far it was willing to push the boundaries of conventional propaganda operations. Additionally, the very existence of such a specifically targeted piece of propaganda shows just what a refined and wide-reaching understanding of the war's global dimensions this newly established intelligence unit possessed. As such, the Moshi Pamphlet represents a truly creative response to German activities thousands of miles from the Arab Bureau's usual sphere of operations, and the project demonstrates not just the Bureau's willingness to adapt its methods for audiences beyond the Arab world, but the ability and a keenness to do so.

Internal Arab Bureau discussions about the pamphlet's creation reveal an educated and urbane understanding of the target audience, which was presumably informed to some extent by connections with colleagues in other branches of the Foreign Office, specialists in the cultural and political dynamics of German East Africa and its Chinese Muslim population. Arab Bureau officers and colleagues debated not just translation issues but deeper questions of cultural resonance. Recognising that Chinese Muslims inhabited a unique cultural space, maintaining Islamic religious identity within a broader Chinese cultural context, meant moving cautiously, giving careful consideration about how best to present religious arguments in culturally appropriate ways. What the Arab Bureau was chasing was to speak to their target audience as both Muslims and Chinese, understanding that these identities were intertwined in ways different from Arab Muslims, and indeed that East Asian forms of Islam were distinct from Arab forms of Islam.

The pamphlet's content reveals masterful cultural adaptation. It opens with the traditional Islamic greeting, "*Bismillah al-Rahman al-Raheem*", or "In the name of God, Most Gracious, Most Merciful",[24] which for the Moshi Pamphlet was rendered in both Arabic and Chinese characters, immediately establishing its dual cultural identity. The text then presents carefully constructed arguments about Germany's treatment of Muslims, citing specific examples that would resonate with its target audience: "Let it be known to our Chinese Muslim brothers," one passage declares, "that while the British Empire has built mosques in Hong

Kong and Singapore, the Germans in East Africa have converted our places of worship into storage houses for pork meat."[25] Whether or not this is true is less important, for the purposes of anti-German propaganda, than the circulation of the story itself.[26]

Skilfully drawing on Chinese cultural concepts to explain Islamic principles, the Moshi Pamphlet also draws on Confucian ideas about righteous governance in order to compare the relationship between the Caliph and Muslim communities to traditional Chinese concepts of imperial authority. As one section puts it, "Just as the Son of Heaven must protect all under heaven, so must the true Caliph protect the faithful. Ask yourselves: who truly protects Muslim rights? The British who allow free worship, or the Germans who mock our traditions?"

The linguistic features of the pamphlet merit special attention, with intelligence officials discussing appropriate terminology and debating how to express Islamic concepts in Chinese while also maintaining their theological accuracy, in the process consulting with Chinese Muslim scholars to ensure the religious terminology would resonate with the target audience and remain doctrinally sound. The resulting text employed an erudite mix of traditional Chinese Islamic terms and more contemporary political language.

Distribution replicated methods of circulating other propaganda materials discussed previously. Rather than solely using British military channels to distribute the pamphlet, the Arab Bureau worked through existing networks of Muslim merchants who travelled the trade routes that connected East Africa with the Indian Ocean rim and south-east Asia. These Muslim merchants, used to moving between different Muslim communities for business, provided natural and credible channels for the pamphlet's circulation, carrying copies along with their regular goods and distributing them through existing social and commercial networks. British consular reports note the pamphlet appearing in ports from Zanzibar to Singapore, spreading through communities connected by trade and religious ties.[27]

The pamphlet's most powerful sections detail specific German transgressions against Islamic practice, describing as it does incidents—whether invented or otherwise, it has not been possible to establish—of German officers forcing Muslim soldiers to handle pork during food preparation, in clear violation of Islamic dietary laws. By contrast, the Moshi Pamphlet posits, "In the British army Muslim soldiers receive halal food and time for their five daily prayers. In the German army, our brothers must choose between their duty to Allah and their military service." These concrete examples of storytelling presented in culturally relevant terms, whether true or false, proved particularly effective.

Scoring an own goal, German responses to the Moshi Pamphlet inadvertently confirmed its impact. Captured German documents reveal increasingly frustrated attempts to counter the pamphlet's influence. It was obvious that British propaganda was at least at an advantage due to its manipulation of concepts of loyalty and religious duty for this Chinese-speaking audience, which also made any possible German counter-arguments come off as strangely foreign and unconvincing. In addition to its content, the pamphlet's distribution through Muslim merchant networks made it nearly impossible for the enemy to intercept, and before long it was appearing in general circulation in markets, cafes, and mosques, and always seeming to arrive through natural channels.

The pamphlet's reach extended far beyond its intended audience, with British diplomatic reports from 1917 noting copies appearing in Chinese Muslim communities in Singapore, Malaysia, and even Indonesia. One British consul in Singapore wrote, "Local Muslim merchants speak of this document as proof that the British understand and respect their faith. They pass copies to their business contacts throughout the region, doing our work for us." This unexpected success in south-east Asia led to discussions within the Arab Bureau about producing similar materials specifically for that region, though the war's end prevented further development of this approach.

The Moshi Pamphlet had evolved from a targeted response to a specific threat into something more significant, namely a demonstration of how a particular item of propaganda could transcend traditional cultural and geographic boundaries. Its success showed how careful attention to cultural authenticity, combined with complex distribution networks, could create propaganda that spread naturally through existing social and commercial channels.

Cross-Cultural Communication Strategies

The Arab Bureau's approach to Arabic propaganda repeatedly shows an understanding of cross-cultural communication that went well beyond simple translation of messages. Its success lay in the recognition that effective propaganda required deep cultural understanding and careful adaptation of both content and delivery methods, so that all the Arab Bureau's propaganda efforts—from newspapers to stamps to pamphlets—demonstrated consistent attention to cultural authenticity while advancing strategic objectives. As Aldous Huxley once noted, "The propagandist is a man who canalises an already existing stream. In a land where there is no water, he digs in vain."[28]

Returning to what we saw in the case of the three main newspapers discussed above—*al-Haqiqa*, *al-Qibla*, and *al-Kawkab*—each demonstrated distinct strategies for reaching different Arab audiences while maintaining credibility and advancing British objectives.

The case of *al-Qibla* provides a prime example of this nuanced approach, so that rather than simply creating a pro-British newspaper in Arabic, the Arab Bureau developed a publication that authentically engaged with Arab intellectual and religious traditions. This dual approach manifested in its content strategy, where scholarly arguments supporting Arab nationalism appeared alongside traditional religious discussions. The paper's content strategy demonstrated remarkable sophistication in balancing multiple audiences and objectives. This required careful calibration of content and language, and this dual approach manifested in its mixture of content.

The Arab Bureau's handling of religious content likewise proved particularly thoughtful, whereby religious discussions employed classical Arabic and traditional Islamic references, while political news used more contemporary language. *Al-Qibla*'s handling of Ottoman criticism was particularly subtle. For instance, when criticising the CUP, rather than focusing on purely political matters, the newspaper delved into its alleged religious transgressions. Those articles which reported on Ottoman intentions, whether true or false, to translate the Quran into Turkish, as well as discussions about replacing the names of the Caliphs displayed in Constantinople's mosques, were successful in part because it was Ottoman government policy at that time to favour the Turkish language over Arabic. Framing Ottoman actions as threats to Islamic tradition, rather than a more straightforward charge of political oppression, was an approach that allowed the paper to advance anti-Ottoman messages while maintaining its religious credibility.

Al-Haqiqa took quite a different approach, relying heavily on visual impact, with Edward Long, one of those involved in the paper's editorial procedures, offering the reasoning: "the native of the countries with which we are concerned is generally unable to read, and often, he mistrusts both the person who is reading to him and that which is written. Pictures, however, awaken in his mind impressions which are not easily effaced." *Al-Kawkab*, meanwhile, represented a middle ground, aiming for sophisticated political discourse while maintaining credibility with urban readers. Produced in Cairo by Arabs for Arabs, it engaged in complex political arguments while avoiding the obvious British connection that might have undermined its effectiveness. Its "specially [sic] pro-Arab and anti-Turk"[29] policy focused particularly on exposing Turkish oppression of Arabs in Syria and Turkey's pan-Turanian ambitions.

The visual elements of these publications demonstrated careful attention to cultural authenticity, from *al-Qibla*'s classical *thuluth* masthead conveying religious authority combined with an overall layout that adopted contemporary journalistic conventions familiar to urban Arab readers. *Al-Haqiqa*'s European-influenced design was thought more appropriate to its overtly pro-British stance, while *al-Kawkab* adopted a hybrid approach combining traditional Arab publishing aesthetics with modern elements.

The Arab Bureau's understanding of these cultural sensitivities extended beyond newspapers to those more deliberately visual aspects of their propaganda outputs, such as the Hijaz postage stamps. The design of these demonstrated remarkable attention to Islamic artistic traditions. As Storrs noted, in designing the stamps the Bureau deliberately avoided pictorial elements that "never formed part of Arab decoration",[30] instead incorporating authentic motifs from prayer niches and mosque doors. This careful attention to cultural authenticity made the stamps effective not just as propaganda but as symbols of Arab political identity. In addition, the very material used to print these stamps conveyed messages about the wealth of resources supporting the Arab cause.

The Moshi Pamphlet represents perhaps the Arab Bureau's most refined example of cross-cultural communication. In creating propaganda for Chinese Muslims in East Africa, the Bureau didn't simply translate existing materials but developed content that specifically addressed the unique cultural position of its target audience. The pamphlet went so far as to employ Chinese cultural concepts to explain Islamic principles, drawing on Confucian ideas about righteous governance to frame arguments about religious authority, concurrently balancing Chinese and Islamic terminology to reach its unique audience.

Distribution strategies likewise showed enormous cultural awareness. When concerns arose that free distribution of publications was undermining credibility, due to the belief that the 'oriental mind' distrusted anything given away freely, the Arab Bureau adapted by developing commercial distribution channels. So it was that, rather than relying on official channels that might mark materials as propaganda, they nimbly altered course. Muslim merchants carried propaganda materials along with their regular goods, allowing distribution to occur through natural and credible channels. This approach demonstrated an understanding that the credibility of propaganda depends not just on content but on how it reaches its audience: materials were considered more plausible, and so carried more weight, when they moved through existing commercial networks, rather than being pushed via official channels.

The Arab Bureau's wider work with Arab intellectuals further demonstrates the depth of its understanding of local cultural dynamics, despite this understanding being harnessed to further British imperial and wartime goals. Rather than simply creating propaganda in isolation, the Bureau engaged with existing Arab intellectual discourse. It worked through respected figures like Rashid Rida, reprinting articles from his influential *al-Manar* magazine.[31] The Arab Bureau also drew upon the established cultural networks developed by earlier pioneer journalists like Jurji Zaydan[32] and Ya'qub Sarruf,[33] whose publications had helped shape modern Arabic literary and journalistic traditions. This engagement with established Arab voices provided credibility that purely British-created content could never achieve.

As noted above, the Arab Bureau's handling of religious and political sensitivities showed remarkable sophistication. When crafting messages about the Arab Revolt, they balanced Hussein's religious authority as Sharif of Mecca with emerging Arab nationalist aspirations. His proclamations needed to present him as simultaneously a religious leader and a nationalist figure, while avoiding any taint of being too closely associated with his British backers. The effectiveness of these strategies was manifested in multiple ways. For one thing, propaganda materials achieved higher credibility when they emerged from seemingly independent Arab sources. For another, Arab nationalist movements were provided with resources and platforms while maintaining their autonomy.

In addition, these strategies created a framework for intelligence gathering that went beyond simple information collection to include deeper understanding of Arab political thought and aspirations.

The effectiveness of these strategies can also be measured by examining contemporary responses, which loudly trumpeted the efficiency of the Arab Bureau's approach. For instance, typically sceptical Indian Muslim-orientated publications acknowledged the religious legitimacy of messages in *al-Qibla*, while German intelligence reports expressed frustration at their inability to counter propaganda that so effectively employed local cultural references. The spread of these materials through commercial networks also indicated their cultural resonance. However, and most significantly in this regard, the networks of Arab intellectuals and activists who engaged with these publications continued to influence regional politics long after the war ended.

Finally, what made the Arab Bureau's cross-cultural communication strategy particularly significant was how it departed from conventional colonial administrative approaches to propaganda. Rather than simply translating messages into different languages, by creating propaganda in Arabic the Bureau developed mechanisms for collaboration that not only worked within existing cultural frameworks, but which allowed both British and Arab strategic objectives to be advanced simultaneously. This understanding of cross-cultural communication represented a significant innovation in how intelligence services could operate in complex cultural environments.

Legacy for Modern Information Operations

While the broader legacy of the Arab Bureau's intelligence operations will be discussed in full in a later chapter, we will mention here in passing how their approach to Arabic-language propaganda operations offers useful lessons for modern information operations, particularly regarding effective engagement with diverse cultural audiences while maintaining credibility. To begin with, its recognition of authentic voices and credible distribution channels speaks directly to contemporary challenges, as does the principle of working through existing networks of influence as opposed to creating artificial channels or imposing external narratives. The realisation that propaganda carried more weight when distributed through commercial channels rather than given away freely also demonstrates an enduring principle surrounding the more general issue of the credibility of materials being produced and circulated.

The Arab Bureau's multi-layered approach, whereby they created and or worked through the pages of three distinct newspapers, each with its own character and apparent level of independence, is a clear and powerful demonstration of the value of multiple voices. Its approach to visual propaganda, particularly the Hijaz stamps and Union Flag postcard, demonstrates the importance of cultural adaptation, as does its clear-sighted and deliberate decision to use authentic Islamic design elements rather than European artistic styles, to enhance propaganda effectiveness. Conversely, the debate around its world map, which some officials feared might inadvertently suggest Allied inefficiency, highlights the importance of considering how visual messages might be interpreted differently by different audiences.

The fact that the Arab Bureau produced, and carefully calibrated, different Arabic registers for different audiences, integrated traditional literary and religious references, and adapted content for different readership levels speaks volumes. Rather than simply translating existing messages into Arabic, the Bureau developed content that worked within Arab cultural frameworks. What makes all these lessons particularly significant is how they display absolutely the importance of deep cultural understanding. The Arab Bureau's success came not from simply creating propaganda in Arabic, but through developing approaches that worked within existing cultural frameworks while advancing strategic objectives. The Arab Bureau's occasional missteps, such as the world map that generated internal debate, demonstrate the challenges of creating cross-cultural propaganda and the importance of understanding how messages might be received differently by dissimilar groups.

The legacy of these operations extended well beyond the war. The networks of journalists, intellectuals, and political activists who collaborated with the Arab Bureau continued to influence regional politics in the post-war period. Their pioneering approaches to cross-cultural communication and propaganda would reshape how Britain engaged with the Middle East for decades to come. As we will see in the next chapter, the Arab Bureau's impact transcended its short operational lifespan, establishing new paradigms for intelligence gathering, cultural diplomacy, and regional engagement that would resonate throughout the complex landscape of the modern Middle East. In many ways, the propaganda efforts described here were merely the most visible manifestation of a profound transformation in how imperial powers understood and interacted with the diverse cultural and political realities of the region.

The Arab Bureau's propaganda operations revealed an organisation that understood propaganda not merely as a tool of persuasion but as a complex system for engaging with foreign cultural and political environments. Its advanced approaches to cross-cultural communication anticipated methods that would not become standard practice in intelligence and information operations until decades later. This revolutionary reimagining of how intelligence units could engage with foreign audiences paralleled equally profound innovations in how intelligence itself was gathered, analysed, and applied. As the war in the Middle East reached its conclusion, the question became whether these innovations would endure beyond the immediate crisis that had spawned them.

PART V

IMPACT AND LEGACY

11

POST-WAR POSTMORTEM

MODERN MIDDLE EAST

In which we examine the Arab Bureau's legacy after its closure in 1920 and consider the various impacts on British victory and regional developments made by this radically original intelligence unit. This chapter also explores the Arab Bureau's long-term influences on intelligence practices and British Middle East policy, assessing both its successes and controversies. The end of the Arab Bureau can also be seen as the conclusion of a short-lived era of intelligence gathering that combined scholarly expertise with operational needs, raising questions about what lessons, if any, were learned from this unique experiment.

Opening: Closing

In the summer of 1920, the Arab Bureau's doors closed for the final time. The organisation that had played such a pivotal role in shaping British intelligence and policy in the Middle East during the First World War was unceremoniously shuttered. With the First World War long since finished, members of the Arab Bureau cleared their desks, before either being reassigned to other units or preparing to leave uniformed life, many of them no doubt reflecting on their activities of the past four years, both their personal journeys and the sometimes tumultuous trajectory of the Arab Bureau itself.

From its creation in early 1916, via operations across the span of the Arab Revolt, to this moment of post-war mothballing, the Arab Bureau had been a lightning rod for both praise and criticism. Its unorthodox methods and approach to intelligence gathering, more rooted in academia than martial traditions, had rankled traditional military minds while its deep cultural understanding of the region had provided invaluable insights to British policymakers.

Yet its legacy would prove far more complex and enduring than its brief institutional life might suggest. The Arab Bureau had fundamentally reimagined how intelligence could operate in culturally distinct environments, challenging traditional approaches to knowledge production and application. Understanding its post-war impact requires examining not just its immediate military contributions, but also its long-term influence on intelligence practices, regional politics, and cross-cultural engagement.

Long after the war, one of the Arab Bureau's fiercest critics, Arnold Talbot Wilson,[1] claimed that "The Arab Bureau in Cairo died unregretted in 1920, having helped to induce His Majesty's Government to adopt a policy which brought disaster to the people of Syria, disillusionment to the Arabs of Palestine and ruin to the Hijaz."[2] Wilson, a loyal member of the Indian Political Department, opposed any views supportive of Arab nationalism and maintained that British direct rule over Arabs was the only logical approach. Further, as Civil Commissioner in Baghdad (1918–20) in the immediate post-war period and fully supportive of the India Office perspective, his criticism is both predictable and grossly unfair. At the same time, his harsh assessment raises important questions about the Arab Bureau's impact and legacy that we will now consider.

Wilson's dismissive assessment of the Arab Bureau was not the only criticism it received. From an Arab perspective, George Antonius[3] in his influential *The Arab Awakening* (1938)[4] accused the Arab Bureau of fostering an "elaborate deception" that created false expectations among Arab nationalist movements. That said, and without wishing to be seen as an apologist for the Arab Bureau, one might posit that, even accepting this criticism as fair, this is surely just a part of the broader question of British imperial aims and the exigencies of war, however duplicitous these may be.

The Iraqi nationalist Sati al-Husri[5] similarly charged that the Arab Bureau's cultural engagement was ultimately "merely a more elegant form of imperial control". Even former Arab Bureau personnel acknowledged limitations. Gertrude Bell, writing to her father after the war, said the Bureau's approach had created an "impossible position of having encouraged Arab national sentiment and then denying its logical conclusion".[6] All such critiques highlight the fundamental contradiction at the heart of the Arab Bureau's work, which is to say, however insightful their understanding of Arab aspirations, ultimately it was all in the service of British imperial objectives that were designed to constrain—even refute—those very aspirations.

The closure of the Arab Bureau came as British priorities shifted in the post-war landscape. With the Ottoman Empire dismantled, new political realities were emerging across the Middle East, and London was now looking to consolidate its influence, at least in part, through more traditional diplomatic and administrative channels. The Arab Bureau's blend of academic expertise and intelligence gathering, once crucial for navigating the complexities of wartime Arabia, now seemed less essential to policymakers focused on establishing formal mandates and drawing new borders.

Comparing the Arab Bureau's legacy with other First World War intelligence units highlights its distinctive impact. For instance, while Wellington House's propaganda operation was much larger and better funded, its institutional legacy proved remarkably limited. Like the Arab Bureau, with the war over Wellington House was quickly disbanded, its techniques largely forgotten until the reestablishment of the Ministry of Information in 1939.[7] By way of contrast, many of the Arab Bureau's methods, though sometimes overlooked, continued to influence British engagement with the Middle East through both formal channels and individual practitioners. Similarly, the Naval Intelligence Division's approach to geographic intelligence produced valuable wartime handbooks but failed to establish enduring methodological innovations. The Arab Bureau's distinctive contribution lay in its integration of cultural understanding with intelligence requirements, creating not just information products but a new framework for regional engagement that transcended the immediate conflict in spite of the Bureau's disbandment.

The Arab Bureau's impact lingered. Its comparatively deeper understanding of Arab politics and culture had altered British perceptions of the region, while the network of pre-war contacts and informants that was added to during the war years remained a valuable resource for British officials grappling with the challenges of post-war administration. Indeed, many former Arab Bureau personnel found themselves in influential positions, their expertise shaping policy decisions in ways both subtle and profound.

THE ARAB BUREAU

Immediate Impact: Transforming Intelligence and Regional Dynamics

The Arab Bureau's immediate impact on the First World War's Middle Eastern theatre went beyond simple military achievement, representing a transformation of how intelligence could be gathered, understood, and applied in complex cultural environments, and in the process challenging fundamental assumptions about intelligence gathering and regional engagement.

At its core, the Arab Bureau revolutionised intelligence by demonstrating that effective information gathering required cultural comprehension rather than mere data collection. Its network blended academic expertise with strategic intelligence in an approach that proved particularly effective in understanding tribal politics, in which capacity the Arab Bureau developed frameworks for comprehending relationships, motivations, and internal dynamics that were far more nuanced than traditional intelligence methods.

The immediate military impact was also evident in the success of both the Arab Revolt and Allenby's campaigns, where Arab Bureau knowledge of tribal politics, regional geography, and local power dynamics provided British commanders with tactical advantages that traditional intelligence simply could not match. The Bureau's ability to disrupt Ottoman supply lines demonstrated the power of its approach, while its work in contextualising intercepted communications went beyond simple translation to provide valuable insights into Ottoman plans.

However, this tactical success came with significant political complications. The Arab Bureau's wartime focus on mobilising Arab support for the anti-Ottoman Arab Revolt had led to a series of overlapping and sometimes contradictory promises, and the expectations it had helped create among Arab leaders, both through carefully crafted propaganda and political engagement, would inevitably lead to tensions that complicated British rule in the coming years. As one Foreign Office official noted in a 1920 memorandum, "We find ourselves in the unfortunate position of having made commitments to various Arab factions that are fundamentally incompatible with both our imperial interests and our agreements with the French."[8]

This tension between wartime expediency and post-war reality revealed a fundamental contradiction in the Arab Bureau's approach, and its remit, over which it of course had no say. While its cultural expertise and ground-breaking methods proved valuable for winning the war, the Bureau created expectations that British policy could not, or would not, fulfil in peacetime. The romantic vision of Arab unity it promoted through propaganda publications like *Thawrat al-Arab* collided with the pragmatic approach of post-war British administration, creating massive disillusionment among Arab leaders who had been close personal allies to many members of the Arab Bureau.

Long-Term Influence: Questions of Institutional Learning

The Arab Bureau's long-term legacy presents a complex story of innovation, institutional resistance, and partial adoption. Its approach to intelligence as a multidisciplinary, culturally informed practice challenged traditional views of intelligence as mere data collection, instead demonstrating that comprehensive understanding requires cultural comprehension and contextual analysis.

The concept of an 'imperial epistemic community', a network of intelligence personnel sharing specialised knowledge in the service of the empire, helps frame the Arab Bureau's novel approach.[9] They functioned not just as an intelligence unit but as a knowledge production system that bridged academic expertise, military intelligence, and cultural understanding. By integrating archaeological, linguistic, and cultural knowledge with operational intelligence, it created a model of regional analysis that anticipated later approaches in both Intelligence Studies and Middle East Studies.

However, the Arab Bureau's most innovative methods faced significant barriers to institutional adoption, with traditional military and colonial administrators often viewing its academic approach with scepticism, preferring more conventional methods. Such resistance highlights what scholars call the 'institutional learning paradox'—the difficulty organisations face in adopting and preserving new practices, particularly when they challenge established institutional cultures, even if they can be demonstrated to be an improvement on previous practises.

As one writer has noted, "The Arab Bureau represented a moment of imperial imagination that could not be sustained within the broader structures of British imperial governance. Its innovative approaches were ultimately absorbed into—and diluted by—more traditional colonial frameworks."[10] This observation points to a fundamental limitation. Arab Bureau methods, while effective in the specific context of wartime operations, proved difficult to integrate into peacetime imperial administration.

Despite this institutional resistance, elements of the Arab Bureau's methodology gradually influenced British intelligence practices. Its approach to tribal intelligence proved particularly enduring, continuing, as it did, to inform British operations throughout the 1920s and 1930s. Notable administrators, even critics, like Percy Cox drew on Arab Bureau methodologies in managing tribal politics in Iraq, demonstrating the lasting impact of its approach.

Perhaps no individual better exemplifies the Arab Bureau's lasting influence than Gertrude Bell, whose post-war role as Oriental Secretary in Iraq allowed her to directly apply Arab Bureau methodologies to nation-building. Drawing on her wartime experience mapping tribal territories and allegiances, Bell played a crucial role in Iraq's boundary demarcation, employing the Arab Bureau's, and her own, understanding of tribal dynamics to create borders that, while both imperfect and imposed, may be said to have shown greater sensitivity to local realities than other post-Ottoman arrangements. Her comprehensive knowledge of regional history and culture, cultivated during her Arab Bureau service, also informed the development of Iraq's archaeological service and national museum.

Letters Bell wrote from Baghdad reveal how deeply Arab Bureau practices continued to shape her own approach, particularly in her continuing cultivation of networks among influential Iraqis across religious and tribal divisions. When she wrote to her father, "you begin by building up a closely knit and well-organized intelligence service",[11] she was explicitly advocating for Arab Bureau methods in the new Iraqi state, and her influence offers a clear demonstration of how Arab Bureau principles continued to shape British policy through the personal legacy of its former members.[12]

The most tangible institutional embodiment of the Arab Bureau's legacy was the Middle East Centre for Arab Studies (MECAS),[13] established in Lebanon in 1947. Though coming nearly three decades after the Arab Bureau's dissolution, MECAS reflected remarkably similar principles, combining academic expertise with intelligence requirements, seeking to create officers who understood the region as thoroughly as the likes of Hogarth, Bell, and Lawrence in a previous generation. The institution became known to locals, perhaps unhelpfully, as the 'British spy school', though its curriculum genuinely prioritised deep cultural immersion and linguistic proficiency. Like the Arab Bureau before it, MECAS understood that effective regional operations required more than tactical intelligence; they demanded comprehensive cultural understanding.[14] The centre's closure in 1978 amid the Lebanese civil war ironically mirrored the Arab Bureau's own fate, where due to taking a modern approach to regional expertise the organisation struggled to maintain institutional support amid shifting political priorities.

Yet these adoptions were selective and incomplete. The broader philosophical challenges posed by the Arab Bureau, such as their fundamental reimagining of how intelligence should function, remained largely unaddressed. The tension between innovative methods and traditional imperial approaches was never fully resolved, leading to what Christopher Andrew describes as a "partial and inconsistent application of lessons that should have transformed British intelligence practices".[15]

Reshaping British Middle East Policy: Promise and Contradiction

The Arab Bureau's influence on British Middle East policy represented a significant, albeit lowkey, reimagining of imperial engagement in the region, challenging colonial assumptions and introducing greater nuance to Britain's approach. However, this influence was marked by fundamental contradictions that limit claims of transformative impact. Traditional British colonial administration approached the Middle East as a monolithic entity to be controlled through direct military and administrative power. The Arab Bureau, on the other hand, introduced a very different paradigm, advocating for a more refined understanding of local power dynamics, tribal relationships, and emerging nationalist sentiments. Its approach recognised the agency of local political actors in ways that were well ahead of their time, suggesting that effective imperial control depended on cultural comprehension and political negotiation rather than mere imposition.

This influence was most evident in specific policy areas. The Arab Bureau's approach to state formation in the Middle East, particularly in Transjordan, provided a blueprint for indirect rule that would shape British colonial administration for decades. The Bureau's carefully cultivated relationships with Hashemite leaders offered a model for working through existing political structures rather than imposing entirely new ones. While in Iraq, former Arab Bureau officers played crucial roles in developing administrative approaches that engaged with tribal hierarchies rather than attempting to completely remake local political systems.

The practical application of Arab Bureau methodologies was particularly evident in Sir Percy Cox's administration of Iraq during his tenure as High Commissioner (1920–23). Cox, who had maintained close correspondence with the Arab Bureau throughout the war, to a large degree implemented their approach to tribal politics when faced with widespread tribal uprisings in 1920. Rather than relying solely on military force, Cox employed tribal mapping techniques pioneered by the Arab Bureau, in the process identifying key influencers and power relationships among tribal confederations. His creation of an 'honourable peace' with tribal sheikhs drew directly on Arab Bureau reports about tribal honour codes and obligation systems. Indeed, when establishing Iraq's administrative structure, Cox recruited former Arab Bureau personnel, notably Gertrude Bell as Oriental Secretary, ensuring that their expertise directly informed the development of Iraqi governance frameworks.[16] This application of Arab Bureau methods in post-war Iraq demonstrates how its innovations influenced British administration well beyond its formal existence.

However, this influence coexisted with serious contradictions. The very policies that the Arab Bureau helped shape often reproduced imperial power dynamics in more subtle forms. As Elizabeth Monroe argued, "The appearance of greater cultural sensitivity masked a continuing commitment to imperial control. The new methods simply represented more sophisticated approaches to maintaining British dominance."[17] This assessment highlights a fundamental tension within the Bureau's legacy: while innovative, its methods ultimately served traditional imperial ends.

The Arab Bureau's handling of Arab nationalist movements may be seen as the best possible illustration of this contradiction. While the Arab Bureau demonstrated a more detailed understanding of nationalist sentiments than traditional colonial administrators, its approach remained fundamentally instrumental, as it sought to channel nationalist energy in the service of British interests during the war, but in the post-war period quickly pursued policies that required backing away from promises of Arab independence. Inevitably, this created a legacy of distrust that undermined British influence in the region for years to come, even down to, depending on who one asks, the present day.

The gap between wartime rhetoric and post-war reality became particularly evident in the administration of Palestine. The Arab Bureau's earlier engagement with Arab nationalist aspirations stood in stark contrast to policies that facilitated Jewish immigration, while suppressing Arab political demands. This contradiction created tensions that would shape regional politics for decades to come, and again which may be regarded as unresolved now.

Many former Arab Bureau officers recognised these contradictions, not least Bell. Again writing to her father, she wrote candidly, "We are in the impossible position of having encouraged Arab national sentiment and then denying its logical conclusion. I do not see how we can hope to maintain our influence if we continue to pursue such fundamentally inconsistent policies."[18]

Development of Intelligence Practices: Innovation and Limitation

The Arab Bureau's approach to intelligence represented a fundamental reimagining of information gathering and analysis in complex operational environments. Its methods integrated academic expertise with practical operational requirements in ways that challenged traditional boundaries between scholarly research and intelligence work. Where previous intelligence practices relied on narrow, even superficial, information gathering the Arab Bureau developed a comprehensive framework for regional analysis. The intelligence reports we read in the *Arab Bulletin* were not simple tactical summaries but nuanced interpretations that wove together military, political, cultural, and social insights. This interdisciplinary method allowed for levels of understanding that traditional intelligence frameworks simply could not achieve.

The Arab Bureau's approach to intelligence networks similarly broke new ground, so that rather than viewing informants simply as sources of raw data, it developed original frameworks for managing and interpreting complex information flows. In the process, Arab Bureau networks grew, extending beyond traditional military intelligence channels to incorporate local intellectuals, tribal leaders, and cultural experts into a dynamic information ecosystem.

The integration of propaganda with intelligence gathering demonstrated particular innovation. The Arab Bureau created a feedback loop where intelligence informed propaganda creation, and propaganda distribution channels provided new sources of intelligence. As we have already explored, publications like *Thawrat al-Arab* engaged with local intellectual traditions, religious discourse, and emerging political narratives in ways that allowed them to simultaneously influence opinion and gather cultural intelligence.

However, their model of intelligence faced significant limitations in institutional adoption, as has been mentioned, its methods often meeting resistance from military authorities who viewed its interdisciplinary approach with scepticism. Ironically, it was the very qualities that made the Arab Bureau effective—its flexible structure, reliance on academic expertise, and comprehensive approach—which made it hard to fathom for the more hidebound, and more difficult to integrate into conventional intelligence structures.

Intelligence historian Philip Davies notes this fundamental tension when he writes, "The Arab Bureau represented an intelligence approach that was simultaneously too academic for military authorities and too operational for scholarly comfort. This boundary-crossing character explains both its innovative power and its institutional vulnerability."[19] This appraisal succinctly and perfectly highlights the challenge of sustaining pioneering intelligence practices within traditional organisational frameworks.

The Arab Bureau's integration of intelligence gathering with propaganda dissemination prefigured later British organisations, though direct institutional influence remains difficult to trace. The PWE, established in 1941, adopted similar approaches to combining regional expertise with information operations, as well as innovative propaganda. The PWE's Middle East operations adopted remarkably similar techniques to those pioneered by the Arab Bureau, and also it should be said Wellington House, particularly its strategy of working through respected local intellectuals.

In Egypt, Freya Stark implemented what she explicitly described as an 'Arab Bureau approach' to counter Axis propaganda, creating reading rooms that distributed carefully crafted materials through seemingly independent Arab cultural channels.[20] Like their First World War predecessors, PWE officers recognised that effective propaganda required cultural authenticity rather than obvious external messaging. Via their *Sharq al-Adna*, or Near East Broadcasting Station,[21] radio broadcasts from Jaffa employed Arab broadcasters and cultural content in a direct echo of the Arab Bureau's newspaper strategy. This resurgence of Arab Bureau methods during another global conflict underscores how its innovations, while sometimes forgotten in peacetime, proved valuable enough to be rediscovered when similar challenges arose.

Meanwhile, the Cold War-era IRD likewise emphasised cultural knowledge in propaganda efforts which closely mirrored the Arab Bureau's earlier integration of intelligence gathering and propaganda production. Whether these similarities represent conscious adoption of Arab Bureau methods or parallel evolution in response to similar challenges requires further archival investigation.

The Arab Bureau's experience reveals a fundamental challenge in intelligence innovation that persists today. While its methods demonstrated the value of cultural understanding and interdisciplinary expertise, these qualities proved difficult to institutionalise. The result was what Michael Herman describes as "islands of innovation that never fully transformed the mainland of intelligence practice".[22]

The Arab Bureau and the Emergence of Arab Nationalism: A Complex Entanglement

The Arab Bureau's engagement with Arab nationalism was neither simple manipulation nor mere observation, but a complex interaction that shaped nationalist discourse during a critical period of political transformation. This far from disinterested relationship reveals the intricate ways imperial powers influenced, while not fully controlling, emerging political movements.

Contrary to simplistic narratives of colonial manipulation, Arab nationalism had deep indigenous roots in late Ottoman intellectual circles, with origins that clearly predated British intervention. The Arab Bureau recognised and engaged with an already emerging political consciousness, its extensive documentation revealing nationalist currents developing within Syrian and Iraqi intellectual circles. As Rashid Khalidi argues, "Arab nationalism emerged through a complex dialogue between local intellectual traditions and external political opportunities. The Arab Bureau did not create this movement but entered into a relationship with it that transformed both sides."[23]

This relationship is best described as catalytic rather than causative. The Arab Bureau's propaganda efforts and intelligence analysis amplified and reshaped existing political tendencies rather than manufacturing nationalist sentiment. Publications like *Thawrat al-Arab* were complex political texts that engaged with Arab intellectual traditions while subtly advancing British strategic interests. The Arab Bureau worked closely with local intellectuals, creating materials that spoke to emerging nationalist sentiments in ways that 'simple' propaganda could not have achieved.

This engagement nevertheless created significant contradictions. The Arab Bureau needed to support Arab nationalist aspirations sufficiently to maintain wartime alliances while ensuring these aspirations did not entirely undermine British imperial interests, a delicate balancing act which created a fundamental tension that would shape post-war politics. The Arab Bureau's wartime promotion of Arab independence created expectations that post-war British policy, particularly the Sykes-Picot(-Sazanov) Agreement and the Balfour Declaration, could not fulfil.

Albert Hourani precisely captured this contradiction: "The British encouraged Arab nationalism as a wartime strategy while simultaneously making arrangements that would frustrate nationalist aspirations after the war. This fundamental dishonesty created a legacy of distrust that would poison Anglo-Arab relations for generations."[24] This evaluation faultlessly highlights the ethical complications of the Arab Bureau's wartime engagement with nationalist movements, and its post-war retreat from support of the same.

This gap between wartime promises and post-war realities also created significant resentment among Arab leaders who had been Arab Bureau allies. King Faisal, who worked closely with them during the Arab Revolt, later remarked, "The British gave us fair words during the war, but their deeds afterward proved those words to be empty."[25]

And yet, the Arab Bureau's impact on nationalist discourse went beyond simple betrayal narratives. Its engagement with Arab intellectuals created spaces for political dialogue that continued to influence nationalist thinking after the war. The very language of Arab nationalism bears traces of this complex interaction between indigenous political thought and external influences, demonstrating what Gelvin calls "the entangled origins of modern political identities",[26] a colourful concept that provides a useful framework for understanding the complex development of Arab nationalism.

POST-WAR POSTMORTEM

Modern Regional Resonance: Lessons Unlearned

The Arab Bureau's approach to understanding the Middle East offers critical insights into contemporary regional challenges, highlighting both the value of its methods and the consequences of failing to apply them consistently in modern interventions. The high importance the Arab Bureau placed on cultural intelligence stands in stark contrast to more recent Western approaches to the region. Modern interventions in Iraq and Afghanistan demonstrate the potentially catastrophic, and generational, consequences of cultural misunderstanding. The 2003 Iraq invasion particularly illustrates this failure, with post-invasion planning demonstrating little of the cultural sensitivity or local knowledge that characterised the Arab Bureau's approach. As Juan Cole observed, "The architects of the Iraq War might have avoided catastrophic errors had they applied even the most basic lessons from the Arab Bureau's approach to regional understanding."[27]

The Arab Bureau's analysis of political identity formation remains equally relevant to contemporary Middle Eastern politics. Its understanding of how national, religious, and transnational identities interact provides a framework for comprehending current regional challenges. The ongoing tensions between state sovereignty and transnational movements—whether pan-Arab nationalism in the mid-twentieth century or religious movements today—echo dynamics first mapped by the Arab Bureau in the First World War.

The Arab Bureau's approach to information operations similarly foreshadowed contemporary challenges. Its development of culturally resonant narratives that worked through existing communication networks anticipated many aspects of modern information warfare, while its understanding of how to create persuasive political messages that respected cultural context offers lessons for engagement in today's complex information landscape. Alas, these lessons remain largely unheeded. Contemporary Western engagement with the Middle East too often continues to demonstrate many of the same patterns of cultural misunderstanding that the Arab Bureau sought to overcome. Despite occasionally offering rhetoric about cultural sensitivity, modern military and political approaches often revert to simplistic frameworks that fail to capture regional complexity.

The Arab Bureau's enduring relevance to modern military operations is strikingly evident in the *U.S. Army/Marine Corps Counterinsurgency*

Field Manual,²⁸ published in 2006 in the midst of the wars in Iraq and Afghanistan. The manual explicitly, if not exactly pertinently, cites Lawrence's "twenty-seven Articles" alongside other Arab Bureau insights, presenting them as foundational wisdom for operating in Arab cultural contexts. More significantly, the manual's approach to cultural intelligence directly parallels Arab Bureau methodologies, emphasising the need for deep regional knowledge, respect for local customs, and understanding of tribal dynamics. One section advises commanders to "map the human terrain" using methods remarkably similar to those employed in Arab Bureau tribal analyses. General David Petraeus, who oversaw the manual's development, acknowledged drawing inspiration from the Arab Bureau's integration of cultural expertise with military operations. This direct application of Arab Bureau principles a century after their development demonstrates their continued relevance to modern asymmetric conflicts in culturally complex environments.

This represents what Robert Jervis called "the tragedy of repeated errors",²⁹ the tendency to make similar mistakes across different historical contexts due to institutional failures of learning. The Arab Bureau offered an original model for regional engagement, but the institutional barriers to adopting its methods remain largely intact. As Roger Owen once wrote, emphasising the importance of historical understanding in contemporary regional analysis, "The most tragic aspect of recent Western interventions in the region is not that they ignored history, but that they ignored the very tools for understanding that history had provided."³⁰

The Arab Bureau's legacy thus serves as both a model and a warning. It demonstrates the possibility of more nuanced approaches to regional understanding while highlighting the institutional and political barriers that prevent their adoption. In an era of continuing Western involvement in the Middle East, the gap between the understanding the Arab Bureau pioneered and the often-reductive approaches that characterise modern interventions remains a concerning feature of international engagement with the region.

The Arab Bureau's legacy can thus be said to present a pattern of selective rather than transformative influence. Its most enduring impacts came in three specific areas. First, its approach to tribal politics, which continued to inform British engagement with tribal structures throughout the mandate period; second, its propaganda methods, which influenced subsequent information operations during and after the Second

World War; and third, its model of integrating academic expertise with intelligence requirements, which would be periodically rediscovered during later conflicts. However, the Bureau's more ambitious innovations—particularly its vision of culturally informed intelligence as fundamental to strategic planning—faced greater institutional resistance. Traditional military structures largely reverted to conventional intelligence methods after the war, while the Foreign Office maintained some aspects of the Arab Bureau's approach through individual practitioners rather than systematic adoption. This uneven pattern of influence reflects broader tensions within intelligence organisations, between innovation and institutional tradition, explaining why some Arab Bureau methods became standard practice while others had to be repeatedly rediscovered.

A Complex Legacy

The Arab Bureau's legacy defies simple assessment. Its approaches to intelligence, cultural understanding, and regional engagement represented a significant departure from traditional imperial methods, yet these innovations operated within, and ultimately served, an imperial framework that limited their transformative potential.

The Arab Bureau's most enduring contribution was methodological rather than political. It demonstrated the value of interdisciplinary approaches to regional understanding, bringing together academic expertise and operational intelligence in ways that anticipated modern approaches to area studies, while its integration of archaeological, linguistic, and cultural knowledge with strategic intelligence created a model of comprehensive regional analysis that remains relevant today.

The Arab Bureau's approach challenged what Edward Said would later call the "latent Orientalism" of colonial knowledge production.[31] However, by engaging seriously with Arab intellectual traditions and political aspirations, the Bureau at least demonstrated possibilities for more nuanced cross-cultural understanding. This engagement was obviously never entirely free from imperial power dynamics, but it represented a more sophisticated approach to cultural difference than traditional colonial frameworks had previously allowed.

This isn't to say that Arab Bureau innovations were not constrained by the broader imperial context in which they operated: of course they were. All its cultural sensitivity, insights, or erudite methodologies ultimately served British strategic interests, often at the expense of the very Arab aspirations it claimed to support. As such, this fundamental contradiction must limit any claims around the Bureau's transformative impact on British imperial practice or regional development.

The gap between the Arab Bureau's wartime promises and post-war realities created significant political complications. Its propaganda efforts and alliance-building activities generated expectations among Arab leaders that post-war British policy could not fulfil. This created a consequential tension, a stress point that shaped Anglo–Arab relations for decades, and which unarguably also contributed in some degree to the instability and conflict that have characterised much of the modern Middle East, from the dissolution of the Ottoman Empire to the present day.

The institutional adoption of Arab Bureau methods was similarly limited. While specific techniques and approaches influenced subsequent British intelligence practices, broader philosophical challenges to how knowledge is produced and applied remained largely unaddressed. Traditional institutional boundaries between academic expertise and operational intelligence quickly reasserted themselves after the Arab Bureau's closure.

As we assess the Arab Bureau's impact, we must recognise both its innovative potential and its practical limitations. The Bureau offered glimpses of other possible approaches to cross-cultural understanding and regional engagement, yet these glimpses never fully transformed British imperial practice or resolved the fundamental contradictions of colonial rule.

Perhaps the most valuable aspect of the Arab Bureau's legacy is not what it achieved, but what it suggested was possible. Its interdisciplinary approach to knowledge production, its engagement with cultural complexity, and its recognition of local agency all pointed towards more nuanced forms of cross-cultural understanding. These possibilities remain relevant in our contemporary moment of global interconnection and cultural tension.

The insights explored in this chapter demonstrate how the Arab Bureau established approaches to intelligence that, despite uneven adoption, continue to offer relevant lessons for modern practitioners. Its integration of cultural expertise with operational requirements, its ground-breaking propaganda methods, and its nuanced regional analysis all represent enduring contributions to intelligence practice. These innovations were not merely tactical adjustments but reflected fundamental principles about effective intelligence in complex cultural environments.

The Arab Bureau's legacy thus presents a pattern of selective rather than transformative influence. Its most enduring impact came through individual practitioners who carried their methods into new institutional settings, and through periodic rediscovery of its approaches during subsequent conflicts. Yet its more profound innovation—its fundamental reimagining of intelligence as cultural understanding—remained difficult to institutionalise within traditional frameworks. This tension between revolutionary methods and institutional constraints points towards the final question: What enduring wisdom can be distilled from the Arab Bureau's experience for contemporary practitioners operating in complex cultural environments?

In Chapter Twelve we will distil these principles into 'Seven Pillars of Intelligence Wisdom', producing a comprehensive framework derived from the Arab Bureau's experience that provides practical guidance for understanding and operating in culturally distinct regions in the contemporary setting. In doing so, this framework radically alters the Arab Bureau's historical significance, taking it from being simply the intelligence unit in which T.E. Lawrence served during the First World War, and instead creating a practical, global roadmap for navigating today's complex intelligence challenges in the MENA region or anywhere else.

12

SEVEN PILLARS OF INTELLIGENCE WISDOM

LESSONS FROM THE ARAB BUREAU

In which we explore how the Arab Bureau, that most unconventional unit, transcended traditional military intelligence, and how by prioritising cultural understanding it revolutionised intelligence practices. Here we draw directly from its pioneering wartime methods to reveal how interdisciplinary expertise and flexible organisational structures—bridging academic knowledge with operational requirements—remains critically important for contemporary intelligence practitioners, as well as anyone working in, or wishing to understand, complex global environments. Drawing directly on the Arab Bureau's experience and approach, this chapter offers us a blueprint for that very purpose, a set of practical principles that are more relevant to more people than ever before ... Seven Pillars of Intelligence Wisdom.

Lessons Learned?

There is an Arabic proverb that says, "Ask the experienced rather than the learned." In the case of the Arab Bureau, by the end of its life, its membership can justly be considered both learned and experienced. Wisdom and right action are other issues, but in the pursuit of their goals, the men—and one woman—who made up the Arab Bureau had developed a unique set of experiences which they were able to add to their already advanced and varied professional backgrounds and formal education.

The Arab Bureau's emphasis on cultural expertise and academic-intelligence collaboration became standard practice in later British operations, though tracing direct causal links proves challenging.[1] The establishment of university–intelligence partnerships during and after the Second World War, the emphasis on area studies in Cold War intelligence, and the integration of propaganda with intelligence gathering all echo Arab Bureau innovations, whether through conscious emulation or similar operational necessities.

Either way, the Arab Bureau's significance extends well beyond its historical moment. Its novel approaches to intelligence gathering, cultural engagement, and information operations offer profound insights for contemporary practitioners navigating complex global environments. While Lawrence distilled tactical advice for engaging with Arab allies in his famous "Twenty-Seven Articles", the Arab Bureau's collective experience suggests a broader set of strategic principles, which I'm calling 'Seven Pillars of Intelligence Wisdom'. These principles transcend their specific historical context, offering a comprehensive framework for understanding and operating in culturally distinct environments that remains remarkably relevant a century later.

Throughout this book we have been arguing that the Arab Bureau was a more innovative and original unit of military intelligence than has previously been fully understood. Such an appreciation is only now fully possible because we have produced, for the first time, a close examination of the Bureau's English-language intelligence reports as well as its various Arabic-language outputs and co-productions. In doing so, the story of the Arab Bureau can now be told more fully. Ignoring its Arabic-language propaganda created an effect akin to chiaroscuro, whereas we have shined an equal degree of light on the different aspects of its work, revealing it as it was never meant to be seen.

Intelligence is never just about collecting information. It is a profound act of understanding, a complex negotiation between knowledge, power, and human complexity. In the midst of the First World War, a small, unconventional group of British intelligence officers discovered this fundamental truth in consultation with colleagues in Cairo and other offices, as well as via cooperation with Arab allies in the deserts and urban centres of Arabia, and as they moved northward on the road to Damascus. Through what they learned, they created an approach to intelligence that would resonate far beyond their organisation's immediate, and ephemeral, historical moment.

The Arab Bureau emerged at a critical juncture in intelligence history. Traditional military intelligence was a rigid, hierarchical system focused primarily on enemy capabilities and movements. The Arab Bureau represented a radical departure, namely, an intelligence unit that recognised cultural understanding as an operational capability more powerful than any technological intervention.

The Arab Bureau's innovative approach to intelligences was not accidental. The First World War created unprecedented challenges that demanded new approaches to understanding complex regional dynamics. As Herman astutely said, "Wartime conditions often enable intelligence organisations to transcend traditional institutional boundaries, creating opportunities for innovation that would be impossible in peacetime."[2] The Arab Bureau embodied this principle, developing an approach to intelligence that was simultaneously a response to immediate wartime challenges and a profound reimagining of how human knowledge could be gathered and used.

Theoretical frameworks can help us understand the Arab Bureau's significance. The novel concept we introduced earlier in this book of an imperial epistemic community describes a network of experts sharing specialised knowledge in an imperial and intelligence setting, and as such provides us with a powerful lens through which to study the Bureau's work. The Arab Bureau was more than just an intelligence unit; it was a knowledge-production system that challenged existing boundaries between academic expertise, military intelligence, and cultural understanding.

This chapter distils the Arab Bureau's revolutionary practices into seven fundamental principles—Seven Pillars of Intelligence Wisdom—that remain critically important for contemporary intelligence practitioners and anyone working in complex global environments. While Lawrence's "Twenty-Seven Articles"[3] offered tactical advice for a specific context, the Seven Pillars of Intelligence Wisdom we offer here provide a much broader, strategic set of insights that are applicable in diverse operational settings.

My approach deliberately bridges academic analysis with practical application, drawing directly from the Arab Bureau's wartime methods to reveal how interdisciplinary expertise and flexible organisational structures can transform intelligence practices. By integrating perspectives from Intelligence Studies and Middle East Studies, I feel more able to offer a thoughtful, reasoned, and fully supported reassessment of how knowledge is produced, circulated, and transformed in complex cultural contexts.

THE ARAB BUREAU

Seven Pillars of Intelligence Wisdom

1. Cultural Understanding as Operational Capability
2. Diversify Intelligence Sources and Expertise
3. Develop Flexible Organisational Structures
4. Recognise Language as Cultural Intelligence
5. Build Networked, Authentic Information Ecosystems
6. Balance Secrecy with Strategic Engagement
7. Cultivate Continuous Institutional Learning

It is important to acknowledge that these Seven Pillars of Intelligence Wisdom emerge from a complex historical context. The Arab Bureau operated within British imperial structures and power dynamics that obviously informed and influenced its methods and perspectives. Its innovations in intelligence practice coexisted with the limitations of colonial frameworks that often subordinated local interests to imperial objectives. This tension between methodological innovation and imperial context offers a valuable lens through which to critically examine Arab Bureau practices. By acknowledging these complexities, we can better appreciate both the groundbreaking nature of its approach and the constraints within which it operated. Thus, the following Seven Pillars of Intelligence Wisdom represent not an uncritical celebration of the Arab Bureau, but a nuanced assessment of its enduring contributions to intelligence practice.

Moreover, these Seven Pillars should not be seen as historical footnotes but, rather, as a blueprint for understanding intelligence in our increasingly complex global environment. Each pillar represents a critical insight into how intelligence can transcend traditional boundaries, bridging academic expertise with operational requirements and cultural understanding with strategic objectives.

The parallels to present-day intelligence challenges are remarkably pronounced. In an era of geopolitical complexity, where traditional boundaries blur and cultural dynamics shift rapidly, the Arab Bureau's approach offers more than historical insight. It provides a roadmap for navigating the intricate landscapes of human information and interaction. Modern intelligence agencies continue to grapple with challenges[4] the Arab Bureau addressed a century ago: How do you develop genuine cultural intelligence? How can organisations break down institutional barriers? How can specialised knowledge be transformed into operational capabilities?

SEVEN PILLARS OF INTELLIGENCE WISDOM

Our journey begins in the deserts of Arabia, but its implications extend far beyond any single time or place. These Seven Pillars of Intelligence Wisdom are an invitation to reimagine intelligence—not as a tool of power, but as a profound act of understanding.

First Pillar: Cultural Understanding as Operational Capability

In the complex terrain of intelligence gathering, knowledge is more than information, it is a nuanced understanding of human landscapes. The Arab Bureau's most revolutionary contribution was not a technological breakthrough, but a radical reimagining of what intelligence could be: a deep, contextual comprehension of cultural dynamics that transforms operational capabilities.

Consider the challenge of tribal intelligence in the Arabian Peninsula. Rejecting conventional doctrine that reduced tribal groups to mere military assets or obstacles, the Arab Bureau developed what scholars now term "deep cultural intelligence".[5] It didn't just collect data about tribes; it understood the intricate webs of relationships, obligations, and conflicts that shaped regional politics.

This approach went far beyond superficial cultural awareness. As one contemporary intelligence theorist notes, "Cultural intelligence requires a fundamental shift from viewing culture as context to understanding it as a primary operational consideration."[6] The Arab Bureau exemplified this principle decades before it became a recognised intelligence paradigm.

The Bureau's method was erudite and pragmatic, as we can see if we take its approach to tribal leaders as an example. Instead of transactional relationships focused solely on military objectives, the Arab Bureau developed frameworks that recognised tribal honour codes, complex social obligations, and the nuanced motivations behind political allegiances. Further, it understood that tribal decision-making operated according to internal logics that couldn't be understood through purely external lenses.

This approach is vividly illustrated in the *U.S. Army/Marine Corps Counterinsurgency Manual*, which explicitly draws on Arab Bureau methods. The manual demonstrates how understanding cultural contexts is not a peripheral skill, but a core operational capability. As the manual suggests, intelligence operations must transcend mere information gathering to truly comprehend social terrains.

THE ARAB BUREAU

The parallels to current challenges are unmistakable. Modern intelligence services continue to struggle with what has been termed the 'cultural-operational integration challenge'.[7] How do you transform cultural knowledge into actionable intelligence? The Arab Bureau's experience offers a convincing plan. Its success also stemmed from an unconventional recruitment approach, one that prioritised cultural and linguistic expertise over traditional military backgrounds, where archaeologists worked alongside military officers, and linguists collaborated with field agents and local contacts. In the process, the Bureau created what researchers today call a 'hybrid knowledge structure',[8] a means of bridging cultural understanding and operational requirements.

This wasn't just about collecting information, but was instead about creating a fundamentally different approach to intelligence. The Arab Bureau recognised that effective intelligence work requires more than linguistic skills: it demands a deep, empathetic understanding of local dynamics, social structures, and cultural nuances.

As such, this lesson couldn't be clearer for contemporary intelligence operators. Cultural understanding is not a soft skill or 'nice-to-have', but an operational capability as critical as any technological intelligence method. One scholar perfectly captured this point and its historical precedent, stating that the "challenges of integrating cultural expertise with intelligence requirements remain as pertinent today as they were during the Arab Bureau's time".[9]

This first pillar of intelligence wisdom challenges traditional paradigms. It suggests that the most powerful intelligence comes not from sophisticated technology but from a profound, nuanced understanding of human complexity. In an increasingly complex global landscape, where traditional boundaries blur and cultural dynamics shift rapidly, this lesson is more crucial than ever. Intelligence is not about collecting data points but about comprehending the human landscape in all its rich, nuanced complexity.

The Arab Bureau didn't just gather information about the Middle East: they sought to understand its intricate social fabric, its hidden motivations, and its unspoken dynamics.

Second Pillar: Diversify Intelligence Sources and Expertise

Traditional intelligence units are bureaucratic machines, rigidly structured and narrowly focused. The Arab Bureau shattered this model, creating what researchers would later call a 'hybrid knowledge structure'[10] that bridged academic expertise with operational intelligence in unprecedented ways.

Imagine an intelligence unit where archaeologists work alongside military officers, linguists collaborate with field agents, and scholarly knowledge is as valued as tactical information. This was not a theoretical exercise, but the daily reality of the Arab Bureau. Its radical approach to intelligence gathering challenged fundamental assumptions about what constitutes valuable intelligence expertise.

David Hogarth, the unit's leader, embodied this interdisciplinary ethos. As Keeper of Antiquities at the Ashmolean Museum, he brought a scholarly approach to intelligence reporting that set new standards for regional analysis, and his pre-war archaeological networks became intelligence-gathering channels, with expedition sites serving as both research locations and information exchange hubs.

The unit's approach to recruitment was also revolutionary, as it did not seek out those with traditional military experience but instead prioritised the search for individuals with deep regional knowledge, exemplified by the historian, traveller, and author Gertrude Bell and the budding archaeologist and scholar-cum-adventurer T. E. Lawrence. The expertise of such individuals went far beyond language skills, being able as a matter of course to offer insight and understanding of regional dynamics that traditional intelligence units could rarely if ever achieve. This approach had tangible operational consequences that transformed intelligence gathering. As one scholar notes, "Effective intelligence requires the successful integration of different forms of knowledge and expertise."[11] The Arab Bureau demonstrated that institutional innovation emerges when you break down disciplinary barriers. While such interdisciplinary diversity represented a methodological innovation, it remained constrained by imperial power structures and the predominant cultural assumptions of the era, which tensions would continue to shape both the Arab Bureau's successes and limitations.

Nevertheless, its interdisciplinary approach yielded tangible operational advantages. Consider, for instance, the Arab Bureau's response to the 1916 Arab Revolt. While conventional military intelligence focused narrowly on troop movements and supply lines, the Arab Bureau integrated first-hand topographical and archaeological knowledge of the desert terrain with an enhanced anthropological understanding of tribal dynamics. When Hogarth was busy analysing potential routes for Arab forces, he drew not just on maps but on his pre-war surveying experience, identifying water sources and travel routes unknown to conventional military planners. Similarly, Bell's extensive pre-war travels among Mesopotamian tribes enabled the Arab Bureau to anticipate with remarkable accuracy which tribal leaders would support the Revolt and which would remain loyal to Ottoman authorities. This integration of diverse expertise transformed abstract knowledge into concrete strategic advantage, demonstrating how interdisciplinary intelligence transcended the capabilities of traditional military units.

Archaeological sites became more than research locations, more closely resembling intelligence-gathering points, while personal networks developed during scholarly expeditions transformed into information channels and academic expertise became an operational capability.

While such methods anticipated modern intelligence approaches by decades, contemporary intelligence challenges still mirror these historical insights. Today, intelligence practitioners still grapple with what researchers have termed the 'cultural-operational integration challenge'.[12] How do you transform specialised knowledge into actionable intelligence? Ask no more: the Arab Bureau's experience offers a precise, actionable methodology.

As was the case with its interdisciplinary approach, so too did the Arab Bureau's organisational flexibility yield concrete operational benefits. For instance, when intelligence indicated growing anti-Ottoman sentiment in the Hijaz in early 1916, the Arab Bureau rapidly reallocated resources, having the means of establishing new communication channels without waiting for formal authorisation from further up the chain of command. Within weeks, the Bureau had redirected personnel, developed new information networks, and established content-sharing arrangements with local Arab notables in both town and country, which rapid and successful operational pivot would have been nigh on impossible under a traditional command structure. For proof of this, we can look at the India Office, whose response stands in stark contrast: while the Arab Bureau had already established functioning intelligence networks, the India Office was still drafting formal communication protocols. Clayton later noted that this 'organisational adaptability' had accelerated British support for the Arab Revolt by nearly twi months, providing a critical strategic advantage that traditional structures simply could not match.

Naturally, this approach wasn't without challenges and did not always operate in perfect harmony with that of other British units. Traditional military authorities viewed these 'amateurs' with scepticism, and yet the Arab Bureau's diverse expertise allowed it to develop intelligence approaches that traditional units could not comprehend, let alone replicate.

Consider its handling of tribal intelligence. Where conventional military reports might offer simple strategic assessments, the Arab Bureau provided complex analyses integrating historical, anthropological, and linguistic insights. In doing so, it didn't just collect information, it was actively creating comprehensive understanding for all who cared to read, listen, and learn. This approach extended beyond individual expertise to create complex information networks. By integrating academic connections with military intelligence requirements, the Arab Bureau established what researchers term 'integrated regional intelligence networks'.[13] Pre-war scholarly connections became wartime intelligence channels.

These principles remain vitally relevant to twenty-first-century security operations. As one intelligence scholar argues, intelligence organisations must recognise that "cultural knowledge can enhance rather than impede operational effectiveness".[14] The Arab Bureau didn't just understand this principle, they lived it. The second pillar of intelligence wisdom is clear: true intelligence transcends disciplinary boundaries. It requires a fundamental reimagining of what expertise means. Knowledge should not be compartmentalised but instead a dynamic, interconnected resource that gains power through diverse perspectives.

For modern intelligence agencies, the message is transformative. Break down institutional silos. Value diverse expertise. Recognise that typically the most powerful intelligence emerges not from narrow specialisation, but from rich, interdisciplinary understanding.

The Arab Bureau didn't just collect intelligence: it created a new way of understanding the world.

Third Pillar: Develop Flexible Organisational Structures

In the rigid world of military intelligence, the Arab Bureau was a radical experiment. It challenged the fundamental assumption that effective intelligence requires strict hierarchical structures, demonstrating instead that innovation thrives in flexible, adaptive environments.

THE ARAB BUREAU

Traditional military units are monuments to bureaucracy, with layers of command, rigid protocols, and unyielding chains of communication. The Arab Bureau was different. As one organisational theorist notes, "The ability to transform operational methods in response to changing circumstances is often more important than maintaining established procedures."[15]

The Bureau's organisational structure was itself an act of innovation. In contrast to established intelligence practices, the Arab Bureau fostered collaboration among specialists who in conventional hierarchies would have remained separated. Archaeologists worked alongside military officers, linguists sat with agents, and academic experts were given equal standing with career intelligence professionals.

Clayton embodied this novel approach. With a background spanning military affairs and colonial administration, he created a leadership model that bridged traditional military intelligence and more unconventional methods. His experience in Egypt and Sudan provided crucial insights, while his military credentials lent legitimacy to the unit's unorthodox approach.

The revolutionary recruitment process mentioned above (where instead of prioritising military experience the Arab Bureau sought individuals with deep regional knowledge, cultural understanding, and interdisciplinary expertise) meant that they were able to create what one scholar described as a 'hybrid knowledge structure'[16] that challenged every existing notion of intelligence organisation.

The Arab Bureau's methods transcended theoretical innovation, yielding concrete advantages in the field. Modern intelligence agencies continue to struggle with what researchers call the 'cultural-operational integration challenge',[17] i.e. how to create organisational structures that can effectively integrate diverse expertise, for which Arab Bureau methods offer a tried and tested prototype.

Its flexibility extended to operational methods, so that where more traditional units saw rigid boundaries between intelligence gathering, analysis, and propaganda, the Arab Bureau created approaches that were seamlessly interconnected. The net result of this meant intelligence networks became propaganda channels, cultural understanding informed strategic planning, and academic expertise directly supported military objectives. Modern military doctrine, particularly in the realm of counterinsurgency, bears the unmistakable imprint of the Arab Bureau's organisational innovations.

Given the dramatic organisational shift the Arab Bureau exhibited, institutional resistance was inevitable, with the India Office in particular viewing the Arab Bureau with deep suspicion, challenging its unorthodox methods at every turn. Yet even this resistance would become a catalyst for further innovation. As one scholar notes, "Intelligence organisations are shaped not only by operational requirements but by deeply embedded institutional cultures that both enable and constrain innovation."[18]

Today's security organisations face remarkably similar challenges, despite a century of technological and methodological advancement. How do organisations create space for creativity within traditional hierarchical structures? If we look closely at the Arab Bureau's experience, this suggests that the answer lies in valuing expertise over rank, and adaptability over rigid protocol; and its implementation has been proven to work. The Bureau's overall approach anticipated modern theories of organisational innovation, demonstrating what researchers call 'adaptive intelligence organisation',[19] in other words the ability to rapidly reconfigure capabilities in response to changing environments. Alternatively, one can see the Arab Bureau less as a fixed structure than a dynamic network of expertise.

The third pillar of intelligence wisdom is clear: organisational effectiveness requires flexibility. In this line of thinking, rigid hierarchies kill innovation; traditional boundaries between disciplines are artificial barriers to understanding; and true intelligence emerges when organisations can rapidly adapt and integrate diverse perspectives, breaking down institutional silos.

For modern intelligence agencies, the message is transformative. Create structures that prioritise adaptability over tradition and value diverse expertise over hierarchical rank. Finally on this point, recognise that the most powerful intelligence organisations are those that can quickly reconfigure themselves in response to complex, changing environments.

The Arab Bureau didn't just do things the way they'd always been done; they reimagined how intelligence organisations could work better, and in the process do better work.

Fourth Pillar: Recognise Language as Cultural Intelligence

Language is more than a communication tool, and it needs to be seen and appreciated as such. For the Arab Bureau, foreign languages were a gateway to understanding complex cultural landscapes, a nuanced instrument of intelligence that went far beyond mere translation.

Lawrence epitomised this approach even if—or, arguably, perhaps because—his own Arabic was far from perfect. As was discussed earlier, having received just two months of formal instruction at the American Mission School in Jebail, Lebanon, Lawrence was brutally honest about his linguistic limitations, acknowledging that he had "never heard an Englishman speak Arabic well enough to be taken for a native of any part of the Arabic-speaking world, for five minutes".[20] But this was okay. He had a functional grasp of the language that was suited to his needs.

The Arab Bureau understood what modern intelligence theorists would later articulate, which is that language is not just about words but about deep cultural interpretation. As has been noted elsewhere, "Cultural intelligence requires more than mere familiarity with local customs; it demands a sophisticated understanding of how cultural knowledge can be operationalized."[21]

This linguistic approach contrasted sharply with previous colonial administrative practices. For instance, in India, many British officials viewed alien languages with serious misgivings. The Arab Bureau, by contrast, recognised that linguistic capability was a gateway to cultural understanding. This was never about achieving, or claiming to achieve, native-level fluency, but was instead about developing what researchers call 'operational cultural intelligence',[22] in other words the ability to navigate complex cultural landscapes through linguistic engagement.

The Arab Bureau's propaganda materials demonstrate such an approach. Rather than producing direct translations, they worked with local writers to create culturally resonant messaging. It understood that effective communication requires more than linguistic accuracy—it demands cultural authenticity.

These methodologies foreshadowed approaches that have become essential in our current intelligence paradigm, with modern intelligence agencies still struggling with what has been described as the "fundamental challenge of maintaining sophisticated cultural intelligence capabilities".[23] The Arab Bureau's approach offers a compelling model: language is not a technical skill, but a sophisticated tool of cultural interpretation.

Consider too the Arab Bureau's approach to written propaganda, where local agents were commissioned to carefully craft Arabic-language documents that engaged with local intellectual traditions—such as

SEVEN PILLARS OF INTELLIGENCE WISDOM

Thawrat al-Arab—instead of simply translating texts that had been written in English. In so doing, the Arab Bureau demonstrated that it recognised language as carrying cultural memory, political sentiment, and complex social dynamics.

This approach extended beyond Arabic. Arab Bureau members were multilingual scholars who understood that each language represents a unique way of perceiving the world. Their recruitment prioritised not just language skills, but the ability to think across cultural boundaries.

Today, the Joint Military Intelligence Training Center's (JMITC) emphasis on cultural contextualisation of intelligence gathering mirrors the Arab Bureau's approach, where the JMITC trains analysts to integrate linguistic nuance with regional cultural knowledge, thus developing intelligence networks that prioritise local knowledge systems and cultural frameworks, rather than imposing external analytical structures. Both approaches recognise that effective intelligence work requires interpreters who can navigate not just language barriers but conceptual and cultural ones as well.

As such, the fourth pillar of intelligence wisdom couldn't be clearer: language is not a peripheral skill, but a fundamental operational capability. True cultural intelligence requires more than translation: it demands a profound, empathetic understanding of how language shapes perception, identity, and social dynamics. Members of the Arab Bureau demonstrated that linguistic capability is the deepest form of intelligence, a way of understanding human experience that transcends mere words and touches on the cultural nuances embedded in language. Likewise, there is a tangible need for modern intelligence agencies to invest in linguistic training that goes beyond technical proficiency, to recognise that language is a window into cultural complexity, and to train staff not simply to speak another language but to think through it, and in so doing acquire real insight.

Fifth Pillar: Build Networked, Authentic Information Ecosystems

Intelligence is not, and never has been, a solitary pursuit. Intelligence is fundamentally about connection. It is a complex, interconnected web of relationships, trust, and strategic communication: the ability to create and maintain original networks of information exchange that transcend traditional boundaries of communication. This is a vital principle which the Arab Bureau understood, creating what scholars would call 'integrated regional intelligence networks' decades before network theory became a mainstream concept.[24] Further, the Arab Bureau also demonstrated that truly effective intelligence demands building complex, trust-based information ecosystems.

The Arab Bureau's approach was novel, and instead of relying on traditional hierarchical information channels it developed complex and multi-layered networks that blurred the lines between intelligence gathering, propaganda, and cultural engagement. Its network included Cairo-based journalists, Syrian and Lebanese émigrés, local intellectuals, and strategic allies, a diverse ecosystem of information exchange.

Consider *al-Muqattam*, a prominent Cairo newspaper. Through its relationship with *al-Muqattam*'s publisher, Faris Nimr, the Arab Bureau didn't just disseminate information, but created collaborative platforms for shaping political discourse. This was not a simple propaganda channel, but a complex information ecosystem that allowed for nuanced cultural communication.

The Arab Bureau's network also extended far beyond traditional intelligence boundaries, working as it did with Arab nationalist writers, leveraging existing intellectual networks to advance strategic objectives. Figures like Jurji Zaydan and Ya'qub Sarruf, who had established numerous Arabic journalistic traditions for the modern era, became critical collaborators in information operations.

Arab Bureau propaganda efforts demonstrate this networked approach perfectly. Rather than creating overtly British materials, the Bureau worked through respected local voices. Rashid Rida's articles in *al-Manar*, for instance, were strategically reprinted to advance British interests while maintaining intellectual authenticity. Nor was this mere manipulation, but a sophisticated understanding of information ecosystems. As one scholar notes, "The success of wartime propaganda often depended on its ability to operate within existing cultural and social networks."[25]

The Arab Bureau mastered this principle, its approach surpassing traditional intelligence practices to create what researchers describe as 'effective knowledge circulation' networks,[26] meaning scenarios in which information flows through multiple channels, gaining credibility and nuance with each transmission. This goes to show that the Arab Bureau's networks were not just about gathering intelligence, but also about creating meaningful cultural dialogues. Intelligence communities worldwide still confront what scholars have identified as the 'information network integration challenge'.[27] How do you create authentic, trustworthy information networks in complex cultural environments? The Arab Bureau's experience offers a powerful paradigm.

The operational impact of these networked information ecosystems was dramatically demonstrated during Allied campaigns against Ottoman forces, perhaps most notably in 1917. When British intelligence identified growing concerns among Arab tribal leaders about post-war British intentions, the Arab Bureau activated multiple communication channels simultaneously. Within days, carefully crafted messaging appeared in *al-Qibla*, reassurances were conveyed through trusted intermediaries like Rashid Rida, and supporting materials were distributed through commercial networks. This coordinated response across multiple information channels effectively neutralised Ottoman counter-propaganda that had been gaining traction. Ottoman intelligence officers, bound by more rigid information hierarchies, found themselves consistently outmanoeuvred by the Arab Bureau's nimble, multi-channel approach.

A considerable portion of social network analysis techniques employed by intelligence agencies have evolved from the Arab Bureau's relationship mapping methods, while the 'pattern of life' analysis employed in contemporary intelligence work—where behavioural patterns and social connections are examined to understand group dynamics—can be said to share methodological DNA with the Arab Bureau's careful documentation of tribal alliances, rivalries, and kinship networks. The Arab Bureau understood that effective networks require more than technological connections. They needed trust, cultural understanding, and strategic alignment. The Bureau's network included not just information sources, but cultural interpreters who could navigate complex social landscapes. This approach was particularly evident in its Arabic-language propaganda. Newspapers like *al-Qibla* and *al-Kawkab* weren't simple messaging platforms, but information ecosystems that could simultaneously serve multiple strategic objectives. They maintained apparent independence while subtly advancing British interests.

The lesson of the fifth pillar of intelligence wisdom for contemporary intelligence couldn't be any clearer. Don't just gather intelligence; build comprehensive, trust-based networks in order to create intelligence that is a networked, collaborative endeavour. Recognise that the most powerful information flows through relationships, not hierarchies. And create platforms that allow for nuanced, multidirectional communication. Further, note should be made that effective information operations require more than collecting data, demanding instead the creation of authentic, trusted communication ecosystems that can navigate complex cultural terrains.

The Arab Bureau didn't just collect information. They created living information ecosystems that could shape political understanding, influence cultural narratives, and transform strategic landscapes.

Sixth Pillar: Balance Secrecy with Strategic Engagement

Intelligence has always existed in a delicate balance between concealment and communication, a complex dance which it can be said the Arab Bureau mastered to a greater degree than its predecessors, developing as it did an approach that simultaneously protected sensitive information while engaging meaningfully with diverse audiences.

For instance, considering its propaganda efforts, while orthodox intelligence doctrine elevated absolute secrecy above all other considerations, the Arab Bureau recognised that true strategic impact requires more carefully calibrated engagement. Its approach demonstrated the delicate balance between preserving operational security and conveying strategic messages.

Arab Bureau-backed newspapers exemplified this approach. Mecca-based *al-Qibla* maintained an appearance of complete independence while subtly advancing British strategic objectives, whereas *al-Kawkab* occupied an even more sophisticated middle ground, presenting seemingly autonomous content that aligned with broader intelligence goals. The challenge was intricate. How could an intelligence unit communicate effectively while protecting its most sensitive information? The Arab Bureau developed what researchers describe as an 'operational security paradox',[28] balancing source protection with analytical transparency.

Wellington House maintained such strict secrecy that even Cabinet-level members of the British Government were initially unaware of its existence. By way of contrast, the Arab Bureau took a subtler, smarter approach, creating multiple propaganda channels with varying degrees of apparent independence, thereby allowing for more cultured information operations.

SEVEN PILLARS OF INTELLIGENCE WISDOM

Contemporary intelligence challenges mirror these historical insights. How do organisations maintain operational security while creating meaningful communication channels? The Arab Bureau's experience suggests that the answer lies in creating multiple, interconnected information platforms with carefully managed visibility. Contemporary information operations doctrine emphasises the integration of physical and psychological effects in a way that directly parallels the Arab Bureau's holistic approach. Whereas the Arab Bureau intuitively understood the need to align military actions, intelligence gathering, and narrative dissemination, today's strategic communication frameworks have formalised this relationship.

For instance, the Defense Information School's approach to strategic communication emphasises that effective messaging must be culturally resonant and contextually appropriate, principles embraced by the Arab Bureau decades before they were formalised, and in anticipation of modern practices of audience segmentation and cultural adaptation in information warfare.

The Arab Bureau's approach to information management yielded concrete operational advantages, as can be seen during preparations for the Aqaba campaign in 1917, where the Arab Bureau faced a critical dilemma: How to coordinate complex military operations while maintaining operational security? Rather than imposing rigid secrecy, the Bureau created a tiered information system. Operational details were compartmentalised among key military planners, while broader strategic objectives were shared with tribal leaders through trusted intermediaries, an approach that allowed for essential coordination without compromising security. As such, the Arab Bureau's finessed tack on information management enabled broader coordination with local allies while still protecting critical operational details.

The sixth pillar of intelligence wisdom is easily defined: effective intelligence requires a sophisticated approach to information management. Secrecy is not about total concealment, but about strategic communication. The most powerful intelligence operations create information ecosystems that can simultaneously protect and engage.

For modern intelligence agencies, the message must be: do not see secrecy and communication as opposing goals, but instead develop multiple, interconnected information channels. Understand that true strategic impact comes from carefully calibrated engagement, not absolute concealment.

THE ARAB BUREAU

The Arab Bureau didn't just protect information, it transformed the very concept of intelligence communication in order to create a model of strategic engagement that continues to resonate a century later.

Seventh Pillar: Cultivate Continuous Institutional Learning

Intelligence organisations have a chronic disease: historical amnesia, meaning the loss of critical insights with each generational shift. To tackle this, the Arab Bureau offers a profound alternative: a model of institutional learning that transcends the typical cycles of forgetting and rediscovery.

As one intelligence scholar bluntly observed, "Western intelligence services too often fail to learn from historical precedents, repeatedly 'reinventing the wheel' when confronting cultural and linguistic challenges."[29] The Arab Bureau offers us the opportunity to learn from its experience, which illustrates both the possibilities, and demonstrates the limitations of, institutional knowledge transfer.

The Arab Bureau's pioneering approaches emerged from a unique wartime context, in which established intelligence practices dissolved under the pressure of global conflict and created space for unconventional expertise, allowing archaeologists, linguists, and scholars of all types to transform into intelligence operatives. In so doing, they brought academic rigour to military objectives. Yet the Arab Bureau's greatest challenge was not in gathering intelligence, but preserving and transmitting the knowledge it created. What historians call the 'institutional learning paradox'[30] became its central struggle: how to maintain innovative practices within rigid institutional frameworks?

The Arab Bureau's legacy is a complex narrative of partial success and institutional resistance, with its approaches to cultural intelligence and regional understanding often forgotten or deliberately marginalised in peacetime, so that, as is often the case in other theatres, wartime innovations frequently fail to become permanently integrated into organisational practices.[31] A prime example of this might be the Bureau's approach to tribal intelligence, where the frameworks it developed for understanding tribal dynamics influenced British operations for decades—particularly through figures like Percy Cox in Iraq—and yet these insights were never systematically preserved or institutionalised.

In addition, the Arab Bureau's linguistic and cultural expertise represented another critical area of potential institutional learning. Its success in this arena demonstrated the greater need for cultural understanding over simply technical skills, and yet subsequent intelligence units struggled to maintain the Bureau's holistic approach. By contrast, contemporary security doctrine—including influential counterinsurgency manuals—explicitly acknowledges an intellectual debt to Arab Bureau methodologies, which shows how institutional learning can transcend generational boundaries, even across different national intelligence approaches.

The hurdles facing today's intelligence services echo these century-old dilemmas with striking similarity. How do organisations capture and transfer innovative practices? How can they prevent the loss of critical knowledge with personnel turnover? The Arab Bureau offers a persuasive model favouring continuous institutional learning.

Its most significant legacy may be methodological, in so far as it showed that intelligence is not just about collecting information, but about creating frameworks for understanding. This approach anticipated modern Intelligence Studies' emphasis on cultural intelligence, with the development of MECAS representing just one tangible example of its institutional learning. Although short-lived, MECAS showed how the Arab Bureau's innovative approaches could be partially preserved and transmitted.

The seventh pillar of intelligence wisdom is well-defined: institutional learning is not automatic, but instead requires intentional mechanisms for knowledge preservation, transfer, and adaptation. To this we might add that the most effective intelligence organisations create frameworks that can capture, validate, and transmit innovative practices across generations. In a contemporary setting, the message is that one should not just collect information, but rather create systems for preserving and transmitting institutional knowledge; recognise that innovation dies without intentional preservation; and build organisational cultures that value historical insights and continuous learning. The story of the Arab Bureau is a reminder that the most powerful intelligence emerges not from individual brilliance, but from organisations that can systematically learn, adapt, and evolve.

The Arab Bureau didn't just gather intelligence. It created a model of institutional learning that challenges how we understand knowledge transfer in complex operational environments.

THE ARAB BUREAU

The Enduring Wisdom of the Arab Bureau

A century ago, in the Arabian sands, a small group of unconventional officers rewrote the fundamental rules of understanding and intelligence. The Arab Bureau was more than a wartime intelligence unit: it became a profound experiment in human comprehension, a testament to how deeply we can understand complex cultural landscapes when we break down institutional barriers. Far more than a mere historical footnote, the Bureau's example is a living blueprint for navigating our increasingly complex global environment. As one intelligence scholar put it, the Arab Bureau demonstrated "how intelligence services can innovate effectively while operating within traditional military structures".[32]

The Seven Pillars of Intelligence Wisdom I have presented here represent a great deal more than historical insights. They are a roadmap for contemporary intelligence operations facing unprecedented global challenges. In an era of rapid technological change and cultural complexity, the Arab Bureau's approach remains startlingly relevant.

Consider what is arguably the Arab Bureau's most fundamental innovation: the recognition that true intelligence is not about collecting data points, but understanding human complexity. The Arab Bureau transformed intelligence from a technical exercise into a profound act of cultural interpretation. Its approach anticipated modern theoretical frameworks for understanding how knowledge is produced, circulated, and transformed, and our novel concept of an 'imperial epistemic community' offers a powerful lens for better understanding their unique contributions.

As such, the Arab Bureau's experience suggests several critical directions for future research to explore:

- Exploring Cultural Intelligence: How can intelligence organisations develop deeper, more nuanced cultural understanding?
- Interdisciplinary Knowledge Integration: What mechanisms can organisations create to break down institutional silos?
- Institutional Learning Mechanisms: How can innovative practices be systematically preserved and transmitted?
- Network-Based Intelligence: How can intelligence agencies develop more sophisticated, trust-based information networks?
- Balancing Operational Requirements With Cultural Expertise: What frameworks can help organisations maintain both strategic effectiveness and deep cultural understanding?

SEVEN PILLARS OF INTELLIGENCE WISDOM

These are not just academic questions, but rather a set of critical challenges facing contemporary intelligence services around the world. The experience of the Arab Bureau demonstrates both the possibilities and limitations of innovation within complex institutional environments. At the same time, any success it enjoyed was not just due to the individual brilliance of its officers, but the fact that they were part of an organisational structure that could adapt, integrate diverse expertise, and maintain a deep commitment to understanding cultural complexity. In doing all of this, the Arab Bureau perfectly demonstrated the importance of blending academic expertise and intelligence operations.

Future Legacy?

The Arab Bureau's most profound lesson is a deceptively simple one. Intelligence is fundamentally about human understanding. In an era of artificial intelligence, big data, and global interconnectedness, the Arab Bureau's approach reminds us that technology (as yet) cannot replace deep cultural comprehension.

Contemporary intelligence challenges mirror the complexities the Arab Bureau navigated a century ago, from counterinsurgency operations to diplomatic negotiations, and the need for informed cultural intelligence remains critical. As such, the Bureau's experience offers crucial insights for organisations operating in culturally complex environments, and it is of vital importance that intelligence agencies see culture as a fundamental aspect of operational effectiveness, and not merely the place where things happen. The Arab Bureau did more than recognise this principle; they lived it.

Of course, the broader implications extend well beyond intelligence operations, with the Arab Bureau's approach challenging how we understand knowledge production, cultural engagement, and institutional innovation. The Arab Bureau demonstrated that the most powerful insights emerge when we break down disciplinary boundaries, create flexible organisational structures, and commit to deep, empathetic understanding.

For academic disciplines, the Arab Bureau's legacy is equally transformative. It anticipated contemporary approaches in Middle East Studies, Intelligence Studies, and as far as I'm concerned interdisciplinary research too. Its work suggests new theoretical frameworks for understanding how knowledge is created, circulated, and transformed across cultural boundaries.

Yet we must be careful not to romanticise its achievements. The Arab Bureau operated within the constraints of British imperial power, and its insights were inevitably shaped by colonial perspectives. Its innovations existed alongside significant limitations and cultural blind spots. Understanding their legacy requires a nuanced, critical approach that recognises both its groundbreaking insights and its historical constraints.

With this caveat in mind, perhaps the most powerful tribute to the Arab Bureau is not uncritical praise, but a commitment to continuing its most fundamental approach, viz. seeing intelligence as a profound act of human understanding. In a world increasingly divided by cultural misunderstandings, the Arab Bureau's approach remains a beacon of possibility. Its story is a reminder that the most effective intelligence comes not from technological sophistication, but from a deep, empathetic commitment to understanding human complexity. In other words, the Arab Bureau demonstrated that intelligence, in whatever setting, is about helping humans navigate complex, uncertain, and often confusing environments.

Modern intelligence agencies face unprecedented challenges. Rapid technological change, global political complexity, and cultural diversification demand new approaches to understanding. Inspired by the Arab Bureau, my Seven Pillars of Intelligence Wisdom offer a compelling roadmap: cultivate cultural expertise, break down institutional barriers, develop flexible networks, and recognise that true intelligence is fundamentally about human connection.

In an era when technological sophistication often overshadows human understanding, the Arab Bureau's emphasis on cultural knowledge, organisational flexibility, and authentic engagement provides a powerful counter-narrative. The Seven Pillars of Intelligence Wisdom distilled from the Arab Bureau's experience offer not just abstract principles but practical guidance for intelligence practitioners, diplomats, military officers, and anyone engaged in cross-cultural operations. In this sense, the Arab Bureau's true significance may lie not in what it achieved a century ago, but in what it can teach us today about understanding and engaging with an increasingly complex world.

NOTES

PREFACE

1. My previous supervisor was the equally wonderful Professor Eugene Rogan, St Antony's, Oxford, a stalwart ally. I only left his camp once it became clear that Intelligence Studies would have equal weight in my DPhil as Middle East Studies, thus placing me beyond a single specialism.
2. Writing as Dr Gearon, I offer the opinion that Dr Johnson deserves a Chair and a pay rise.
3. Ursula K. Le Guin, *Steering the Craft: A 21st-Century Guide to Sailing the Sea of Story* (2015).
4. Abby Aguirre, "Ursula K. Le Guin on Writing in the 21st Century", *Vogue* (31 August 2015): https://www.vogue.com/article/ursula-le-guin-steering-the-craft (Accessed 7 January 2025).
5. *A Reassessment of the Arab Bureau: Innovative Approaches to Military Intelligence Reporting and Propaganda Production in the Arab Context, 1916–1920* (University of Oxford, 2025).
6. Elmore Leonard, "Easy on the Adverbs, Exclamation Points and Especially Hooptedoodle", *New York Times* (16 July 2001): https://www.nytimes.com/2001/07/16/arts/writers-writing-easy-adverbs-exclamation-points-especially-hooptedoodle.html?searchResultPosition=1 (Accessed, 7 January 2025).
7. This first encounter was so powerful that—along with a week in bed with COVID, and a strong desire to do something even more fun than DPhil research (?!)—it is the starting point of another book I've written, working title *Lawrence of Arabia: A Love Story* (2026).
8. T.E. Lawrence, *Seven Pillars of Wisdom* (1926).

INTRODUCTION

1. Roger Owen, "British and French Military Intelligence in Syria and Palestine, 1914–1918: Myths and Reality", in *British Journal of Middle Eastern Studies* 38, no. 1 (2011): 1–6.
2. CAB 4/6, CID 230-B, 10 January 1916.

3. "Members of the India Office and the government of India were often strident in their opposition to bureau objectives," Bruce Westrate, *The Arab Bureau* (1992), 3.
4. Without permanent status, no intelligence bureau could meaningfully settle into its work. As Gertrude Bell wrote to her father, "We want to establish here a permanent Intelligence Bureau for the Near East, which shall endure after the war is over—it would be invaluable; but it could not work properly without the sympathy and help of India." 24 January 1916. E. Burgoyne, *Gertrude Bell From Her Personal Papers: 1914–1926*, (1961), 34.
5. T.E. Lawrence, *Seven Pillars of Wisdom: A Triumph* (1935).
6. David Lean, *Lawrence of Arabia* (1962).
7. FO 882/2. Minutes of a 7 January 1916 meeting, entitled "Establishment of an Arab Bureau in Cairo".
8. Arnold Wilson, quoted in Westrate, *The Arab Bureau* (1992), 201.
9. The PWE (1941–45) was a secret body reporting to the Foreign Office, created to produce and disseminate propaganda during wartime, which was wound up at the end of the war.
10. The IRD (1948–77) was a secret propaganda department of the Foreign Office.

1. THE GALLOWS AT DAWN: DAMASCUS AND BEIRUT

1. From "Burnt Norton" (1935), one of *Four Quartets*, by T.S. Eliot (1888–1965).
2. In both Damascus and Beirut, these squares were subsequently renamed 'Martyrs' Square' (Sahat ash-Shuhada), with the anniversary memorialised in both countries every 6 May. In Beirut, a memorial statue on the site of the executions was inaugurated in 1960, created by Italian sculptor Marino Mazzacurati in an unashamedly heroic style.
3. Ahmed Djemal Pasha, or Ahmed Djemal (in Turkish Cemâl Pasha, or Ahmet Cemal Paşa) (1872–1922), was one of the so-called Three Pashas who ruled the Ottoman Empire during the First World War. The triumvirate consisted of Mehmed Talaat Pasha (1874–1921) as Grand Vizier (or prime minister) and Minister of the Interior; Ismail Enver Pasha (1881–1922), as Minister of War and Commander-in-Chief to the Sultan; and Djemal Pasha, Minister of the Navy and Governor General of Syria, and effectively ruler of the empire after the 1913 Ottoman coup d'état.
4. The CUP was a political group in the Ottoman Empire that aimed to reform and modernise the state, and which played a key role in the Young Turk Revolution of 1908. Active from 1889, it eventually became the ruling party

in the empire, responsible for both significant changes as well as for controversial policies, including the Armenian Genocide (1915–17).

5. Born in Mecca and raised in Constantinople (now Istanbul), Faisal bin al-Hussein bin Ali al-Hashemi (1885–1933) was Hussein's third son who played a major role in the Arab Revolt (1916–18). After the war, in 1919, he led the Arab delegation at the Paris Peace Conference. From March to July 1920, he ruled as the unrecognised King of the Arab Kingdom of Syria until he was expelled by the French. With British backing, he was then appointed first King of Iraq, which title he held from August 1921 until his death in 1933.

6. The text of the Damascus Protocol was first translated into English by George Antonius and published in his landmark text *The Arab Awakening* (1938). His translation was based on a copy of the protocol given to him by Faisal, which required the following:

> The recognition by Great Britain of the independence of the Arab countries lying within the following frontiers:
>
> North: The Line Mersin–Adana to parallel 37N and thence along the line Birejek–Urga–Mardin–Midiat–Jazirat (Ibn 'Unear)–Amadia to the Persian frontier;
>
> East: The Persian frontier down to the Persian Gulf;
>
> South: The Indian Ocean (with the exclusion of Aden, whose status was to be maintained);
>
> West: The Red Sea and the Mediterranean Sea back to Mersin.
>
> The abolition of all exceptional privileges granted to foreigners under the capitulations.
>
> The conclusion of a defensive alliance between Great Britain and the future independent Arab state.
>
> The grant of economic preference to Great Britain.

7. The French official was none other than François Georges-Picot, co-signatory of what Arabs would soon know as, and for evermore characterise as one of the most perfidious documents in the modern history of the Middle East, the Sykes-Picot Agreement.
8. Jan Morris, *Farewell the Trumpets* (1978), 3–4.
9. Christopher Catherwood, *The Battles of World War I* (2014), 51–2.
10. Chapter 10, The Paper War.
11. Chapter 9, *Thawrat al-Arab*.
12. Chapter 4, The Scholar Spies.
13. Bruce Westrate, *The Arab Bureau* (1992).
14. Priya Satia, *Spies in Arabia* (2008).

15. Polly Mohs, *Military Intelligence and the Arab Revolt* (2008).
16. Philip Walker, *Behind the Lawrence Legend: The Forgotten Few Who Shaped the Arab Revolt* (2018).
17. James Barr, *Setting the Desert on Fire* (2006).
18. For comprehensive treatments of orientalism and imperial knowledge production, see Said, *Orientalism* (1978); Satia, *Spies in Arabia* (2008); and the extensive literature on colonial discourse analysis. This study builds on these insights while focusing on operational rather than discursive analysis.
19. George Antonius, *The Arab Awakening: The Story of the Arab National Movement* (1938).
20. Albert Hourani, *A History of the Arab Peoples* (1991).
21. Eugene Rogan, *The Fall of the Ottomans* (2015).
22. Rashid Khalidi, *Palestinian Identity: The Construction of Modern National Consciousness* (1997).
23. James Gelvin, *Divided Loyalties: Nationalism and Mass Politics in Syria at the Close of Empire* (1998).
24. Christopher Andrew, *The Secret World: A History of Intelligence* (2018).

2. UNPREPARED FOR WAR: BLACK SEA, CONSTANTINOPLE, EGYPT, INDIA

1. SMS—or *Seiner Majestät Schiff*, German for 'His Majesty's Ship'—was the prefix used by both the Imperial German Navy (*Kaiserliche Marine*) and the Austro-Hungarian Navy (*Kaiserliche und königliche Kriegsmarine*) during the First World War.
2. For a classic account of the *Goeben* and *Breslau*, see Paul Halpern, *The Naval War in the Mediterranean, 1914–1918* (1987); and David Fromkin, *A Peace to End All Peace* (2001).
3. For valuable context on intelligence structures in these years, see Jim Beach, *Haig's Intelligence: GHQ and the German Army, 1916–1918* (2015).
4. Kim Wagner, *The Great Fear of 1857: Rumours, Conspiracies and the Making of the Indian Uprising* (2010); for more on India in this period, see William Dalrymple, *The Anarchy: The Relentless Rise of the East India Company* (2019).
5. The Indian Rebellion of 1857 was a major uprising in India against the East India Company, which functioned as a sovereign power on behalf of the British Crown. The rebellion posed a threat to British power in that region and was contained only with the rebels' defeat in June 1858. The name of the revolt is contested, being variously described as the Indian Mutiny (when this author was at school), the Sepoy Mutiny, the Great Rebellion, the Revolt of 1857, the Indian Insurrection, and the First War of Independence.
6. For useful context for understanding information networks in imperial

settings, see C.A. Bayly, *Empire and Information: Intelligence Gathering and Social Communication in India, 1780–1870* (1996).
7. For an insightful overview of intelligence organisational theory, see John Ferris, *Intelligence and Strategy: Selected Essays* (2005).
8. Abbas Hilmi (also Helmy) II (1874–1944; r. 1892–19 December 1914) was the last Khedive of Egypt and the Sudan. His removal by the British marked the de jure end of four centuries of Egypt as a province of the Ottoman Empire, which had begun in 1517.
9. Sir Joshua Milne Crompton Cheetham (1869–1938) served in Madrid, Paris, Tokyo, Berlin, Rome, and Rio de Janeiro before being sent to Cairo in January 1910. When the United Kingdom declared a protectorate over Egypt in December 1914, he became acting High Commissioner, pending the arrival of Sir Henry McMahon. He took charge of the British Residency during the spring and fall of 1919, and thus had to confront the Egyptian Revolution in 1919.
10. General Sir John Grenfell Maxwell (1859–1929) was a British Army officer and colonial governor. He served in the Mahdist War (1881–99) in the Sudan, the Second Boer War (1899–1902), the First World War, and, as Commander-in-Chief, Ireland. He also had a key role in Britain's response to the 1916 Easter Rising.
11. FO 471/1970, 5 November 1914. Cheetham.
12. Hussein Kamel (also Husayn Kamil) (1853–1917; r. 19 December 1914–9 October 1917) was appointed Sultan of Egypt under the British protectorate, the first person to hold that title since the Ottoman conquest in 1517. When Hussein died, his only son, Prince Kamal el-Dine Hussein, declined the succession, which instead passed to Hussein's half-brother Ahmed Fuad, who ruled as Fuad I.
13. The singular form of the word, *fallāḥ*, derives from an Arabic word for a ploughman.
14. Mark Sykes minute on Arabian Report, 15 October 1916: I.O.L., L/P&S/10/586, file 705/1916.
15. Martin Thomas, *Empires of Intelligence: Security Services and Colonial Disorder After 1914* (2007), remains one of the best studies of this area.
16. Mustafa Kemal Atatürk (c. 1881–1938) a founding father of the Republic of Turkey, or Türkiye as it has been known officially since June 2022. Atatürk served as the country's first president from 1923 until his death. He undertook sweeping modernisation reforms that turned the country into a secular, industrialised nation.
17. For an account of the campaign that remains fresh and insightful, see Alan Moorehead, *Gallipoli* (1989).
18. Major General Sir Charles Vere Ferrers Townshend (1861–1924).

19. The Revolutionary War, American Revolutionary War, or American War of Independence (19 April 1775–3 September 1783) was the conflict that saw the British Army beaten by the Continental Army, commanded by George Washington, which resulted in independence for what had been the American colonies.
20. Charles Cornwallis, 1st Marquess Cornwallis (1738–1805), the British Army officer, Whig politician, and colonial administrator whose surrender at Yorktown marked the end of major hostilities and the start of negotiations that would eventually end the American War of Independence.
21. Andrew Syk, "The 1917 Mesopotamia Commission: Britain's First Iraq Inquiry", *RUSI Journal* 154:4 (2009).
22. Field Marshal Horatio Herbert Kitchener (1850–1916) was, in addition to being a senior staff officer, a colonial administrator before the First World War. On 5 June 1916, while sailing to Russia for talks with Tsar Nicholas II, HMS *Hampshire* struck a German mine 1.5 miles (2.4 kilometres) west of Orkney, Scotland, and sank. Kitchener was among 737 dead, and he would remain the highest-ranking British officer to die in action in the entire war.
23. Sir Maurice William Ernest de Bunsen (1852–1932) was a British diplomat. His grandfather was Baron von Bunsen, Prussian ambassador to London, the family later removing the German 'von', instead preferring to adopt the French 'de'.
24. Early discussions about the formation of the Arab Bureau can be found in FO/882/2 ARB/16: 6 January 1916.
25. The lack of experience, or cultural insight, or linguistic expertise, on the part of the so-called experts remains alive and problematic to this day. Beware the expert who lacks expertise.
26. Baron Max von Oppenheim (1860–1946) was a German lawyer, diplomat, archaeologist, historian of the ancient Near (or Middle) East, intelligence officer, and promoter of pan-Islamism as a tool of German foreign policy.
27. *Denkschrift betreffend die Revolutionierung der islamischen Gebiete unserer Feinde* (October 1914).
28. For details of Oppenheim's propaganda bureau, and German operations more broadly, see Tilman Lüdke, *Jihad Made in Germany: Ottoman and German Propaganda and Intelligence Operations in the First World War* (2006); Benjamin Fortna, *The Circassian: The Life of Esref Bey, Late Ottoman Insurgent and Special Agent* (2016); Curt Prüfer, *Germany's Covert War in the Middle East: Espionage, Propaganda and Diplomacy in World War I* (2018); and Sean McMeekin, *Berlin–Baghdad Express* (2010).
29. For one interesting article about the London-based unit responsible for British propaganda, see Sorin Radu, "Wellington House and British Propaganda during the First World War", *Studia Politica: Romanian Political Science Review* 9 (2009), 63–80.

30. Antonin Jaussen (1871–1962), a Dominican priest, ethnologist, and archaeologist specialising in the Near East, and an eager and willing gatherer of local intelligence for French intelligence.
31. For more on French intelligence operations in the Middle East, see Henry Laurens, "Jaussen et les services de renseignement français, 1915–1919", in Géraldine Chatelard and Mohammed Tarawneh, *Antonin Jaussen, Western Social Sciences and Arab Heritage—Jaussen and the French Intelligence Service 1915–1919* (1999); and Roberto Mazza and Idir Ouhes, "For God and La Patrie: Antonin Jaussen, Dominican Priest and French Intelligence Agent in the Middle East", *First World War Studies* 3:2 (2012), 145–64. French material can be verified through Laurens' work on Jaussen (1999), and Mazza's studies (2012, 2016).
32. Russian intelligence operations are covered in Yigal Sheffy, *British Military Intelligence in the Palestine Campaign, 1914–1918* (1998).
33. FO 882/2, ARB 16/4, 24. Committee of Imperial Defence meeting, Whitehall Gardens: 7 January 1916.
34. Arnold C. Cooper and Dan Schendel, "Strategic Responses to Technological Threats", *Business Horizons* 19:1 (1976), 61–9, provide an early theoretical framework for organisational innovation that remains valuable.
35. David George Hogarth (1862–1927) was a British orientalist archaeologist and scholar, and Keeper of Antiquities (1909–27) at the Ashmolean Museum, Oxford. At the start of the First World War, he was commissioned into the Royal Naval Volunteer Reserve, serving with the Naval Intelligence Division. When it was formed, Hogarth was brought in as the Arab Bureau's acting director, and it was in this capacity that he recruited Lawrence, whom he knew before the war as a fellow Oxford-based archaeologist.
36. Gertrude Margaret Lowthian Bell (1868–1926) was a writer, traveller, political officer, administrator, and archaeologist, and the only woman member of the Arab Bureau, based for much of this time in Basra, southern Iraq. She had travelled extensively in the Middle East and Persia before the war, and she derived some of her influence through her network of contacts across the region.
37. Chapter 4, The Scholar Spies.
38. Chapter 4, The Scholar Spies.
39. Edited by Isabelle Duyvesteyn, *Intelligence and Strategic Culture* (2013) offers a number of theoretical frameworks that can, to varying degrees, also be applied to the development of the Arab Bureau.

3. "BRITISH DESIDERATA IN TURKEY AND ASIA": FOREIGN OFFICE, WHITEHALL, LONDON

1. For detailed analysis of the de Bunsen Committee's formation and functioning,

see Westrate, *The Arab Bureau* (1992), pp. 11–38; and Fromkin, *A Peace to End All Peace* (1989), pp. 146–9.

2. Details on Maurice de Bunsen's diplomatic background and career can be found in David Cannadine, *The Decline and Fall of the British Aristocracy* (1990), pp. 227–8.

3. On Sykes' role on the committee, and his limited regional experience, see Roger Adelson, *Mark Sykes: Portrait of an Amateur* (1975), pp. 170–5; and James Barr, *A Line in the Sand: Britain, France and the Struggle for the Mastery of the Middle East* (2011), pp. 27–32.

4. From an unpublished archive of personal papers and wartime diaries of Maurice and Berta de Bunsen, Broughton Castle, Oxfordshire. Accessed by the author, 9 July 2018.

5. Ibid.

6. Regarding the Arab Congress of 1913, see C. Ernest Dawn, *From Ottomanism to Arabism: Essays on the Origins of Arab Nationalism* (1973), pp. 148–52; and Rashid Khalidi, "Arab Nationalism: Historical Problems in the Literature", *The American Historical Review* 96:5 (December 1991), 1363–73.

7. From an unpublished archive of personal papers and wartime diaries of Maurice and Berta de Bunsen, Broughton Castle, Oxfordshire. Accessed by the author, 9 July 2018.

8. From an unpublished archive of personal papers and wartime diaries of Maurice and Berta de Bunsen, Broughton Castle, Oxfordshire. Accessed by the author, 9 July 2018.

9. For the development of the concept of 'epistemic communities' more generally, see Peter Haas, "Epistemic Communities and International Policy Coordination", *International Organization* 46:1 (1992), 3; and Steven Wagner, "Intelligence and the Origins of the British Middle East", in *The Journal of Imperial and Commonwealth History* 43:4 (2015), 725.

10. On the changing nature of intelligence requirements in unconventional warfare, see Jim Beach, "No Cloaks, No Daggers: The Historiography of British Military Intelligence", in *Intelligence Studies in Britain and the US: Historiography Since 1945* (2013), eds. Christopher R. Moran and Christopher J. Murphy, pp. 205–7; and Ferris, *Intelligence and Strategy* (2005), pp. 87–92.

11. For the declaration of 'jihad', see Mustafa Aksakal, *The Ottoman Road to War in 1914* (2008), pp. 163–75; and McMeekin, *The Berlin–Baghdad Express* (2010), pp. 121–8.

12. For French claims to Syria and Lebanon, see Barr, *A Line in the Sand* (2011), pp. 12–18; and Christopher Andrew and A.S. Kanya-Forstner, *The Climax of French Imperial Expansion, 1914–1924* (1981), pp. 156–64.

13. On Russian territorial claims and ambitions, see Fromkin, *A Peace to End All Peace* (1989), pp. 137–45; and Sean McMeekin, *The Ottoman Endgame: War,*

Revolution, and the Making of the Modern Middle East, 1908–1923 (2015), pp. 208–15.

14. On balancing strategic requirements against diplomatic commitments, see Robert H. Lieshout, *Britain and the Arab Middle East: World War I and Its Aftermath* (2016), pp. 82–8; and John Darwin, *Britain, Egypt and the Middle East: Imperial Policy in the Aftermath of War 1918–1922* (1981), pp. 124–32.

15. On the Foreign Office's European diplomatic orientation, see John R. Ferris, *The Evolution of British Strategic Policy, 1919–26* (1989), pp. 12–18; and Elizabeth Monroe, *Britain's Moment in the Middle East* (1981), pp. 34–9.

16. For detailed analysis of the options presented by the de Bunsen Committee, see Monroe, *Britain's Moment in the Middle East* (1981), pp. 34–9; and Marian Kent (ed.), *The Great Powers and the End of the Ottoman Empire* (1996), pp. 172–8.

17. On Britain's traditional approach of 'informal empire', see John Gallagher and Ronald Robinson, "The Imperialism of Free Trade", *The Economic History Review* 6:1 (1953), 1–15; and Darwin, *The Empire Project: The Rise and Fall of the British World-System, 1830–1970* (2009), pp. 112–24.

18. FO 141/817/1 3830/3: 10 September 1916; "Pan-Islamic Propaganda Meeting in Berlin".

19. FO 882/2, ARB 16/4, 24: 7 January 1916. Committee of Imperial Defence meeting, Whitehall Gardens.

20. On Britain's 'veiled protectorate' in Egypt, see Roger Owen, *Lord Cromer: Victorian Imperialist, Edwardian Proconsul* (2004), pp. 271–84; and Robert L. Tignor, *Modernization and British Colonial Rule in Egypt, 1882–1914* (1966), pp. 245–56.

21. Regarding the 'Exclusive Agreement' of 1892 with the Trucial States and the Kuwait Convention of 1899, see James Onley, *The Arabian Frontier of the British Raj: Merchants, Rulers, and the British in the Nineteenth-Century Gulf* (2007), pp. 172–84; and Briton Cooper Busch, *Britain and the Persian Gulf, 1884–1914* (1967), pp. 213–25.

22. Regarding the India Office's anxiety about Muslim opinion in India, see Richard J. Popplewell, *Intelligence and Imperial Defence* (1995), pp. 170–84; and Judith M. Brown, *Modern India: The Origins of Asian Democracy* (1985), p. 152, quoted in Christopher Andrew, *The Secret World: A History of Intelligence* (2018), p. 410.

23. On the Baghdad Railway question, see McMeekin, *The Berlin–Baghdad Express* (2010), pp. 34–52; and for a very early text, Edward Mead Earle, *Turkey, the Great Powers, and the Bagdad Railway: A Study in Imperialism* (1923), pp. 182–96.

24. For French claims to Syria and Lebanon, see Barr, *A Line in the Sand* (2011),

pp. 12–18; and Andrew and Kanya-Forstner, *The Climax of French Imperial Expansion* (1981), pp. 156–64.

25. On the evolution of British military intelligence practices, see John Ferris, *British Army and Signals Intelligence During the First World War* (1992), p. 55; and Beach, *Haig's Intelligence* (2015), pp. 8–9.

26. On British intelligence failures at Gallipoli, see Sheffy, *British Military Intelligence in the Palestine Campaign* (1998), pp. 42–58; and Satia, *Spies in Arabia* (2008), pp. 103–12.

27. For the conversion of the Royal Navy to oil fuel and its strategic implications, see Daniel Yergin, *The Prize: The Epic Quest for Oil, Money, and Power* (1991), pp. 153–64; and Satia, *Spies in Arabia* (2008), pp. 56–62.

28. For analysis of the 'institutional provincialism' in British administration, see Michael Herman, *Intelligence Power in Peace and War* (1996), pp. 103–5; and Philip Davies, *Intelligence and Government in Britain and the United States* (2012), pp. 142–7.

29. For more on Kut al-Amara and associated intelligence failures, see Peter Morris, "Intelligence and Its Interpretation: Mesopotamia, 1914–16", in Christopher Andrew and Jeremy Noakes (eds), *Intelligence and International Relations* (1987), pp. 77–101; and Nikolas Gardner, *The Siege of Kut-al-Amara: At War in Mesopotamia, 1915–1916* (2014), pp. 114–26.

30. For the India Office's preoccupation with Muslim opinion, see Popplewell, *Intelligence and Imperial Defence* (1995), pp. 170–84; and Satia, *Spies in Arabia* (2008), pp. 103–7.

31. For analysis of Arabic language skills among British officers, see Satia, *Spies in Arabia* (2008), pp. 106–8; and Wagner, "Intelligence and the Origins of the British Middle East" (2015), pp. 725–30.

32. For the cultural limitations of British officials, see Martin Thomas, *Empires of Intelligence: Security Services and Colonial Disorder After 1914* (2007), pp. 156–62; and Simon Willmetts, "The Cultural Turn in Intelligence Studies", *Intelligence and National Security* 34:6 (2019), pp. 804–6.

33. The concept of 'operational cultural intelligence' is explored in Thomas, *Empires of Intelligence* (2007), pp. 156–62; and Satia, *Spies in Arabia* (2008), pp. 103–12.

34. For Sykes's conception of an 'Islamic Bureau', see Barr, *Setting the Desert on Fire* (2006), pp. 27–33; and Westrate, *The Arab Bureau* (1992), pp. 22–8.

35. On the need for improved language capabilities, see Satia, *Spies in Arabia* (2008), pp. 106–8; and Ferris, *Intelligence and Strategy* (2005), pp. 87–92.

36. On the 'wandering scholars' recruited by Hogarth, see Satia, *Spies in Arabia* (2008), pp. 45–50; and Westrate, *The Arab Bureau* (1992), pp. 106–10.

4. THE SCHOLAR SPIES: OXFORD

1. On Hogarth's concept of "wandering scholars", see Satia, *Spies in Arabia* (2008), pp. 45–50; and Wagner, "Intelligence and the Origins of the British Middle East" (2015), pp. 725–30.
2. For more on the Ashmolean's role, see D.W.J. Gill, "Harry Pirie-Gordon: Historical research, journalism and intelligence gathering in the Eastern Mediterranean (1908–18)", *Intelligence and National Security* 21 (2006), pp. 26–31; and Thomas, *Empires of Intelligence* (2007), pp. 156–62.
3. Davies, *Intelligence and Government in Britain and the United States* (2012); and Herman, *Intelligence Power in Peace and War* (1996).
4. Herman, *Intelligence Power in Peace and War* (1996), pp. 103–7; and Polly Mohs, *Military Intelligence and the Arab Revolt* (2008), pp. 125–31.
5. The tension between academic and military approaches is examined in Radha Kumar, "Seeing Like a Policeman", in *Police Matters: The Everyday State and Caste Politics in South India, 1900–1975* (2018), pp. 1–18, & 21ff; and Duyvesteyn (ed.), *Intelligence and Strategic Culture* (2011), pp. 524–7.
6. On institutional setting and operational challenges, see Ronald Storrs, *Orientations* (1937), pp. 220–3; and Westrate, *The Arab Bureau* (1992), pp. 106–10.
7. On interdisciplinary approach, see Willmetts, "The Cultural Turn in Intelligence Studies" (2019), pp. 804–6; and Beach, "No Cloaks, No Daggers" (2013), pp. 205–7.
8. Brigadier-General Sir Gilbert Falkingham Clayton (1875–1929), was a career British Army intelligence officer, head of multiple agencies, and colonial administrator.
9. Mohs, *Military Intelligence and the Arab Revolt* (2008), pp. 125–31; and Walker, *Behind the Lawrence Legend* (2018), pp. 104–7.
10. On the 'new imperial expert', see Satia, *Spies in Arabia* (2008), pp. 106–8; and Edward Said, *Orientalism* (1978), pp. 206–10.
11. On Leonard Woolley's dual roles in archaeology and intelligence, see his *Dead Towns and Living Men* (1920), pp. 57–68; and H.V.F. Winstone, *The Illicit Adventure: The story of Political and Military Intelligence in the Middle East, From 1898 to 1926* (1987), pp. 176–83.
12. Mohs, *Military Intelligence and the Arab Revolt* (2008), pp. 73–9; and Thomas, *Empires of Intelligence* (2007), pp. 156–62.
13. Scott Anderson, *Lawrence in Arabia* (2013), pp. 47–56; and Lawrence's own *Crusader Castles* (1936).
14. More on Lawrence's specific methodological contributions in Anderson, *Lawrence in Arabia* (2013), pp. 177–86; and Wilson, *Lawrence of Arabia: The Authorised Biography of T.E. Lawrence* (1990), pp. 312–21.

15. Mohs, *Military Intelligence and the Arab Revolt* (2008), pp. 107–18; and Michael Heffernan, "Geography, Cartography and Military Intelligence: The Royal Geographical Society and the First World War", *Transactions of the Institute of British Geographers* 21:3 (1996), 520–38.
16. For more on Lawrence's pre-war archaeological work see Wilson, *Lawrence of Arabia* (1990); and Anderson, *Lawrence in Arabia* (2013).
17. The Arab Bureau's collaborative approach to intelligence is captured in Westrate, *The Arab Bureau* (1992); and Peter Gill and Mark Phythian, *Intelligence in an Insecure World* (2006), p. 84.
18. Leonard Woolley, *Dead Towns and Living Men: Being Pages From an Antiquary's Notebook* (1920).
19. Technological limitations and their impact on intelligence are discussed in Ferris, *Intelligence and Strategy* (2005), pp. 87–92; and Beach, *Haig's Intelligence* (2015), pp. 156–9.
20. The specific methodological innovations are detailed in Thomas, *Empires of Intelligence* (2007), pp. 156–62; and Satia, *Spies in Arabia* (2008), pp. 45–50.
21. The postcolonial critique of imperial intelligence is a well-trodden field, and while this study acknowledges these important perspectives it should be clear by now that we do not intend to make the ground any muddier by walking back and forth across it, preferring instead to walk along another, complementary path. The broader intellectual context of orientalist scholarship is critiqued in Said, *Orientalism* (1978), pp. 206–10; and Zachary Lockman, *Field Notes: The Making of Middle East Studies in the United States* (2016), pp. 28–33.
22. FO 371/2781, 18 August 1916.
23. Hogarth's application of archaeological methods to intelligence work is detailed in Gill, "Harry Pirie-Gordon" (2006), pp. 26–31; and Satia, *Spies in Arabia* (2008), pp. 45–50.
24. For a complete biography, see Timothy Paris' wonderful *In Defence of Britain's Middle Eastern Empire: A Life of Sir Gilbert Clayton* (2015).
25. Satia, *Spies in Arabia* (2008), pp. 116–18; and Westrate, *The Arab Bureau* (1992).
26. For more on Clayton et al., see Westrate, *The Arab Bureau* (1992); and Walker, *Behind the Lawrence Legend* (2018).
27. Bell's genealogical research is detailed in Georgina Howell, *Gertrude Bell: Queen of the Desert, Shaper of Nations* (2008), pp. 270–85; and Satia, *Spies in Arabia* (2008), pp. 116–18.
28. Howell, *Gertrude Bell* (2008), pp. 254–67; and Liora Lukitz, *A Quest in the Middle East: Gertrude Bell and the Making of Modern Iraq* (2006), pp. 112–4.

29. Bell's relationships with tribal leaders are analysed in Howell, *Gertrude Bell* (2008), pp. 254–67; and Westrate, *The Arab Bureau* (1992), pp. 115–19.
30. The interdisciplinary approach to regional understanding is discussed in Thomas, *Empires of Intelligence* (2007), pp. 156–62; and Willmetts, "The Cultural Turn in Intelligence Studies" (2019), pp. 804–6.
31. Post-war Arab Bureau legacies are explored in Andrew, *The Secret World* (2018), pp. 542–5; and R. Gerald Hughes, Philip Murphy, and Philip H.J. Davies, "The British Secret Intelligence Service, 1909–1949", *Intelligence and National Security* 26:5 (2011), pp. 705–9.
32. The concept of regional experts as intelligence assets is analysed in Wagner, "Intelligence and the Origins of the British Middle East" (2015), pp. 725–30; and Davies, *Intelligence and Government in Britain and the United States* (2012), p. 147.
33. The academic foundations of Intelligence Studies are examined in Stephen Marrin, "Improving Intelligence Studies as an Academic Discipline", *Intelligence & National Security* 31:2 (2014), pp. 1–14; and Duyvesteyn, *Intelligence and Strategic Culture* (2011), pp. 524–7.
34. For more on Ruhi, see Walker, *Behind the Lawrence Legend* (2018).
35. On integrating cultural expertise with military operations, see Kumar, "Seeing Like a Policeman" (2018), pp. 135–7; and Thomas, *Empires of Intelligence* (2007), pp. 156–62.
36. Philip Walker, *Behind the Lawrence Legend: The Forgotten Few Who Shaped the Arab Revolt*, Oxford, 2018. See in particular chapters 1–3.
37. Ibid.
38. Ibdi.
39. MECA, St Antony's College, Oxford, GB 165–0310, John Young, *A Little to the East: Experiences of an Anglo-Egyptian Official, 1899–1925*, p. 14.
40. Abdullah Bin Sulaiman Al Hamdan (1887–1965), Saudi Arabia's first Minister of Finance (1932–1955).
41. IWM, Private Papers of Major-General Sir Arthur Lynden-Bell. 7826, pp. 176–7: 31 August 1916. Lynden-Bell to Major-General Frederick Maurice, Director of Military Operations, War Office.
42. Wilson to Clayton, 22 November 1916, SAD C.P. 470/4.
43. Comparative intelligence approaches are examined in Sheffy, *British Military Intelligence in the Palestine Campaign* (1998), pp. 156–68; and Andrew, *The Secret World* (2018), pp. 542–5.
44. 1 December 1916; FO 371/2781.
45. Hubert Young Papers; King's College Archives, London.
46. David Hogarth Papers, Magdalen College Archives, Oxford: P/452/MIL/2.
47. Clayton's management approach of 'structured flexibility' is discussed in Satia,

Spies in Arabia (2008), pp. 106–8; and Westrate, *The Arab Bureau* (1992), pp. 106–10.
48. Westrate, *The Arab Bureau* (1992).
49. The broader implications for intelligence theory are discussed in Herman, *Intelligence Power in Peace and War* (1996), pp. 143–6; and Gill and Phythian, *Intelligence in an Insecure World* (2006), p. 84.
50. See Clifford Geertz's seminal essay 'Thick Description: Toward an Interpretive Theory of Culture,' in The Interpretation of Cultures (1973).

5. ROOMS AT THE SAVOY: CAIRO

1. On the Arab Bureau's establishment in Cairo, see Westrate, *The Arab Bureau* (1992).
2. Darwin, *Britain, Egypt and the Middle East* (1981); and Lanver Mak, *The British in Egypt: Community, Crime and Crises: 1882–1922* (2012).
3. Storrs, *Orientations* (1937).
4. Storrs, *Orientations* (1937), pp. 220–3; and Mohs, *Military Intelligence and the Arab Revolt* (2008), pp. 107–18.
5. On challenges of communications infrastructure, see Tom Standage, *The Victorian Internet* (1999); and David Kahn, *The Codebreakers* (1967), pp. 617–39.
6. The technological context of wartime intelligence is examined in Ferris, *Intelligence and Strategy* (2005), pp. 87–92; and Priya Satia, "War, Wireless, and Empire: Marconi and the British Warfare State, 1896–1903", *Technology and Culture* 51 (2010), 829–53.
7. For the development of signals intelligence, see John Ferris, "The Road to Bletchley Park: The British Experience With Signals Intelligence, 1892–1945", *Intelligence and National Security* 7:1 (2002), 53–84; and Herman, *Intelligence Power in Peace and War* (1996), pp. 143–6.
8. The role of wireless technology in imperial intelligence is explored in Daniel Headrick, *The Tentacles of Progress: Technology in the Age of Imperialism, 1850–1940* (1988); and Satia, *Spies in Arabia* (2008).
9. See Andrew and Noakes (eds), *Intelligence and International Relations* (1987); and Richard J. Aldrich, "Strategic Culture as a Constraint", *Intelligence and National Security* 32:5 (2017), 625–35.
10. For inter-agency tensions more generally, see Hughes et al., "The British Secret Intelligence Service, 1909–1949" (2011); and Keith Jeffery, *MI6: The History of the Secret Intelligence Service* (2010).
11. On the concept of an imperial epistemic community, see Mai'a K. Davis Cross, "Rethinking Epistemic Communities Twenty Years Later", *Review of International Studies* 39:1 (2013), 137–60; and Haas, "Epistemic Communities and International Policy Coordination" (1992).

12. Institutional resistance to innovation is analysed in Duyvesteyn, "Intelligence and Strategic Culture" (2011), 521–30; and Marrin, "Improving Intelligence Studies" (2016), pp. 266–79.
13. Arab Bureau administrative challenges are detailed in Paris, *In Defence of Britain's Middle East Empire* (2016); and Thomas, *Empires of Intelligence* (2007).
14. Lawrence, *Seven Pillars of Wisdom* (1926); Chapter 6, p. 29.
15. Sirdar was the rank assigned to the British Commander-in-Chief of the British-controlled Egyptian Army 1882–1937. The Sirdar resided at the Sirdaria, a three-block-long property in Zamalek which was also the home of British military intelligence in Egypt.
16. During the First World War, there were two Sirdars: Sir Reginald Wingate (1861–1954; Sirdar 1899–1916) and Sir Lee Stack (1868–1924), Sirdar from 1916 until his assassination in 1924. Stack was the last Sirdar to also be Governor General of Sudan.
17. Davies, *Intelligence and Government in Britain and the United States* (2012); and Peter Gill, Stephen Marrin, and Mark Phythian, *Intelligence Theory: Key Questions and Debates* (2009).
18. On the development of intelligence networks, see Kristan J. Wheaton and Melonie K. Richey, "The Potential of Social Network Analysis in Intelligence", *e-International Relations* (2014); and Ian McCulloh, Helen Armstrong, and Anthony Johnson, *Social Network Analysis with Applications* (2013).
19. Willmetts, "The Cultural Turn in Intelligence Studies" (2019).
20. For intelligence as knowledge production, see Michael Warner, "Documenting the History of Intelligence", *Intelligence and National Security* 24:3 (2009), 458–63; and Robert Clark, *Intelligence Analysis: A Target-Centric Approach* (2003).
21. On technological adaptations of wartime intelligence, see Cooper and Schendel, "Strategic Responses to Technological Threats" (1976); and Ruggie, "International Responses to Technology: Concepts and Trends", *International Responses to Technology* 29:3 (1975), 557–83.
22. For aerial reconnaissance and intelligence, see James Streckfuss, *Eyes All Over the Sky: Aerial Reconnaissance in the First World War* (2011); and Heffernan, "Geography, Cartography and Military Intelligence: The Royal Geographical Society and the First World War", (1996).
23. On translation and linguistic intelligence, see Kees Versteegh, *The Arabic Language* (2014); and Edward T. Hall, *Beyond Culture* (1976).
24. On imperial knowledge production, see Christopher Murray, "Imperial Dialectics and Epistemic Mapping: From Decolonisation to anti-Eurocentric IR", *European Journal of International Relations* 26:2 (2020), 419–42; and Wagner, "Intelligence and the Origins of the British Middle East" (2015).

25. Kumar, "Seeing Like a Policeman" (2018); and Richard Deacon, *A History of the British Secret Service* (1969).
26. Davies, *Intelligence and Government in Britain and the United States* (2012), p. 147.
27. For more on the imperial epistemic community concept, see Cross, "Rethinking Epistemic Communities" (2013), pp. 137–60; and Haas, "Epistemic Communities and International Policy Coordination" (1992), pp. 1–35.
28. The institutional transformation of intelligence is discussed in Rory Cormac, *Disrupt and Deny* (2021); and Calder Walton, *Empire of Secrets: British Intelligence, the Cold War and the Twilight of the Empire* (2013).
29. For post-war legacies, see Andrew, *The Secret World* (2018); and Hughes et al., "The British Secret Intelligence Service, 1909–1949" (2011).

6. NETWORKS OF KNOWLEDGE

1. Philip Graves (1876–1953) was an Anglo-Irish journalist and writer who, while based in Constantinople, exposed *The Protocols of the Elders of Zion* as a fraudulent hoax. He was a correspondent for *The Times* in Constantinople (1908–1914) and Cairo (1919–1932), and the older half-brother of the authors Robert Graves and Charles Graves.
2. Leonard Wolley, *The Wilderness of Zin* (1936).
3. *Arab Bulletin*, Issue 6 (23 June 1916) discusses of networks.
4. FO 882/2, ARB 16/4, 24: 7 January 1916. Committee of Imperial Defence meeting, Whitehall Gardens.
5. Hogarth's archaeological background significantly shaped Arab Bureau approaches.
6. For German and Ottoman propaganda in this period, see Tilman Lüdke, *Jihad Made in Germany: Ottoman and German Propaganda and Intelligence Operations in the First World War* (2005); and McMeekin, *Berlin–Baghdad Express* (2010).
7. Woolley, *Dead Towns and Living Men* (1920). Woolley's memoir provides insights into how archaeological networks transformed into intelligence infrastructure.
8. The archaeology–intelligence connection is examined in Gill, "Harry Pirie-Gordon" (2006); and Thomas, *Empires of Intelligence* (2007).
9. Satia's *Spies in Arabia* is one of the most thorough analyses of the relationship between scholarly networks and intelligence operations.
10. Herbert Garland (1880–1921), metallurgist and Army Ordnance Corps officer, joined the Arab Bureau and was posted to the Hijaz in September 1916. His linguistic skills and demolition expertise both proved invaluable.

11. *Arab Bulletin*, Issue 45 (23 March 1917). Garland's report "Arabic Dialects and Identification Methods" shows the intelligence value of linguistic expertise.
12. *Arab Bulletin*, Issue 60 (20 August 1917) includes discussions of linguistic methods.
13. Thomas, *Empires of Intelligence* (2007), and Satia, *Spies in Arabia* (2008), both analyse methodological innovations of this approach to linguistics.
14. Wilson, *Lawrence of Arabia* (1990), provides a good assessment of Lawrence's linguistic capabilities as functional rather than fluent.
15. Christopher Andrew and David Dilks (eds), *The Missing Dimension: Governments and Intelligence Communities in the Twentieth Century* (1984), p. 102.
16. T.E. Lawrence Papers, Bodleian Library, Oxford. MS. Eng. c.6710, fols. 1–53: "Crusader Castles", and T.E. Lawrence, *Crusader Castles* (1936); see also Anderson, *Lawrence in Arabia* (2013).
17. Gertrude Bell, *Letters* (1927). Her correspondence reveals her self-assessment of her role within regional networks.
18. Mohs, *Military Intelligence and the Arab Revolt* (2008), pp. 107–18.
19. FO 141/817: 11 February 1917. "Report on 'Moslem Propaganda'", an anonymous Arab Bureau memo, reveals its understanding of regional information networks.
20. Heffernan, "Geography, Cartography and Military Intelligence: The Royal Geographical Society and the First World War", (1996).
21. *Arab Bulletin*, Issue 25 (7 October 1916, 340–1) contains discussion of information verification.
22. Faris Nimr (1856–1951), Syrian-born journalist and founder of *al-Muqattam* newspaper in 1889, became an important intellectual collaborator with the Arab Bureau. See also Chapter 9.
23. Ya'qub Sarruf (1852–1927), pioneering Lebanese writer, publisher, and translator, co-founded the influential journal *al-Muqtataf* in 1876.
24. Rashid Rida (1865–1935), influential Islamic reformer and publisher of *al-Manar* (1898–1935), had a complex relationship with the Arab Bureau, and indeed the British more broadly.
25. FO 882/14, 16/9: 25 July 1916. Clayton to Symes, correspondence detailing their approach to working with Arab intellectuals.
26. Jurji Zaydan (1861–1914) was a prolific Lebanese novelist, journalist, editor and teacher, and one of the first to formulate a theory of Arab nationalism. His historical novels were particularly influential.
27. *Al-Hilal* (*The Crescent*), established in 1892, was Zaydan's platform for publishing serialisations of his twenty-plus historical novels and promoting pan-Arab ideas.

28. FO 141/773/6: 24 June 1916. Hogarth to Clayton.
29. Butrus al-Bustani (1819–83), Lebanese writer and scholar, was one of the leading figures of the Nahda Movement (Arabic Renaissance), whose legacy influenced intellectual networks the Arab Bureau engaged with.
30. For instance, Mayy Ziyade (1886–1941), a Lebanese-Palestinian poet, essayist and translator who hosted an influential literary salon in Cairo and represented an important node in intellectual networks.
31. *Arab Bulletin*, Issues 40 (29 January 1917), 97 (16 July 1918), and 100 (20 August, 1918) on verification methods and systems.
32. *Arab Bulletin*, Issue 100 (20 August 1918).
33. *Arab Bulletin*, Issue 48 (21 April 1917).
34. Hughes et al., "The British Secret Intelligence Service, 1909–1949", (2011).
35. *Arab Bulletin*, Issue 49 (30 April 1917) includes discussion around information networks.
36. *Arab Bulletin*, Issue 93 (15 June 1918) includes discussion of geographic limitations.
37. Ferris, *Intelligence and Strategy* (2005); and Beach, *Haig's Intelligence* (2015), both discuss technological limitations and the impact on intelligence operations.
38. For broader theoretical context, see Willmetts, "The Cultural Turn in Intelligence Studies" (2019).
39. Christopher Bayly, *Empire and Information: Intelligence Gathering and Social Communication in India, 1780–1870* (1996), examines the colonial knowledge–intelligence nexus.
40. *Arab Bulletin*, Issue 112 (24 June 1919) reflects on Arab Bureau methodological innovations.
41. *Arab Bulletin*, Issues 113 and 114 (17 July and 30 August 1919) partly summarise their legacy.

7. "READING THE ENEMY'S MAIL": INTELLIGENCE BREAKTHROUGHS

1. Ferris, *Intelligence and Strategy* (2005) discusses technological context of First World War intelligence operations, including the limitations and capabilities of wireless telegraphy.
2. *Arab Bulletin*, Issue 47 (11 April 1917) on Ottoman wireless communications and their intelligence value.
3. FO 882/25: August 1916. "Report on Wireless Intercept Operations, Jeddah Station."
4. *Arab Bulletin*, Issue 60 (20 August 1917) Herbert Garland, "Linguistic Analysis of Ottoman Communications".

5. *Arab Bulletin*, Issue 60 (20 August 1917) documents linguistic analysis methods.
6. For analysis of academic methods transforming into intelligence methodologies, see Mohs, *Military Intelligence and the Arab Revolt* (2008), pp. 107–18.
7. For more on archaeological methods and intelligence analysis, see Woolley, *Dead Towns and Living Men* (1920), pp. 45–8.
8. For an examination of urban intelligence networks, see Anna Danielson, "The Emergence of a Military Urban in and of War", *Annals of the American Association of Geographers* 115:2 (2025), 404–18 (published online: 18 November 2024).
9. For considerations on the scholarly–military nexus, see Heffernan, "Geography, Cartography and Military Intelligence: The Royal Geographical Society and the First World War" (1996).
10. Lawrence, *Seven Pillars of Wisdom* (1935), Chapter 16, on the complex nature of tribal intelligence networks.
11. For an examination of approaches to tribal intelligence, see C. C. R. Murphy, *Soldiers of the Prophet* (2008).
12. Westrate, pp. 11–38, examines Arab Bureau's institutional position and innovative approach.
13. *Arab Bulletin*, Issue 57 (24 July 1917). Extensive analysis of Hijaz Railway operations.
14. FO 141/734/3: September 1916. Graves' report and analysis of Ottoman wireless operations.
15. DUA 136/5: 17 April 1916. Clayton to Wingate, in Westrate, p. 106. On the strategic significance of railway intelligence.
16. *Arab Bulletin*, Issue 45 (23 March 1917) "Raid on the Hejaz Railway".
17. BL IOR L/PS/11/110: 30 September 1916. Clayton to Hogarth, details technical challenges.
18. *Arab Bulletin*, Issue 96 (9 July 1918). Discussion on the challenges of network operations.
19. *Arab Bulletin*, Issue 40 (29 January 1917). On verification methods for intelligence from diverse sources.
20. *Arab Bulletin*, Issue 93 (15 June 1918). Discusses geographic limitations to intelligence gathering.
21. *Arab Bulletin*, Issues 97 and 100 (16 July and 20 August 1918). Insights into verification systems.
22. *Arab Bulletin*, Issue 65 (23 July 1917). On dialectal variations and their intelligence implications.
23. Bell, *Letters* (1927), includes correspondence revealing her assessment of intelligence limitations.

24. For more context on intelligence operations, see Storrs, *Orientations* (1937), 220.
25. Bayly, *Empire and Information* (1996), examines information networks in imperial contexts.
26. For more on the Arab Bureau's distinctive methodological approach, see Beach, "No Cloaks, No Daggers" (2013), p. 205.
27. Eugene Rogan, *The Arabs: A History* (2009), 152–7; Impact of intelligence operations on the Arab Revolt.
28. Richard Meinertzhagen, *Army Diary 1899–1926* (1960). A controversial source, it nevertheless provides insights into Hijaz Railway operations.
29. *Arab Bulletin*, Issue 49 (30 April 1917) discusses information network management.
30. Anderson, *Lawrence in Arabia* (2013), pp. 177–86, on Lawrence's application of Arab Bureau methods.
31. WO 157/717: 26 September 1917. Allenby to War Office shows integration of Arab Bureau intelligence into conventional military operations.
32. Donald McKale, *War by Revolution: Germany and Great Britain in the Middle East in the Era of World War I* (1998); On German intelligence operations, and British countermeasures.
33. For more on the intelligence foundations of this operation, see Maxwell Orme Johnson, "The Arab Bureau and the Arab Revolt: Yanbu' to Aqaba", *Military Affairs* 46:4 (December 1982), 194–201.
34. Leonard Woolley, *As I Seem to Remember* (1962), 87–92, provides perspective on intelligence innovation.
35. For insights into the Arab Bureau's multi-source approach, see *Arab Bulletin*, Issue 100 (20 August 1918).
36. Monroe, *Britain's Moment in the Middle East* (1981), on British regional policy.
37. Satia, *Spies in Arabia* (2008), on the impact of Arab Bureau methods on subsequent British operations.
38. Thomas, *Empires of Intelligence* (2007), on the influence of Arab Bureau cultural intelligence methods.
39. IOR L/PS/10/581/521: 7 June 1916. Official recognition of influence of Arab Bureau's approaches.
40. Hall, *Beyond Culture* (1976), provides a theoretical framework for understanding cultural intelligence.
41. Willmetts, "The Cultural Turn in Intelligence Studies" (2019), p. 804, for theoretical context.
42. Brian Reid's 'T.E. Lawrence and His Biographers' (1991) considers Lawrence's intelligence contributions; in *The First World War and British Military History*, ed. Brian Bond.

43. Wagner, *Intelligence Transformation* (2011), 113–17, on network theory in intelligence operations, with reference to historical precedents.
44. Christopher Andrew, "Intelligence Analysis Needs to Look Backwards Before Looking Forward", *History & Policy* (2004), 12–15, discussing institutional memory, or the lack thereof, in intelligence organisations.
45. *Arab Bulletin*, Issues 113 and 114 (17 July and 30 August 1919); final issues reflect on the Arab Bureau's methodological innovations and legacy.
46. Philip S. Khoury, *Syria and the French Mandate* (1987); on legacy of wartime intelligence networks in post-war administration.

8. THE *ARAB BULLETIN* AS INTELLIGENCE INNOVATION: CAIRO

1. *Arab Bulletin*, Issue 100 (20 August 1918), 276.
2. *Arab Bulletin*, Issue 1 (6 June 1916) references the original distribution list of twenty-five, including a single copy for the Arab Bureau files.
3. See *Arab Bulletin*, Issue 100 (20 August 1918), p. 276, for Hogarth's comments about French and Italian access making certain discussions impossible.
4. *Arab Bulletin*, Issue 100 (20 August 1918), pp. 275–6.
5. *Arab Bulletin*, Issue 48 (21 April 1917), pp. 172–87.
6. *Arab Bulletin*, Issue 54 (22 June 1917), 280–5, for presentation of differing accounts of Ottoman troop strengths in Syria.
7. *Arab Bulletin*, Issue 37 (4 January 1917), p. 6.
8. *Arab Bulletin*, Issue 60 (20 August 1917), 353–4 for Garland's survey from Yambo to Abu Markha.
9. *Arab Bulletin*, Issue 25 (7 October 1916), 340–1. Reprint of Ottoman delegation's statement in Berne that failed to acknowledge their loss of Mecca.
10. *Arab Bulletin*, Issue 98 (23 July 1918), 256–66.
11. *Arab Bulletin*, Issue 5 (18 June 1916), 43–4, earliest Arab Bureau reporting on the Arab Revolt.
12. *Arab Bulletin*, Issue 5 (18 June 1916), 43–4, on straightforward reporting of military developments.
13. *Arab Bulletin*, Issue 25 (7 October 1916), 332.
14. *Arab Bulletin*, Issue 50 (13 May 1917).
15. *Arab Bulletin*, Issue 50 (13 May 1917), 207–17, for Lawrence's report.
16. *Arab Bulletin*, Issue 6 (23 June 1916).
17. *Arab Bulletin*, Issue 9 (9 July 1916), 8–9. First-hand report from an Arab officer who visited Mecca, and honest reporting about Medina.
18. *Arab Bulletin*, Issue 9 (9 July 1916), 1. Intercepted German wireless message denying any rebellion in the Hijaz.

19. *Arab Bulletin*, Issue 9 (9 July 1916), 1.
20. *Arab Bulletin*, Issues 37 and 38 (8 and 12 January 1917), 3–5; 13, on guerrilla operations against the Hijaz Railway.
21. *Arab Bulletin*, Issue 57 (24 July 1917), 307–9. Analysis connecting the capture of Aqaba to broader strategy and Ottoman force deployments.
22. Arab Bulletin, Issue 97 (16 July 1918), 255–6; and Issue 100 (20 August 1918), 277–9, demonstrating Harry St John Philby's (1885–1960) observations that Ibn Saud's ambitions did not always align with Sharif Hussein's.
23. *Arab Bulletin*, Issue 45 (23 March 1917).
24. *Arab Bulletin*, Issue 49 (30 April 1917), 191–3.
25. *Arab Bulletin*, Issue 65 (23 July 1917), 395–9, on Hussein's position regarding the Holy Cities and the Ottoman fatwa.
26. *Arab Bulletin*, Issue 96 (9 July 1918), 245–6. Notes from Lawrence highlighting competing interests among central Arabian tribes.
27. *Arab Bulletin*, Issue 48 (21 April 1917), 179–87.
28. *Arab Bulletin*, Issues 99–104 (6 August–24 September 1918), on the evolving concept of Arab unity and competing political aspirations.
29. *Arab Bulletin*, Issue 54 (22 June 1917), 275–80.
30. *Arab Bulletin*, Issues 108–14 (11 January–30 August 1919).
31. Born Ömer Fahrettin Türkkan (1868–1948), he was a Turkish career officer, commander of the Ottoman garrison, and governor of Medina, commonly known as Fakhri Pasha. He earned the nickname 'Defender of Medina', and from his British and Arab opponents either the 'Lion' or the 'Tiger of the Desert' for his defence of the city while under siege, lasting from 10 June 1916–10 January 1919.
32. *Arab Bulletin*, Issue 110 (30 April 1919), 32–53, devoted to Medina, the lifting of the siege, and interrogations of Fakhri Pasha.
33. *Arab Bulletin*, Issue 44 (12 March 1917), pp. 117–21.
34. *Arab Bulletin*, Issue 100 (20 August 1918), 275.
35. *Arab Bulletin*, Issue 100 (20 August 1918), 275–7.

9. *THAWRAT AL-ARAB*: CREATING AN ARABIC-LANGUAGE PROPAGANDA MASTERPIECE

1. Hereafter, for stylistic reasons, where *Thawrat al-Arab* is rendered into English it will be as *The Arab Revolt*, rather than *The Arabs' Revolt*, which while arguably having greater immediacy of tone is not how these events are remembered today.
2. FO 141/817: "Report on 'Moslem Propaganda'", anonymous Arab Bureau memo (11 February 1917). This document provides crucial evidence of the

Arab Bureau's direct involvement in commissioning and distributing *Thawrat al-Arab*, confirming its status as an official British propaganda instrument.

3. Gary S. Messinger, *British Propaganda and the State in the First World War* (1992), while offering a solid study of British propaganda, overlooks *Thawrat al-Arab*, highlighting the text's neglect until now.
4. As'ad Khalil Daghir (1860–1935), a Lebanese Orthodox Christian journalist, editor, and author born in Kfarshima, 6 miles south-east of Beirut. See also Daghir's memoir, *Mudhakkirati 'ala hamish al-qadiyya al-'arabiyya*; *My Memoirs on the Margins of the Arab Cause* (1959).
5. Faris Nimr (1856–1951) was an intellectual, pioneer of Lebanese journalism, and co-founder of *al-Muqattam* newspaper (established 1888), whose pro-British views made his publications a reliable outlet for British messaging in Egypt.
6. Thomas, *Empires of Intelligence* (2007), 156. Thomas's concept of 'intelligence epistemic communities' helps explain the Arab Bureau's integration of academic expertise with intelligence operations.
7. Westrate, *The Arab Bureau* (1992), 108 notes that the speed of publication suggests both the priority given to influencing Arab opinion and the effectiveness of the Arab Bureau's working relationship with local Arab intellectuals.
8. James Gelvin, *Divided Loyalties: Nationalism and Mass Politics in Syria at the Close of Empire* (1998), 124–6 looks at the impact of the executions on Arab politics and the precipitation of the Arab Revolt.
9. Joshua Teitelbaum, "The Man Who Would Be Caliph: Sharifian Propaganda in WWI", in Erik J. Zürcher (ed.), *Jihad and Islam in World War I* (2016), 275–304. Teitelbaum examines Hussein's claim to the title 'King Among the Arabs' and its religious and political implications.
10. Arabic for 'martyr'.
11. P.J. Vatikiotis, *The History of Modern Egypt* (1991), 241–3 discusses territorial ambitions expressed in early Arab nationalist literature and how this complicated British plans for post-war settlement.
12. FO 882/2, ARB 16/4, 24, Foreign Office report explicitly identifying propaganda as a key function of the Arab Bureau.
13. FO 882/2, ARB 16/4, 24 (7 January 1916), Committee of Imperial Defence meeting, Whitehall Gardens, explicitly identifying propaganda as a central function of the Arab Bureau, indicating that information operations were considered a core mission from the agency's inception.
14. Eitan Bar-Yosef, "The Last Crusade? British Propaganda and the Palestine Campaign, 1917–18", *Journal of Contemporary History* 36:1 (2001), 87–109. Examines how the martyrs of 1916 became powerful symbols in British and Arab propaganda.

15. *Al-Muqattam* was named after a range of hills and an associated district on Cairo's eastern perimeter. The newspaper was established, in 1888, by three Syrian Christians with the support of Lord Cromer (1841–1917), then British Consul-General.
16. Malcolm Yapp, *The Making of the Modern Middle East, 1792–1923* (1987), 210.
17. Hasan Kayali, *Arabs and Young Turks: Ottomanism, Arabism, and Islamism in the Ottoman Empire, 1908–1918* (1997), 165–8, looking at the spectrum of Arab nationalist thought, from reformists to revolutionaries.
18. Rashid Khalidi, "The Press as a Source for Modern Arab Political History: A Case Study of Beirut", *Arab Studies Quarterly* 3:1 (1981), 22–42, examines how colonial powers engaged with and influenced Arabic-language publications during this period.
19. C.S. Forester (b. Cairo, 1899–1966).
20. Forester, *Hornblower During the Crisis* (1967), p. 109.
21. A. Terence McEvoy, "Influencing the Muslim world: British wartime propaganda in the Middle East, 1914–1918", *The Muslim World* 111:2 (2021), 241–63 offers a view of the relationship between British intelligence and Arab intellectuals during the war.
22. Ask any publisher waiting for an academic to submit a manuscript!
23. Ami Ayalon, *The Press in the Arab Middle East* (1995), 141 provides important background on Faris Nimr's role as owner of both *al-Muqattam* newspaper and its printing press, making him a central figure in British-sponsored Arabic publishing during the war.
24. A battle that took place near Vienna on 12 September 1683, which saw a combined force from the Holy Roman Empire, led by the Habsburg monarchy, and the Polish–Lithuanian Commonwealth, both under the command of King Jan—or John—III Sobieski, defeat the Ottomans, which was the end of any further Ottoman expansion in Europe. In the ensuing war, which lasted until 1699, the Ottomans ceded most of Ottoman Hungary to Leopold I, Holy Roman Emperor.
25. Mustafa Aksakal, "The Ottoman Empire and the Armenian Genocide", in Donald Bloxham and A. Dirk Moses (eds), *The Oxford Handbook of Genocide Studies* (2011), pp. 365–85. This chapter provides context for Daghir's treatment of the 'Armenian Question' and other imperial 'questions'.
26. Peter Wien, "Those Who Pronounce the *Ḍād*", *Die Welt des Islams* 60 (2020), 109–32 analyses how linguistic markers became powerful symbols of Arab cultural identity and nationalism in early twentieth-century discourse.
27. C. Ernest Dawn, *From Ottomanism to Arabism* (1973), pp. 148–52 provides valuable context for understanding the 1913 Arab Congress and its significance in pre-war Arab-Ottoman relations.

28. Peter Wien, *Arab Nationalism: The Politics of History and Culture in the Modern Middle East* (2017), pp. 45–8 includes an analysis of 'defensive nationalism' that helps contextualises the speeches quoted in *Thawrat al-Arab*.
29. Muhammad Rashid Rida (1865–1935), Lebanese-born Islamic reformer who advocated for modernising Islam while returning to its fundamentals. A disciple of Muhammad Abduh, his ideas greatly influenced twentieth-century Islamic thought and reform movements.
30. *Al-Manar*, or *The Lighthouse*, was an influential Islamic journal (1898–1935) founded and edited by Rashid Rida in Cairo. It served as the primary platform for Islamic modernist thought, discussing religious interpretation, social reform, and Muslim engagement with modernity.
31. FO 141/817: Arab Bureau memorandum discussing the significance of the al-Idrīsī letter in demonstrating that even reluctant Arab leaders had sought compromise with Ottoman authorities.
32. Satia, *Spies in Arabia* (2008), pp. 332–33, acknowledges the Arab Bureau's propaganda efforts but does not examine *Thawrat al-Arab*.
33. Timothy J. Paris, *Britain, the Hashemites, and Arab Rule, 1920–1925: The Sherifian Solution* (2003), pp. 37–42, discusses the religious and political significance of the moderate reform proposals in the pre-war context.
34. Harold D. Lasswell, *Propaganda Technique in the World War* (1927), pp. 43–6. Lasswell's classic study provides a useful comparison for understanding *Thawrat al-Arab* and the Arab Bureau's innovative approach to wartime propaganda.
35. Olivia Saunders, "Wellington House and British Propaganda during the First World War", *The Historical Journal* 18:1 (1975), 119–46, provides context for understanding how *Thawrat al-Arab* fitted within broader British propaganda efforts.
36. For more on Arab Bureau reports, see Andrew, *The Secret World* (2018), p. 737.
37. Kurt A. Hatlebrekke, *The Problem of Secret Intelligence* (2021), pp. 156–8, discusses how intelligence organisations balance operational flexibility with strategic constraints.
38. Wien, *Arab Nationalism* (2017), pp. 45–8, has analysis of nationalist rhetoric that helps contextualise Daghir's literary devices.
39. See note in earlier chapter about Djemal Pasha.
40. Abd al-Qadir ibn Muhyi al-Din (1808–83), known as the Emir Abdelkader or Abd al-Qadir al-Hassani al-Jaza'iri, was an Algerian religious and military leader who led a struggle against the French colonial invasion of Algiers in the early nineteenth century. His regard for what would now be called human rights, including those of Christians, drew widespread admiration; in 1860, his intervention saved many Christians in Damascus from a massacre, for

which he received honours from around the world, earning him the epithet "defender of the Christians".

41. Joshua Teitelbaum, "The Man Who Would Be Caliph: Sharifian Propaganda in WWI", in Erik J. Zürcher (ed.), *Jihad and Islam in World War I* (2016), pp. 275–304, examines Ottoman desecration allegations as wartime propaganda.
42. *Thawrat al-Arab*, Chapter 7: "Aggravated Sermons".
43. Eitan Bar-Yosef, "The Last Crusade? British Propaganda and the Palestine Campaign, 1917–18", in *Journal of Contemporary History* 36:1 (2001), pp. 87–109, on how martyrdom narratives functioned in wartime propaganda.
44. Mustafa Aksakal, "The Ottoman Empire and the Armenian Genocide", pp. 365–85, comparative analysis of Middle Eastern responses to famine and atrocity during the war.
45. The *hijri* is a lunar Islamic calendar that begins with Muhammad's emigration in 622 CE. With 12 months and 354–355 days per year, it's roughly 11 days shorter than the solar calendar, causing Islamic dates to shift seasons over time.
46. See Paris, *Britain, the Hashemites, and Arab Rule, 1920–1925* (2003), pp. 37–42, for a discussion of the religious and political significance of Hussein's early government appointments.
47. Ayalon, *The Press in the Arab Middle East* (1995), p. 141.
48. Benjamin C. Fortna, "Learning to Read in the Late Ottoman Empire and Early Turkish Republic", in Cyrus Schayegh and Andrew Arsan (eds), *The Routledge Handbook of the History of the Middle East Mandates* (2018), pp. 44–62. Fortna provides nuanced analysis of literacy rates in the early twentieth-century Middle East; see also Ayalon, *The Press in the Arab Middle East* (1995).
49. CO 323/760/57. Details Arab Bureau distribution network for *Thawrat al-Arab*.
50. FO 141/817. Arab Bureau memorandum suggesting some success in reaching intended audiences.
51. A. Terence McEvoy, "Influencing the Muslim World: British Wartime Propaganda in the Middle East, 1914–1918" *The Muslim World* 111:2 (2021), 241–63.
52. Hindawi Foundation for Education and Culture (Beirut, 2016).
53. Mustafa Aksakal, "The Ottoman Empire and the Armenian Genocide", pp. 365–85. Comparative analysis of Middle Eastern responses to the Armenian Genocide.
54. Tony Shaw, "The Information Research Department of the British Foreign Office and the Korean War, 1950–53", *Journal of Contemporary History* 34:2

(1999), 263–81. Work on the IRD demonstrates the Arab Bureau's legacy of approaches to information gathering.
55. Westrate, *The Arab Bureau* (1992), pp. 204–8 acknowledges the Arab Bureau's propaganda efforts but does not examine *Thawrat al-Arab*.
56. Ayalon, *The Press in the Arab Middle East* (1995), on Nimr's role in British-sponsored Arabic publishing.
57. Andrew, *The Secret World* (2018), p. 737, where the author describes the Arab Bureau's outputs as "the best-written intelligence reports in British history".
58. Thomas, *Empires of Intelligence* (2007); see Chapter 2
59. Patrick Wagner, "Intelligence and the Origins of the British Middle East", *Intelligence and National Security* 30:6 (2015), pp. 725–52, argues these methodological innovations continue to influence modern intelligence practices.

10. THE PAPER WAR: LONDON–CAIRO–MECCA

1. FO 141/817, 11 February 1917: "Report on 'Moslem Propaganda'". This memorandum provides a comprehensive overview of various propaganda materials produced and distributed by the Arab Bureau.
2. The archives favour *al-Hakikat*, using transliteration conventions from the time. This book follows the current International Journal of Middle East Studies (IJMES) conventions, with the Arabic letter *qaf* represented by the English 'q'.
3. FO 141/475/8. Contemporary reports highlight the deliberate use of high production values to create a visual impression of British power and resources.
4. BL IOR L/PS/11/110; 30 September 1916. Clayton, to Hogarth, observed that *al-Haqiqa* was "obviously produced by us", indicating an awareness of the need for different publications to have varying degrees of apparent independence.
5. FO 141/738/6 outlines *al-Kawkab*'s editorial focus on Turkish oppression and pan-Turanian ambitions.
6. (Miss M.) Reeves Palmer, "The Kibla [sic]: A Meccan Newspaper", *The Moslem World*, April 1917, p. 185.
7. Pan-Turanianism was a nationalist movement that sought to unite Turkic peoples across Central Asia; the Ottoman embrace of this ideology threatened to sideline Arabs, Armenians, and other non-Turkic peoples within the empire.
8. 'Abd al-Rahman al-Kawakibi (c. 1854–c. 1902), Syrian author, supporter of Pan-Arab solidarity, and one of the most prominent intellectuals of his time. His work *Taba'i' al-istibdad* (*The Nature of Despotism*, 1902; English translation published by Hurst, 2021), provided intellectual foundations for Arab nationalist criticism of Ottoman rule.

9. FO 141/475/8. Long's commentary regarding *al-Hakikat* reveals certain orientalist assumptions that nevertheless informed effective propaganda strategies.
10. FO 141/475, 2047, 18 August 1916: Clayton to War Office. This assumption led to important adaptations in distribution strategy.
11. Cf. the haggling scene in *Monty Python's Life of Brian* (1979), written by the Monty Python team (Graham Chapman, John Cleese, Terry Gilliam, Eric Idle, Terry Jones, and Michael Palin). Brian: "That's four for the gourd." Harry the Haggler: "Four? For this gourd? Four?! Look at it. It's worth ten if it's worth a shekel." Brian: "But you just gave it to me for nothing." Harry the Haggler: "Yes, but it's worth ten!"
12. FO 141/375, 2047; 12 June 1917. De Bunsen to Wingate, correspondence detailing distribution across various territories.
13. Storrs, *Orientations* (1937), p. 220. Storrs's memoir provides valuable insight into the strategic thinking behind this.
14. Ibid. For additional perspective on this project, see also Lawrence, *Seven Pillars of Wisdom* (1935), Chapter 16.
15. Kerry Webber, "The Life & Times of Colonel Stewart Francis Newcombe, BE, R.E., D.S.O.: Soldier, Explorer, Surveyor, Adventurer and Loyal Friend to Lawrence of Arabia", from the blog *In the Shadow of the Crescent* (2015). Accessed 7 November 2024: https://shadowofthecrescent.blogspot.com/2015/06/te-lawrence-and-hejaz-postage-stamps.html
16. David R. Beech, "Hejaz: The First Postage Stamps of 1916 and T.E. Lawrence", *The London Philatelist* 114: November (2005), 323–7.
17. CO 323/732. Macnaghten's sardonic critique highlighting internal debates about propaganda effectiveness that informed the Arab Bureau's nascent approaches.
18. Ayalon, *The Press in the Arab Middle East* (1995), p. 141. Despite low literacy rates, newspapers reached wider audiences through public readings, extending their influence beyond direct readership.
19. CO 323/732, 46. File on postcard propaganda, combining British imperial symbolism with Arabic text.
20. Arabic, *'alim dawlat britania*.
21. FO 141/776, 787; 11 February 1917. The "Arab Bureau Report on Muslim Propaganda" offers one official perspective, as well as important feedback about reception that informed future propaganda efforts.
22. CO 323/720/21. English translation of the Moshi Document.
23. CO 323/719/97. The Moshi Document, and the original German memo that prompted the Arab Bureau response, also provides an exchange showing the reactive, as well as proactive, nature of wartime propaganda.
24. The *bismillah* is one of the most important phrases in Islam, frequently recited

by Muslims before performing religious practices, including prayer, but also before daily activities such as eating.
25. CO 323/719/97.
26. Compare with accounts of tallow used for cartridges, made in Britain with beef and pork fat and sent overseas, as one cause of unrest that led to the Indian Rebellion of 1857.
27. CO 323/731, pp. 302–6. Memoranda on reception of Chinese materials, which reports indicate the pamphlet's reach into South-East Asia.
28. Aldous Huxley, "Notes on Propaganda" (1936), cited in James R. Vaughan, *The Failure of American and British Propaganda in the Arab Middle East, 1945–1957* (2005), p. 238.
29. BL IOR L/PS/11/110: "Report on Moslem Propaganda", 11 February 1917.
30. Storrs, *Orientations* (1937), p. 220.
31. See note in earlier chapter on Rashid Rida and *al-Manār* (*The Lighthouse*; 1898–1935), an Egyptian-based publication espousing an Islamic political worldview, most notably supporting a renewed, pan-Islamic caliphate.
32. Jurji Zaydan (1861–1914) was a prolific Lebanese novelist, journalist, editor and teacher, and one of the first to formulate a theory of Arab nationalism. His magazine *al-Hilal* (est. 1892) was influential in spreading nationalist ideas.
33. Yaqub Sarruf (1852–1927) was a pioneering Lebanese writer, publisher, and translator. He co-founded the science-based monthly *al-Muqtataf* in Beirut in 1876 with Faris Nimr.

11. POST-WAR POSTMORTEM: MODERN MIDDLE EAST

1. Arnold Talbot Wilson (1884–1940), British soldier, colonial administrator, Conservative politician, and author. He served under Percy Cox, the colonial administrator of Mesopotamia, a.k.a. Mandatory Iraq, during and after the First World War, including during the Iraqi revolution or uprising of 1920.
2. A.T. Wilson, *Mesopotamia 1917–1920: A Clash of Loyalties* (1931), p. 324.
3. George Habib Antonius (1891–1942), Lebanese author and diplomat, later based in Jerusalem as a civil servant in the British Mandate of Palestine. One of the first historians of Arab nationalism.
4. Antonius, *The Arab Awakening: The Story of the Arab National Movement* (1938), pp. 248–9. In spite of its age, and flaws, this remains one of the most influential Arab perspectives on British wartime promises.
5. Sāṭi' al-Ḥuṣrī (1880–1968) was a Syrian intellectual best known for creating the idea of a united Arab nation built on a shared language and culture, rather than religion.
6. Gertrude Bell Archive, Newcastle University Library. Letter to her father, 29 May 1921. Bell's correspondence offers candid reflections on the contradictions of post-war British policy.

7. For more comparative analysis of First World War intelligence units, see Andrew, *The Secret World* (2018), pp. 534–42.
8. FO 371/5032; 14 August 1920. "The Arab Question" memorandum explicitly acknowledging the tensions created by wartime commitments.
9. The concept of an 'epistemic community' was developed by Peter Haas but has been adapted here to describe the Arab Bureau's particular function. See Haas, "Epistemic Communities and International Policy Coordination" (1992), 1–35.
10. Satia, *Spies in Arabia* (2008), p. 245.
11. Gertrude Bell Archive, Newcastle University Library. Letter to her father, 29 May 1921.
12. For more on Bell and Arab Bureau methodologies in post-war Iraq, see Liora Lukitz, *A Quest in the Middle East* (2006), pp. 142–65.
13. Initially established by the British Army in Jerusalem during the Second World War, after the war MECAS was relocated to Lebanon and reinvented as a civilian institution, operating outside of Beirut from 1947 to 1978.
14. On MECAS and its relationship to the Arab Bureau legacy, see Robert Mabro, "The London and Durham Universities Intelligence Centre and Middle East Centre for Arab Studies", *British Journal of Middle Eastern Studies* 40:4 (2013), pp. 437–52.
15. Christopher Andrew, "Intelligence Analysis Needs to Look Backwards Before Looking Forward", in Loch Johnson and James Wirtz (eds), *Intelligence and National Security: The Secret World of Spies* (2015), pp. 101–17. Andrew has consistently emphasised intelligence organisations' failure to learn from historical precedents.
16. For details on Cox's application of Arab Bureau methods in Iraq, see Peter Sluglett, *Britain in Iraq: Contriving King and Country* (2007), pp. 40–58.
17. Elizabeth Monroe, *Britain's Moment in the Middle East, 1914–1971* (1981), pp. 76–7. Monroe's critique of the British cultural approach remains influential.
18. Gertrude Bell Archive, Newcastle University Library. Letter to Hugh Bell, 4 September 1921.
19. Davies, *Intelligence and Government in Britain and the United States* (2012), p. 147. His work on intelligence organisations provides useful theoretical frameworks for understanding institutional resistance to innovation.
20. On the PWE's adoption of Arab Bureau techniques, see David Garnett, *The Secret History of PWE: The Political Warfare Executive 1939–1945* (2002), pp. 218–27. Freya Stark's papers at the Middle East Centre Archive, St Antony's College, Oxford, document her explicit references to Arab Bureau precedents.
21. Roger Hardy, "Remembering *Sharq Al-Adna*: British Radio Propaganda in the Middle East, 1941–1956", in *Asian Affairs* 51: 1 (2023), 106–24.

22. Herman, *Intelligence Power in Peace and War* (1996), p. 143. Herman's 'islands of innovation' concept aptly describes the Arab Bureau's legacy.
23. Rashid Khalidi, "Arab Nationalism: Historical Problems in the Literature", *The American Historical Review* 96:5 (1991), 1363–73. Khalidi's view of the development of Arab nationalism avoids both purely indigenous and purely external explanations.
24. Albert Hourani, *A History of the Arab Peoples* (1991), pp. 316–17.
25. Quoted in Ali Allawi, *Faisal I of Iraq* (2014), p. 382.
26. James Gelvin, *Divided Loyalties: Nationalism and Mass Politics in Syria at the Close of Empire* (1998), p. 124.
27. Juan Cole, "The United States and Shi'ite Religious Factions in Post-Ba'thist Iraq", *The Middle East Journal* 57:4 (2003), 543–66. Cole was an early, prescient, and outspoken critic of cultural misunderstandings in post-2003 Iraq.
28. David Petraeus and James Amos, *U.S. Army and Marine Corps Counterinsurgency Field Manual* (FM 3–24) (2007), pp. 27–38.
29. Robert Jervis, *Why Intelligence Fails: Lessons From the Iranian Revolution and the Iraq War* (2010), pp. 123–5.
30. Roger Owen, *State, Power and Politics in the Making of the Modern Middle East* (2004), pp. 8–9.
31. Said, *Orientalism* (1978), pp. 206–7. The Arab Bureau's approach can be viewed as both challenging and reinforcing the orientalist frameworks which Said later critiqued.

12. SEVEN PILLARS OF INTELLIGENCE WISDOM: LESSONS FROM THE ARAB BUREAU

1. The question of direct institutional influence versus parallel evolution deserves further research. While similarities between Arab Bureau methods and later PWE/IRD practices are striking, further archival investigation is required if conscious transmission is to be incontrovertibly demonstrated.
2. Herman, *Intelligence Power in Peace and War* (1996), p. 227.
3. T.E. Lawrence, "Twenty-Seven Articles", *The Arab Bulletin*, Issue 60 (20 August 1917), pp. 347–53.
4. Robert R. Tomes Rand, "Informing U.S. national security transformation discussions: An argument for balanced intelligence, surveillance and reconnaissance," *Defence Studies* (2003), 3:2, pp. 20–35.
5. David J. Kilcullen, "Twenty-Eight Articles: Fundamentals of Company-Level Counterinsurgency", *Military Review* 86:3 (2006), pp. 103–8.
6. David Price, "Cultural Intelligence in Asymmetric Conflict", *Intelligence and National Security* 24:2 (2009), pp. 195–215.
7. Christopher E. Claus, "Assessing Cultural Intelligence Training in the United States Military", *Journal of Intelligence Studies* 5:2 (2018), pp. 37–54.

8. Robert Johnson, *The Great War and the Middle East: A Strategic Study* (2016), pp. 183–7.
9. Peter Jackson, "Intelligence and Empire: The Imperial Defence and Security Network, 1918–1939", in Christopher R. Moran and Christopher J. Murphy (eds), *Intelligence Studies in Britain and the US* (2013), pp. 54–78.
10. Satia, *Spies in Arabia* (2008), pp. 121–4.
11. Steven C. Roach and James Pattison, "Empowering the Individual? International Relations, the Public, and Bridging the Capabilities-Expectations Gap", *Intelligence and National Security* 24:5 (2009), 714–35.
12. William R. Johnson, "Clandestinity and Current Intelligence", *Studies in Intelligence* 20:3 (1976), 15–69.
13. Timothy J. Paris, "British Middle East Strategy-Making During World War I: The Sykes-Picot Agreement", in Michael J. Cohen and Martin Kolinsky (eds), *Decision Making in the Middle East* (2013), pp. 7–33.
14. Philip H.J. Davies, "Intelligence Culture and Intelligence Failure in Britain and the United States", *Cambridge Review of International Affairs* 17:3 (2004), 495–520.
15. Paul R. Pillar, *Intelligence and U.S. Foreign Policy: Iraq, 9/11, and Misguided Reform* (2011), pp. 89–92.
16. James Pattison, *The Morality of Private War: The Challenge of Private Military and Security Companies* (2014), pp. 173–5.
17. Christopher Andrew, "Intelligence, International Relations and 'Under-theorisation'", *Intelligence and National Security* 19:2 (2004), 170–84.
18. Richard J. Aldrich, "Beyond the Vigilant State: Globalisation and Intelligence", *Review of International Studies* 35:4 (2009), 889–902.
19. Michael Goodman, "Learning to Walk: The Origins of the UK's Joint Intelligence Committee", *International Journal of Intelligence and Counter Intelligence* 21:1 (2008), 40–56.
20. T.E. Lawrence, *Seven Pillars of Wisdom* (1935), p. 147.
21. Robert Irwin, "Cultural Intelligence and the Understanding of Middle Eastern Politics"," in Steve Tsang (ed.), *Intelligence and Human Rights in the Era of Global Terrorism* (2008), pp. 118–32.
22. James S. Corum, "Building the Wehrmacht's Operational Intelligence: The German Abwehr Legacy", *Intelligence and National Security* 22:5 (2007), 647–65.
23. David Omand, *Securing the State* (2010), pp. 207–12.
24. Mark Phythian, "Intelligence Theory and Theories of International Relations: Shared World or Separate Worlds?", in Peter Gill, Stephen Marrin, and Mark Phythian (eds), *Intelligence Theory: Key Questions and Debates* (2009), pp. 54–72.
25. Philip M. Taylor, *British Propaganda in the 20th Century: Selling Democracy* (1999), pp. 78–82.

26. Christopher R. Moran, "The Pursuit of Intelligence History: Methods, Sources, and Trajectories in the United Kingdom", *Studies in Intelligence* 55:2 (2011), 33–55.
27. Michael Warner, "Building a Theory of Intelligence Systems", in Gregory F. Treverton and Wilhelm Agrell (eds), *National Intelligence Systems: Current Research and Future Prospects* (2009), pp. 11–37.
28. Michael Herman, *Intelligence Services in the Information Age* (2001), pp. 45–8.
29. Robert Jervis, *Why Intelligence Fails: Lessons From the Iranian Revolution and the Iraq War* (2010), p. 123.
30. Richard K. Betts, *Enemies of Intelligence: Knowledge and Power in American National Security* (2007), pp. 87–93.
31. Len Scott and Peter Jackson, "The Study of Intelligence in Theory and Practice", *Intelligence and National Security* 19:2 (2004), 139–69.
32. Wyn Q. Bowen, "Intelligence Reform and Organizational Change: The British Experience", in Steve Tsang (ed.), *Intelligence and Human Rights in the Era of Global Terrorism* (2008), pp. 214–39.

BIBLIOGRAPHIC ESSAY

My original DPhil Bibliography ran to more than thirty pages, including numerous closely annotated lists of archives, hundreds of articles, and more arcane theses than anyone could wish to know. This Bibliographic Essay instead highlights texts that were either of greatest use in my research, or else were just good reads, and as such I recommend to you as someone who enjoyed them.

The Arab Bureau: Specialised Research

Works looking in detail at the Arab Bureau are thin on the ground. That said, the few that do tackle the subject in detail are rather good. Bruce Westrate's *The Arab Bureau: British Policy in the Middle East, 1916–1920* (1992) provides the most comprehensive institutional history of the organisation, detailing its formation, structure, and influence on British policy. Westrate convincingly argues that the Arab Bureau was more than just an intelligence-gathering agency, but also functioned as a key advisory body that significantly shaped British regional policy during the final years of the war and immediate post-war period.

Building on Westrate's institutional approach, Polly Mohs' *Military Intelligence and the Arab Revolt: The First Modern Intelligence War* (2008) offers a more focused examination of aspects of Arab Bureau operations. Mohs innovatively frames the Arab Bureau's work within the context of modern intelligence practice, seeing its operations as a watershed moment in the development of intelligence tradecraft. The most theoretically inclined treatment of the Arab Bureau (albeit not to everyone's taste) is Priya Satia's *Spies in Arabia: The Great War and the Cultural Foundations of Britain's Covert Empire in the Middle East* (2008). Satia examines the cultural and epistemological dimensions of British intelligence in the region, arguing that the Arab Bureau's work was fundamentally shaped by romanticised colonial imaginaries and cultural assumptions about the Arab world.

Yigal Sheffy's *British Military Intelligence in the Palestine Campaign, 1914–1918* (1998) provides an essential and meticulous analysis of intelligence operations in the Palestinian theatre, including significant discussion of the Arab Bureau's role. Sheffy's examination of intelligence gathering, assessment, and dissemination reveals the complex relationship between field intelligence and strategic

BIBLIOGRAPHIC ESSAY

decision-making. Timothy Paris' work provides crucial insights into key personalities and policy formation related to the Arab Bureau, such as his meticulously researched biography, *In Defence of Britain's Middle East Empire: A Life of Sir Gilbert Clayton* (2016).

One of the most influential figures in British Middle East policy during this period, and head of the Arab Bureau from 1916 to 1917, Clayton played a pivotal role in shaping both Arab Bureau operations and broader British policy. Paris also wrote the article "British Middle East Policy-Making After the First World War: The Lawrentian and Wilsonian Schools" (*The Historical Journal*, 1998), which provides a sophisticated analysis of the competing ideological frameworks that influenced British policy in the region, including the significant impact of Arab Bureau personnel on post-war policy formation. Also useful in this area was Robert Blyth's *Empire of the Raj: Eastern Africa and the Middle East, 1858–1947* (2003).

Roger Owen's seminal contributions have been foundational to critical scholarship on British intelligence operations in the Middle East. His article "British and French Military Intelligence in Syria and Palestine, 1914–1918: Myths and Reality" (*British Journal of Middle Eastern Studies*, 2011) provides a crucial reassessment of conventional narratives about British intelligence success, challenging what he terms the 'Lawrence myth' while offering a more nuanced understanding of the actual effectiveness and limitations of British intelligence operations. Owen's broader work on Middle Eastern history, including *Lord Cromer: Victorian Imperialist, Edwardian Proconsul* (2004), further contextualises British imperial governance in the region, providing background for understanding the institutional framework within which the Arab Bureau operated.

These core texts are supplemented by works that address specific aspects of the Arab Bureau. For instance, James Barr's *Setting the Desert on Fire: T.E. Lawrence and Britain's Secret War in Arabia, 1916–18* (2006), provides an engaging narrative of Arab Bureau involvement in the wider Arab Revolt, while Philip Walker's *Behind the Lawrence Legend: The Forgotten Few Who Shaped the Arab Revolt* (2018) is a brilliant piece of research, which provides an important corrective to Lawrence-centric accounts by highlighting the roles and activities of other key Arab Bureau personnel. Meanwhile, Steven Wagner's *Intelligence and the Origins of the British Middle East* (2015) connects the work of the Arab Bureau to the longer trajectory of British regional involvement.

The First World War in the Middle East: Context and Campaigns

Understanding the Arab Bureau requires situating it within the broader context of the First World War in the Middle East. Several comprehensive histories provide this essential framework. Eugene Rogan's *The Fall of the Ottomans* (2015) offers an authoritative and accessible overview of the Ottoman Empire's wartime

BIBLIOGRAPHIC ESSAY

experience, balancing military, political, and social dimensions. Rogan's work is particularly valuable for understanding the conflict from perspectives beyond the British imperial gaze. Robert Johnson's *The Great War and the Middle East* (2016) provides a detailed strategic analysis of the various Middle Eastern campaigns, placing them within the broader context of imperial rivalries and global strategic considerations. His examination of the campaigns in Mesopotamia, Palestine, and the Dardanelles reveals the complex interplay between local military operations and higher strategic imperatives.

For studies specifically focused on military aspects, Kristian Coates Ulrichsen's *The First World War in the Middle East* (2014) offers a thorough treatment of the various campaigns and their logistical challenges. Matthew Hughes' *Allenby and British Strategy in the Middle East, 1917–1919* (1999) provides valuable insights into the Palestine campaign, while Ian Rutledge's *Enemy on the Euphrates: The Battle for Iraq, 1914–1921* (2015) covers the Mesopotamian front in depth. The social and cultural dimensions of the conflict are addressed in Leila Tarazi Fawaz's brilliant *A Land of Aching Hearts: The Middle East in the Great War* (2014), which examines the war's impact on civilian populations.

Middle East Studies: Region, Identity, and Empire

The Arab Bureau operated within complex regional dynamics involving emergent Arab nationalism, Ottoman governance, and British imperial interests. Several key works in Middle East Studies provide essential context for these dynamics. Rogan's *The Arabs: A History* (2009) offers a comprehensive survey of Arab history with particular attention to the late Ottoman period and the emergence of Arab nationalism, while James Gelvin's *Divided Loyalties: Nationalism and Mass Politics in Syria at the Close of Empire* (1998) provides a nuanced analysis of Arab political identity during this pivotal period.

For understanding Ottoman governance and the empire's final years, Mustafa Aksakal's *The Ottoman Road to War in 1914* (2006) and Ryan Gingeras' *Fall of the Sultanate: The Great War and the End of the Ottoman Empire, 1908–1922* (2016) offer complementary perspectives. Aksakal examines how Ottoman decision-making led to participation in the war, while Gingeras analyses the empire's ultimate dissolution. Referencing and intellectual engagement with other authors is extremely basic. Another important recent work in this arena is *The Last Ottoman Generation* (2017) by Michael Provence.

The emergence of Arab nationalism, crucial to understanding the political context of the Arab Bureau's work, is thoroughly examined in Rashid Khalidi's *Palestinian Identity: The Construction of Modern National Consciousness* (1997) and *The Origins of Arab Nationalism*, edited by Rashid Khalidi, Lisa Anderson, Muhammad Muslih, and Reeva S. Simon (1993). George Antonius' classic *The Arab Awakening: The Story of the Arab National Movement* (1965), though dated in some respects and controversial in others, remains valuable for understanding contemporary Arab perspectives.

British imperial frameworks are analysed in John Darwin's *The Empire Project: The Rise and Fall of the British World System, 1830–1970* (2011) and Robert Fletcher's *British Imperialism and 'The Tribal Question': Desert Administration and Nomadic Societies in the Middle East, 1919–1936* (2015), which examines how imperial powers conceptualised and governed tribal populations—a key concern for Arab Bureau officials.

Intelligence Studies: Theory, Practice, and History

Placing the Arab Bureau within the broader development of intelligence institutions requires engagement with key works in Intelligence Studies. Christopher Andrew's *The Secret World: A History of Intelligence* (2018) provides comprehensive historical context for intelligence practices, while his earlier work, *Secret Service: The Making of the British Intelligence Community* (1985), offers detailed analysis of British intelligence institutions. For First World War intelligence specifically, Michael Occleshaw's *Armour Against Fate: British Military Intelligence in the First World War* (1989) provides a thorough overview, complemented by Keith Jeffery's *MI6: The History of the Secret Intelligence Service, 1909–1949* (2010), which includes discussion of early MI6 operations in the Middle East. Daniel Larsen's "Intelligence in the First World War: The State of the Field" (*Intelligence and National Security*, 2014) offers a valuable historiographical survey.

Theoretical perspectives on intelligence can be found in Peter Gill and Mark Phythian's *Intelligence Theory: Key Questions and Debates* (2009) and Michael Handel's *War, Strategy, and Intelligence* (1989). These works provide conceptual frameworks for understanding the Arab Bureau's activities and significance.

The relationship between intelligence and empire is explored in Richard Popplewell's *Intelligence and Imperial Defence: British Intelligence and the Defence of the Indian Empire 1904–1924* (1995) and Martin Thomas's *Empires of Intelligence: Security Services and Colonial Disorder After 1914* (2007). Both examine how intelligence practices emerged from and supported imperial governance.

The emergence of military intelligence as a distinct practice is addressed in Jim Beach's *Haig's Intelligence: GHQ and the German Army, 1916–1918* (2015) and Terrence Finnegan's *The Origins of Modern Intelligence, Surveillance, and Reconnaissance: Military Intelligence at the Front, 1914–18* (2009), providing important context for understanding the military dimensions of the Arab Bureau's work.

Primary Sources and Archives

Research on the Arab Bureau requires engagement with several key archival collections. The most essential primary sources are found in the National Archives at

BIBLIOGRAPHIC ESSAY

Kew, London, particularly the Foreign Office series FO 882 (Arab Bureau papers), which contains the complete run of the *Arab Bulletin* as well as memoranda, intelligence reports, and correspondence produced by Arab Bureau personnel. Complementary materials can be found in the FO 371 series (general Foreign Office correspondence), the War Office series WO 106 (Directorate of Military Operations papers), and the Cabinet Office series CAB 24 (Cabinet memoranda).

The British Library's India Office Records house crucial materials in the L/P&S (Political and Secret) series, including reports and correspondence that reveal the critical relationship between the Government of India and the Arab Bureau. The Imperial War Museum contains personal papers of several Arab Bureau personnel and others, as does the Middle East Centre Archives, St Antony's College, Oxford. It was also on the shelves of the Middle East Centre Library that I discovered *Thawrat al-Arab* (*The Arab Revolt*) (Cairo, 1916). This rare Arabic source provided a crucial counterbalance to British-dominated narratives of the period. The forthcoming English translation of this seminal text (Hurst, 2026) will make this essential primary source accessible to a much wider scholarly audience, allowing for more detailed assessments of Arab Bureau intelligence activities than have been conducted at any point since its disbandment.

Conclusion

This Bibliographic Essay highlights key works across four interconnected areas relevant to the study of the Arab Bureau. Together, these sources provide a comprehensive foundation for understanding the Arab Bureau's formation, operations, and significance within the broader contexts of the First World War, Middle Eastern politics, British imperialism, and the development of modern intelligence practices. While Westrate, Mohs, Satia, Sheffy, Paris, and Owen offer the most focused examinations of the Arab Bureau itself and the key figures who shaped its direction, their work is enriched and contextualised by engagement with broader historiographical traditions in military history, regional studies, and intelligence history. Owen's critical reassessment of British intelligence operations has been particularly inspiring in adopting a new scholarly approach to this field, challenging established narratives and encouraging more nuanced interpretations of the Arab Bureau's actual effectiveness and historical significance.

INDEX

Note: Page numbers followed by "*n*" refer to notes.

Abduh, Muhammad, 293*n*29
Abu Markha, 155
Abyssinia, 159
Aden Protectorate, 159
aerial observations, 103, 133–4, 137, 138, 139
aerial photography, 29, 134
Afghanistan, xv, xx, 210, 241, 242
al-Ahram (newspaper), 27, 32, 121
al-Azhar Mosque complex, 90, 205, 210
Albanian Question, 186
Alexandria, 27, 82
Algeria, 193
al-Haqiqa (newspaper), 206, 208–10, 213, 221–2, 295*n*4
al-Hilal (magazine), 121, 122, 285*n*27, 297*n*32
Ali, Abd al-Aziz bin, 195–6
Ali, Agami Effendi, 211
al-Kawkab (The Star) (newspaper), 206, 208–9, 221, 222, 261, 262, 295*n*5
Allenby, Edmund, 144, 166, 232
al-Manar (journal), 120, 188, 223, 260, 293*n*30
al-Mufid (newspaper), 14, 17, 22
al-Muqattam (newspaper), 32, 121, 180, 184, 193, 198, 201, 260, 293*n*15

al-Qibla (newspaper), 32, 206–9, 222, 221, 224, 261, 262
Amin, Sheikh Muhammad, 196
Amoon, Alexander Bey, 189–90
Andrew, Christopher, xiv, 32, 146, 235
Antonius, George, 31, 230, 271*n*6, 297*n*3, 305
Aqaba campaign (1917), 144, 166, 263, 290*n*21
Aqaba, 131, 144, 160
Arab Awakening, The (Antonius), 230, 271*n*6, 297*n*4
Arab Bulletin, xiv, 142–3, 148
    complexity as strategic advantage, 173–5
    coverage of the Arab Revolt, 159–65
    emergence of, 149–53
    impacting strategy, 165–6
    intelligence challenges and limitations, 166–9
    invisible networks mapping, 153–7
    tactical reports to strategic vision, 157–9
    wartime innovation, 169–73
Arab Bureau, The (Westrate), 30, 303, 307
Arab Bureau

INDEX

aerial reconnaissance and visual intelligence, 133–4
approach to wireless communication, 130–2
arab intellectual partnerships, 119–20
challenges and limitations, 124–5
challenges in coordination between departments, 99–101
codebreaking and linguistic analysis, 132–3
conflict between India Office and, 104–6
cross-cultural communication strategies, 220–4
cultural and operational challenges, 142–3
human intelligence networks and tribal intelligence operations, 134–6
imperial epistemic community, 106–8, 125–6
information ecosystems, 122–4
intelligence fusion, 137–9
intelligence innovations and strategic influence, 143–4
intelligence network managements, 102–4
intelligence practice transformation, 108–10
linguistic research and cultural translation, 116–17
long-term legacies, 144–7
map and postcards, 212–17
Moshi Pamphlet, 217–20
newspapers, 205–10
physical infrastructure and communication networks, 98–9
scholar–spies legacy, 93–5
stamps, 210–11

technological constraints and cultural limitations, 140–2
transformation of scholarly networks, 126–7
urban networks and ottoman intelligence, 136–7
Arab Congress (1913), 14–15, 17, 65, 71–2, 180, 187, 189–90, 276n6, 292
Arab Revolt, 19–21, 30, 130, 139–40, 158, 253
  Arab Bulletin's coverage of, 159–65
  Arab Bureau impacts on, 143–4
Arab Revolt, The (Daghir), xiv, 16, 28, 179–204
Arab Spring (2011), 23–4
Arabian Peninsula, 52, 136, 141, 167
Arabs, 18, 20, 37, 54–6, 169
Armenian Question, 186
Armenians, 20, 295n7, 198
Army Intelligence, 166
Ashmolean Museum, 80, 81, 253, 275n35, 279n2
Asia, 62
al-Azm, Shafiq Muayyad, 14

Baghdad Railway, 73, 277n23
Baghdad, 26, 47–9, 216, 230, 234
Balfour Declaration, 240
Balkan wars, 46
Balkans, 27
Banaga, Sheikh Ahmed bin Abdul Rahman, 196
Basra, 62, 47, 87, 197, 201, 216, 275n36
Bayhum, Mukhtār, 189
Behind the Lawrence Legend (Walker), 30, 304
Beirut, xx, 9, 13–18, 21–3, 25–7, 34, 181–2, 291n4, 297n33, 298n13

INDEX

Bell, Gertrude, xv, 53, 86–7, 94, 99, 118, 225, 130, 137, 230, 234–5, 236–7, 253–4, 270n4, 275n36, 280n27
Berlin, 36, 51, 218
Berne, 155, 158
Black Sea, 35–7
Bosnian and Herzegovinian Question, 186
Bray, Norman, 89
British Embassy, 44, 73
British Empire, 2, 36–7, 68, 108
British India, 3, 51–2
British Military Intelligence, 180
British Union Flag, 213–14
British
 administrative paralysis, 72
 influence over Egypt, 41–3, 62–3
 intelligence failure, 24–7, 37–40, 74–6
 Middle East Policy, reshaping, 235–7
 new approaches for intelligence capabilities, 49–54
 See also Arab Bureau; de Bunsen Committee
Buchan, John, 37
Burundi, 217
al-Bustani, Butrus, 121, 286n29

Cairo Residency, 27, 98, 101, 166, 273n9
Cairo, xiv, xviii, xix-xxi, 1, 5, 8, 14, 182, 248
 executions impacts on networks, 21–2, 24
 operating as a hub of British operations, 53
 See also Arab Bureau
Carchemish, 84, 86, 115, 117
Central Asia, 51–2
Cheetham, Milne, 40

Chinese Muslims, 218–7, 219, 220, 222
cholera, 152
Christians, 17, 54, 293n40
Cilicia, 70
Clayton, Gilbert, 82–3, 86–7, 92, 99, 100, 254, 256, 279n8, 280n24, 304
Cold War era, xx, 8, 239, 247
Cole, Juan, 241
Colonial Office, 94, 109, 126, 152
Committee of Union and Progress (CUP), 17–18, 187, 192, 201, 207, 221, 270–1n4(ch.1)
Constantinople, 18, 20, 35–8, 40, 44–5, 62–3, 187, 207, 216, 221, 271n5, 284n1
Cornwallis, Kinahan, xv, 47, 86
Cox, Percy, 87, 145, 234, 236, 264, 297n1
Ctesiphon, 47
cultural analysis, 29, 88, 132, 137, 145, 171
cultural gaps, 54–7
cultural insights, 38, 87, 107, 121, 122
CUP. *See* Committee Union and Progress (CUP)
cyber threats, 174
Cyprus, 82

Daghir, Asʻad, 16, 115, 180, 182–199, 201, 291n4, 292n25, 293n38
Thawrat al-Arab, chapters, 186–96
Damascus Protocol, 20, 271n6
Damascus, 9, 181, 192, 216, 248
 executions impacts on networks, 21–2
 mass executions, 13–14, 18
Dardanelles, 25, 36, 45, 62, 71, 305

311

INDEX

Davies, Philip, 238
de Bunsen Committee, 49–50, 63–6
  context and challenges, 67–8
  formation of, 61–3
  new approaches made by, 68–72
de Bunsen, Maurice, 50, 63, 274n23, 276n2
Decentralization Party, 189
al-Din, Abd al-Qadir ibn Muhyi, 293–4n40

East Africa, 222
  Moshi Pamphlet, 217–20
Eastern Question, 186
economic patterns, 133
economic reports, 122
Egypt, 15, 26, 37, 40–4, 53–4, 184, 189, 256
  British influence, 62–3, 65
  growth of publishing networks, 121
  veiled protectorate, 101
  war impacts, 40–1
Egyptians, xviii, 40–2, 44, 99
Ephesus, 82
Euphrates Group Intelligence Organisation, 156
Europe, 35, 36, 40, 50, 53, 68, 292n24
Ezbekiyya Gardens, 98

Faisal, Emir, 18–19, 20, 240, 271n5, n6
field observations, 104, 122, 153
Field Service Regulations of 1909, 25
Foreign Office, 36, 39, 44, 71, 75, 77
  challenges faced by, 73, 79
Forester, C.S., 184–5
France, 36, 46, 62, 70, 73

Gallipoli, 4, 18, 73, 98, 118, 130
  British defeats at, 21, 25, 49, 55–6
  intelligence failures, 45–7
Garland, Herbert, 86–7, 116, 122, 132, 153, 165, 284n10
Geertz, Clifford, 93–4, 282n50
Gelvin, James, 31, 240m 291n8, 305
general officer commanding (GOC), 101
geographical challenges, 141
George V (King), 212
Germans, 51, 219
Germany, 36, 69
  Moshi Pamphlet, 217–20
Giza, 102, 211
Gozlan, Mustafa Effendi, 211
Grand Continental Hotel, 98
Graves, Philip, 86, 88, 113, 284n1
Greenmantle (Buchan), 37
Guillaume, Alfred, 86

Harb tribe, 135
'HASDD (Historical Attention Span Deficit Disorder)', 146
Hashemites, 19, 20, 235, 271n5
al-Hashimi, Hussein bin Ali, 17–21, 271n5
Hellespont, 36
Herman, Michael, 239, 249
Hijaz Handbook, 90
Hijaz Railway, 20, 144, 161
  Arab Bureau operations against, 139–40
  guerrilla operations against, 165
Hijaz, 18, 32, 42, 164
Hilmi II, Abbas, 40–1, 273n8
Hirtzel, Arthur, 63
Hogarth, David, xv, 53, 80–2, 86, 88, 92, 99, 109, 114, 137, 169, 234–5, 253–4, 275n35
  archaeological experience, 84, 86, 115, 133–4, 280n23

INDEX

challenges faced by, 149–51, 154, 167
Hollis, Stanley, 22
Holy Roman Empire, 292n24
Hong Kong, 218–19
Hourani, Albert, 31, 240
HUMINT (human intelligence), 102–3
al-Husri, Sati, 230
Hussein, Sharif, 17–21, 136, 143, 162–3, 181, 184, 187, 194–6, 201, 206, 209, 223, 271n5
Hussein–McMahon Correspondence, 19–20, 184, 187, 273n9
Huxley, Aldous, 221

al-Idrīsī, al-Sayyid, 188, 190
India Office, 36,-7, 39, 44, 48–9, 70–1, 98, 100, 168, 254, 307
  conflict between Arab Bureau and, 52–3, 79, 97, 104–6, 257
  views on Middle East, 69, 72–4, 78, 230
India, 4, 36, 52, 68, 73–4, 105, 258
Indian Army, 52, 72, 105
Indian Rebellion (1857), 38, 52, 72, 104, 272n5, 297n26
Indonesia, 220
Influence of the Crusades on European Military Architecture to the End of the XII Century, The (Lawrence), 83
Information Research Department (IRD), 8, 145, 239, 270n10, 294n54, 299n1
Iraq invasion (2003), 241
Iraq War, 241
Iraq, 145, 236, 241, 242, 264

Jackson, Henry, 63

Jan (King) a.k.a. Jan Sobieski, 292n24
Jaussen, Père Antonin, 51, 154, 275n30, 275n31
al-Jazairi, Abd al-Qadir, 192–3
al-Jazā'irī, Salīm Bey, 188
Jebail, 258
Jeddah Great Mosque, 89
Jeddah, 89, 131, 136, 201, 206
Jervis, Robert, 242
Jews, 54
Joint Military Intelligence Training Center's (JMITC), 259

Kahlenberg, Battle of. *See* Vienna, Battle of
Kemal, Hussein, 41, 42, 273n12
Kemal, Mustafa, a.k.a.Atatürk, 46, 273n16
Kew, National Archives, ix-x, xix, xxi, 32, 214, 307
Khalidi, Rashid, 31, 239, 292n18, 299n23, 305
al-Khalil, Abdul Karim, 187
Khartoum, 197, 201
Kitchener (Lord), 50–1, 63, 274n22
Kurds, 54
Kut al-Amara, 21, 25–6, 47–9, 55, 73, 118, 130

Lawrence, T.E., xiv, xv, xviii-xx, 1, 3, 5, 7, 83–6, 98, 100, 102, 113, 115–17, 130, 150, 159, 165, 169, 199, 211, 234–5, 242, 245, 248, 249, 253, 258, 269n7, 275n35, 280n16, 304
  approach to warfare, xiii, 103, 140, 143–4, 171, 279n14
  tension between Wilson and, 92
Lean, David, xviii, 5, 30, 159
Lebanese civil war, 235
Lebanon, 16, 22, 23, 62, 194, 258

INDEX

Leopold I (Holy Roman Emperor), 292*n*24
Levant, 14, 62
Libya, 46, 159
London, xix, xx, xxi, 2, 4, 27, 37, 44, 53, 61, 71, 97, 99, 114, 183, 205–6, 213, 231, 274*n*23, 274*n*29
Long, Edward, 208, 221–2, 296*n*29
Lowther, Gerard, 64
Lynden-Bell, Arthur, 91–2

Macedonian Question, 186
Macnaghten, T.C., 213
al-Maḥmaṣānī, Muḥammad, 189
Malaysia, 220
Maliki, Sheikh Ali, 195–6
Marjeh Square, 13–14
Martyrs' Day, 23–4
al-Masri, Aziz Bey Ali, 188
Maxwell, John, 40, 273*n*10
McMahon, Arthur Henry, 19, 184, 187
Mecca, 19, 21, 155, 201, 205, 206
Medina, 19, 20, 21, 139
Memorandum on Revolutionising the Islamic Territories of Our Enemies (von Oppenheim), 51
MENA, 1–2, 171, 197
Mesopotamia Commission (1917), 48–9
Mesopotamia, 25, 48–9, 62, 69–70, 118
Middle East Centre for Arab Studies (MECAS), xxi, 234–5, 265, 298*n*13, 298*n*14
Middle East Department, 94, 109, 126
Middle East, 107–8, 197, 203, 205, 225–6, 229, 238
  British failure in, 24–6
  British Middle East Policy, reshaping, 2, 3–4, 235–7

  long-term Influence, 233–5
  modern regional resonance, 241–3
  transforming Intelligence and regional dynamics, 232–3
  See also Arab Bureau
Military Intelligence and the Arab Revolt (Mohs), 30, 303, 307
Monroe, Elizabeth, 236, 277*n*16
Morris, Jan, 25
Moshi, 217
Muntefiq Mission, 156
Murray, Archibald, 83, 92

Nahda Movement, 121, 286*n*29
National Archives, ix,-x, xix, xxi, 32, 307, 214
Naval Intelligence Division, 231, 275*n*35
Negev, 85, 113
New Delhi, 37, 44
Newcombe, Stewart F., 82, 85, 113, 296*n*15
Nile, 102
Nimr, Faris, 115, 119–20, 121–2, 180, 182, 184–5, 198, 201, 260, 285*n*22, 291*n*5, 292*n*23, 297*n*33
North Africa, 5, 6, 37, 99
Notes on the Middle East, 158

Odessa, 35
Opera Square, 98
Ottoman Empire, 24, 50, 68, 75, 136
  entry into war, 1–2, 35
  India Office's approach to, 44
  Russia war declaration on, 36
Ottomans, 14, 18–20, 36–7, 52, 160
  British efforts against, 25
  British High Command remarks on, 4

INDEX

pre-First World War defeats, 46
views on Arab nationalism, 15
Owen, Roger, vii, ix, 1, 3, 242, 304

Palestine Exploration Fund, 113
Palestine, 1, 51, 70, 83, 113, 144, 151, 160, 184, 230, 237, 297n3, 303–5
Paris, 14, 15, 17, 63, 65–6, 71–2, 271n5, 273n9
Parthians, 47
Pasha, Djemal, 16, 18, 23, 192, 270n3
Pasha, Fakhri 164, 290n31
Persia, 44, 72
Persian Gulf, 39, 52, 62, 69–70, 75
Petraeus, David, xx, 242
Political Warfare Executive (PWE), xx, 8, 238, 270n9, 298n20, 299n1
Protocols of the Elders of Zion, 86

Quran, 86, 194, 187, 207, 209, 211, 221

regional dynamics, 123, 126, 130, 138
regional geography, 117, 143–4, 153, 232
regional infrastructure, 133
religious sensitivities, 55, 76, 78, 82
Residentur Urundi (German), 217
Rida, Muhammad Rashid, 120, 188, 189, 223, 260, 261, 285n24, 293n29, 297n31
Rightly Guided Caliphs, 207
River Tigris, 47
Rogan, Eugene, x, 31, 269, 304–5
Royal Navy, 35–6, 69, 73, 278n27
Ruhi, Hussein, 88–90, 281n34
Rushdi, Hussein, 40
Russia, 36, 44, 62, 65, 70, 73
Russians, 51–2

Sāḥat ash-Shuhadā (Martyrs' Square), 14, 182
Said, Edward, 243
Salem, Sheikh Yusuf Bin, 196
Salisbury (Lord), 44
Sarruf, Ya'qub, 120, 121, 223, 260
Sasanians, 47
Satia, Priya, 30, 33, 115, 303
Savoy Hotel, xvi, xxi, 33, 41, 97–8, 102, 108, 149–50, 206
Schnee, Heinrich, 217
Secret Service Bureau, 38
Serbian Question, 186
Setting the Desert on Fire (Barr), 30, 278n34, 304
Sevastopol, 35
Seven Pillars of Intelligence Wisdom, xv, 247–268
　balance secrecy with strategic engagement, 262–4
　build networked, authentic information ecosystems, 259–62
　cultivate continuous institutional learning, 264–5
　cultural understanding as operational capability, 251–2
　develop flexible organisational structures, 255–7
　diversify Intelligence sources and expertise, 252–5
　recognise language as cultural intelligence, 257–9
Seven Pillars of Wisdom (Lawrence), 4–5, xviii
Shepheard's Hotel (Egypt), 41
SIGINT (signals intelligence), 102–3
Simla, 99
Sinai, 4, 85, 113

INDEX

Singapore, 218–19, 220
Siraj, Sheikh Abdullah, 195
Sirdar, 101, 283n15, 283n16
smallpox, 152
SMS Breslau, 35
SMS Goeben, 35–6
social network analysis (SNA), 156
social structures, 56, 76, 78, 118, 252
Spies in Arabia (Satia), 30, 33, 303
Stark, Freya, xx, 238, 298n20
Storrs, Ronald, xv, 210–12, 222, 296n13
Sudan Civil Service, 86
Sudan Intelligence, 166
Sudan, 77, 100, 198, 256, 273n8, 283n16
Suez Canal, 2, 3–4, 16, 27, 36, 97
al-Sulayman, Abdullah, 90
Sykes, Mark, 43, 49–50, 63, 72, 77, 276n3
Sykes-Picot (Sazanov) Agreement, 240, 271n7
syphilis, 152
Syria, 18, 65, 151, 187, 208
   Arab merchants arrival from, 14
   British policy, 161
   French ambitions in, 70, 73
   killings in, 23
   Ottoman forces' activities in, 153, 163–4

Tabbarah, Sheikh Ahmad, 15, 187–8
Tangier, 201
Thawrat al-Arab (The Arabs' Revolt) (Arabic book), 28–9, 31, 179–80
   chapters, 186–8
   distribution of, 197–9
   dual-Purpose Propaganda, 199–203

   Ottoman Oppression Vs. Arab Dignity, 188–93
Times, The (newspaper), 86, 113
Townshend, Charles, 25, 47–8, 273n18
trade routes, 107, 115, 133–4, 162, 169–70
tribal dynamics, 55, 142–4, 168, 171
tribal movements, 133, 135, 167
tribal politics, 8, 55, 75–6, 78, 103, 151
   British understanding of, 48, 161
   Arab Bureau's approach to, 101, 145, 168, 232
tribal relationships, 77, 144
Tunisia, 23
Turkey, 208
Turks, 37, 54, 169
typhus, 152

U.S. Army/Marine Corps Counterinsurgency Field Manual, 241–2, 251
Union Flag postcard, 213–5, 225
United States, 27, 72
al-Uraysi, Abd al-Ghani, 14, 17

Vienna, 63, 292n24
Vienna, Battle of, 186
von Oppenheim, Max, 51, 274n26

'wandering scholars', 29, 80, 81–2, 114
War Office, 27, 38, 98, 101
   focus on military objectives, 72, 73, 74–5
Wellington House, 231, 262
Western Asia, 20
Western India, 47
Westrate, Bruce, 30, 92–3, 303, 307
Wilderness of Zin survey, 113

INDEX

Willmetts, Simon, 145–6, 286*n*38
Wilson, Arnold Talbot, 230, 297*n*1
Wilson, Cyril Edward (C.E.), 88–9, 92
wireless intercepts, 102–4, 122, 133–4, 137, 138
Woolley, Leonard, 84–6, 87–8, 113, 115, 119, 279*n*11
World War I, 52, 114, 130, 149, 173–4, 180, 182, 188, 198, 201, 206, 229, 238, 241
    Arab Bureau's position in, 30
    Britain's entry into, 38
    British intelligence operations in, 152
    impacts on scholars, 117
    long-term Influence, 233–5
    Ottoman Empire entry, 1–2, 35
    transforming Intelligence and regional dynamics, 232–3
World War II, 32, 201, 242–3, 247–8

Yahyá, Imam, 188, 190
Yambo, 155
Yorktown, 47
Young Turk movement, 64
Young, Hubert, 63, 92
Young, John, 89–90

al-Zahrāwī, Abd al-Ḥamīd, 14, 17, 189
Zanzibar, 219
Zaydan, Jurji, 121, 223, 260